Exercise Adherence

ITS IMPACT ON PUBLIC HEALTH

Exercise Adherence

ITS IMPACT ON PUBLIC HEALTH

Rod K. Dishman, PhD
Editor
University of Georgia

Human Kinetics Books
Champaign, Illinois

Library of Congress Cataloging-in-Publication Data

Exercise adherence.

  Includes bibliographies and index.
  1. Exercise—Hygienic aspects.   2. Health
promotion.   I. Dishman, Rod K. [DNLM: 1. Exertion.
2. Health Promotion—methods.   3. Physical Fitness.
QT 255 E955]
RA781.E89   1988   613.7'1   86-33731
ISBN 0-87322-102-8

197720793

Developmental Editor: Jan Progen, EdD; Production Director: Ernie
Noa; Projects Manager: Lezli Harris; Assistant Editor: Julie Anderson;
Copy Editor: Patrick O'Hayer; Proofreader: Kimberly Sands; Text Design:
Keith Blomberg; Typesetter: Sonnie Bowman; Text Layout: Denise
Mueller; Cover Design: Jack Davis; Printed By: Versa Press, Inc. and R &
R Bindery, Inc.

ISBN: 0-87322-102-8

Printed in the United States of America   10   9   8   7   6   5   4   3   2

Human Kinetics
P.O. Box 5076, Champaign, IL 61825-5076
1-800-747-4457

Canada: Human Kinetics, Box 24040, Windsor, ON N8Y 4Y9
1-800-465-7301 (in Canada only)

Europe: Human Kinetics, P.O. Box IW14, Leeds LS16 6TR, England
(44) 532 781708

Australia: Human Kinetics, 2 Ingrid Street, Clapham 5062, South
Australia
(08) 371 3755

New Zealand: Human Kinetics, P.O. Box 105-231, Auckland 1
(09) 309 2259

Contents

Contributors

William B. Baun, MS

Tenneco, Inc.
P.O. Box 2511, Suite 1047
Houston, TX 77001

Edward J. Bernacki, MD, MPH

Corporate Medical Director
Tenneco, Inc.
P.O. Box 2511, Suite 1047
Houston, TX 77001

Steven N. Blair, PED

Director, Epidemiology
Institute for Aerobics Research
12200 Preston Road
Dallas, TX 75230

Rod K. Dishman, PhD

Director, Behavioral Fitness Laboratory
Department of Physical Education
The University of Georgia
Athens, GA 30602

Andrea L. Dunn, MS

Department of Physical Education
The University of Georgia
Athens, GA 30602

Leonard H. Epstein, PhD

University of Pittsburgh School
  of Medicine
Western Psychiatric Institute and Clinic
3811 O'Hara Street
Pittsburgh, PA 15213

Barry A. Franklin, PhD

Director, Cardiac Rehabilitation
  and Exercise Laboratories
William Beaumont Hospital
3601 West 13 Mile Road
Royal Oak, MI 48072

Larry R. Gettman, PhD

National Health Enhancement Systems
3200 N. Central Avenue
Suite 1750
Phoenix, AZ 85012

Robert T. Hyde, MS

Department of Family, Community,
and Preventive Medicine
Stanford University
Stanford, CA 94305

Dorothy N. Knapp, PhD

Department of Medical Psychology
Oregon Health Sciences University
3181 S.W. Sam Jackson Park Road
Portland, OR 97201

William P. Morgan, EdD

Director, Sport Psychology Lab
University of Wisconsin
2000 Observatory Drive
Madison, WI 53706

Patrick J. O'Connor, MS

University of Wisconsin
2000 Observatory Drive
Madison, WI 53706

Neil B. Oldridge, PhD

Director, Exercise Rehabilitation
Programs
Mount Sinai Medical Center
950 N. 12th Street
P.O. Box 342
Milwaukee, WI 53233

Ralph S. Paffenbarger, Jr.,
MD, DrPH

Department of Family, Community,
and Preventive Medicine
Stanford University
Stanford, CA 94305

Kenneth A. Perkins, PhD

University of Pittsburgh School
of Medicine
Western Psychiatric Institute and Clinic
3811 O'Hara Street
Pittsburgh, PA 15213

Michael Pollock, PhD

Departments of Medicine
and Physiology
University of Florida
College of Medicine
Box J-277
Gainesville, FL 32610

Kenneth E. Powell, MD, MPH

Chief, Behavioral Epidemiology &
Evaluation Branch
Centers for Disease Control
1600 Clifton Road
Atlanta, GA 30333

Roy J. Shephard, MD, PhD

Department of Preventive Medicine
  and Biostatistics
University of Toronto
Toronto, Ontario M5S 1A1
CANADA

Robert J. Sonstroem, PhD

Department of Physical Education,
  Health and Recreation
University of Rhode Island
Kingston, RI 02881

Leonard M. Wankel, PhD

Department of Recreation and
  Leisure Studies
University of Alberta
Edmonton, Alberta T6G 2H9
CANADA

Preface

This book grew out of a career-long interest in the relationship between physical activity and health and the things that distinguish a physically active life from a sedentary one. I became interested in health-related exercise during my undergraduate studies with Harold B. Falls, Jr. Then, while a graduate student studying sport psychology with William P. Morgan at the University of Wisconsin, I was introduced to the problem of poor compliance in medically supervised exercise programs. I first learned about the problem by reading the early writings of many of the contributors to this book. Motivated by their work and by the fact that our accumulated knowledge of the subject was minimal considering its significance, I have pursued the study of exercise adherence as one of my main research interests.

It has been rewarding for me to see that the solid foundations of inquiry laid by the contributors to this book, and by others, have been built upon by those in the many public health related fields who have shown a growing interest in exercise adherence. It is now clear that the need to understand the determinants and outcomes of exercise adherence extends beyond medically supervised settings to the domain of public health. Specialists from exercise science and preventive medicine still contribute the bulk of the research, but scientists from epidemiology, behavioral medicine, and health psychology have helped to expand and strengthen the field. However, as recently as 1984, literature published in other fields on the subjects of medical compliance and lifestyle change has not considered exercise adherence, or has given inadequate attention to existing pertinent literature on the subject. These conspicuous exclusions were key considerations in preparing this book.

Although the terms *exercise adherence* and *exercise compliance* have been adopted by the exercise sciences and have become recognizable catchwords in the popular fitness domain, a search in the literature for studies on exercise adherence remains a scholar's nightmare. An earlier, related topic heading in *Index Medicus* was *compliance*, but the National Library of Medicine now lists *compliance* under the topic of *elasticity*, while *compliant behavior* is listed under *cooperative behavior*. Neither is a heading that will lead to fruitful research of the topic at hand. *Psychological Abstracts*, published by the American Psychological Association, still retains the topic heading of *treatment compliance*, but this also remains an inefficient index for exercise and physical activity studies. Moreover, the literature on exercise and physical activity has historically vacillated between the terms *compliance* and *adherence* so that indexing of pertinent articles has been, and continues to be, inconsistent and confusing. Problems exist with each term. Compliance implies forced coercion, while adherence is synonomous with stickiness! Probably, each connotation is relevant to the understanding of habitual exercise, but I have chosen *adherence* for traditional reasons and for personal preference—and because its definition seems self-evident to most people.

It has been gratifying to see exercise adherence become a common topic of symposia and original research sessions at the meetings of scientific and professional organizations, as well as an increasingly popular topic for graduate student research. The interest expressed in this area by scholars, professionals, and graduate students has grown exponentially. Over the past 8 years, I have answered more than 1,000 inquiries about the study of exercise adherence. I know that the other contributors to this book have also answered many inquiries about the subject.

It is also noteworthy that a branch of the National Centers for Disease Control has been established with the principal purpose of monitoring our nation's progress toward meeting some important physical activity and fitness objectives—the *Public Health Service 1990 Objectives for the Nation*. This branch is known as the Behavioral Epidemiology and Evaluation Branch of the Center for Health Promotion and Education, and its director, Kenneth E. Powell, has prepared the first chapter for this book. It is also timely for the purposes of this book that the newly stated *Objectives for the Nation by the Year 2000*, recommended by the Behavioral Epidemiology and Evaluation Branch as well as by the President's Council on Physical Fitness and Sports, now include as an objective the understanding of determinants of physical activity and exercise adherence. We hope that this book makes a contribution to attaining this important objective.

Exercise adherence is now an established area of study with clearly defined questions and developing methods. Emerging theoretical models will soon begin to keep pace with the pragmatic problems of promoting physical activity in the population, delivering exercise programs in supervised settings, and studying the efficacy and effectiveness of exercise adherence among the many segments of the population that might benefit.

Credits for this volume extend to many people. As Ecclesiastic stated, "We have all drunk from wells we did not dig and have been warmed by fires we did not build." The contributions of the authors and of the other scholars that they cite are obvious. My own students' ideas and inquiries and the support of my family are less obviously, but equally, important. Thanks also go to Rainer Martens, Publisher, Jan Progen, Editor, and the staff of Human Kinetics Publishers, and to Donna Smith and Andrea Dunn of the University of Georgia for their production assistance.

Rod K. Dishman
Athens, Georgia

Overview

Rod K. Dishman

Study and facilitation of exercise adherence are fundamental for promoting the health potential of physical activity and determining its true health impact for the public. Both high dropout rates from exercise programs and sedentary leisure time present a two-fold problem. They first limit the delivery of a public health service to a select segment of the population. This self-selection in turn exerts a bias on controlled research. The measurable health impact (efficacy) of exercise training and habitual activity is diluted when dropouts and the inactive are included in follow-up evaluations, whereas the generalizability of this impact (effectiveness) is limited when dropouts or the inactive are excluded (Feinstein, 1975).

At a given time about 40% of Americans do not exercise during leisure time, another 40% are active at levels probably too low and infrequent for fitness and health gains, while just 20% exercise regularly and intensely enough (Stephens, Jacobs, & White, 1985) to meet current guidelines for fitness (American College of Sports Medicine, 1978) or reduced risk for several chronic diseases and premature death (Powell, Spain, Christenson, & Mollenkamp, 1986; Paffenbarger, Hyde, Wing, & Hsieh, 1986). Available estimates indicate that about one-half of those who begin or renew a personal exercise program will fail to maintain it at the level initially intended, and a like proportion have failed in previous attempts. In the typical supervised exercise setting, about 50% of the clients or patients will drop out of the program within 6 months to a year. Although some medically supervised programs report adherence rates exceeding 80% as long as 2 to 4 years after entry, this is unusual. Roughly 20 to 40% of the employees eligible to use worksite exercise facilities will do so, but only one-third to one-half of the users will exercise on a regular basis at vigorous intensities. For all age groups current activity patterns in the population base appear to fall far below optimal goals set for 1990 by the United States Public Health Service (see Figures 1 and 2). Powell et al. (1986) have concluded it is unlikely these physical activity goals will be reached. One barrier to implementing public health promotions of exercise as well as uniform interventions in exercise programs is the absence of a consensus over the methods that might be effectively employed and the exercise determinants to be targeted.

Adherence rates and patterns differ in various settings and types of programs. It is noteworthy, however, that adherence statistics overall are very similar for apparently healthy adults in community, worksite, and unsupervised self-initiated exercise programs; for patients in supervised exercise programs for primary and secondary prevention of cardiopulmonary diseases; and for persons being treated with exercise for obesity, diabetes, and depression. In general it is remarkable that the rate of dropout observed for exercise programs is very similar in magnitude and form to those observed for other behavior-change programs including smoking and alcohol/drug abstinence, weight loss, and psychotherapy (see Figures 3 and 4). It is not known, however, to what extent the deter-

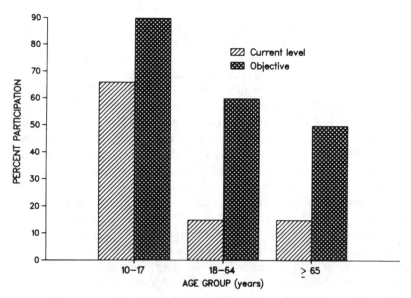

Figure 1   Current prevalence and 1990 objectives for appropriate physical activity by age group. *Note.*   From ''The Status of the 1990 Objectives for Physical Fitness and Exercise'' by K.E. Powell, K.G. Spain, G.M. Christenson, and M.P. Mollenkamp, 1986, *Public Health Reports*, **101**, p. 17. Copyright 1986 by U.S. Public Health Service. Reprinted by permission.

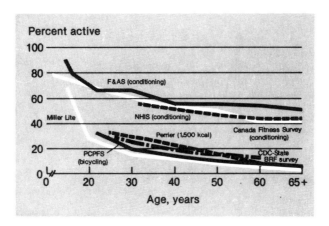

Figure 2   Leisure-time physical activity in North America across age groups. *Note.* From ''A Descriptive Epidemiology of Leisure-Time Activity'' by T. Stephens, D.R. Jacobs, Jr., and C.C. White, 1985, *Public Health Reports*, **100**, p. 150. Copyright 1985 by U.S. Public Health Service. Reprinted by permission.

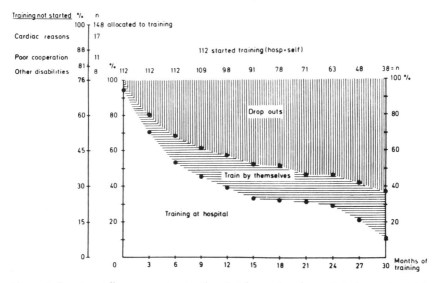

Figure 3   Exercise adherence rates in the Goteborg, Sweden, clinical exercise trial. *Note.* From ''Exercise Tolerance and Physical Training of Non-Selected Patients After Myocardial Infarction'' by H.M. Sanne, D. Elmfeldt, G. Grimby, C. Rydin, and L. Wilhelmsen, 1973, *Acta Medica Scandinavica*, **551**(Suppl.), p. 60. Copyright 1973 by *Acta Medica Scandinavica*. Reprinted by permission.

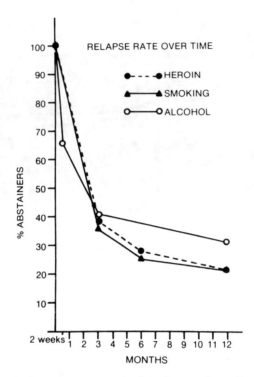

Figure 4   Relapse rates in treatment programs for substance abuse. *Note.*   From "Relapse Rates in Addiction Programs" by W.A. Hunt, L.W. Barnett, and L.G. Branch, 1971, *Journal of Clinical Psychology, 27*, p. 456. Copyright 1971 by The Clinical Psychology Publishing Co., Inc. Reprinted by permission.

minants of habitual physical activity or, conversely, of dropout from exercise programs are similar to those of other compliance patterns seen in medical or behavior modification settings. It is also unclear what proportion of those who drop out of supervised exercise programs are physically active elsewhere. Likewise, similarities in the incidence, prevalence, and correspondence between exercise behaviors and other health related habits in the population base are poorly described.

Public health interest in exercise adherence has grown exponentially in the past several years. This is evidenced not only by the number of published articles in the world literature but also by inclusion of exercise adherence topics on the scientific programs of national meetings held by numerous exercise professional groups. Exercise adherence was a main theme of the 1986 meeting of the Canadian Association of Sport Sciences. Symposia and original research papers on exercise adherence have become increasingly prevalent at meetings of the Society of Behavioral Medicine, the American Public Health Association, the American Psychological Association, the North American Society for the Psychology of Sport and Physical Activity, the International Society of Sport Psychology, and the American Alliance for Health, Physical Education, Recreation and Dance, to name a few. At the 1979 national meeting of the American College of Sports Medicine (ACSM), a symposium on exercise compliance (including several of the authors in this volume) was attended by about 40 people (4% of the 938 registrants at the convention). A similar symposium (again presented by several of the contributors to this book) held at the 1984 ACSM meeting attracted nearly 400 (17% of the 2,352 registrants).

Recent emphasis has been given to exercise adherence and its public health outcomes by the Public Health Service and the National Institutes of Health (U.S. Department of Health and Human Services, 1983). Government agencies in Canada (Fitness Ontario, 1984) and South Australia (Owen & Lee, 1986) have published handbooks on promoting exercise adherence for exercise leaders. Despite these efforts the determinants of exercise adherence are not understood sufficiently to guide public health interventions toward predictable ends (Dishman, Sallis, & Orenstein, 1985). As Figures 5 and 6 reveal, published articles on exercise

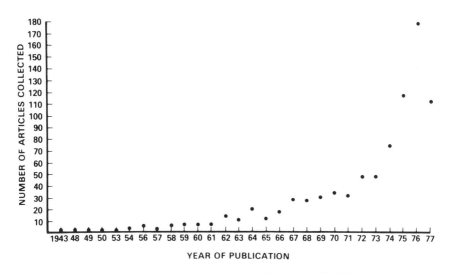

Figure 5 Annual publication rates of articles on compliance with health care prescriptions and advice. *Note.* From "Introduction" by R.B. Haynes to *Compliance in Health Care* (p. 2) edited by R.B. Haynes, D.W. Taylor, and D.L. Sackett, 1979, Baltimore: The Johns Hopkins University Press. Copyright 1979 by The Johns Hopkins University Press. Reprinted by permission.

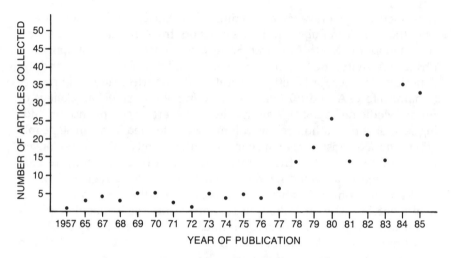

Figure 6 Annual publication rates of articles on exercise adherence/compliance in both supervised programs and population based activity. *Note.* These rates are estimates based on computer searches of biomedical, psychological, and social science literatures. Because exercise adherence is not a topic area that has been well indexed, a personal retrieval system has been more fruitful. Although the world literature has been canvassed, omissions are likely.

adherence/compliance have lagged far behind those on medical compliance both in number and in time. Recent reviews of compliance in health care (Haynes, Taylor, & Sackett, 1979), behavioral interventions and compliance with treatment regimes (Benfari & Eaker, 1981), health promotion and disease prevention at the worksite (Fielding, 1984), and modifying and developing health behavior (Green, 1984) all focus on public health concerns but do not discuss theories or interventions designed with exercise and physical activity as the target behaviors.

An empirical base has accumulated that describes correlates of exercise adherence, and several comprehensive reviews of this literature have appeared in scientific and professional periodicals (e.g., Morgan, 1977; Oldridge, 1982; Martin & Dubbert, 1982, 1985; Dishman, 1982). Nevertheless, scientific reviews collectively reveal that existing information on exercise adherence is largely descriptive. These studies have not yet been able to predict or explain exercise adherence with the precision or reproducibility required to design systematic interventions aimed at changing current physical activity and exercise patterns in the various population segments and settings that constitute the public health domain. Noticeably lacking are theoretical formulations derived from exercise adherence research that can guide new research hypotheses and practical interventions to facilitate exercise adherence in ways that will identify and promote healthy outcomes. For these reasons this book was planned.

The authors assembled are consensus experts in the known outcomes of exercise adherence believed to be related to health and longevity and in the theories and principles that have guided interventions designed to understand, predict, and facilitate exercise adherence as a public health behavior.

With a very few exceptions leading authorities were willing and able to include this book as a priority in their already committed schedules. As a group their past efforts arguably have forged the field of exercise adherence by describing its associated determinants and health outcomes, by critically evaluating published articles, and by charting new directions in contemporary questions and research methods. Most have long histories as the preeminent scholars in their areas of study. All are uniquely qualified to provide firsthand accounts of the material they review, and it is a privilege for me to join them as a student and colleague. It is our hope that the chapters that follow will help define the current and potential roles of exercise adherence in public health by describing the following:

1. The known health outcomes and health habits associated with exercise adherence
2. The known personal, environmental, and activity characteristics associated with exercise adherence
3. Theoretical views of determinants of exercise adherence and principles for exercise behavior change
4. Practical suggestions and guidelines for increasing exercise adherence through exercise prescription and fitness programming
5. Representative views of exercise adherence in worksite, community, and clinical settings
6. Critical evaluations of past research methods and traditions
7. Recommendations for future questions, approaches, methods, and applications

References

American College of Sports Medicine. (1978). The recommended quantity and quality of exercise for developing and maintaining fitness in healthy adults. *Medicine and Science in Sports*, **10**(3), vii–ix.

Benfari, R.C., Eaker, E., & Stoll, J.G. (1981). Behavioral interventions and compliance to treatment regimes. *Annual Review of Public Health*, **2**, 421–471.

Dishman, R.K. (1982). Compliance/adherence in health-related exercise. *Health Psychology*, **1**, 237–267.

Dishman, R.K., Sallis, J.F., & Orenstein, D.R. (1985). The determinants of physical activity and exercise. *Public Health Reports*, **100**, 158–171.

Feinstein, A.R. (1975). Clinical biostatistics: Biostatistical problems in 'compliance bias'. *Clinical Pharmacology and Therapeutics*, **16**(5), 846–857.

Fielding, J.E. (1984). Health promotion and disease prevention at the worksite. *Annual Review of Public Health*, **5**, 237–265.

Fitness Ontario. (1984). *Sticking with fitness: What to do about the adherence problem in fitness programs.* Toronto: Ministry of Tourism and Recreation, Government of Ontario.

Green, L.W. (1984). Modifying and developing health behavior. *Annual Review of Public Health*, **5**, 215–236.

Haynes, R.B., Taylor, D.W., & Sackett, D.L. (Eds.). (1979). *Compliance in health care.* Baltimore: The Johns Hopkins University Press.

Hunt, W.A., Barnett, L.W., & Branch, L.G. (1971). Relapse rates in addiction programs. *Journal of Clinical Psychology*, **27**, 455.

Martin, J.E., & Dubbert, P.M. (1982). Exercise applications and promotion in behavioral medicine: Current status and future directions. *Journal of Consulting and Clinical Psychology*, **50**, 1004–1017.

Martin, J.E., & Dubbert, P.M. (1985). Adherence to exercise. *Exercise and Sport Sciences Reviews*, **13**, 137–167.

Morgan, W.P. (1977). Involvement in vigorous physical activity with special reference to adherence. In G.I. Gedvilas & M.E. Kneer (Eds.), *National College of Physical Education Association proceedings* (pp. 235–246). Chicago: University of Illinois Press.

Oldridge, N.B. (1982). Compliance and exercise in primary and secondary prevention of coronary heart disease: A review. *Preventive Medicine*, **11**, 56–70.

Owen, N., & Lee, C. (1984). *Why people do and do not exercise: Recommendations for initiatives to promote regular, vigorous physical activity in Australia.* Adelaide: Department of Recreation and Sport, South Australia, Sport and Recreation Minister's Council.

Paffenbarger, R.S., Jr., Hyde, R.T., Wing, A.L., & Hsieh, C.C. (1986). Physical activity, all-cause mortality, and longevity of college alumni. *New England Journal of Medicine*, **314**, 605–613.

Powell, K.E., Spain, K.G., Christenson, G.M., & Mollenkamp, M.P. (1986). The status of the 1990 objectives for physical fitness and exercise. *Public Health Reports, 101,* 15–21.

Stephens, T., Jacobs, D.R., Jr., & White, C.C. (1985). A descriptive epidemiology of leisure-time physical activity. *Public Health Reports, 100,* 147–158.

U.S. Department of Health and Human Services. (1983). Promoting health/preventing disease: Public health service implementation plans for attaining the objectives for the nation. *Public Health Reports, 98* (Suppl.).

PART 1

Health and Exercise Adherence: Outcomes and Influences

Understanding exercise adherence and defining the health potential of physical activity are intertwined problems. The benefits of exercise cannot accrue for the inactive, and the true effectiveness of exercise as a health intervention cannot be determined if only a select portion of the population is willing or able to participate in studies of exercise effects. Important questions of who will best benefit from a physically active lifestyle, what form this activity should take, and how exercise may complement other health-affecting behaviors such as nutrition control, smoking, substance abuse, and stress management are just now being framed in meaningful ways. There is also reason to believe that whereas objective aspects of health and feelings of well-being may be facilitated by exercise, the decision to initiate and maintain regular activity may in turn be influenced by the expectation and the attainment of these benefits. Thus health represents at once a desired outcome and a likely motivator (intrinsically and extrinsically) of exercise adherence. This section will provide a rationale for and a means of understanding exercise adherence from a broad population perspective of health outcomes associated with physical activity.

The papers in this section address aspects of both outcome and motivation at the health and exercise adherence interface. Perspectives will include epidemiology and public health, lifestyle change in health behaviors, and mental health. Each paper will survey and critically evaluate what is known and what needs to be examined, the theory and methods needed to further knowledge and application, and the public impact of understanding exercise and physical activity as health behaviors. This section provides not only a rationale for the study and promotion of exercise adherence but also a beginning for understanding what determines an active rather than sedentary lifestyle.

Chapter 1

Kenneth E. Powell's "Habitual Exercise and Public Health: An Epidemiological View" surveys current data on the epidemiological significance of being active, contrasts the health potential of different types and volumes of activities, discusses the role of exercise within public health policy, suggests the motivational potential of mass exercise promotions for increasing activity levels, and charts directions for future study. It also provides the encompassing public health basis for exercise adherence upon which the remaining chapters build.

Chapter 2

"Exercise Adherence, Coronary Heart Disease, and Longevity" by Ralph S. Paffenbarger, Jr. and Robert T. Hyde presents an in-depth account of the authors' persuasive epidemiological analyses of health outcomes associated with physical activity patterns among large cohorts of Harvard alumni and San Francisco longshoremen. Their original research findings are examined in relation to the world literature on the epidemiology of physical activity in heart disease and its major risk factors and longevity. The data base presented and its quantitative implications for exercise adherence and health planning provide a basis for interpreting the public health significance of many of the other chapters included in this text.

Chapter 3

In "Exercise Within a Healthy Lifestyle" Steven N. Blair outlines the evidence supporting the importance for public health of controlling various health-related behaviors including smoking, poor diet, substance abuse, and coping with excessive stress. The focus highlights the potential of physical activity for augmenting the health outcomes of lifestyle management and speculates about the facilitative effects of health behavior change on chronic exercise patterns.

Chapter 4

Cross-sectional, correlational, and experimental evidence from human and comparative research supports a potential for exercise as a means for coping with mental stress. ''Exercise and Mental Health'' by William P. Morgan and Patrick J. O'Connor summarizes and evaluates this research and discusses the management of stress emotions as a model for understanding motivation for habitual exercise in both normal and clinical populations. Psychometric, neurophysiological, and biochemical aspects of the affective states associated with acute and habitual exercise are addressed. Exercise dependence is described as both a health risk of exercise and a model for understanding exercise adherence as a process.

CHAPTER 1

Habitual Exercise and Public Health: An Epidemiological View

Kenneth E. Powell

Habitual exercise is beneficial to health. Although many important questions remain, data of sufficient quality and quantity are available to conclude that regular physical activity is a salubrious behavior. The list of probable benefits is broad and includes prevention of several of the leading causes of morbidity and mortality in the United States. As a result, the U.S. Public Health Service has identified physical fitness and exercise as an area of major importance to the health status of the people of the United States. This chapter summarizes the relationship between habitual exercise and public health. It includes a brief definition of public health, epidemiology, and habitual exercise; summaries of the health benefits and risks of habitual exercise; an epidemiological analysis of habitual exercise in the United States; and a discussion of the national objectives in the area of physical fitness and exercise and some of the leading problems and issues from a public health perspective.

Public health is the combination of organizations and individuals whose actions are concerned with the level of function and wellness of a community as a whole. This is in contrast with the more familiar concept of a medical practitioner whose concern is focused upon the individual patient. Although most public health workers are in the fields of medical and social sciences, public health encompasses a broad spectrum of agencies and vocations. The public health importance of various conditions is judged by their impact on the vitality of society as a whole rather than on any individual. Diseases that are both common and frequently fatal, for example, coronary heart disease, are of primary public health importance. Diseases or problems that are common but rarely fatal, such as low back pain, have public health importance because they have a significant overall impact on the economics and function of society. Diseases or problems that are uncommon and rarely fatal generally have low public health importance. Diseases that are uncommon but often fatal have intermediate positions; their relative rank is determined by their potential for becoming widespread. Frequently fatal conditions that are insufficiently understood to know the future incidence are of great public health importance. The acquired immunodeficiency syndrome (AIDS) is an example of such a condition. The common thread through all of these examples is that the public health importance is determined by the actual or potential impact on the community rather than on an individual. Prevention has generally been a more effective public health strategy than treatment. Habitual exercise, therefore, has become of interest to the public health community because it appears to prevent or at least retard the development of several diseases or conditions of public health importance.

Epidemiology is the science that has grown from the efforts of public health workers to understand and to serve the needs of the community. It is a systematic approach to the collection and analysis of health data that has seen increasingly broad application. The essence of the epidemiological method is the calculation of rates. These may be rates of events, conditions, or diseases for the community as a whole or, when appropriate, for selected subgroups of the population.

Two kinds of rates are used. Incidence rates pertain to the number of new cases during a specified period of time. Prevalence rates pertain to the total number of cases, new or old, that exist at a specific point in time or over a given period of time. To be properly used and understood, incidence and prevalence rates must provide not only the number of cases but also the size of the population from which those cases arose and the time period during which the cases occurred. All epidemiological studies must have a rate or an estimate of a rate. Although some studies produce only a single rate, others produce two or more so that the rate of a problem in one population can be compared with the rate of the same problem in a different population.

The rates provide the information that is necessary to determine the public health importance of a problem. Epidemiology also makes important contributions to the understanding of the causes of the events, conditions, or diseases and to the determination of the efficacy of potential preventive measures.

Epidemiological studies fall into two broad categories, experimental and observational. In experimental studies different treatments or exposures are given to individuals or groups that have been randomized by the investigator to eliminate systematic differences between them. In observational studies the exposure or treatment groups have been determined by someone other than the investigator. In some cases the exposure may be determined by the individual (e.g., smoking); in others, by another source (e.g., the administration of a drug by a physician). Observational studies may engender disquiet or skepticism because the groups being compared may differ in ways unknown to and out of the control of the epidemiologist. The epidemiologist must therefore take special care in the selection of the groups under investigation to be sure that the variables known or reasonably presumed to be crucial are taken into consideration.

A solitary observational study may observe and report an association between exposure and disease. Causal inference can be made, however, only when the association is repeatedly observed in carefully designed studies and when the association is strong, consistent, temporally appropriate, biologically graded, plausible, and coherent.

Habitual exercise is the regular and planned performance of physical activity with the final or intermediate objective of improving or maintaining levels of physical fitness. It is a complex behavior. One of the major deficiencies of past research in this area has been the absence or imprecision of a clear definition of the behavior being studied. At the very least, exercise should be described in terms of the type, frequency, duration, and intensity at which it is conducted. The variable specificity of the definition of activity has made it difficult to compare the results of previously reported studies.

Conditions of Public Health Importance That May Be Related to Habitual Exercise

One of the salient aspects of habitual physical activity is the broad spectrum of conditions upon which it has an allegedly favorable influence. The conditions include diseases of large public health importance such as coronary heart disease (Table 1) and behaviors that have important public health consequences such as proper weight control and smoking (Table 2). Moreover, the benefits of habitual activity may be manifested in terms of primary prevention (e.g., a reduced incidence of coronary heart disease [CHD] or via the use of exercise as a treatment for already established disease (e.g., blood pressure reduction, maintenance of function of persons with rheumatoid arthritis or chronic pulmonary disease).

Table 1   Prevalence, Mortality, and Estimated Costs of Selected Conditions That May Be Ameliorated by Habitual Exercise

Disease	Age group (yrs)	Prevalence (cases per 1,000)	Annual death rate (deaths per 100,000)	Estimated annual cost (in billions of dollars)
Ischemic heart disease	All ages	24	294.3[a]	14.6
Hypertensive disease	All ages	260[b]	7.3[a]	8–10[b]
Osteoporosis	50–64	550	0.1[a]	3.8
Diabetes mellitus	All ages	24	15.5[a]	17.9
Acute respiratory disease	All ages	10	NA	>5[c]
Back pain of more than 1 month	25–74	10	NA	13.4
Depression	Adults	30 to 40	7.1[d]	16.5

Note.   Unless otherwise specified, data are from The Carter Center of Emory University (1984).
[a]U.S. vital statistics 1983. [b]Department of Health and Human Services (1981). [c]Foy & Grayston (1981). [d]Based on an estimate of 60% of all suicide deaths.

Table 2   Diseases and Conditions Commonly Associated With Obesity or Cigarette Smoking

Obesity	Cigarette smoking
Cardiovascular disease including hypertension	Cardiovascular disease
Diabetes	Cancer
Gall bladder stones	Chronic obstructive pulmonary disease
Osteoarthritis	Infant mortality
Complications of pregnancy	Fires and burns
Endometrial cancer	
Surgical risk	
Psychological disturbances	

Claims have also been made that habitual exercise provides a broad spectrum of psychological benefits such as improved confidence, feeling of well-being, sexual satisfaction, anxiety reduction, intellectual function, and others (Taylor, Sallis, & Needle, 1985). Clearly, even if exercise provides only a portion of the alleged benefits, it already has had a major influence on the health of the public and could have an even greater impact.

Unfortunately, the scientific evidence supporting the alleged associations and measuring their impact has been slow in coming. As a result, some health workers are reluctant to vigorously promote physical activity as an established method of maintaining or improving health. Many questions remain and more research is needed. The ability to provide quantitative estimates of the benefits and risks is rudimentary. Evidence, however, is accumulating that the benefits significantly outweigh the risks.

Cardiovascular Disease

A number of studies have examined the relationship between coronary heart disease and levels of physical activity. Several more complete reviews are available (Haskell, 1984; Paffenbarger & Hyde, 1984; Siscovick, LaPorte, & Newman, 1985; see also chapter 2). Taken altogether, the studies document the inverse relationship between level of physical activity and incidence of CHD. The relationship has been observed in a variety of population groups, using a variety of CHD end points, and using several different methods to measure physical activity. The general consistency of the findings obtained in a variety of settings with a variety of instruments is persuasive evidence of the validity of the relationship.

An important and difficult epidemiological issue concerns self-selection. Persons with a proclivity for CHD may shun physical activity. Taken to its logical extreme, the issue can be resolved only by one or more experimental trials. However, observational studies have contributed and can continue to contribute information on the issue of selection versus protection. Several studies (Morris, Everitt, Pollard, & Chave, 1980; Paffenbarger & Hyde, 1975; Paffenbarger, Wing, & Hyde, 1978; Siscovick, Weiss, Hallstrom, Inui, & Peterson, 1982) have begun with presumably healthy populations in all levels of activity. Excluding cases of CHD that occurred early in the follow-up and accounting for changes in job classification did not modify the findings. Assuming that participation in college athletics reflects a positive constitutional attitude toward physical activity or exercise, such participation provided no protection unless the behavioral pattern either persisted or was reinstituted later in life (Paffenbarger et al., 1978). Finally, several studies have controlled in the analysis for other established risk factors such as age, smoking, hypertension, and family history (Garcia-Palmieri, Costas, Cruz-Vidal, Sorlie, & Havlik, 1982; Kannel & Sorlie, 1979; Morris et al., 1980; Paffenbarger et al., 1978; Siscovick, Weiss, Fletcher, Schoenbach, & Wagner, 1984). These factors did not account for the reduction in risk of CHD. Therefore, to the extent that epidemiologists have been able to examine the issue of self-selection, available evidence suggests that the association between increased levels of activity and a reduced risk of CHD is not due to self-selection.

It has also been noted that the difference between the risk for inactive persons and the risk for active persons is greater for persons who were older (Morris et al., 1980; Siscovick et al., 1984), hypertensive (Paffenbarger et al., 1978; Paffenbarger, Hyde, Wing, & Steinmetz, 1984; Siscovick, Weiss, Fletcher, Schoenbach, & Wagner, 1984), or obese (Siscovick, Weiss, Fletcher, Schoenbach, & Wagner, 1984). This suggests that persons with these other risk factors for CHD reduce their risk the most by habitual vigorous activity.

Siscovick and co-workers have also noted that the risk of primary cardiac arrest is greater during vigorous physical activity than at rest even for persons who are regularly active (Siscovick, Weiss, Fletcher, & Lasky, 1984). However, persons who expended the most calories per week in habitual high-intensity activity had both the lowest rate of primary cardiac arrest during less active periods and the smallest increase in risk during episodes of activity. Thus, even though vigorous activity temporarily increases the risk of an adverse cardiac event, people who regularly engage in vigorous physical activity are still at the least risk overall.

Hypertension

Currently available evidence suggests that regular vigorous physical activity is associated with a small but significant decrease in blood pressure, approximately 2–5 mmHg average diastolic pressure (Siscovick et al., 1985). The modest decrease would have a large effect if applied to the entire population. More definitive studies are necessary.

Osteoporosis

Physical activity may be inversely related to the development of osteoporosis and the risk of fracture. Clinical studies of persons temporarily immobilized and comparisons of marathon runners and nonrunners suggest that activity is associated with higher bone density (Aloia et al., 1978; Dalen & Olsson, 1974; Krolner & Taft, 1983). Higher bone density has yet to be shown to be associated with reduced incidence of fractures. The type of activity generally considered to be associated with higher bone density is simple weight-bearing activity (e.g., walking or standing) as opposed to the more vigorous activity generally recommended for cardiovascular benefits (Siscovick et al., 1985).

Diabetes

Physical activity reduces blood glucose levels, increases the number of insulin receptors, and increases the effect of insulin in noninsulin-dependent diabetes (Siscovick et al., 1985). A cross-sectional study of a population on a Pacific island noted a higher prevalence of diabetes among the sedentary than among the active population. The association was independent of obesity (King et al., 1984). No other data are available for estimating whether habitual physical activity might prevent or postpone the development of noninsulin-dependent diabetes or its complications (Siscovick et al., 1985).

Clinical observations suggest that physical activity improves glucose control in children with insulin-dependent diabetes mellitus. However, no data are available for estimating changes in the rate of complications of diabetes (Siscovick et al., 1985).

Acute Respiratory Disease

Simon (1984) has recently reviewed the effects of exercise on various defenses against infectious diseases. Vigorous physical activity produces a transient increase in the concentration of white blood cells in the circulation. Some laboratory studies also have shown enhanced lymphocyte function, which may be induced via endogenous pyrogen released during exercise (Cannon & Kluger, 1983). Endogenous pyrogen is a protein that appears to mediate the febrile response to infection. Whether or not these findings have any clinical importance is not known. A study of competitive rowers and ROTC cadets indicated that the high-exercise group experienced more upper respiratory symptoms than the low-exercise group (Hanson, 1984). Nevertheless, a common belief is that vigorous physical exercise reduces the incidence or severity of minor, acute illnesses. Although rarely life threatening, acute respiratory disease has major economic consequences in terms both of medical costs and of loss of wages and productivity (Table 1). If vigorous physical activity reduces the incidence or severity of acute respiratory illness, it would be a significant public health benefit.

Low Back Pain

Low back pain is a common cause of discomfort and disability. Strength and flexibility exercises of various types have been advocated for the management of low back pain for many years. The value of these exercises has not been firmly established (Deyo, 1983). Similarly, although anatomically and physiologically plausible, the role of prophylactic strength and flexibility exercises or an overall conditioning program is not established in the prevention of low back pain.

Mental Illness

More than 1,000 articles have been written about the psychological effects of sport and exercise (Hughes, 1984). Several recent reviews are available (Dishman, 1985; Folkins & Sime, 1981; Hughes, 1984; Morgan, 1982; Taylor et al., 1985). A reduction in the symptoms of anxiety and mild to moderate depression and an improved self-concept are consistently observed findings. Improvements in the aspects of mental health among normally functioning persons in our society are likely to be difficult to show because the overall level of malfunction is low and most of our objective measures are limited to the assessment of malfunction as opposed to an improvement in normal function. Hence, the potential benefits of regular exercise in the general population may be large but are difficult to measure. Further discussion of this topic is found in chapter 4.

Indirect Benefits

Increased levels of physical activity may provide indirect benefits to health by influencing other health-related behaviors. The beneficial effects of physical activity on weight control are established whereas its effect on smoking prevention and cessation, alcohol and substance abuse, or healthy behavior in general requires additional study (Blair, Jacobs, & Powell, 1985). Further discussion of this topic is found in chapter 3.

Adverse Effects

The overall assessment of the impact of habitual exercise on the health of the public requires an assessment of both benefits and risks at the population level. The likely benefits of exercise adherence cover a broad spectrum, but the spectrum of potential adverse effects is also large. The adverse effects may be acute or chronic, and they may be mechanical, metabolic, or psychological. They are likely to be dependent upon the age and sex of the participant and the activity in question.

The incidence of adverse effects of the most commonly practiced adult exercise activities—walking, running, swimming, cycling, calisthenics, and racket sports—is generally not available (Koplan, Siscovick, & Goldbaum,

1985). The annual incidence among recreational runners of injuries severe enough to cause a reduction in mileage, use of medication, or a visit to a physician has been estimated at about 30% in one study (Koplan, Powell, Sikes, Shirley, & Campbell, 1982). Incidence rates of adverse acute musculoskeletal injury for these sports are not otherwise known (Koplan et al., 1985). Some adverse consequences have been hypothesized but not established; for example, it has been suggested that osteoarthritis of the knee among runners will be a common malady in the future. The preliminary report, however, of one study found no supportive evidence for the hypothesis (Sohn & Micheli, 1984). In other cases metabolic effects have been noted but the health significance is not known. Amenorrhea has developed among some vigorously active women, but its cause is unknown (Loucks & Horvath, 1985) as is its apparent relationship with reduced bone mineral content (Caldwell, 1984).

It seems reasonable to assume that the adverse effects of habitual exercise are either minor, rare, or so unusually obscure that they have not yet been detected. However, even minor afflictions like the common cold may have significant economic consequences if they are widespread. Therefore, the adverse effects of habitual exercise deserve more careful epidemiological study than they have received. On balance, the apparent benefits of physical activity appear to outweigh heavily the apparent risks. The community at large, however, is poorly served if both are not studied and described with equal care.

The Epidemiology of Physical Activity

Given the evidence that increased levels of physical activity are beneficial to the overall health of the community, the epidemiological study of the behavior itself is appropriate (Mason & Powell, 1985). One important public health issue is the distribution of physical activity behaviors within the population. Rational planning and promotional efforts require that the activity practices of the population and selected subgroups of the population be known with a reasonable degree of accuracy. The results of several surveys and polls have been reported. The available data, however, are noted more for their quantity than their quality (Stephens, Jacobs, & White, 1985). The major problem is the definition of *active*. The proportion of active persons in the population depends on how active is defined. A list of the definitions used in several major surveys of adults and the results from each of the surveys are shown in Table 3 and Figure 1. Stephens et al. (1985) have pointed out that, not surprisingly, the proportion who are active is inversely related to the strictness of the definition. As a rough approximation, about 20% of the population exercise

Table 3 Principal National Surveys of Leisure-Time Activity for Adults Ages 18-64, 1972-1984

Source	Year of survey	Age coverage	Sample size	Definition of active	Percent active
President's Council on Physical Fitness and Sports (1974)	1972	22+	3,875 (incl. 979 60+ years)	"Now doing" one or more of six listed exercises (walking, bicycling, swimming, calisthenics, jogging, weight lifting)	55
National Health Interview Survey (National Center for Health Statistics, 1978)	1975	20 to 64	10,080 (approx.)	Participation in one or more of six listed exercises "on a regular basis" (bicycling, calisthenics, jogging, weight lifting, swimming, walking)	50
Pacific Mutual Life Ins. Co. (Louis Harris and Associates, Inc., 1978)	1978	18 to 49	1,001	Participation in "any regular exercise activities at the present time"	42
Perrier-Great Waters of France, Inc. (1979)	1978	18 to 64	1,270 (approx.)	1,500 kcal/week or 3+ kcal/Kg-day on sports and conditioning for an average size person	18
General Mills Inc. (1979)	1978-79	18 to 64	1,700 (approx.)	"Regular exercisers" are those who "get some planned physical exercise at least several times a week"	35
Nationwide Precursor of the CDC-State Behavioral Risk Factor Survey (C.C. White, personal communication, 1984)	1981-83	18 to 64	13,698	3+ kcal/Kg-day of expenditure on single major activity	22
Miller Lite Report 1982 (Miller Brewing Company, 1983)	1982	18 to 64	886	Athletic index score = 12+, where 1 point given for weekly participation, 4 points for "daily or almost daily" participation in 29 listed activities	15
Prevention Magazine, (Louis Harris and Associates, 1983)	1983	18 to 64	1,056	Participation in strenuous exercise 3+ days/week in which "you breathe heavily and your heart and pulse rate are accelerated for a period lasting at least 20 minutes"	36
CDC-State Behavioral Risk Factor Surveillance System (C.J. Caspersen & R.A. Pollard, personal communication, 1985)	1984	18 to 64	8,062	3+ days/week, 20+ min/session at 60% maximal capacity or more	9

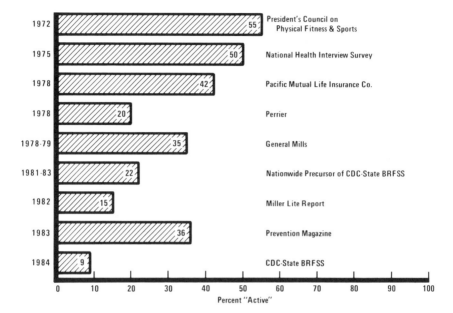

Figure 1   Principal national surveys of leisure-time physical activity for adults ages 18–64, percent active 1972–1984.

at the level frequently recommended for cardiovascular benefit, another 40% are less active but may achieve some health benefits, and about 40% are presumably sedentary (Stephens et al., 1985).

In spite of variations in the definition of an active person, age, socioeconomic status, and gender have consistently been associated with level of activity in various surveys of adults over the past 13 years. Younger age and higher socioeconomic status, whether measured by income, occupation, or educational level, are associated with more leisure-time physical activity. Males are more likely than females to be classified as physically active, especially if frequency or intensity of activity is taken into account (Stephens et al., 1985).

Activity status does not appear to differ between whites and other races once age and socioeconomic status are taken into account. Surburbanites have been reported to be more active than urban or rural residents, and persons in the western United States have been reported to be more active than others. The findings, however, may be attributable to differences of age distribution, socioeconomic status, or other factors.

Although incontrovertible supportive data are not available, leisure-time activity appears to have increased in the U.S. population over the past two decades. The best data come from surveys of midwestern men and Harvard alumni (Powell & Paffenbarger, 1985). Both indicate that the increase in vigorous leisure-time activity is particularly marked. The Harvard alumni study confirms that the increases are both between and within cohorts. That is, men 45–49 years of age reported doing more sport activity in 1977 than men of identical age span reported doing a decade earlier, and men 55–59 years of age reported doing more sport activity in 1977 than the same men reported approximately 10 years earlier at ages 45–49. Generalization from Harvard alumni and midwestern men to the U.S. population would not be warranted in most situations. Therefore, even though the evidence seems strong that leisure-time activity has increased, it is not possible to quantify the increase or to be sure if the increase applies to all subgroups of the population. Furthermore, whether the increase in leisure-time activity has been large enough to counterbalance the decrements in occupational energy expenditure and the reduced energy expenditure due to the widespread availability of mechanized transportation is not known (Koplan & Powell, 1984).

The overall activity level of an individual is determined by the type, frequency, duration, and intensity of the activities in which he or she participates. In most surveys reported values for some or all of these variables have been used to estimate the activity level and in turn to determine if the individual is active. In general, surveys have applied the same criteria across all age and sex groups. However, this does not account for differences in capacity by age and sex. Surveys that estimate energy expenditure show particularly sharp decrements in the proportion of active persons in older age groups (Perrier-Great Waters of France, Inc., 1979; C.C. White, personal communication, 1984). The question naturally arises whether or not the decrease in proportion would persist if capacity were taken into account. Preliminary analysis of telephone survey data from 16 states in 1984 suggests that when decrements of $\dot{V}O_2$max are taken into account with age, essentially equal proportions of persons 18–64 years and 65+ years of age achieve the definition of active recommended in the 1990 Objectives (C.J. Caspersen & R.A. Pollard, personal communication, 1985).

Determinants of Habitual Exercise

Rational public health planning also requires knowledge about the factors that appear to be causally related to physical activity. Considerable research has produced a rather long list of potentially important determinants of physical activity (Table 4) (Dishman, Sallis, & Orenstein, 1985). Unfortunately, variable methods and definitions make it impossible to say which are the most important independent factors.

Table 4 Summary of Variables That May Determine the Probability of Exercise

Personal characteristics	Environmental characteristics	Activity characteristics
Past program participation	Spouse support	Activity intensity
Past extraprogram activity	Perceived available time	Perceived discomfort
School athletics, 1 sport	Access to facilities	
School athletics, > 1 sport	Disruptions in routine	
Blue-collar occupation	Social reinforcement (staff, exercise partner)	
Smoking	Family influence	
Overweight	Peer influence	
High risk of coronary heart disease	Physical influences	
Type A behavior	Cost	
Health, exercise knowledge	Medical screening	
Attitudes	Climate	
Enjoyment of activity	Incentives	
Perceived health		
Mood disturbance		
Education		
Age		
Expect personal health benefit		
Self-efficacy for exercise		
Intention to adhere		
Perceived physical competence		
Self-motivation		
Evaluating costs and benefits		
Behavioral skills		

Note. From ''The Determinants of Physical Activity and Exercise'' by R.K. Dishman, J.F. Sallis, and D.R. Orenstein, 1985, *Public Health Reports*, **100**, p. 161. Copyright by U.S. Public Health Service. Adapted by permission.

Some of the potential determinants in Table 4 have more immediate potential than others for public health intervention activities. Participation in school athletics, knowledge about health and exercise, and access to facilities are variables with obvious, immediate policy implications. For example, if participation in high school sports can be shown to be associated with a more active adult lifestyle beyond factors attributable to self-selection, then high school athletics can be modified to ensure participation by a larger proportion of students. Similarly, if knowledge about the health benefits of exercise and knowledge about how to begin and continue an exercise program are important factors in the adoption and maintenance of an active lifestyle, then educational campaigns can be conducted. The availability of facilities is another important issue. People cannot swim without water or play tennis without courts. It does not necessarily follow, of course, that people without access to water or tennis courts will do nothing; they may seek out activities for which facilities are available or not needed. Conversely, people with access to water or tennis courts may not use them. If, however, the availability of certain facilities can be shown to be associated with more widespread participation in an active lifestyle and not merely with increased use by persons already physically active, then resources should be allocated to increase the availability of facilities. Availability can be improved by constructing new facilities or removing cost and other barriers to the use of existing facilities. Cost of participation, availability of time, and certain aspects of social reinforcement (e.g., attitude of employer) are other factors that may readily be influenced by public health policy decisions. More definitive evidence on the value of these factors may lead to specific public health actions.

The refinement in understanding the relative importance of these and other probable determinants of habitual exercise is of great importance to our efforts to achieve the health benefits of increased levels of physical activity at the societal level. These and similar issues form the substance of many chapters in this book.

Important Epidemiological Concerns

As previously noted, variable definitions of an active person have impeded comparison of data from different surveys. A single definition satisfactory for all surveys and other research is unlikely because physical activity is such a complex behavior. Various components of that behavior are likely to have independent effects on different health outcomes. For example, the type of activity that retards osteoporosis is probably different from that which reduces the risk of CHD. Therefore, in order for research to rapidly promote our understanding of the various effects of the various components of exercise, considerably more attention must be given to describing the nature and extent of the physical activity being examined. The type, frequency, duration, and intensity are all important characteristics of activity. Similarly, it is important to know if the activity is occupational or leisure-time in origin or if it is voluntarily conducted or is demanded by a force outside personal control. A more thorough discussion of these issues is available (Caspersen, Powell, & Christenson, 1985). If the benefits of physical activity are to be more fully understood, greater attention to the description of the components of the activity being studied is necessary.

Dose-Response Effects of Exercise

More detail also is necessary on the dose-response effects of the various components of physical activity. Most dose-response curves are smooth, continuous functions. Thresholds above which benefits occur and below which benefits are absent probably do not exist. The need to group data for analytical purposes and, perhaps more important, to make specific conclusions and recommendations often forces us to specify levels at which benefits occur. Methodological limitations such as sample size often limit the conclusions that can be supported by a single study. Statistically significant differences may be present only between the most active and the least active groups. Examination of the actual data, however, usually reveals a graded response. The changes or benefits at the lower end of the activity scale are not large enough to achieve statistical significance for the size of the population studied and are not mentioned.

This may have inadvertently led to the erroneous conclusion that lesser levels of activity are not helpful. Examination of the data from several studies of physical activity and CHD indeed suggests that reduction in overall morbidity and mortality may actually accrue more rapidly at the lower end of the activity scale than at the upper end (Figure 2). The level of activity at which a statistically significant improvement is shown should not be equated with a threshold below which there are no benefits. That benefits accrue at all levels—except perhaps at the very highest—seems likely.

National Objectives for Physical Fitness and Exercise

In 1975 Milton Terris observed that "physical fitness and physical education have no respected place in the American public health movement."

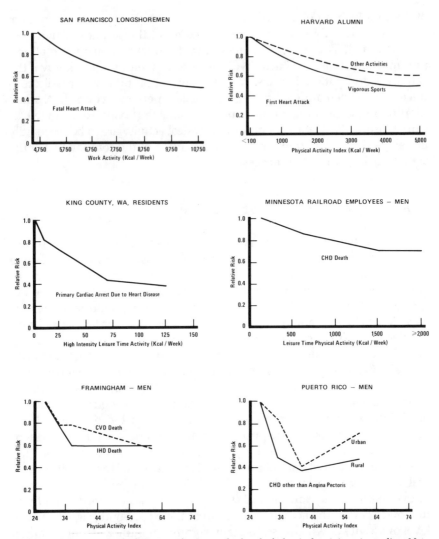

Figure 2   Relative risk of adverse cardiac event by level of physical activity, six studies. *Note.* The San Francisco Longshoremen and Harvard Alumni studies are from *Exercise and Health: The Evidence and The Implications* by G.S. Thomas, P.R. Lee, P. Franks, and R.S. Paffenbarger, 1981, Cambridge, MA: Oelgeschlager, Gunn & Hain. Copyright 1981 by Oelgeschlager, Gunn & Hain. Reprinted by permission.

His comment was factual and without judgmental implication. It serves, nevertheless, as a mark against which current conditions can be compared. By 1980 specific national objectives for physical fitness and exercise had been set by the U.S. Public Health Service (USPHS), and during 1984 and 1985 at least four USPHS agencies held important workshops on fitness or exercise.

The 1990 Physical Fitness and Exercise Objectives

In 1979 the USPHS involved more than 500 individuals from both the private and public sectors in a year-long project to identify important public health problems and to establish realistic yet challenging objectives that, if achieved, would result in major improvements in the health of the nation. The results of the deliberations are published in *Healthy People: The Surgeon General's Report on Health Promotion and Disease Prevention* (Department of Health, Education, and Welfare, 1979) and *Promoting Health/Preventing Disease: Objectives for the Nation* (Department of Health and Human Services, 1980). These documents identify 223 discrete objectives in 15 general areas such as immunization, pregnancy and infant health, and smoking. As a group these objectives are often referred to as the 1990 Objectives, and 11 of the objectives are in the area of physical fitness and exercise (Table 5). By 1985 a few of the physical fitness and exercise objectives had been achieved, but several others seemed out of reach (Centers for Disease Control, 1985).

The gist of these documents is that we must shift our emphasis from traditional to contemporary health problems and that we must change our attitudes and approaches to health. Infectious diseases were formerly the leading causes of death in our society. Although infectious diseases still require surveillance, containment, and research efforts, they are no longer the leading killers and cripplers in our society. The dramatic success in the control of infectious diseases has been called the first public health revolution. These documents call for a second public health revolution using a new approach for modern problems. The leading killers and cripplers in today's society are largely chronic disease, accidents, and violent events. The 10 leading causes for years of potential life lost before age 65 now include only one infectious disease category (Centers for Disease Control, 1980). (Note: The number for years of potential life lost before age 65 is calculated for each death by subtracting the age at death from 65. For example, a person who dies at age 25 in an automobile accident loses 40 years of potential life before age 65. Such a death would be classified under the category "Motor Vehicle Accidents.") For the 10 leading causes, lifestyle is estimated to account for 53% of the years of potential life lost before age 65 (Figure 3) (Centers for Disease Control, 1980). As a result, the second public health revolution emphasizes modification of the lifestyles that result in premature loss of life.

Two aspects of *Healthy People* and *Objectives for the Nation* deserve special mention. First, the objectives are "designed primarily for well people . . . to reduce their risks of becoming ill or injured at some future date"

Table 5 Physical Fitness and Exercise Objectives to be Accomplished by 1990

Reduced risk factors	Increased public/professional awareness	Improved services/protection	Improved surveillance/ evaluation systems
1. The proportion of children and adolescents ages 10 to 17 participating regularly in appropriate physical activities, particularly cardiorespiratory fitness programs that can be carried into adulthood, should be greater than 90%.	1. The proportion of adults who can accurately identify the variety and duration of exercise thought to promote cardiovascular fitness most effectively should be greater than 70%.	1. The proportion of employees of companies and institutions with more than 500 employees offering employer sponsored fitness programs should be greater than 25%.	1. A methodology for systematically assessing the physical fitness of children should be established, with at least 70% of children and adolescents ages 10 to 17 participating in such an assessment.
2. The proportion of children and adolescents ages 10 to 17 participating in daily school physical education programs should be greater than 60%.	2. The proportion of primary-care physicians who include a careful exercise history as part of their initial examination of new patients should be greater than 50%.		2. Data should be available with which to evaluate the short- and long-term health effects of participation in programs of appropriate physical activity.
3. The proportion of adults 18 to 65 participating regularly in vigorous physical exercise should be greater than 60%.			3. Data should be available to evaluate the effects of participation in programs of physical fitness on job performance and health care costs.
4. 50% of adults 65 years and older should be engaging in appropriate physical activity, for example, regular walking, swimming, or other aerobic activity.			4. Data should be available for regular monitoring of national trends and patterns of participation in physical activity, including participation in public recreation programs in community facilities.

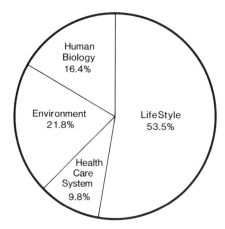

Figure 3 Percent contribution to years of life lost before ages 65 by the four elements of the health field, total population 1+ years of age, U.S.A., 1977. *Note.* From "The Status of the 1990 Objectives for Physical Fitness and Exercise" by K.E. Powell, K.G. Spain, G.M. Christenson, and M.P. Mollenkamp, 1986, *Public Health Reports, 101*, p. 19. Copyright 1986 by U.S. Public Health Service. Reprinted by permission.

(Department of Health and Human Services, 1980). This reflects the nature of current health problems. Today's leading killers and cripplers must be attacked long before they become manifest because our postmanifestation treatments are inadequate. To wait until a person has had a heart attack or has been killed in an auto accident is to wait too long. Physical activity patterns need to be in place years before a heart attack might occur, and seatbelts need to be buckled each time one gets into a car.

Second, the goals and objectives constitute a national commitment, not a federal imperative (Department of Health and Human Services, 1980). From the beginning many individuals from outside the government participated actively in the conception and development of *Healthy People* and the *Objectives for the Nation*. Now, at the implementation stage, participation by nongovernmental sources is essential. Schools, churches, consumer groups, industry, and labor—as well as local legislators and officials—must support, promote, and participate.

The adoption of physical fitness and exercise as one of the 15 priority areas in which implementation of current knowledge can lead to important reductions in premature morbidity and mortality has led to increased interest by scientists and public health officials. The interest at the federal level is reflected in a series of workshops conducted by USPHS agencies. In April 1984 the National Institute of Mental Health sponsored a workshop on "Coping with Stress: The Potential and Limits of Exercise Intervention"; in May the National Heart, Lung, and Blood Institute held a "Workshop on Activity Assessment Methods for Use in Epidemiologic Studies"; in September the Center for Health Promotion and Education conducted the "Workshop on Epidemiologic and Public Health Aspects of Physical Activity and Exercise" (Powell & Paffenbarger, 1985); and in June 1985 the National Center for Health Statistics (NCHS) held the "Workshop on Physical Fitness and Activity Assessments in NCHS General Population Surveys." The workshops are patent manifestations of the interest and program development in the area of physical activity and health at the federal level. This presumably both reflects and stimulates similar concerns at other levels of government and in the private sector.

The document *Objectives for the Nation* contains a variety of measures to improve the current situation (Department of Health and Human Services, 1980). Programs in schools, worksites, medical settings, and communities are all likely to increase the proportion of the population benefiting from regular exercise (Iverson, Fielding, Crow, & Christenson, 1985). However, no single agency or organization can accomplish much by itself. To enlarge the proportion of our population that benefits from being physically active will require the involvement of multiple agencies using a variety of methods.

Impediments to Public Health Interventions

As noted in the previous section, the public health community has made important policy (decisions) to promote the adoption of a more active lifestyle by the U.S. population. Nevertheless, several important impediments to the successful accomplishments of the objectives exist.

First, quantitative estimates about the reduction in morbidity and mortality that accrue with increased exercise are largely not available. The probable beneficial effects of physical activity on a variety of diseases of public health importance is established. With the exception of CHD, however, the data are insufficiently developed to quantitatively predict the magnitude of the benefits. We do not know, for example, whether the reduction in symptoms among depressed patients also means a reduction in the number of depressive episodes or an improved level of function and, if so, to what degree. Similarly, while the reduction in osteoporosis seems likely, no data are available with which to estimate the reduction in osteoporosis-related fractures that is associated with increased exercise. Only by comparing quantitative estimates for benefits and risks can we make fully enlightened policy decisions. In order to achieve quantitative estimates, greater care must be taken to characterize the physical activity being studied and to produce quantitative estimates of incidence and relative risks from which estimates of the overall impact on the population can be made.

A second major impediment to public health intervention is the uncertainty concerning the solution to the problem. The determinants of a physically active lifestyle are largely speculative, and many of the apparent determinants seem relatively impervious to change. For example, male sex, younger age, and more years of education regularly are found to be associated with higher activity levels (Stephens et al., 1985). Sex is for all practical purposes immutable. Age is forever changing but in a constant direction at an invariable pace. The number of one's years of education is modifiable but certainly not easily so. Previous exercise experiences are similarly unchangeable although one's attitude toward and interpretation of those experiences is likely to be always in flux. Much of the remainder of this book pertains to the methods by which a more vigorously active lifestyle or, more specifically, an exercise regimen can be effectively and efficiently promoted.

Given the fact that almost all of the benefits and risks remain to be quantified and that the determinants readily subject to policy change are not definitely shown to be important, the proper course of public health policy is unclear. One could argue that the public health activities outlined previously have already exceeded the scientific foundation for the area. However, this is not the case (Mason & Powell, 1985). Although not yet well quantified, the evidence in support of the public health importance of physical activity and exercise is well enough established to deserve public support. In addition to epidemiological research to supply the needed quantitative estimates, promotional efforts to provide the knowledge, skills, and facilities are appropriate.

References

Aloia, J.F., Cohn, S.H., Babu, T., Abesamis, C., Kalici, N., & Ellis, K. (1978). Skeletal mass and body composition in marathon runners. *Metabolism, 27,* 1793-1796.

Blair, S.N., Jacobs, D.R., Jr., & Powell, K.E. (1985). Relationships between exercise or physical activity and other health behaviors. *Public Health Reports, 100,* 172-180.

Caldwell, F. (1984). Light-boned and lean athletes: Does the penalty outweigh the reward? *Physician and Sportsmedicine, 12*(9), 139-149.

Cannon, J.G., & Kluger, M.J. (1983). Endogenous pyrogens activity in human plasma after exercise. *Science, 220,* 617-619.

The Carter Center of Emory University. (1984). *Closing the gap, health policy project, interim summary.* Atlanta: Emory University.

Caspersen, C.J., Powell, K.E., & Christenson, G.M. (1985). Physical activity, exercise, and physical fitness: Definitions and distinctions for health-related research. *Public Health Reports,* **100,** 126–131.

Centers for Disease Control. (1980). *Ten leading causes of death in the United States, 1977.* Atlanta: Author.

Centers for Disease Control. (1985). The status of the 1990 Objective for Physical Fitness and Exercise. *Morbidity and Mortality Weekly Report,* **34,** 521–524, 529–531.

Dalen, N., & Olsson, K.E. (1974). Bone mineral content and physical activity. *Acta Orthopaedica Scandinavica,* **45,** 170–174.

Department of Health and Human Services. (1980). *Promoting health/ preventing disease: Objectives for the nation.* Washington, DC: U.S. Government Printing Office.

Department of Health and Human Services. (1981). *Cardiovascular primer for the work place* (NIH Publication No. 2210). Washington, DC: U.S. Government Printing Office.

Department of Health, Education, and Welfare. (1979). *Healthy people: The surgeon general's report on health promotion and disease prevention* (DHEW [PHS] Publication No. 79-55071). Washington, DC: U.S. Government Printing Office.

Deyo, R.A. (1983). Conservative therapy for low back pain: Distinguishing useful from useless therapy. *Journal of the American Medical Association,* **250,** 1057–1062.

Dishman, R.K. (1985). Medical psychology in exercise and sport. *Medical Clinics of North America,* **69,** 123–143.

Dishman, R.K., Sallis, J.F., & Orenstein, D.O. (1985). The determinants of physical activity and exercise. *Public Health Reports,* **100,** 158–171.

Folkins, C.H., & Sime, W.E. (1981). Physical fitness training and mental health. *American Psychologist,* **36,** 373–389.

Foy, H.M., & Grayston, J.T. (1981). Acute respiratory infections. In D.W. Clark & B. MacMahon (Eds.), *Preventive and community medicine* (p. 309). Boston: Little, Brown.

Garcia-Palmieri, M.R., Costas, R., Jr., Cruz-Vidal, M., Sorlie, P.D., & Havlik, R.J. (1982). Increased physical activity: A protective factor against heart attacks in Puerto Rico. *The American Journal of Cardiology,* **50,** 749–755.

General Mills, Inc. (1979). *The General Mills American family report 1978–79: Family health in an era of stress.* Minneapolis: Author.

Hanson, P. (1984). Illness among athletes: An overview. In R.H. Strauss (Ed.), *Sports medicine* (pp. 79–90). Philadelphia: W.B. Saunders.

Haskell, W.L. (1984). Cardiovascular benefits and risks of exercise: The scientific evidence. In R.H. Strauss (Ed.), *Sports medicine* (pp. 57–75). Philadelphia: W.B. Saunders.

Hughes, J.R. (1984). Psychological effects of habitual aerobic exercise: A critical review. *Preventive Medicine, 13*, 66–78.

Iverson, D.C., Fielding, J.E., Crow, R.S., & Christenson, G.M. (1985). The promotion of physical activity in the U.S. population: The status of programs in medical, worksite, community, and school settings. *Public Health Reports, 100*, 212–224.

Kannel, W.B., & Sorlie, P. (1979). Some health benefits of physical activity: The Framingham study. *Archives of Internal Medicine, 139*, 857–861.

King, H., Taylor, R., Zimmet, P., Pargeter, K., Raper, L.R., Beriki, T., & Tekanene, J. (1984). Non-insulin-dependent diabetes (NIDDM) in a newly independent Pacific nation: The Republic of Kiribati. *Diabetes Care, 7*, 409–415.

Koplan, J.P., & Powell, K.E. (1984). Physicians and the Olympics. *Journal of the American Medical Association, 252*, 529–530.

Koplan, J.P., Powell, K.E., Sikes, R.K., Shirley, R.W., & Campbell, C.C. (1982). An epidemiologic study of the benefits and risks of running. *Journal of the American Medical Association, 248*, 3118–3121.

Koplan, J.P., Siscovick, D.S., & Goldbaum, G.M. (1985). The risks of exercise: A public health view of injuries and hazards. *Public Health Reports, 100*, 189–195.

Krolner, B., & Taft, B. (1983). Vertebral bone loss: An unheeded side effect of therapeutic bed rest. *Clinical Science, 64*, 537–540.

Loucks, A.B., & Horvath, S.M. (1985). Athletic amenorrhea: A review. *Medicine and Science in Sports and Exercise, 17*, 56–72.

Louis Harris & Associates. (1978). *Health maintenance.* For Pacific Mutual Life Insurance Company.

Louis Harris & Associates. (1984). *The prevention index: A report card on the nation's health.* For The Prevention Research Center, Prevention Magazine.

Mason, J.O., & Powell, K.E. (1985). Physical activity, behavioral epidemiology and public health. *Public Health Reports, 100*, 113–115.

Miller Brewing Company. (1983). *The Miller Lite report on American attitudes towards reports.* Milwaukee: Author.

Morgan, W.P. (1982). Psychological effects of exercise. *Behavioral Medicine Update, 4,* 25–30.

Morris, J.N., Everitt, M.G., Pollard, R., & Chave, S.P.W. (1980). Vigorous exercise in leisure-time: Protection against coronary heart disease. *Lancet, No. 8206,* 1207–1210.

National Center for Health Statistics. (1978). *Exercise and participation in sports among persons 20 years of age and over, United States, 1975* (Advancedata No. 19). Washington, DC: U.S. Government Printing Office.

Paffenbarger, R.S., Jr., & Hyde, R.T. (1975). Work activity and coronary heart mortality. *New England Journal of Medicine, 292,* 545–550.

Paffenbarger, R.S., Jr., & Hyde, R.T. (1984). Exercise in the prevention of coronary heart disease. *Preventive Medicine, 13,* 3–22.

Paffenbarger, R.S., Jr., Hyde, R.T., Wing, A.L., & Steinmetz, C.H. (1984). A natural history of athleticism and cardiovascular health. *Journal of the American Medical Association, 252,* 491–495.

Paffenbarger, R.S., Jr., Wing, A.L., & Hyde, R.T. (1978). Physical activity as an index of heart attack risk in college alumni. *American Journal of Epidemiology, 108,* 161–175.

Perrier—Great Waters of France, Inc. (1979). *The Perrier study: Fitness in America.* New York: Author.

Powell, K.E., & Paffenbarger, R.S., Jr. (1985). Workshop on epidemiologic and public health aspects of physical activity and exercise. *Public Health Reports, 100,* 118–126.

President's Council on Physical Fitness and Sports. (1974). National adult fitness survey. *Physical Fitness Research Digest, 4,* 1–27.

Simon, H.B. (1984). The immunology of exercise. *Journal of the American Medical Association, 252,* 2735–2738.

Siscovick, D.S., LaPorte, R.E., & Newman, J.M. (1985). The disease-specific benefits and risks of physical activity and exercise. *Public Health Reports, 100,* 180–188.

Siscovick, D.S., Weiss, N.S., Fletcher, R.H., & Lasky, T. (1984). The incidence of primary cardiac arrest during vigorous exercise. *New England Journal of Medicine, 311,* 874–877.

Siscovick, D.S., Weiss, N.S., Fletcher, R.H., Schoenbach, V.J., & Wagner, E.H. (1984). Habitual vigorous exercise and primary cardiac arrest: Effect of other risk factors on the relationship. *Journal of Chronic Diseases, 37*, 625–631.

Siscovick, D.S., Weiss, N.S., & Hallstron, A.P. (1982). Physical activity and primary cardiac arrest. *Journal of the American Medical Association,* **248**, 3113–3117.

Slattery, M.L., & Jacobs, D.R. (1985, January). Association of leisure-time physical activity and coronary heart disease incidence: The U.S. railroad study. Abstract submitted for the 25th Conference on Cardiovascular Disease Epidemiology. *CVD Epidemiology Newsletter,* No. 37, p. 81.

Sohn, R.S., & Micheli, L.J. (1984). The effect of running on the pathogenesis of osteoarthritis of the hips and knees. *Medicine and Science in Sports and Exercise,* **16**, 150.

Stephens, T., Jacobs, D.R., Jr., & White, C.C. (1985). A descriptive epidemiology of leisure-time physical activity. *Public Health Reports,* **100**, 147–158.

Taylor, C.B., Sallis, J.F., & Needle, R. (1985). The relation of physical activity and exercise to mental health. *Public Health Reports,* **100**, 195–202.

Terris, M. (1975). Approaches to an epidemiology of health. *American Journal of Public Health,* **65**, 1037–1045.

CHAPTER 2

Exercise Adherence, Coronary Heart Disease, and Longevity

Ralph S. Paffenbarger, Jr. and Robert T. Hyde

Numerous independent contributors to the development of relative risk for coronary heart disease (CHD) have been identified by epidemiological research. Habitual physical inactivity is one contributor that has particular importance for public health because it should be modifiable by behavioral interventions. Because physical inactivity may also interact with or influence unfavorably other behaviorally linked risk factors such as (a) cigarette smoking, (b) obesity, (c) hypertension, and (d) hyperlipidemia, it has an added significance for behavioral epidemiology. In this paper we review pertinent research findings on the relationships among physical inactivity, hypertension, cigarette smoking, obesity, adverse family history, cardiovascular disease, and mortality. Specific discussion of our prospective studies of San Francisco longshoremen and Harvard University alumni is provided in detail.

Primary Prevention of Coronary Heart Disease

Epidemiological research on physical activity and the risk of coronary heart disease has varied in subjects, activity, methods, and scope. The work of Professor J.N. Morris in England is regarded as the pioneering attempts to understand how both vocational and leisure-time physical activity relate to cardiovascular fitness and risk of CHD. Morris and his colleagues found that highly active conductors on London buses were at lower risk for CHD than the bus drivers who worked by sitting at the wheel (Morris, 1975; Morris, Heady, Raffle, Roberts, & Parks, 1953; Morris, Kagan, Pattison, Gardner, & Raffle, 1966). Similar findings were reached when these investigators later showed that the varying leisure-time exercise patterns of thousands of civil servants inversely paralleled their rates of CHD during a follow-up period (Chave, Morris, Moss, & Semmence, 1978; Epstein, Miller, Stitt, & Morris, 1976; Morris, Chave, Adam, Sirvey, Epstein, & Sheehan, 1973; Morris, Everitt, Pollard, Chave, & Semmence, 1980). Morris's studies attracted wide attention to the probable importance of exercise and the need for further investigations. From his studies of transport workers and civil servants Morris found that a moderate amount of physical work, whether on or off the job, could reduce the risk of CHD. This finding appeared to be particularly true when considering sudden, unexpected death and when some vigorous exercise was included. Morris also considered other variables such as cigarette smoking, somatotypes, blood pressure, family history, and blood lipids in concluding that contemporary habits of vigorous exercise make an independent contribution in lowering CHD risk.

Subsequent investigators of CHD rates and job- or leisure-related physical activity have sampled letter carriers and mail clerks, farmers and nonfarmers, workers in various occupations in Israeli kibbutzim, railroad trackmen and clerks, health insurance subscribers in various jobs, San Francisco cargo handlers and warehousemen, college students and alumni in various activities, residents of Framingham, Massachusetts, and various regions of Finland, Oslo, Norway, and many others (Breslow & Buell, 1960; Brunner, Manelis, Modan, & Levin, 1974; Cassel, Heyden, Bartel, 1971; Costas, Garcia-Palmieri, Nazario, & Sorlie, 1978; Dawber, 1980; Hammond & Garfinkel, 1969; Kahn, 1963; Kannel & Sorlie, 1979; Karvonen, 1983; Leven et al., 1975; Marmot, Rose, Shipley, & Hillman, 1978; Menotti & Puddu, 1976; Morris et al., 1953; Paffenbarger & Hale, 1975; Paffenbarger, Laughlin, Gima, & Black, 1970; Paffenbarger, Wing, & Hyde, 1978; Paffenbarger, Wolf, Notkin, & Thorne, 1966; Pomrehn, Wallace, & Burmeister, 1982; Punsar & Karvonen, 1976; Salonen, Puska, & Tuomilehto, 1982; Shapiro, Weinblatt, & Frank, 1969; Siscovick, Weiss,

Hallstrom, Inui, & Peterson, 1982; Taylor, Klepetar, Keys, Parlin, Blackburn, & Pachner, 1962; Zukel et al., 1959). Although these studies showed that lower CHD risk corresponded with higher exercise level, they were often not uniform in considering pertinent questions of diet, heredity, stress, cigarette smoking, and other potentially confounding factors that might account for the associations seen. Also, relatively few prospective studies have included female subjects although findings for women have generally paralleled those of men. However, several seemingly important contributions to gender differences in risk profiles or gender-by-risk factor interactions have not yet been adequately investigated. This is noteworthy in view of contemporary changes in lifestyle among women in some populations (Dawber, 1980; Kannel & Sorlie, 1979; Salonen et al., 1982).

For some time, variations in study design, methodology, and sampling rendered the associations between physical activity and CHD risks unclear. Some studies failed to show appreciable differences in CHD risks. Among groups of civil service workers in Los Angeles and among industrial workers in Chicago, this may have been due to insufficient range of differences in physical activity in their jobs or because other influences such as leisure-time exercise were not considered (Chapman & Massey, 1964; Paul, Lepper, Phelan, & Dupertuis, 1963; Stamler, Lindberg, Berkson, Shaffer, Miller, & Poindexter, 1960; Thomas, Lee, Franks, & Paffenbarger, 1981). A 10-year follow-up of men constituting 16 culturally varied cohorts in seven countries also produced mixed results (Keys, 1980), but assessments of physical activity were minimal in the program. When difficulties arise in defining or assessing physical activity levels in diverse international settings, comparisons within or among international groups are complicated (Fox, Naughton, & Haskell, 1971). On a global scale the relationships of CHD and its predisposing characteristics are complex. Because they at times may appear contradictory, lifestyles and work styles must be carefully characterized and closely studied if valid conclusions concerning them are to be drawn.

Occupational Activity: The San Francisco Bay Area Longshoremen Study

The work activity and fatal CHD records of the San Francisco longshoremen involve a wide range of energy expenditures that were evaluated by physical measurements taken in actual on-the-job situations. The study of these men included a 22-year follow-up of work assignments and CHD and began with a 1951 initial multiphasic screening examination of several thousand cargo handlers and dockworkers (Brand,

Paffenbarger, Scholtz, & Kampert, 1979; Paffenbarger, 1972; Paffenbarger, 1977; Paffenbarger, Brand, Scholtz, & Jung, 1978; Paffenbarger, Gima, Laughlin, & Black, 1971; Paffenbarger & Hale, 1975; Paffenbarger, Hale, Brand, & Hyde, 1977; Paffenbarger et al., 1970). Choice of a longshoring career might reflect a sturdy inherited constitution, but union rules assigned all men to physically demanding jobs as cargo handlers for at least their first 5 years of service. Some continued in that heavy work much longer; the average time was 13 years. Because this record was available for analysis, an interaction between hereditary cardiovascular differences and job selection could be evaluated. There was little or no reason to accept selection bias as a persuasive explanation for the differences in CHD rates observed when the longshoremen were grouped by their levels of energy output at work during the follow-up interval.

Figure 1 gives rates of fatal CHD among 3,686 San Francisco longshoremen during the years 1951 to 1972. These are expressed per 10,000 man-years of work, by age at death, and by job energy-output status. Energy-output calculations represented evaluations of various longshoring tasks on the job; allowances were made for rest periods and slack mo-

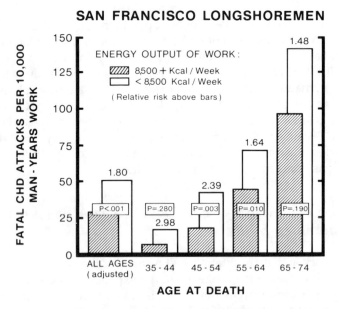

Figure 1   Fatal attacks of coronary heart disease per 10,000 man-years of work among San Francisco longshoremen, 1951–1972, by work energy output and age at death.

ments between heavy work episodes (Hale & O'Hara, 1959). Job assignments were checked annually to adjust for transfers, but those changes did not greatly alter the findings.

About 11% (395) of the longshoremen died of CHD during the 22-year period. Men who expended 8,500 or more kilocalories per week (kcal/week) at work (contributing 32% of the man-years of follow up) had significantly less risk of fatal CHD at any age than men whose jobs required less exercise. The effect was proportionately strongest at the younger ages but important at all ages studied; this is especially meaningful because the longshoremen were a stable work population who stayed in that industry and worked hard all their lives. The study did not include data on their leisure-time exercise, but from a sampling checkup this was considered to be relatively minimal (Paffenbarger & Hale, 1975).

A somewhat different risk pattern was seen in a birth-cohort analysis. Fatal CHD rates were significantly lower for vigorous job holders only in the two younger cohorts: men who were aged 35 to 44 and 45 to 54 in 1951 when the 22-year follow-up began (Paffenbarger et al., 1977). Several plausible explanations exist for this observation. The older longshoremen may have been allowed to ease their work effort even on heavy jobs, or experience may have taught them to work more efficiently or casually, reducing the distinction between their classifications of energetic and less energetic. On the other hand, younger cohorts may have been presented a new and different pattern of risk that was unknown to the older cohorts who in youth performed much manual labor in all jobs. Conversely, the older cohorts may have represented what the younger cohorts would become; the young groups may have included men at high risk of fatal CHD whose counterparts had already vanished from the older cohorts before the study began. Because cargo handling now relies more on machinery than on muscle power, the younger cohorts have been losing opportunity for high-energy output on their jobs, and the need for vigorous exercise in leisure-time activities has become as important for longshoremen as for more sedentary populations and their risks of CHD at any age.

Figure 2 presents data abstracted from official death certificates indicating the interval between CHD onset and death of San Francisco longshoremen who died of CHD during the 22-year interval from 1951 to 1972. Those dead on hospital arrival (or within one hour) following an observed attack were classified as "sudden death" cases. Those who died more than an hour after an attack were considered "delayed" deaths. Those for whom the interval was unknown were classed as "unspecified"; their relative risk resembled that of the "delayed" category.

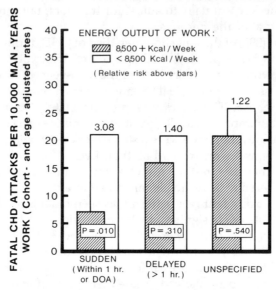

SAN FRANCISCO LONGSHOREMEN

Figure 2   Fatal attacks of coronary heart disease per 10,000 man-years of work among San Francisco longshoremen, 1951–1972, by work energy output and interval from symptom onset to death (DOA = dead on arrival). *Note.*   From ''Physical Activity as a Defense Against Coronary Heart Disease'' by R.S. Paffenbarger, 1985. In W.E. Connor and J.D. Bristow (Eds.), *Coronary Heart Disease: Prevention, Complications and Treatment* (p. 137), New York: J.B. Lippincott. Copyright 1985 by J.B. Lippincott. Reprinted by permission.

The sudden deaths were perhaps less likely to have involved prodromal symptoms that might have influenced work activity or job assignment. Figure 2 shows that high-energy workers had much less risk of sudden death from CHD than their less active companions. Although data on nonfatal CHD among the longshoremen were not available, the vigorous cargo handlers might have been less likely to have the disease or better able to survive a cardiac event if it occurred (Morris et al., 1966; Siscovick et al., 1982). In either instance, fewer cases would be found in the sudden death category. This is seen in Figure 2. The birth-cohort-specific analysis mentioned previously revealed also that the association of vigorous exercise with lower risk of sudden death was especially pronounced in the younger cohorts (Paffenbarger et al., 1977).

The association of vigorous occupational activity with lower risk of fatal CHD appears independent of other risk factors viewed as predictors of the disease. Given high-energy output, CHD risk is lower both in the presence and in the absence of heavy cigarette smoking, obesity, high blood pressure, abnormal glucose metabolism, excessive blood cholesterol content, and prior CHD. With respect to secondary prevention of fatal CHD, it is worth noting that high-energy output cargo handlers with a history of prior attack were at half as much risk of CHD death as were less active longshoremen with diagnosed heart disease. Under union rules it was standard practice for men who had been ill to return to their same jobs even when the work required strenuous exertion; many did so. The policy does not appear to have been unwise for those assigned to heavy work.

A multiple logistic regression analysis was used to control statistically the influence of age, follow-up interval, cigarette smoking, obesity, high blood pressure, and prior CHD in order to reveal the unique pattern of energy output with lower risk of fatal CHD. A reference level of 4,750 kcal/week was chosen, well below the 8,500 kcal breakpoint used to define low- and high-output categories. This minimum represented the exercise level of dockmen in light duties. Figure 3 shows that risk of fatal CHD is progressively lowered to 50% as energy output is doubled to 9,500 kcal/week.

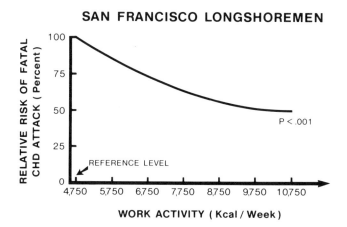

Figure 3 Multiple logistic regression analysis of percent reduction in risk of fatal attacks of coronary heart disease among San Francisco longshoremen, 1951–1972, by work energy output. The effects of age, follow-up interval, cigarette smoking, body mass index, blood pressure, and prior coronary heart disease are held constant.

In comparison with other populations the work-energy output of the San Francisco longshoremen was a relatively high level of occupational physical activity. The cargo-handling jobs frequently involved repeated bursts of strenuous exertion—heavy lifting, pushing, hauling, and gang work. Whether or not assisted by machinery, this manual labor of loading and unloading ships was necessarily dynamic and often rhythmic activity. It employed the large muscles for prolonged energy expenditure in motion; aerobic and isotonic applications of bodily power therefore predominated over demands for isometric stress.

It is of public health interest to consider how the absence or reduction among these men from the longshoremen population of the three major characteristics predisposing to CHD (low energy output, heavy smoking, and higher blood pressure) might have lowered death rates from CHD over the 22-year period of follow-up. To address this question Table 1 gives attributable risk percentages. These are the estimated theoretical reductions in rates of fatal CHD that might have been achieved if various combinations of these characteristics had been changed from high-risk to low-risk levels. If all longshoremen had worked at the level of 8,500 or more kcal/week, the death rate from CHD might have been reduced by a third or up to a half. If all had worked at high energy levels, smoked

Table 1 Potential Reduction in Fatal Coronary Heart Disease (CHD) Rates Among San Francisco Longshoremen With the Elimination of Specific Combinations of Low Work-Energy Output, Heavy Cigarette Smoking, and Higher Levels of Systolic Blood Pressure

Characteristics eliminated	Prevalence of characteristic (%)	CHD deaths per 10,000 man-years[a]	Potential reduction in fatal CHD rates[b] (% ± 1SE)
1. Low energy output[c]	68.9	69.7	48.8 ± 9.1
2. Heavy cigarette smoking[d]	37.7	94.3	27.9 ± 3.9
3. Higher systolic blood pressure[e]	40.2	89.1	28.8 ± 4.1
1, 2, or both	80.1	95.7	64.7 ± 10.1
1, 3, or both	81.8	91.5	73.5 ± 8.3
2, 3, or both	63.6	161.6	50.3 ± 5.3
1, 2, 3, or combinations	88.3	151.9	88.2 ± 9.0
None present	11.7	6.7	

Note. From "Physical Activity as a Defense Against Coronary Heart Disease" by R.S. Paffenbarger, 1985. In W.E. Connor and J.D. Bristow (Eds.), *Coronary Heart Disease: Prevention, Complications and Treatment* (p. 139), New York: J.B. Lippincott. Copyright 1985 by J.B. Lippincott. Reprinted by permission.
[a]Age- and cohort-adjusted. [b]Attributable risk (community). [c]<8,500 kcal/wk energy expenditure. [d]1 + pack per day. [e]≥ mean level for age.

less than a pack of cigarettes per day or not at all, and had had systolic blood pressures below average for longshoremen of their age, the total reduction might have approached 75% or more. This estimate, of course, represents a marked gain over the observed experience and is idealistic but of some guidance value. The attributable risk analysis assumes (a) a causal and dose-response relationship between each of the measured characteristics and fatal CHD, (b) that the characteristics can indeed be modified to the low-risk level, and (c) that other unmeasured influences on CHD risk are distributed equally between high- and low-risk groups. Interacting variables would tend in practice to reduce percentage estimates somewhat, but they remain useful and important for comparative purposes and policy making.

On balance, the attributable risk connected with low energy expenditure among the longshoremen is larger than the corresponding risk for the heavy cigarette habit or high systolic blood pressure level.

Leisure Activity: The United States College Alumni Health Study

Patterns of leisure-time exercise, other lifestyle elements, and health status have been examined among 50,000 former students from Harvard University and the University of Pennsylvania in order to determine how past and contemporary physical activity relate to CHD risk. Data extending from 1900 to the present time have been obtained from physical examination and other college records for students who matriculated during the years 1916 to 1950, from alumni responses to self-administered mail questionnaires, and from death certificates. Subsets of the total population have been studied for personal characteristics of college days and for present-day exercise habits and physician-diagnosed CHD. Analysis has shown that current and continuing adequate exercise adherence rather than a history of youthful or hereditary vigor and athleticism is associated inversely with risk of CHD in all age groups studied.

Rates of first attack of CHD among 16,936 Harvard University alumni during 10 years (1962 to 1972) or 6 years (1966 to 1972) were expressed per 10,000 man-years. There were 572 first attacks. Age-specific rates of CHD declined consistently with increases in energy expenditure by stair-climbing, walking, and sports play (as determined from mail questionnaires) and with increasing kcal/week in a composite physical activity index. Similar trends were found for both nonfatal and fatal clinical events (angina pectoris, myocardial infarction, and, to a lesser degree, sudden death). Overall CHD risk patterns were similar in each 10-year age group from 35 through 74 years. The cardiovascular health advantage from exercise adherence was seen over a wide range of lifestyles and at all ages studied. The effect was augmented, moreover, by vigorous sports play. In summary, alumni still engaging in strenuous activities plus at least a minimum of about 1,000 additional kcal/week of stair-climbing, walking, and other light activities had less than half (0.42) the CHD incidence of their nonathletic, mostly sedentary classmates.

Figure 4 consists of stereograms in which each bar represents an incidence rate of CHD for one of nine categories established by cross-tabulation of two designated characteristics at three levels each. The height of a bar shows the relative risk of CHD for alumni in that particular category as compared with the CHD risk of 1.00 assigned to the incidence rate for the category presumed at greatest risk (the "back corner" bar in each stereogram). Numbers atop bars give percentage of man-years experience involved.

Figure 4 presents relative risks of first CHD attack by cross-tabulations of (A) alumnus vigorous sports play and college student sports play or (B) alumnus physical activity index and college student sports play. In A, vigorous sports exercise by alumni seems important to their cardiovascular health ($p < .01$), but sports play of their student days carries little or no benefit into the later years ($p = .2$). Alumnus exercise index in B gives a broader sampling of energy expenditure: drop of CHD risk is significant with increased index ($p < .001$) but not with increased college sports play ($p < .18$). Ex-varsity athletes who remained active as alumni (2,000+ kcal/week) had less than half the CHD risk of classmates least active during and after college. Ex-varsity athletes inactive as alumni equaled the highest risk. Inactive students becoming active alumni had as low a risk as ex-varsity active alumni.

Exercise and Mortality

For the 1,413 alumni aged 35 through 84 years who died in the 213,716 man-years, 1962 to 1978, underlying causes of death were (a) cardiovascular disease 45%, (b) cancer 32%, (c) other natural causes 13%, and (d) unnatural causes 10%. Table 2 gives age-adjusted totals and cause-specific death rates by three exercise levels. The inverse relationship is strong between exercise level and death from all causes, total cardiovascular diseases (including both CHD and stroke), and total respiratory diseases. The trend is similar but less strong for total cancers but not for

HARVARD ALUMNI

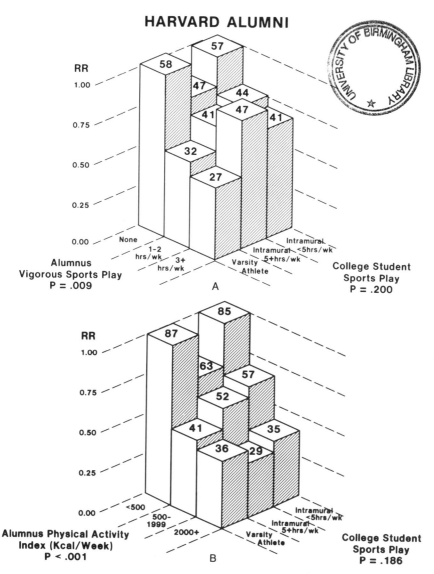

Figure 4 Relative risks (RRs) of first coronary heart disease attack for 16,936 Harvard alumni in 1962–1972 by cross-tabulations of alumnus vigorous sports and college student sports play (A), and alumnus physical activity index (expressed in kilocalories per week) and college student sports play (B). Coronary heart disease incidence rates corresponding to RR of 1.00 (back corner bar) are 57.5 (A) and 85.5 (B) per 10,000 man-years. Numbers atop bars give percent of man-years.

Table 2 Cause-Specific Death Rates per 10,000 Man-Years of Observation Among 16,936 Harvard Alumni, 1962 to 1978, by Physical Activity Index

Cause of death	Physical Activity Index, kcal/wk			One-tail test for trend, p
	<500	500–1,999	2,000+	
All causes (n = 1,413)	84.8	66.0	52.1	<.001
Total cardiovascular diseases (n = 640)	39.5	30.8	21.4	<.001
Coronary heart disease (n = 441)	25.7	21.2	16.4	.002
Stroke (n = 103)	6.5	5.2	2.4	.001
Total respiratory diseases (n = 60)	6.0	3.2	1.5	.001
Total cancers (n = 446)	25.7	19.2	19.0	.026
Lung (n = 89)	6.2	3.7	4.0	.116
Colorectal (n = 58)	2.2	2.3	3.5	.091[b]
Pancreas (n = 41)	1.8	2.4	1.0	.085
Prostate (n = 36)	2.2	1.5	1.6	.359
Total unnatural causes (n = 146)	8.7	7.1	5.9	.032
Accidents (n = 78)	3.6	3.9	3.0	.147
Suicides (n = 68)	5.1	3.2	2.9	.049

Note.   From "A Natural History of Athleticism and Cardiovascular Health" by R.S. Paffenbarger, R.T. Hyde, A.L. Wing, and C.H. Steinmetz, 1984, *Journal of the American Medical Association, 252,* p. 494. Copyright 1984 by the American Medical Association. Reprinted by permission.
[a]Adjusted for differences in age, cigarette smoking, and hypertension. [b]Opposite trend.

those site-specific cancers (lung, colon-rectum, pancreas, and prostate) common enough to be analyzed separately. The trend is weak for total unnatural causes including accidental deaths and suicides.

To allow for disease-rate self-selection that might affect exercise adherence (i.e., by persons choosing sedentary habits because of illness) rather than exercise adherence affecting disease rate, death rates were recomputed for major causes of death (1,270 decedents). The first 2 years of follow-up after exercise assessment were omitted. In 179,961 man-years a strong inverse relation remained between exercise and death from cardiovascular diseases ($p < .001$), including both CHD and stroke, and from respiratory causes ($p < .01$), but a dwindling association was found between exercise and death from cancer ($p < .05$) or unnatural causes ($p > .05$). The persistently strong inverse relation between exercise and specific cardiovascular mortality but not most other causes of death testifies to the specificity of the association for CHD and supports the hypothesis of "exercise as heart protection" over alternative hypotheses of constitutional or behavioral preselection.

Although not depicted here, when adjustment is made also for the adverse influences of cigarette smoking, hypertension, and obesity, the reduced risk of CHD remains strongly related to vigorous sports play, but the strength of the relationship is reduced somewhat for less vigorous activities. As assessed, the level of physical activity characterizing the lifestyle of Harvard alumni varied over a modest range of energy expenditure at work and at leisure. Because these alumni were sedentary workers or retired, their spare-time activity represented a large share of their total energy output per week and characterized their level of effort. Because of their lifestyle contrasts with that of the San Francisco longshoremen of the 1950s and 1960s, the associations seen support the finding that the association between vigorous exercise and cardiovascular health is a robust one that is not limited to a single population or type of exertion.

The community or public health view of intervention was computed to represent the potential reduction in first CHD attack from elimination of various combinations of characteristics in Harvard alumni (Table 3). As for longshoremen, shown in Table 1, similar theoretical considerations (cause-and-effect, proportional changes, risk alterability, and equivalent distributions of other risk factors) apply to the three most prominent risk characteristics—sedentary lifestyle, cigarette smoking, and hypertension. Other things being equal, if all alumni had expended 2,000 or more kcal/week, the number of CHD attacks might have been reduced by about 26%. If none had smoked cigarettes, about 25% fewer first attacks might have

Table 3 Potential Reduction in First Attacks of Coronary Heart Disease (CHD) Rates Among Harvard Alumni With the Elimination of Specific Combinations of Sedentary Lifestyle, Cigarette Smoking, and Hypertension

Characteristics eliminated	Prevalence of characteristic (%)	Fatal or nonfatal CHD per 10,000 man-years[a]	Potential reduction in CHD rates[b] (% ± 1SE)
1. Sedentary lifestyle[c]	60.0	57.9	26.0 ± 5.9
2. Cigarette smoking[d]	40.0	70.8	25.1 ± 4.0
3. Hypertension[e]	8.2	107.9	16.1 ± 2.5
1, 2, or both	75.6	57.0	44.6 ± 7.0
1, 3, or both	63.0	57.7	31.2 ± 6.2
2, 3, or both	44.9	72.4	36.7 ± 4.4
1, 2, 3, or combinations	77.3	56.5	48.2 ± 7.3
None present	22.7		

Note. From "Physical Activity as a Defense Against Coronary Heart Disease" by R.S. Paffenbarger, 1985. In W.E. Connor and J.D. Bristow (Eds.), *Coronary Heart Disease: Prevention, Complications and Treatment* (p. 144), New York: J.B. Lippincott. Copyright 1985 by J.B. Lippincott. Reprinted by permission.
[a]Age-adjusted. [b]Attributable risk (community). [c]<2,000 kcal/wk energy expenditure. [d]Any amount. [e]Doctor-diagnosed.

occurred. If none had been hypertensive, reduction might have approximated 16%. If all men had been physically active, nonsmoking, and normotensive, the corresponding estimated reduction might have avoided or delayed nearly 50% of the CHD attacks observed among them during the follow-up interval. Over the lifetime of this study population, the gain in man-years by adequate exercise and nonsmoking would be impressive (Paffenbarger, Hyde, Wing, & Hsieh, 1986b).

Secondary Prevention of Heart Attack

The protective role of exercise regarding second or subsequent CHD attack is less clear than that seen in studies of first attacks. Clinical trials often have encountered problems of small numbers, poor compliance, high dropout, and short follow-up. Each of these design problems mitigates conclusive inferences. Epidemiological studies of stevedores and British civil service workers have suggested that differences of two-fold or more may exist between the high risk of death from recurring CHD in sedentary subjects and the lower risk for those with a more energetic lifestyle (Morris et al., 1980; Paffenbarger & Hale, 1975). Whether these differences represent protective as opposed to selective influences is not yet established. Other investigators have addressed this issue in the study of physical activity and secondary prevention of CHD (Karvonen, Rautaharju, Orma, Punsar, & Takkunen, 1961; Rechnitzer et al., 1975; Shaw, 1981; Tibblin, Wilhelmsen, & Werko, 1975; Wilhelmsen, Tibblin, Aunell, Bjure, Ekstrom-Jodal, & Grimby, 1976).

Continuing studies of health status and physical activity ratings of Harvard alumni with clinically recognized CHD have assessed the relationship of their various characteristics to risk of death from CHD and other causes (Paffenbarger, 1982; Paffenbarger & Hyde, 1984; Thomas, Lee, Franks, & Paffenbarger, 1981).

A total of 782 Harvard alumni ages 35 through 74 reported a history of CHD by questionnaire in 1962 or 1966. Among them were 197 CHD deaths (25%) and 82 deaths from other causes (10%) during a 12- to 16-year follow-up interval. As in other studies of this population, relative risks of death from CHD were related to measures of physical activity, including ascending stairs, block walking, sports play, and the composite index of these activities when expressed in kilocalories of energy expenditure per week. Relative risks of death from all other causes, however, were unrelated to these same physical activity measures (Figure 5).

When the 782 CHD patients were classified as having had myocardial infarction with or without angina pectoris ($N = 607$) or angina alone ($N = 175$) as in Table 4, relative risks of death from subsequent CHD were

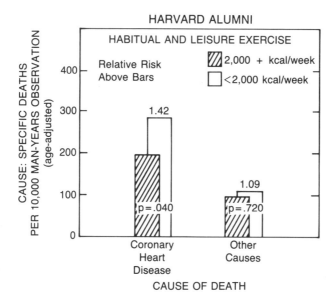

Figure 5   Death rates of coronary heart disease and other causes per 10,000 man-years of observation among 782 Harvard alumni with coronary heart disease, 1962 or 1966 to 1977, by leisure-time energy output. *Note.*   Adapted from "Exercise in the Prevention of Coronary Heart Disease" by R.S. Paffenbarger and R.T. Hyde, 1984, *Preventive Medicine, 13, p. 16.* Copyright 1984 by Academic Press Inc. Adapted by permission.

generally higher for less active men but with variations as to type of activity and disease category. Similar differences were found in relative risks both for death that occurred within 1 hour of symptom onset and for delayed death. Thus it would seem that men who have survived a first attack of CHD will have lower risk of death from a recurrent attack over a period of several years if they maintain habits of adequate exercise than if they do not exercise.

As in the study of the primary prevention of CHD, men with a prior attack of this disease were cross-tabulated by student and alumnus physical activity patterns and followed 12 to 16 years for rates of fatal CHD. Rate trends were lower for patients who expended 2,000 or more kcal/week. This was observed whether or not these men had been active in varsity sports or in intramural sports play for 5 or more hours per week during student years. Neither type of student athleticism showed any prospective relationship with reduced CHD death; this is in contrast to a 40% risk reduction for contemporary sports participation as an alumnus. A current and continuing level of exercise adherence appears to be uniquely associated in an inverse fashion with level of CHD risk for either a first or subsequent attack.

Table 4 Physical Activities and Coronary Heart Disease (CHD) Death Rates Among CHD Patients (Harvard Alumni) in a 12- to 16-Year Follow-Up Interval

Weekly activity	Patients with myocardial infarction (N = 607)		Patients with angina pectoris (N = 175)	
	CHD deaths per 10,000 man-years[a]	Relative risk[a]	CHD deaths per 10,000 man-years[a]	Relative risk[b]
Stair climbing				
<350	319		128	
		1.16		0.88
350+	275		146	
Block walking				
<35	300		157	
		1.03		1.35
35+	291		117	
Sports play				
No	327		149	
		1.33		1.09
Yes	246		136	
Index in kcal				
<2,000	323		151	
		1.34		3.12
2,000+	240		48	

Note. From "Physical Activity as a Defense Against Coronary Heart Disease" by R.S. Paffenbarger, 1985. In W.E. Connor and J.D. Bristow (Eds.), *Coronary Heart Disease: Prevention, Complications and Treatment* (p. 146), New York: J.B. Lippincott. Copyright 1985 by J.B. Lippincott. Reprinted by permission.
[a]Age- and interval-adjusted. [b]Rate for high-risk level of activity divided by low-risk level of activity.

Patients with CHD who exercised less than 2,000 kcal/week were at greater risk of death from this cause than those more active, whether or not they smoked cigarettes, were hypertensive, or were overweight for their height. Moreover, a multiple logistic analysis using a reference level of 100 kcal/week showed a 25% reduction in risk at a 3,000 kcal expenditure and a 35% reduction at 5,000 kcal expenditure. Risk reduction from habitual and leisure exercise persisted when cigarette smoking, hypertension, obesity, parental CHD, and student athleticism were controlled. The salutary influence of exercise was consistent for patients suffering either angina pectoris or myocardial infarction at all ages and in successive 4-year periods of follow-up through 16 years. Men who included vigorous sports play in their weekly activity program experienced no further benefit over those who did not, a departure from the findings for the first attack of CHD.

How plausible are the data that seem to show a meaningful relationship between physical inactivity and increased risk of CHD? This issue was addressed in the 22-year follow-up of the 3,686 San Francisco longshoremen previously described by assessing the roles of occupational activity, the cigarette smoking habit, and systolic blood pressure levels for their independent relationships to rate of death from a wide range of diseases (Paffenbarger et al., 1978). Smoking patterns and blood pressure status were established at the start of observations (1951), and job activities were assessed annually through the end of observations (1972). Holding differences in age, smoking patterns, and blood pressure levels constant, death rates from CHD per 10,000 man-years of observation were twice as high among men who expended less than 8,500 kcal/week in their work performance as compared to CHD death rates among more active cargo handlers. Death rates from stroke were two-thirds higher. On the other hand, death rates among less active and more active longshoremen by such causes as site-specific cancers, accidental death, suicide, and most natural causes other than CHD did not differ statistically. Although numbers were small, death from chronic obstructive respiratory disease was more common among less active longshoremen than among cargo handlers. These observations show that a more sedentary lifestyle took its toll chiefly through hypertensive-arteriosclerotic influences and was less clearly related to other natural and traumatic causes of death. However, a significant inverse association has been shown between physical activity and all-cause mortality in Harvard alumni (Paffenbarger et al., 1984; Paffenbarger et al., 1986).

To test the specificity of the relationship between leisure-time exercise and CHD influence, the relative risks of specific causes of death were examined by level of energy expenditure among Harvard alumni. In the study population of 16,936 men, 695 men died during the 6 to 10 year follow-up from 1962 or 1966 to 1972. The level of energy expenditure was computed, as previously described, from questionnaire data on number of stairs climbed and blocks walked together with the hours of light and vigorous sports played weekly. Age-specific death rates and relative risks of death by selected causes were computed by level of physical activity. Table 5 presents relative risks by cause for alumni who expended less than 2,000 kcal/week in climbing, walking, and sports play as compared with men who were more active. At this breakpoint of leisure-time activity the risk of CHD was twice as common among less active as compared with more active alumni; the risk of stroke was 1.25 times higher.

Table 5 Relative Risks of Death From Specific Diseases Among Harvard Alumni in a 6- to 10-Year Follow-Up, by Leisure-Time Physical Activity Level

Cause of death	Number of decedents	Number of decedents	Relative risk of death[a]	p
All causes	695	500	1.57	<.001
CHD	215	151	2.01	<.001
Stroke	53	38	2.25	.030
All cancer	196	138	1.14	.538
Lung cancer	45	37	1.21	.620
Other natural	137	98	1.14	.512
Accident	44	32	1.94	.166
Suicide	50	43	1.58	.154

Note. From "Physical Activity as a Defense Against Coronary Heart Disease" by R.S. Paffenbarger, 1985. In W.E. Connor and J.D. Bristow (Eds.), *Coronary Heart Disease: Prevention, Complications and Treatment* (p. 147), New York: J.B. Lippincott. Copyright 1985 by J.B. Lippincott. Reprinted by permission.
[a]Age- and interval-specific death rate per 10,000 man-years for high-risk level of physical activity (<2,000 kcal/wk) divided by rate for low-risk level (2,000 + kcal/week).

The risk of death from other causes was not related significantly to the level of energy expenditure although the inverse association was strong for all-cause mortality. Thus, again, the specificity of the relationship would seem to be most pronounced for hypertensive-arteriosclerotic diseases.

Prevention of Hypertension

Exercise adherence is accompanied by a slight lowering of both systolic and diastolic blood pressure in normotensive men (Boyer & Kasch, 1970; Fitzgerald, 1981; Stamler, Farinaro, & Mojonnier, 1980; Wilcox, Bennett, Brown, & MacDonald, 1982). Frequent and vigorous sports play is associated with lower blood pressure levels, with a lower incidence of hypertension, and with reduced focal myocardial fibrosis (Hillman, Levy, Stroud, & White, 1944; Levy, White, Stroud, & Hillman, 1947; Morris & Crawford, 1958; Paffenbarger, 1982; Paffenbarger, Thorne, & Wing, 1968; Paffenbarger, Wing, Hyde, & Jung, 1983; Thomas, 1952; Thomas, Ross, & Higinbotham, 1964). Because hypertension is a strong predictor of increased CHD risk, as is physical inactivity, the influence of student and alumnus exercise patterns on hypertension incidence was studied among Harvard alumni. Physical activity patterns and other selected characteristics from college records, supplemented with post-college health and exercise data from mail questionnaires obtained in 1962 or 1966, provided the potential predictor variables for study. Surviving respondents were questioned again in 1972 about the development of physician-diagnosed hypertension.

Among 14,998 male alumni ages 35 to 74 reportedly free of hypertension in 1962 or 1966, 681 developed hypertension by 1972. Age-adjusted incidence rates computed for each kind and level of physical activity showed no difference for alumni (a) who climbed fewer than 50 stairs per day than for men who climbed more, (b) who walked fewer than five blocks per day than for men who walked farther, and (c) who played no sports than for those who indulged only in light sports. In contrast, the 59% of alumni who did not engage in vigorous sports were at a 35% greater risk of hypertension than the 41% who did. The association of vigorous exercise with lower risk of hypertension persisted in each 10-year age class from 35 through 74. When the data were adjusted for differences in age and body mass index, the incidence of hypertension in the 6- to 10-year follow-up was 48 per 10,000 man-years for alumni who reported playing vigorous sports as contrasted with 72 for those who reported no vigorous activities.

Neither varsity sports play nor intramural student athleticism was associated with lower risk of hypertension unless supplemented by vigorous sports play in postcollege years. However, three youth characteristics—increased weight-for-height, faster pulse rate, and higher blood pressure levels—predisposed students to hypertension in the 6- to 10-year follow-up that began 16 to 50 years after college. A body mass index of 32+ units, representing youths approximately 15% overweight, identified students having a 24% greater risk of developing hypertension as compared with lighter classmates. A student pulse rate of 90+ beats per minute predicted a 26% higher risk than did a slower pulse. Hypertension risk increased 36% with higher systolic blood pressure (130+ mmHg), 27% with higher diastolic blood pressure (80+ mmHg), and 92% with both pressures elevated when contrasted with the risk seen if college-assessed blood pressures were below these levels.

A gradient effect of increasing weight-for-height was apparent among alumni ages 35 to 74 throughout the range of observations, from alumni having ideal weight levels up through the 13% of men who were 40 or more pounds (18.1+ kg) overweight. Gain in body mass index across subjects between college and 1962 or 1966, an interval that ranged from 16 to 50 years, also showed a gradient effect from least to most gain, and the 38% of alumni who gained 25 or more pounds (11.5+ kg) for a constant height were at 60% increased risk of hypertension over those who gained less or not at all.

Alumni reporting a parental history of hypertension represented 38% of the total and were at an 83% increased risk of hypertension over their classmates with a negative parental history.

Figure 6 shows age-adjusted incidence rates of hypertension together with relative risk for that disease for alumni classified by participation in vigorous sports (yes or no) and by gradient of body mass index in two-unit stages from lightest to heaviest. These categories comprised 23%, 25%, 24%, 15%, and 13% of the man-years of observation. Along this gradient the reduced risk of hypertension for vigorous sports players is notable only among men considerably overweight for their height. When compared with the vigorous alumni, nonparticipants who were 20% over ideal weight (body mass index of 36-37) had a 50% higher risk of hypertension. Those 25% or more overweight (body mass index 38+) had a

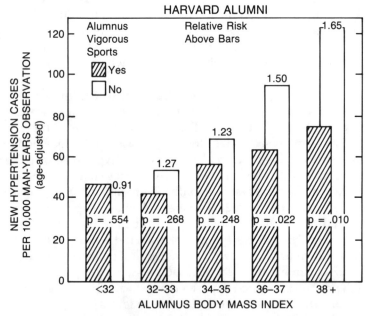

Figure 6 First diagnoses of hypertension per 10,000 man–years of observation among Harvard alumni in a 6- to 10-year follow-up (1962 or 1966–1972), by leisure-time energy output in vigorous sports play and body mass index assessed by questionnaire in 1962 or 1966. *Note.* From "Physical Activity as a Defense Against Coronary Heart Disease" by R.S. Paffenbarger, 1985. In W.E. Connor and J.D. Bristow (Eds.), *Coronary Heart Disease: Prevention, Complications and Treatment* (p. 148), New York: J.B. Lippincott. Copyright 1985 by J.B. Lippincott. Reprinted by permission.

65% higher risk. When the data were adjusted for differences in age, follow-up interval, body mass index gain since college, and parental history of hypertension (in a multiple logistic risk analysis), the odds of this disease in alumni were lowered as weekly hours of vigorous sports play increased, but the reduction was significant only for men 25% or more overweight for their height (Figure 7). Two hours per week of vigorous sports play by heavyweights was associated with one fourth less risk of hypertension, and 4 hours with one-half the risk. It is very likely that the vigorous heavy men tended to be muscular and the inactive to be fat although they were rated alike by body mass index.

Relative risk and attributable risks of this disease were computed (Table 6) to assess the relative importance of vigorous sports play and three other major characteristics of increased hypertension risks. The data were based on a multivariate analysis adjusted for differences in age, follow-up interval, and each of the other characteristics listed when assessing the relationship of participation in vigorous sports: alumnus body

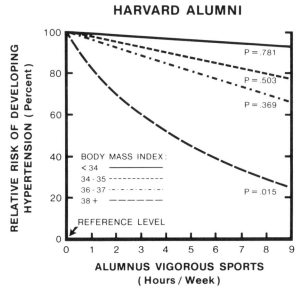

Figure 7   Multiple logistic regression analysis of percent reduction in risk of developing hypertension among Harvard alumni in a 6- to 10-year follow-up (1962 or 1966–1972), by vigorous sports play in hours per week. The effects of age, follow-up interval, body mass index gain since college, and parental history of hypertension are held constant. *Note.*   From "Physical Activity as a Defense Against Coronary Heart Disease" by R.S. Paffenbarger, 1985. In W.E. Connor and J.D. Bristow (Eds.), *Coronary Heart Disease: Prevention, Complications and Treatment* (p. 149), New York: J.B. Lippincott. Copyright 1985 by J.B. Lippincott. Reprinted by permission.

Table 6 Relative Risks and Potential Reductions in Hypertension Incidence Among Harvard Alumni in a 6- to 10-Year Follow-Up, by Selected High-Risk Characteristics

Alumnus characteristic	Prevalence of characteristic (%)	Relative risk of hypertension[a] (95% confidence interval)	Potential reduction in hypertension incidence[b] (%)	p
Lack of vigorous sports play	65.0	1.52 (1.18–1.86)	25.3	<.001
Body mass index of 36 + units	36.3	1.43 (1.13–1.73)	13.5	<.001
Body mass index gain since college of 5 + units	40.8	1.44 (1.34–1.74)	15.2	<.001
Parental history of hypertension	38.8	1.91 (1.55–2.27)	26.1	<.001

Note. From "Physical Activity as a Defense Against Coronary Heart Disease" by R.S. Paffenbarger, 1985. In W.E. Connor and J.D. Bristow (Eds.), *Coronary Heart Disease: Prevention, Complications and Treatment* (p. 149), New York: J.B. Lippincott. Copyright 1985 by J.B. Lippincott. Reprinted by permission.
[a]Incidence rate for high-risk level of characteristic divided by rate for low-risk level. Incidence rates were adjusted for differences in age, follow-up interval, and each of the other characteristics. [b]Attributable risk (community).

mass index, body mass index gain since college, and parental history of hypertension. Each characteristic made an independent contribution to hypertension incidence. Men not vigorously active were at a 52% higher risk than their athletic classmates. Those with a body mass index of 36+ were at a 43% greater risk than lighter men. Weight gain of 5+ units since college predicted a 44% increased risk over a lesser gain. Alumni with one or both parents hypertensive were at 91% greater risk of hypertension than their peers with normotensive parents. Attributable risks within population of Harvard alumni ranged from 14 to 26%.

Cigarette Smoking

As Blair notes in chapter 3, the pattern of association between physical activity and cigarette smoking remains unclear. For this reason it is particularly informative to examine the comparative and interactive influences that both behaviors may exert on CHD risk. This evaluation can help determine the public health importance for establishing their association in future behavioral studies.

Cigarette smoking contributes to the development of atherosclerotic lesions, the predominant underlying cause of cardiovascular disease, and to the clinical manifestations of atherosclerotic vascular disease—coronary, cerebral, aortic, and peripheral vascular disease and sudden, unexpected death. Although understanding of the precise pathophysiological basis of these clinical manifestations is incomplete, it may relate to several deleterious effects of cigarette smoking on cardiovascular health: accelerating the atherosclerotic process, promoting myocardial oxygen insufficiency, inducing abnormal plasma lipoprotein-cholesterol profile, disrupting the hemostatic system, and lowering the threshold for ventricular fibrillation. Although nicotine and carbon monoxide are the constituents of tobacco smoke most prominent as agents, hydrogen cyanide, oxides of nitrogen, and carbon disulfide also are highly suspect in the pathogenesis of coronary heart disease (Paffenbarger, Hyde, Wing, & Hsieh, 1986a).

The epidemiological evidence linking cigarette smoking and cardiovascular diseases is reinforced by pathological findings that smoking aggravates and accelerates development of the underlying lesions and occlusive events in coronary, cerebral, aortic, and peripheral arteries (Auerbach, Carter, Garfinkel, & Hammond, 1976; Auerbach, Hammond, & Garfinkel, 1965; McGill, 1979; McMillan, 1978; Strong & Richards, 1976).

Figure 8-A gives rates and relative risks of fatal cardiovascular disease by alumnus cigarette habit cross-tabulated with student and alumnus blood pressure status. For normotensive alumni risk is 10 to 20% lower with decreasing amounts smoked irrespective of whether student systolic blood pressure was below 130 mmHg or higher. Among alumni with physician-diagnosed hypertension, however, the relative risk of fatal cardiovascular disease is reduced nearly one-half (relative risk 0.55) when smoking level is decreased from heavy (a pack or more per day) to none. The effect of the cigarette habit on risk of fatal cardiovascular disease is strong and independent of the influence of hypertension, which is even stronger.

At each level of cigarette smoking in Figure 8-B cardiovascular disease mortality declines as leisure-time exercise increases, and when the data are adjusted for the influence of smoking exercise continues to be inversely related to death. The cigarette habit is directly related to cardiovascular disease mortality when exercise is held constant. The most physically active nonsmokers have only 30% as much fatal cardiovascular disease as the sedentary heavy smokers, and the least physically active nonsmokers 52%.

Figure 8-C shows that cardiovascular disease mortality is related directly to the cigarette habit when body mass index is held constant. If smoking is held constant, the risk of fatal cardiovascular disease is related directly also to weight-for-height but less strongly than to smoking.

HARVARD ALUMNI

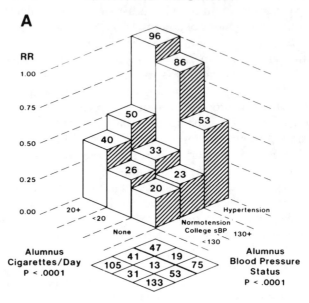

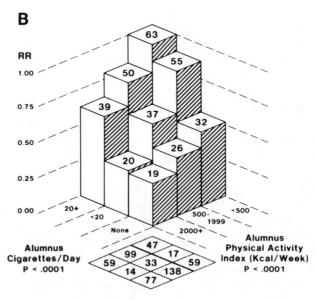

(Cont.)

Epstein, L., Miller, G.J., Stitt, F.W., & Morris, J.N. (1976). Vigorous exercise in leisure time, coronary risk factors, and resting electrocardiogram in middle-aged civil servants. *British Heart Journal*, **38**, 403–409.

Fitzgerald, W. (1981). Labile hypertension and jogging: New diagnostic tool or spurious discovery? *British Journal of Medicine*, **38**, 403–409.

Fox, S.M., Naughton, J.P., & Haskell, W.L. (1971). Physical activity and the prevention of coronary heart disease. *Annals of Clinical Research*, **3**, 404–412.

Hale, F.C., & O'Hara, J.J. (1959, June). *An engineering analysis of cargo handling X. Energy expenditure of longshoremen* (Report No. 59-20). Los Angeles: University of California, Department of Engineering.

Hammond, E.C., & Garfinkel, L. (1969). Coronary heart disease, stroke and aortic aneurysms: Factors in the etiology. *Archives of Environmental Health*, **19**, 167–183.

Hillman, C.C., Levy, R.L., Stroud, W.D., & White, P.D. (1944). Studies of blood pressure in army officers. *Journal of the American Medical Association*, **125**, 699–701.

Kahn, H.A. (1963). The relationship of reported coronary heart disease mortality to physical activity of work. *American Journal of Public Health*, **53**, 1058–1067.

Kannel, W.M., & Sorlie, P. (1979). Some health benefits of physical activity: The Framingham study. *Archives of Internal Medicine*, **139**, 857–861.

Karvonen, M.J. (1983). Physical activity in work and leisure time in relation to cardiovascular diseases. *Annals of Clinical Research*, **14** (Suppl. 34), 118–123.

Karvonen, M.J., Rautaharju, P.M., Orma, E., Punsar, S., & Takkunen, J. (1961). Heart disease and employment. Cardiovascular studies on lumberjacks. *Journal of Occupational Medicine*, **3**, 49–53.

Keys, A. (1980). *Seven countries: A multivariate analysis of death and coronary heart disease*. Cambridge: Commonwealth Fund Harvard University Press.

Leren, P., Askevold, E.M., Foss, O.P., Froili, A., Grymyr, D., Helgeland, A., Hjermann, I., Holme, I., Lund-Larsen, P.G., & Norum, K.R. (1975). The Oslo study: Cardiovascular disease in middle-aged and young Oslo men. *Acta Medicus Scandinavica* (Suppl. 588), 1–38.

Levy, R.L., White, P.D., & Stroud, W.D. (1947). Sustained hypertension. Predisposing factors and causes of disability and death. *Journal of the American Medical Association*, **135**, 77–80.

Marmot, M.G., Rose, G., Shipley, M., & Hillman, C.C. (1978). Employ-ment grade and coronary heart disease in British civil servants. *Journal of Epidemiology and Community Health,* **32**, 244–249.

McGill, H.C., Jr. (1979). Potential mechanisms for the augmentation of atherosclerotic disease by cigarette smoking. *Preventive Medicine,* **8**, 390–403.

McMillan, G.C. (1978). Atherogenesis: The process from normal to lesion. In A.B. Chandler, K. Eruenius, G.C. McMillan, C.B. Nelson, C.J. Schwartz, & S. Wessler, (Eds.), *The thrombotic process in atherogenesis* (pp. 3–10). New York: Plenum.

Menotti, A., & Puddu, V. (1976). Death rates, among the Italian railroad employees, with special reference to coronary heart disease and physi-cal activity at work. *Environmental Research,* **11**, 331–342.

Morris, J.N. (1975). *Uses of epidemiology* (3rd ed., pp. 163–165). New York: Churchill Livingstone.

Morris, J.N., Chave, S.P.W., Adam, C., Sirey, C., Epstein, L., & Sheehan, D.J. (1973). Vigorous exercise in leisure-time: Protection against coro-nary heart disease. *Lancet,* **2**, 1207–1210.

Morris, J.N., & Crawford, M.D. (1958). Coronary heart disease and physi-cal activity of work: Evidence of a national necropsy survey. *British Medical Journal,* **2**, 1485–1496.

Morris, J.N., Everitt, M.G., Pollard, R., Chave, S.P.W., & Semmence, A.M. (1980). Vigorous exercise in leisure-time: Protection against coro-nary heart disease. *Lancet,* **2**, 1207–1210.

Morris, J.N., Heady, J.A., Raffle, P.A.B., Roberts, C.G. & Parks, J.W. (1953). Coronary heart disease and physical activity of work. *Lancet,* **2**, 1053–1057, 1111–1120.

Morris, J.N., Kagan, A., Pattison, D.C., Gardner, M., & Raffle, P.A.B. (1966). Incidence and prediction of ischaemic heart disease in London busmen. *Lancet,* **2**, 552–559.

Paffenbarger, R.S., Jr. (1972). Factors predisposing to fatal stroke in long-shoremen. *Preventive Medicine,* **1**, 522–528.

Paffenbarger, R.S., Jr. (1977). Physical activity and fatal heart attack: Pro-tection or selection? In E.A. Amsterdam, J.H. Wilmore, & A.N. DeMaria (Eds.), *Exercise in cardiovascular health and disease* (pp. 35–49). New York: Yorke Medical Books.

Paffenbarger, R.S., Jr. (1982). Lifestyle patterns as a defense against coro-nary heart disease. In W.P. Santamore & A.A. Bove (Eds.), *Coronary artery disease* (pp. 263–274). Baltimore: Urgan & Schwarzenberg.

Paffenbarger, R.S., Jr. (1982). The role of physical activity in the primary and secondary prevention of coronary heart disease. In H. Weidemann & L. Samek (Eds.), *Bewegungstherapie in der kardiologie.* Darmstadt: Steinkopff Verlag.

Paffenbarger, R.S., Jr. (1983). Physical exercise as protection against heart attack. In G. Schlierf & G. Schettler (Eds.), *Proceedings of the Sixth International Symposium on Atherosclerosis* (pp. 276–280). Berlin: Springer-Verlag.

Paffenbarger, R.S. (1985). Physical activity as a defense against coronary heart disease. In W.E. Connor & J.D. Bristow (Eds.), *Coronary heart disease: Prevention, complications, and treatment* (pp. 135–155). New York: J.B. Lippincott.

Paffenbarger, R.S., Jr., Brand, R.J., Scholtz, R.I., & Jung, D.L. (1978). Energy expenditure, cigarette smoking, and blood pressure level as related to death from specific diseases. *American Journal of Epidemiology,* **108**, 12–18.

Paffenbarger, R.S., Jr., Gima, A.S., Laughlin, M.E., & Black, R.A. (1971). Characteristics of longshoremen related to fatal coronary heart disease and stroke. *American Journal of Public Health,* **61**, 1362–1370.

Paffenbarger, R.S., Jr., & Hale, W.E. (1975). Work activity and coronary heart mortality. *New England Journal of Medicine,* **292**, 545–550.

Paffenbarger, R.S., Jr., Hale, W.E., Brand, R.J., & Hyde, R.T. (1977). Work-energy level, personal characteristics, and fatal heart attack: A birth-cohort effect. *American Journal of Epidemiology,* **105**, 200–213.

Paffenbarger, R.S., Jr., & Hyde, R.T. (1984). Exercise in the prevention of coronary heart disease. *Preventive Medicine,* **13**, 3–22.

Paffenbarger, R.S., Jr., Hyde, R.T., Wing, A.L., & Hsieh, C. (1986a). Cigarette smoking and cardiovascular disease. In D.G. Zaridze & R. Peto (Eds.), *A major international hazard* (IARC Scientific Publications No. 74). Lyon: International Agency for Research on Cancer.

Paffenbarger, R.S., Jr., Hyde, R.T., Wing, A.L., & Hsieh, C.C. (1986b). Physical activity, all-cause mortality, and longevity of college alumni. *New England Journal of Medicine,* **314**, 605–613.

Paffenbarger, R.S., Jr., Hyde, R.T., Wing, A.L., & Steinmetz, C.H. (1984). A natural history of athleticism and cardiovascular health. *Journal of the American Medical Association,* **252**, 491-495.

Paffenbarger, R.S., Jr., Laughlin, M.E., Gima, A.S., & Black, B.A. (1970). Work activity of longshoremen as related to death from coronary heart disease and stroke. *New England Journal of Medicine,* **282**, 1109–1114.

Paffenbarger, R.S., Jr., Thorne, M.C., & Wing, A.L. (1968). Chronic disease in former college students. VIII. Characteristics in youth predisposing to hypertension in later years. *American Journal of Epidemiology,* **88,** 25–32.

Paffenbarger, R.S., Jr., Wing, A.L., & Hyde, R.T. (1978). Chronic disease in former college students. XVI. Physical activity as an index of heart attack risk in college alumni. *American Journal of Epidemiology,* **108,** 161–175.

Paffenbarger, R.S., Jr., Wing, A.L., Hyde, R.T., & Jung, D.L. (1983). Physical activity and incidence of hypertension in college alumni. *American Journal of Epidemiology,* **117,** 245–257.

Paffenbarger, R.S., Jr., Wolf, P.A., Notkin, J., & Thorne, M.C. (1966). Chronic disease in former college students. I. Early precursors of fatal coronary heart disease. *American Journal of Epidemiology,* **83,** 314–328.

Paul, O., Lepper, M.H., Phelan, W.H., Dupertuis, G.W., MacMillan, A., McKean, H., & Park, H. (1963). A longitudinal study of coronary heart disease. *Circulation,* **28,** 20–31.

Pomrehn, P.R., Wallace, R.B., & Burmeister, L.S. (1982). Ischemic heart disease mortality in Iowa farmers: The influence of lifestyle. *Journal of the American Medical Association,* 1073–1076.

Punsar, S., & Karvonen, M.J. (1976). Physical activity and coronary heart disease in populations from East and West Finland. *Advances in Cardiology* (Basel), **18,** 196–207.

Rechnitzer, P.A., Sangal, D.A., Cunningham, D.A., Andrew, G.M., Buck, C.W., Jones, N.L., Kavanagh, T., Oldridge, N.B., Parker, J.O., Shephard, R.J., Sutton, J.R., & Donnor, A.P. (1975). Relation of exercise to the recurrence rate of myocardial infarction in men. *American Journal of Cardiology,* **51,** 65–69.

Salonen, J.T., Puska, P., & Tuomilehto, J. (1982). Physical activity and risk of myocardial infarction, cerebral stroke and death: A longitudinal study in Eastern Finland. *American Journal of Epidemiology,* **115,** 526–537.

Shapiro, S., Weinblatt, E., & Frank, C. (1969). Incidence of coronary heart disease in a population insured for medical care (HIP). *American Journal of Public Health,* **59,** 1–101.

Shaw, L.W. (1981). Effects of a prescribed supervised exercise program on mortality and cardiovascular morbidity in patients after myocardial infarction. The national exercise and heart disease project. *American Journal of Cardiology,* **48,** 39–46.

Siscovick, D.S., Weiss, N.S., Hallstron, A.P., Inui, T.S., & Peterson, D.R. (1982). Physical activity and primary cardiac arrest. *Journal of the American Medical Association*, **248**, 3113–3117.

Stamler, J., Lindberg, H.A., Berkson, H.A., Shaffer, A., Miller, W., & Poindexter, A. (1960). Prevalence and incidence of coronary heart disease in strata of the labor force of a Chicago industrial corporation. *Journal of Chronic Diseases*, **11**, 405–420.

Strong, J.P., & Richards, M.L. (1976). Cigarette smoking and atherogenesis in autopsied men. *Atherosclerosis*, **23**, 451–476.

Taylor, H.L., Klepetar, E., Keys, A., Parlin, M.S., Blackburn, H., & Puchner, T. (1962). Death rates among physically active and sedentary employees of the railroad industry. *American Journal of Public Health*, **52**, 1697–1707.

Thomas, C.B. (1952). The heritage of hypertension. *American Journal of Medical Science*, **224**, 367–376.

Thomas, C.B., Ross, D.C., & Higinbotham, C.Q. (1964). Discriminant function analysis. II. Using parental history as the criterion. *Bulletin of Johns Hopkins Hospital*, **115**, 245–264.

Thomas, G.S., Lee, P.R., Franks, P., & Paffenbarger, R.S., Jr. (1981). *Exercise and health: The evidence and the implications.* Cambridge, MA: Oelgeschlager, Gunn & Hain.

Tibblin, G., Wilhelmsen, L., & Werko, L. (1975). Risk factors for myocardial infarction and death due to ischemic heart disease and other causes. *American Journal of Cardiology*, **35**, 514–522.

Wilcox, R.G., Bennett, T., Brown, A.M., & MacDonald, J.A. (1982). Is exercise good for blood pressure? *British Medical Journal*, **285**, 767–769.

Wilhelmsen, L., Tibblin, G., Aurell, M., Bjure, J., Ekstrom-Jodal, B., & Grimby, G. (1976). Physical activity, physical fitness, and risk of myocardial infarction. *Advances in Cardiology* (Basel), **18**, 217–230.

Zukel, W.J., Lewis, R.H., Enterline, P.E., Painter, R.C., Ralston, L.S., Fawcett, R.M., Meredith, A.P. & Peterson, B. (1959). A short-term community study of the epidemiology of coronary heart disease: A preliminary report on the North Dakota study. *American Journal of Public Health*, **49**, 1630–1639.

CHAPTER 3

Exercise Within a Healthy Lifestyle

Steven N. Blair

Humans have lived on the earth for a few million years. Our species, *Homo sapiens,* has been here less than 500,000 years. For most of human existence life was very much different than it is today. For more than 99.5% of our tenure on this planet we lived in small nomadic or semi-nomadic groups and were sustained by hunting and gathering food. Burke (1980) and Tiger (1979) review how this long evolutionary period is related to current human behavior in exercise and diet respectively. Suffice it to say that most of us are not living the kind of life for which our evolutionary development prepared us.

For this discussion of historical and evolutionary perspectives on lifestyle and health four somewhat arbitrary time periods are considered: (a) the preagricultural period, from the beginning of human existence until about 10,000 years ago; (b) the agricultural period, from 10,000 years ago until about the year 1800; (c) the industrial period, from 1800 to 1945; and (d) the nuclear/technological period, from 1945 to the present. In the following paragraphs brief descriptions of these periods are given, and the major causes of mortality for each are mentioned. Additional information on this topic can be found in Tiger (1979), Burke (1980), and Blair (1979).

During the preagricultural period humans lived by hunting and gathering. They got a lot of exercise and ate a diet high in complex carbohydrates and low in fat. The major causes of mortality were starvation and violent death due to accidents, natural disasters, and wild animals. Infectious disease was virtually nonexistent because population groups were too small to harbor a reservoir of pathogens. (For example, a population group of about 1,000,000 people is required to sustain measles as an epidemic disease.)

As the agricultural period developed, people were able to drop nomadic habits and settle in groups to grow food and raise animals. During the agricultural period most people were physically active, and diets remained simple. Most calories came from complex carbohydrates, and most individuals still had diets low in fat although domestication of animals for meat and milk probably increased saturated fat in the diet.

In the industrial period people moved into cities to work in factories, and the infrastructure for an industrialized society was created. Extensive crowding occurred, and the masses were subjected to inadequate diets, environmental pollution, and an inadequate public health or medical care system. The major causes of morbidity and mortality were malnutrition and infectious diseases. During this period, however, improvements in public health were undertaken (notably the provision of clean water and waste disposal), and medical science began to control the infectious diseases.

The nuclear/technological period developed rapidly in the industrialized world during the last half of the twentieth century. Labor saving devices became increasingly available as a result of the spread of electrical power and the internal combustion engine. Food supplies became generally adequate, and in many cases abundant. Widespread availability of cheap factory-made cigarettes added a new health burden to the population. These trends had begun earlier in this century, and 1945 is a rather arbitrary year to use as the beginning of the nuclear/technological period. That year, however, marks the advent of nuclear power, and soon thereafter the high-speed computer began to have an impact on our lives.

The point of this discussion is that people in the United States have experienced profound and rapid changes in living conditions and factors affecting health. Furthermore, we are not evolutionarily prepared for a sedentary existence with excess food supplies cheaply and readily available. These factors, of course, have led to the epidemic of cardiovascular diseases, cancer, diabetes, and other chronic diseases which we are facing in the latter half of this century. The major causes of mortality during this period are all multifactoral lifestyle diseases. To control the major health problems we should not focus on treating the disease, which is only a symptom. Instead the root causes—unhealthy living habits—must be addressed. In the rest of this chapter the evidence linking lifestyle and health, the place of exercise within a healthy lifestyle, and public health recommendations for exercise are reviewed.

Lifestyle and Health

Quality of health is influenced by living habits. A discussion of diet, smoking, exercise, and risk-taking behavior as lifestyle factors related to health is presented.

Diet

Few disagree that diet is a fundamental building block for good health. The present nutritional problems relate more to excess than to caloric or nutrient deficiencies. The primary way the current U.S. diet affects health is in its impact on coronary heart disease and cancer. In brief, the problem is a diet high in fat (especially saturated fat) and cholesterol, low in complex carbohydrates, high in refined carbohydrates, high in sodium, and high in alcohol. One does not need to be a highly trained nutritionist to recognize the dietary changes that need to be made by the American public: eat less meat and dairy products, eat more fruits and vegetables (preferably fresh) and cereals, eat fewer convenience or highly processed foods, and drink alcohol in moderation (if at all).

The scientific foundation for the preceding generalizations is extensive. The relationship between composition of the diet (especially fats and cholesterol) and a person's blood lipid profile is direct and causal (Keys, 1984). Dietary sodium is probably causally related to the risk of developing hypertension (Blackburn & Prineas, 1983). Blood lipids and blood pressure are primary precursors to coronary atherosclerosis and its clinical manifestations (Kannel et al., 1984). Fat and cholesterol intake has also been shown to be directly associated with coronary heart disease (Gordon et al., 1981; Shekelle, Shryock, et al., 1981). Furthermore, intervention studies have shown a reduction in risk of death from coronary heart disease with change in blood lipids by medication (Lipid Research Clinics Program, 1984) and by diet (Hjermann, Velve Byre, Holme, & Leren, 1981).

Diet is probably also a causal factor for some types of cancer although the existing literature is inconsistent and incomplete (Willett & MacMahon, 1984). Much more work is needed to specifically link individual nutrients or practices to specific cancers. The same high fat and cholesterol, low fiber diet that causes coronary heart disease is generally thought to be associated with colon and breast cancer (Hankin & Rawlings, 1978; Sidney & Farquhar, 1983; Willett & MacMahon, 1984). Some dietary components may be protective against cancer. Shekelle, Lepper, et al. (1981) found a lower risk of lung cancer in men with higher dietary intake of vitamin A.

Smoking

Cigarette smoking is undoubtedly the single most disastrous health habit that an individual can adopt. The major impact of smoking on mortality is via cardiovascular disease and cancer. Other forms of lung disease are also caused almost exclusively by smoking and contribute significantly to the disease burden of the U.S. population.

Cigarette smoking is the greatest single cause of cancer death in the U.S. It is estimated that 30% of all cancer deaths are caused by smoking (Office on Smoking and Health, 1982). This amounts to 129,000 Americans a year or more than 350 persons per day who die from smoking-induced cancer. The major cancer caused by smoking is cancer of the lung; 85% of all cases are attributed to the smoking habit. Smoking also contributes significantly to deaths from cancers of the larynx and oral cavity, esophagus, bladder, kidney, and pancreas. Several of these smoking-induced cancers (lung, esophagus, and pancreas) are invariably fatal; 5 year survival rates are less than 10%.

Smoking causes even more deaths from cardiovascular disease than from cancer (Office on Smoking and Health, 1983). It is estimated that 170,000 Americans die each year of coronary heart disease due to smoking. Risk of sudden death is 2 to 4 times greater in smokers than in nonsmokers. Smoking also contributes to stroke mortality and to peripheral vascular disease. Women who smoke and use oral contraceptives have a greatly increased risk of stroke.

Exercise

Exercise is another behavior that most scientists, physicians, and lay persons believe is related in some way to health. Scientists and physicians may argue about the specific benefits and the magnitude of probable benefits, but even the critics of running usually advise some moderate amount of exercise (frequently walking). Those who criticize running and promote walking are apparently unaware that both activities fall on the same spectrum. The issue of whether one runs or walks is not important; what matters is that an individual exercises at the proper intensity to produce benefits. Running may represent a lower exercise stress for one person than walking represents for another.

Sedentary living is associated with poor health. A sample of almost 7,000 residents of Alameda County, California, was followed for 9.5 years to ascertain the relationship between living habits and health (Breslow & Enstrom, 1980). Lack of exercise was judged to be as important as several other health behaviors in predicting total mortality. Paffenbarger, Wing, and Hyde (1978) and Morris, Everitt, Pollard, Chave, and Semmence (1980) have shown that the risk of dying of heart attack is approximately 2 times greater in sedentary men than in active men. Both studies are large, prospective studies that are carefully controlled. In a case-control study in a defined population (Seattle), Siscovick, Weiss, Hallstrom, Inui, and Peterson (1982) report a significantly increased risk of sudden death in inactive men as compared to their exercising peers. Risk of heart attack has also been related to physical fitness level, and less fit men have been found to be at higher risk (Peters, Cady, Bischoff, Bernstein, & Pike, 1983). We followed 6,000 men and women for an average of 4 years and found that less fit individuals had about a 50% increased risk of developing physician-diagnosed hypertension (Blair, Goodyear, Gibbons, & Cooper, 1984). These studies are all epidemiological investigations, but experimental work helps confirm their findings. Vigorous exercise appears to directly affect the atherosclerotic process. Kramsch, Aspen, Abramowitz, Kreimendahl, and Hood (1981) report that exercising monkeys had larger hearts and wider coronary arteries with much less atherosclerotic involvement than sedentary monkeys.

Risk-Taking Behavior

Violent and accidental death is receiving increasing attention from scientists and public health officials. Injury researchers frequently calculate preretirement years of life lost (death at 20 = 65 − 20 or 45 years of life lost). The impact of injuries on preretirement years of life lost is staggering. Current estimates of the number of years of life lost annually in the U.S. due to injuries is 4.1 million (American Public Health Association, 1985). To put this figure in perspective, note that the number of years of life lost annually due to cancer and cardiovascular disease combined is 3.8 million. Much of the mortality from injuries is due to risk-taking behavior and deliberate actions (nonuse of seat belts; drinking and then driving, swimming, or engaging in other dangerous activities; homicide; and suicide). The Centers for Disease Control and other medical and public health groups are seeking to identify causes and effects of violence (Check, 1985). This area of health behavior will receive increased interest, and we should learn much about how to deal with the problems over the next few years.

Relationships Between Exercise and Other Health Behaviors

The notion that exercise promotes other health behaviors has intuitive appeal and is believed by many people. Vigorous exercise and smoking, for example, appear to be incompatible behaviors. It is important to know whether or not exercise is related to other health behaviors. As stated earlier, the major chronic diseases have multifactoral lifestyle causes. In order to study the independent contribution of regular exercise to protection against coronary heart disease, for example, we need to sort out other possibly confounding behaviors such as diet and smoking. In addition to understanding the relationship between exercise and other health behaviors for epidemiological research, the issue also has important implications for health promotion activities. If it were established that adoption of a regular exercise habit is accompanied by other beneficial lifestyle changes, programs of health promotion could be simplified. Instead of spending scarce resources to effect dietary change, program planners could focus directly on exercise and let diet and other behaviors change spontaneously. Although it is unlikely that exercise is a universal, ideal health behavior change, it would be useful to know the strength of its relationships with other health behaviors. Such knowledge would obviously facilitate program planning, and synergistic effects may exist between behaviors that can be maximized with the proper approach.

We recently made an extensive review of the scientific literature for evidence of associations between exercise and other health behaviors (Blair, Jacobs, & Powell, 1985). In a separate study we added a number of new analyses of data from the National Center for Health Statistics and the Institute for Aerobics Research (Blair & Kohl, in press). In general, little evidence can be found for asserting strong associations between exercise and other health behaviors. One of the more consistent relationships found is between exercise and caloric intake; active individuals are eating more than the sedentary. It is surprising that only a weak association exists between exercise and smoking status, and if occupational physical activity is the exercise measure the association is a positive one. Some limited evidence suggests that individuals who engage in vigorous leisure-time exercise are somewhat more likely to engage in certain preventive health practices. Regular exercisers are more likely to visit a physician for a preventive examination, practice preventive dentistry, and wear seat belts.

The associations between exercise and other health behaviors are summarized in Figure 1. The strength of each association is indicated by + or − signs. The strength of an association is judged by the quality and quantity of evidence for the association and by the magnitude of associations reported in the literature. This is a subjective rating that attempts to summarize available data.

There are numerous problems with the existing studies:

- Few of the studies were specifically designed to investigate relationships among health behaviors. This has led to less than optimal designs and analyses to address the specific problem.

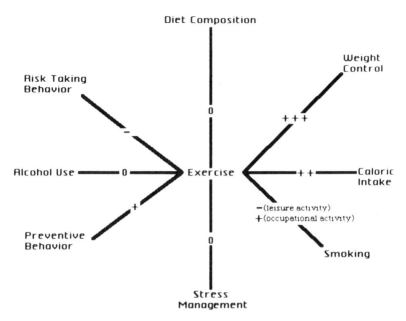

Figure 1 Association between exercise and other risk factors. *Note.* Positive association between exercise and other behavior (+ = weak, + + + = strong); negative association between exercise and other behavior (− = weak, − − − = strong); no consistent effect demonstrated = 0.

- Exercise and other health behaviors are extremely difficult to assess, and few validated methods are available. This leads to much misclassification of the variables of interest and may well attenuate existing relationships. In some of our more recent analyses, for example, we were able to construct exercise indices that identified the most highly active individuals. We also tended to see stronger relationships between exercise and smoking abstinence (Blair & Kohl, in press).

- In many of the papers only crude analyses are presented. Health behaviors are strongly correlated with such demographic characteristics as sex, age, socioeconomic status, and ethnicity. If these and other factors are not taken into account, spurious results may appear.

- All existing studies are observational, and many have a cross-sectional design. Intervention studies, preferably with randomized designs, are needed to strengthen causal inferences.

Very little is known for certain about the relationship between exercise and other health behaviors, and new studies are needed in which the noted deficiencies are corrected. Topics that seem to be especially fruitful for additional work include determining the value of planned exercise to promote better stress management and smoking cessation. Studies dealing with children are also needed, such as assessing the value of using exercise to help prevent the adoption of undesirable health behaviors like cigarette smoking and illegal drug use.

We should not, however, be disappointed if exercise turns out to be of limited or no value in promoting other health behaviors. We do not expect this synergistic effect from most other health-promoting activities. Furthermore, the process of health behavior change is poorly understood and exceedingly complex. It may be unrealistic, therefore, to expect that exercise can exert a powerful influence as a preventive health practice on such behaviors.

Exercise and the Quality of Life

Exercise appears to be related to several quality of life factors. The potential health benefits of regular exercise and physical fitness to longevity, work performance, and the aging process are discussed.

Health and Longevity

The evidence linking exercise habits to risk of dying was briefly reviewed earlier in this chapter. Regular exercise appears to benefit health in numerous ways. It is beyond the scope of this discussion to detail the topic, but several recent publications should be examined by those interesed in the issue (Eckert & Montoye, 1984; White & Mondeika, 1982; Powell & Paffenbarger, 1985).

The effect of exercise on longevity has been assessed by studying former athletes. Athletic participation does not generally appear to be strongly related to longevity (Stephens, Van Huss, Olson, & Montoye, 1984). Although former athleticism does not appear to be related to longevity, current exercise participation appears to decrease the risk of dying prematurely (Paffenbarger et al., 1978; Morris et al., 1980). Direct evidence supporting this assumption is still lacking, but research is now beginning to suggest an extension in longevity in active individuals (Paffenbarger, Hyde, Wing, & Steinmetz, 1984).

Exercise and Work

Very few employees in modern America expend a large number of calories on the job. High levels of physical fitness are not directly required for occupational success. Regular exercise habits and optimal levels of physical fitness may, however, contribute indirectly to work performance and job satisfaction. Health promotion and physical fitness programs in the workplace have increased enormously during the past few years. Most of these programs have been implemented with the assumption that they will lead to improved worker performance and reduced medical care costs. Unfortunately, most of these programs have not been rigorously evaluated, and program effects are somewhat unclear. In recent years, however, evidence has been presented that supports the value of worksite programs.

A properly planned and implemented program can have a major impact on exercise patterns and physical fitness levels of large numbers of employees. The Johnson and Johnson *Live-for-Life* Program increased estimated $\dot{V}O_2$ max levels in employees receiving the full program a net 7 to 8% compared to employees receiving only a health screen (Blair, Piserchia, Wilbur, Crowder, 1986). This result compares very favorably to the 15 to 18% net increase of $\dot{V}O_2$ max levels of treated subjects in small, tightly controlled studies. Furthermore, the changes at Johnson and Johnson extended over a 2-year period and were distributed throughout the work force across all demographic groups.

A review of worksite health promotion programs indicates several potential economic benefits. School employees in the Dallas Independent School District who participated in a health promotion program were absent 1.25 fewer days per year than nonparticipants (Blair, Smith, Collingwood, Reynolds, Prentice, & Sterling, 1986). A multivariate analysis was used to relate reduction in absenteeism to improvement in physical fitness. Other economic benefits attributed to health promotion include less turnover (Cox, Shephard, & Corey, 1981) and reduced medical care costs (Shephard, Corey, Renzland, & Cox, 1982; Bowne, Russell, Morgan, Optenberg, & Clarke, 1984). Assigning an economic or productivity value to psychosocial variables is difficult, but logically such variables are important. We find that employees participating in health promotion activities exhibit significant increases in feelings of general well-being and self-concept (Blair, Collingwood, et al., 1984).

Exercise and Aging

Virtually all published studies show a decline of physical fitness with age. The rate of decline, however, is unclear. Several analyses, including our own, suggest a decline in $\dot{V}O_2$ max of about 10% per decade (Blair, Lavey, Goodyear, Gibbons, & Cooper, 1984). A key issue is whether or not these declines in physiological functioning differ in active and inactive individuals. Published studies are inconsistent: some show a slower decline among the active, some show no difference, and some show a more rapid decline in athletes. Interpretation of existing studies is made difficult by variations in design and study groups. Both cross-sectional and longitudinal studies are available, and special problems in interpretation arise with both types (Shephard, 1978). Cross-sectional studies may be biased by selective recruitment of active and inactive subjects, and longitudinal studies may be confounded by detraining effects in addition to aging. Several of the existing studies used highly selected samples such as physical education majors or athletes; such results are difficult to generalize to the population. Few of the studies have information on lifestyle factors, and in some cases even exercise data are lacking. Many of the earlier studies were conducted when very few adults exercised regularly. The difference, therefore, between active and inactive groups might have been quite small.

In summary, the effect of exercise on the physical fitness decline across the age span is uncertain and much further study is needed to clarify this issue. What is absolutely clear, however, is that at any age the active individuals have greater physical working capacities than their inactive peers. For example, the active 60-year-old person may be as physically fit as the inactive 30- or 40-year-old. Whether this is due to an attenuation of the physical fitness aging curve or totally to training is immaterial. No other health intervention can hope to achieve a 20–30 year gain in functional capability, and the active and physically fit senior citizen is much better able to meet the physical demands of life.

Exercise and the Public's Health

Americans are much more interested today in taking the responsibility for their own health than they were in the past. Although the data are sometimes scanty, it seems clear that millions of individuals have improved their health outlook by stopping smoking, changing their diet, and starting regular exercise. The scientific basis for efficacy has been strengthened considerably by reports such as those from the Alameda County study (Breslow & Enstrom, 1980) that support common sense health habits.

Adoption of regular exercise habits has been one of the significant health habit changes to occur in the last 10 to 20 years. Unfortunately, we do not have good national data to precisely document the extent of the change, but surely few can doubt that many more people are active now than was the case several decades ago. Much remains to be done, however. No more than 20% of the adult population in the United States engages in optimal levels of activity (defined as having a sufficient frequency, intensity, and duration for cardiovascular fitness improvement) (Stephens, Jacobs, & White, 1985). Furthermore, several demographic subgroups (the elderly, blue collar workers, and women) are much less likely to engage in regular exercise than others. If the public health benefits of exercise are to be fully realized, promotion of exercise for these underserved groups must be increased.

The prevalence of inactivity in the United States is much higher than the prevalence of several other deleterious health behaviors. Approximately 80% of Americans are sedentary while less than 40% of the population smoke cigarettes. In theory more may be gained in the population's health status by adoption of exercise than by smoking cessation. This does not apply, obviously, to the sedentary individual who smokes. That person will benefit most from stopping smoking. When we look at the entire population, however, exercise adoption may be most important. Paffenbarger et al. (1984) have applied these concepts to calculations of community attributable risk in their Harvard alumni study data. In the Harvard group, community attributable risk for several risk factors is presented, with the risk expressed as a percent of first heart attacks that presumably could have been prevented if all individuals in the population eliminated that risk factor. The result of this analysis suggests reductions in heart attacks for the following risk factors: sedentary lifestyle 23%, cigarette smoking 13%, overweight 11%, hypertension 10%, and parental history of heart attack 10%. These analyses suggest that if all alumni had been physically active 23% of all first heart attacks would have been prevented; if all hypertension had been eliminated 10% of the heart attacks in the group would have been prevented. These calculations require several assumptions that may or may not be valid, and it is easy to quarrel with the specific figures. The fact remains, however, that due to the strong association between exercise and health, and the high prevalence of sedentary living in the population, lack of exercise is a very significant health problem in the United States. The Harvard data are probably an underestimate of the national impact because only 61% of the alumni were sedentary, which is probably less than in the U.S. population as a whole.

Summary

Ample evidence links regular exercise to health and functional capability throughout life. Exercise may also operate synergistically with other lifestyle factors to promote better health and quality of life. Present data strongly suggest that elimination of sedentary habits in the United States would have a major impact on health for the population. Exercise is an important part of a healthy lifestyle.

References

American Public Health Association. (1985, July). Institute panel calls for center for major research on injuries. *Nation's Health*, p. 9.

Blackburn, H., & Prineas, R. (1983). Diet and hypertension: Anthropology, epidemiology, and public health implications. *Progress in Biochemical Pharmacology*, **19**, 31–79.

Blair, S.N. (1979). A total health-fitness lifestyle. In D.E. Cundiff (Ed.), *Implementation of Aerobic Programs* (pp. 1–16). Washington, DC: American Alliance for Health, Physical Education, Recreation and Dance.

Blair, S.N., Collingwood, T.C., Reynolds, R., Smith, M., Hagan, R.D., & Sterling, C.L. (1984). Health promotion for educators: Impact on health behaviors, satisfaction, and general well-being. *American Journal of Public Health*, **74**, 147–149.

Blair, S.N., Goodyear, N.N., Gibbons, L.W., & Cooper, K.H. (1984). Physical fitness and the incidence of hypertension in healthy normotensive men and women. *Journal of the American Medical Association*, **252**, 487–490.

Blair, S.N., Jacobs, D.R., Jr., & Powell, K.E. (1985). Relationships between exercise or physical activity and other health behaviors. *Public Health Reports*, **100**, 172–179.

Blair, S.N., & Kohl, H.W., III. (in press). Measurement and evaluation of health behaviors and attitudes in relationship to physical fitness and physical activity patterns. In T.F. Drury (Ed.), *Assessing physical fitness and physical activity in NCHS general population surveys.*

Blair, S.N., Lavey, R.S., Goodyear, N., Gibbons, L.W., & Cooper, K.H. (1984). Physiologic responses to maximal graded exercise testing in apparently healthy white women aged 18 to 75 years. *Journal of Cardiac Rehabilitation*, **4**, 459–468.

Blair, S.N., Piserchia, P.V., Wilbur, C.S., & Crowder, J.H. (1986). A public health intervention model for worksite health promotion: Impact on exercise and physical fitness in a health promotion plan after 24 months. *Journal of the American Medical Association*, **255**, 921–926.

Blair, S.N., Smith, M., Collingwood, T.R., Reynolds, R., Prentice, M.C., & Sterling, C.L. (1986). Health promotion for educators: Impact on absenteeism. *Preventive Medicine, 15,* 166–175.

Bowne, D.W., Russell, M.L., Morgan, J.L., Optenberg, S.A., & Clarke, A.E. (1984). Reduced disability and health care costs in an industrial fitness program. *Journal of Occupational Medicine, 26,* 809–816.

Breslow, L., & Enstrom, J.E. (1980). Persistence of health habits and their relationship to mortality. *Preventive Medicine, 9,* 469–483.

Burke, E.J. (1980). Thoughts on heredity and the environment preliminary to a study of exercise. In E.J. Burke (Ed.), *Exercise, science, and fitness* (pp. 1–18). Ithaca, NY: Mouvement Publications.

Check, W.A. (1985). Homicide, suicide, other violence gain increasing medical attention. *Journal of the American Medical Association, 254,* 721–730.

Cox, M., Shephard, R.J., & Corey, P. (1981). Influence of an employee fitness programme upon fitness, productivity and absenteeism. *Ergonomics, 24,* 795–806.

Eckert, H.M., & Montoye, H.J. (Eds.). (1984). *Exercise and health.* Champaign, IL: Human Kinetics.

Gordon, T., Kagan, A., Garcia-Palmieri, M., Kannel, W.B., Zukel, W.J., Tillotson, J., Sorlie, P., & Hjortland, M. (1981). Diet and its relation to coronary heart disease and death in three populations. *Circulation, 63,* 500–515.

Hankin, J.H., & Rawlings, V. (1978). Diet and breast cancer: A review. *American Journal of Clinical Nutrition, 31,* 2005–2016.

Hjermann, I., Velve Brye, K., Holme, I., & Leren, P. (1981). Effect of diet and smoking intervention on the incidence of coronary heart disease. *Lancet, 2,* 1303–1310.

Kannel, W.B., Doyle, J.T., Ostfeld, A.M., Jenkins, C.D., Kuller, L., Podell, R.N., & Stamler, J. (1984). Optimal resources for primary prevention of atherosclerotic diseases. *Circulation, 70,* 157A–204A.

Keys, A. (1984). Serum cholesterol response to dietary cholesterol. *American Journal of Clinical Nutrition, 40,* 351–359.

Kramsch, D.M., Aspen, A.J., Abramowitz, B.M., Kreimendahl, T., & Hood, W.B., Jr. (1981). Reduction of coronary atherosclerosis by moderate conditioning exercise in monkeys on an atherogenic diet. *New England Journal of Medicine, 305,* 1483–1489.

Lipid Research Clinics Program. (1984). The Lipid Research Clinics Coronary Primary Prevention Trial Results: I. Reduction in incidence of coronary heart disease. *Journal of the American Medical Association, 251,* 351–364.

Morris, J.N., Everitt, M.G., Pollard, R., Chave, S.P.W., & Semmence, A.M. (1980). Vigorous exercise in leisure-time: Protection against coronary heart disease. *Lancet, 2,* 1207–1210.

Office on Smoking and Health. (1982). *The health consequences of smoking: Cancer, a report of the Surgeon General* (DHHS [PHS] Publication No. 82-50179). Washington, DC: U.S. Government Printing Office.

Office on Smoking and Health. (1983). *The health consequences of smoking: Cardiovascular disease, a report of the Surgeon General.* (DHHS [PHS] Publication No. 82-50204). Washington, DC: U.S. Government Printing Office.

Paffenbarger, R.S., Jr., Hyde, R.T., Wing, A.L., & Steinmetz, C.H. (1984). A natural history of athleticism and cardiovascular health. *Journal of the American Medical Association, 252,* 491–495.

Paffenbarger, R.S., Jr., Wing, A.L., & Hyde, R.T. (1978). Physical activity as an index of heart attack risk in college alumni. *American Journal of Epidemiology, 108,* 161–175.

Peters, R.K., Cady, L.D., Bischoff, D.P., Bernstein, L., & Pike, M.C. (1983). Physical fitness and subsequent muyocardial infarction in healthy workers. *Journal of the American Medical Association, 249,* 3052–3056.

Powell, K.E., & Paffenbarger, R.S., Jr. (1985). Workshop on epidemiologic and public health aspects of physical activity and exercise: A summary. *Public Health Reports, 100,* 118–126.

Shekelle, R.B., Lepper, M., Liu, S., Maliza, C., Raynor, W.J., Jr., Rossof, A.H., Paul, O., Shryock, A., MacM., & Stamler, J. (1981). Dietary vitamin A and risk of cancer in the Western Electric study. *Lancet, 2,* 1185–1190.

Shekelle, R.B., Shryock, A., MacM., Paul, O., Lepper, M., Stamler, J., Liu, S., & Raynor, W.J., Jr. (1981). Diet, serum cholesterol, and death from coronary heart disease. *New England Journal of Medicine, 304,* 65–70.

Sidney, S., & Farquhar, J.W. (1983). Cholesterol, cancer and public health policy. *American Journal of Medicine, 75,* 494–508.

Siscovick, D.S., Weiss, N.S., Hallstrom, A.P., Inui, T.S., & Peterson, D.R. (1982). Physical activity and primary cardiac arrest. *Journal of the American Medical Association, 248,* 3113–3117.

Shephard, R.J. (1978). *Human physiological work capacity*. London: Cambridge University Press.

Shephard, R.J., Corey, P., Renzland, P., & Cox, M. (1982). The influence of an employee fitness and lifestyle modification program upon medical care costs. *Canadian Journal of Public Health*, **73**, 259–263.

Stephens, K.E., Van Huss, W.D., Olson, H.W., & Montoye, H.J. (1984). The longevity, morbidity, and physical fitness of former athletes—an update. In H.M. Eckert & H.J. Montoye (Eds.), *Exercise and health* (pp. 101–119). Champaign, IL: Human Kinetics.

Stephens, T., Jacobs, D.R., Jr., & White, C.C. (1985). A descriptive epidemiology of leisure-time physical activity. *Public Health Reports*, **100**, 147–158.

Tiger, L. (1979). Anthropological concepts. *Preventive Medicine*, **8**, 600–607.

White, P.L., & Mondeika, T. (Eds.). (1982). *Diet and exercise: Synergism in health maintenance*. Chicago: American Medical Association.

Willett, W.C., & MacMahon, B. (1984). Diet and cancer—An overview. *New England Journal of Medicine*, **310**, 633–638, 697–703.

CHAPTER 4

Exercise and Mental Health

William P. Morgan and
Patrick J. O'Connor

The overall purpose of this chapter is twofold: (a) to provide a rationale for the study and promotion of exercise adherence and (b) to provide a beginning for understanding what determines an active rather than sedentary lifestyle. Several perspectives have been employed in an effort to achieve this objective, and the present study will focus on the interaction of exercise and mental health. The first chapter in this volume noted that exercise may influence health and feelings of well-being and that these effects may actually influence the decision to maintain regular activity. The conceptual framework emphasized in this volume maintains that health represents both a desired *outcome* and a *motivator* of exercise adherence. Although such a view possesses considerable intuitive appeal, whether or not it would generalize to the normal as well as the pathological case is unknown. Furthermore, because no evidence exists that the mental health of sedentary individuals falls outside the normal range, the belief that exercise would lead to an improvement in the mental health of formerly sedentary individuals seems dubious. The conceptual framework just mentioned may be limited to sedentary individuals who do not possess positive mental health at the outset of an exercise program.

The primary objectives of this chapter are to survey and critically evaluate what is currently known about the relationship between exercise and mental health and to propose what we need to know in order to advance knowledge in this area. A secondary purpose is to comment on the theory and methods needed to further knowledge and application. A number of review articles and chapters published during the past two decades have dealt with the relationship of exercise and mental health. The first portion of this chapter will synthesize these earlier reviews and summarize research published since their appearance. This discussion is followed by a summary of a state-of-the-art workshop sponsored by the Office of Prevention at the National Institute of Mental Health (NIMH). This section presents the conclusions advanced by the NIMH consensus panel relative to what we know about the relationship of exercise and mental health. This section also serves as a research agenda for individual investigators and funding agencies. The third purpose is to focus on a topic that has not been included in any of the earlier reviews; this issue involves the related problems of overtraining and exercise abuse. A fairly substantial clinical literature seems to indicate that exercise can, in certain types of individuals, lead to undesirable psychological effects. Whereas this clinical literature must ultimately be evaluated with experimental trials, the preliminary clinical reports are sufficiently compelling to warrant attention. In other words, the very thrust of this volume, adherence, has a darker side that is not widely recognized. Some individuals not only adhere to exercise programs once they adopt them, but their exercise patterns become compulsive and self-destructive.

The next section of the chapter focuses on four hypotheses that can be employed to explain how exercise might provoke psychological change. The hypotheses to be advanced are (a) the monoamine hypothesis with special reference to norepinephrine and MHPG, (b) the endorphin hypothesis, (c) the thermogenic hypothesis, and (d) the distraction hypothesis. Although these hypotheses are advanced as independent explanations, that two or more of these mechanisms operate simultaneously or synergistically is quite possible.

The final section consists of a summary statement designed to integrate each of the major components of the chapter and a discussion of the interaction of exercise and mental health within the context of exercise adherence.

Earlier Reviews

A review of the contributions of exercise and sports to mental health and social adjustment written by Layman (1960) appears to be the first comprehensive examination of the potential impact of exercise on mental health. She emphasized that the principle of mind-body unity is sound, and she pointed out the ''close relationship between organic health and adequate adjustment" (p. 561). She also speculated that if sports and exercise can be shown to enhance the development and maintenance of organic health, these activities "will also prevent poor mental health" (p. 561). The studies reviewed by Layman justify the conclusion that exercise and sports have the potential for contributing positively to mental health. The most compelling research examined in this review, however, dealt with individuals who lacked positive mental health prior to exercise intervention. Furthermore, few of the studies that demonstrated positive effects had adequate controls for comparison purposes, and none of the studies dealt with the widely recognized behavioral artifact known as the Hawthorne effect. The author recognized, moreover, that "there are indications that under some circumstances, with some groups, and for certain individuals, physical education and athletic activities seem to be unrelated to the development of mental health, or may be detrimental to it" (p. 588). This review was updated (Layman, 1972), and the overall conclusions advanced earlier remained essentially the same.

The next review to appear dealt with the improvement of psychological states by means of exercise-fitness programs (Cureton, 1963). This study indicated that personality structure is associated with various physical fitness measures, and these findings were in general agreement with the work of Layman (1960). On the basis of a series of investigations conducted at the University of Illinois, Cureton (1963) stated that "it is certainly suggestive that personality deterioration and physical deterioration parallel one another, and it follows that improvement of physical fitness should minimize both types of deterioration" (p. 17). The research reviewed by Cureton, however, was not characterized by acceptable experimental designs. Control and placebo groups were not routinely employed for comparison purposes, and test subjects were not randomly assigned to treatments.

The findings of Layman (1960) and Cureton (1963) were extended and updated by Morgan (1969), and this review included subsequent research as well as the results of earlier investigations that were not discussed by Layman and Cureton. Morgan's (1969) findings and conclusions were in general agreement with those of Layman and Cureton, and he reported that physical fitness was inversely correlated with psychopathology. Aerobic power, for example, was found to decline as the degree of psychopathology increased, and psychiatric patients were noted to have consistently lower levels of physical fitness, as measured by standard tests of muscular strength and muscular endurance, than nonhospitalized adults.

A fundamental philosophy of science issue emerges if one objectively examines these literature reviews. They were based almost entirely on cross-sectional comparisons and correlational analyses, and essentially no evidence was presented to suggest that a *causal* link exists between fitness measures and psychopathology. Also, even if a causal link had been demonstrated, the results would not be generalizable beyond the psychiatric population studied in these investigations. The review by Morgan (1969) has periodically been updated as new research evidence has become available (Morgan, 1974, 1976, 1979a, 1981, 1982, 1985), and related reviews, which involve somewhat different approaches, have been prepared by Folkins and Sime (1981), Gruber (1986), Mihevic (1981), Raglin and Morgan (1985), Ransford (1982), and Sonstroem (1984). The issue of *causality* versus *association* continues to be identified as a major problem in these recent reviews. Indeed, the reviews by Folkins and Sime (1981) and Sonstroem (1984) suggest that most of this research has been based upon what are known as preexperimental or quasiexperimental designs. Much of the research in this area of inquiry continues to be cross-sectional and correlational. Hence, one cannot attribute differences in mental health observed in active and sedentary groups to differences in exercise patterns because evidence that these groups did not differ initially is lacking. Moreover, significant inverse correlations reported between physical fitness and depression or anxiety may reflect exercise patterns, but they may also reflect initial psychological differences that mediate active or sedentary patterns. Another possibility is that genetic differences in physical fitness may be responsible for the observed relationship (Klissouras, 1970).

The issue of potential differences that may exist from the outset in either physical fitness or mental health is a recognized problem inherent in cross-sectional and correlational designs. The solution, of course, is to conduct longitudinal studies designed to investigate the effect of a selected intervention such as exercise. Unfortunately, the limited longitudinal exercise research has not relied on rigorous experimental designs (Folkins & Sime, 1981; Sonstroem, 1984). Some investigators have simply studied the influence of exercise on the psychological characteristics of a selected group, and comparisons have not been made to untreated controls. When untreated control groups have been included, experimental and control groups have seldom been generated in a random manner. A potential for bias in group composition usually exists from the outset in most of these studies. Finally, with very few exceptions, efforts to quantify the influence of the Hawthorne effect by including some type of placebo or ''special attention'' group have been absent. Indeed, in the few cases where placebo controls have been employed, significant psychological effects have occurred for the subjects in the placebo treatments as well as for those in the exercise treatments (Bahrke & Morgan, 1978; Morgan & Pollock, 1977; Raglin & Morgan, 1985).

In summary, examination of earlier reviews dealing with exercise and mental health yields a number of consistent generalizations. First, reviewers have unanimously concluded that physical fitness and mental health are related in a positive manner—the higher the physical fitness the more desirable the level of mental health. Second, no evidence has been found to demonstrate that the physical fitness–mental health relationship reflects more than a mere association. Reviewers have consistently refrained from suggesting that this relationship involves causality. Third, because the few longitudinal studies dealing with the psychological consequences of exercise interventions have been characterized by preexperimental and quasiexperimental designs, to accept or refute the hypothesis that vigorous exercise leads to an alteration in mental health is impossible at this time.

The NIMH Consensus Panel

In view of the observation that earlier reviews have consistently concluded that we lack empirical evidence to support the view that exercise improves mental health and in view of the report that many health care professionals such as primary-care physicians routinely prescribe exercise in the treatment of emotional disorders such as anxiety and depression (Morgan & Goldston, 1987), it seems important to address the lack of congruence between research and practice. This absence of agreement was responsible in part for a state-of-the-art workshop sponsored by the Office of Prevention at NIMH in which a consensus panel attempted to identify exactly what is known about the influence of exercise on mental health. The complete details of the consensus panel's deliberations appear in a volume edited by Morgan and Goldston (1987).

The NIMH consensus panel comprised individuals with extensive research and clinical experience in exercise science and mental health, and this group developed the following consensus statements concerning what we know about the influence of exercise on mental health (Morgan & Goldston, 1987, p. 156):

1. Physical fitness is positively associated with mental health and well-being
2. Exercise is associated with the reduction of stress emotions such as state anxiety
3. Anxiety and depression are common symptoms of failure to cope with mental stress, and exercise has been associated with a decreased level of mild to moderate depression and anxiety
4. Long-term exercise is usually associated with reductions in traits such as neuroticism and anxiety
5. Severe depression usually requires professional treatment, which may include medication, electroconvulsive therapy, and/or psychotherapy, with exercise as an adjunct

6. Appropriate exercise results in reductions in various stress indices such as neuromuscular tension, resting heart rate, and some stress hormones
7. Current clinical opinion holds that exercise has beneficial emotional effects across all ages and in both sexes
8. Physically healthy people who require psychotropic medication may safely exercise when exercise and medications are titrated under close medical supervision

Several important points are imbedded in most of these consensus statements. First, the statements support the concept that physical fitness is associated with mental health. Second, they support the idea that improvements in physical fitness through regular exercise are associated with improved affect in certain individuals. Third, the panel qualified these statements by emphasizing that the relationships were associational rather than causal. This panel of experts arrived at the same conclusions that individual reviewers had advanced earlier.

Whether or not any beneficial emotional effects occurring with regular exercise would be age or gender specific has not been investigated in a systematic manner; however, the consensus panel stated that current clinical opinion holds that exercise has beneficial emotional effects across all ages and in both sexes. Also, many individuals being treated for emotional problems receive various psychotropic medications as part of their therapy. The consensus panel concluded that such individuals may safely exercise while taking these medications, providing that the exercise and medication are titrated under close medical supervision.

One point that the NIMH consensus panel did not address involves the potential abuse or negative aspects of exercise. A growing clinical literature deals with overtraining and exercise abuse, and this potential problem will be examined in the next section.

Overuse and Abuse of Exercise

One of the most significant problems in sports medicine involves the syndrome known as overtraining or staleness. That athletes who overtrain develop a number of physiological and psychological problems has been recognized for years, and these problems are usually associated with decrements in performance. Overtraining in the athlete involves a paradox because many of the beneficial effects known to accompany the adoption of an exercise program are reversed in the overtrained athlete. Some of the more common symptoms known to accompany overtraining are (a) increase in resting and exercise heart rate, (b) increase in resting blood pressure, (c) decrease in maximal aerobic power, (d) increase in biochemical stress markers at rest (e.g., epinephrine and creatine-phosphokinase), (e) significant increases in mood disturbances, (f) decreased libido, (g) decreased appetite and weight loss, and (h) sleep disturbances.

Noncompetitive athletes who engage in various physical activities for recreational or fitness purposes may also become overtrained. They, of course, would be self-driven as opposed to having a training load imposed by a coach. It has been reported, for example, that some regular exercisers, such as joggers, become *addicted* to the running experience (Morgan 1979b; Peele, 1981a; Yates, Leehey, & Shisslak, 1983).

Sheehan (1983) has argued that the term addiction should not be used to explain the behavior of runners, and terms such as *commitment* and *dedication* are proposed as substitutes. Peele (1981a) has pointed out that no one has presented evidence that "running addicts differ neurologically from nonaddicted runners or from nonrunners" (p. 811) and that the World Health Organization's Committee on Addiction-Producing Drugs has proposed that the term addiction be discarded in favor of *drug dependence*. This taxonomy led Peele to propose that some runners are dependent on running rather than addicted to running. More recently Yates et al. (1983), on the basis of interviews with marathon and trail runners, have identified a subgroup of male athletes that they have labeled obligatory runners. These runners were described as resembling anorexic females in a number of ways, and they were reported (a) to be compulsive exercisers, (b) to be characterized by a bizarre preoccupation with food, and (c) to place an unusual emphasis on lean body mass. These obligatory runners were viewed as having a single-minded commitment to physical effectiveness, and some were observed to run over 100 miles per week. Yates et al. (1983) also reported that running becomes a consuming goal for these individuals and that the running experience "preempts all other interests in life" (p. 252). Furthermore, exercise deprivation was observed to produce anxiety state and depression in these obligatory runners.

It has recently been reported by Katz (1986) that many anorexic patients are quite physically active prior to the onset of their eating disorders. Katz also pointed out that significant increases in physical activity can result in "a biologically mediated reduction in food consumption" (p. 74). Although this view is based largely on the results of animal research (Epling, Pierce, & Stefan, 1983), it is in agreement with observations involving appetite suppression and weight loss in overtrained athletes suffering from the syndrome known as staleness. Katz (1986) has also described two case studies involving male patients who developed eating disorders "after they had become serious long-distance runners" (p. 74). These cases demonstrate that long-distance running can stimulate the onset of anorexia nervosa in runners who are biologically and psychologically vulnerable to the development of eating disorders. Katz postulated that the onset of anorexia in these male runners was mediated by endorphin activity. The endorphin hypothesis will be explored in a subsequent section of this chapter.

In a related paper Little (1969) reported that some individuals require regular exercise, and he observed a striking distinction between neurotic patients with athletic and nonathletic personalities.

> On the one hand were the thirty-nine percent who appeared, to the exclusion of other interests, to overvalue health and fitness, revealing an inordinate pride in their previous sickness-free progress through life and in their excess physical stamina, strength or skill. In complete contrast were the forty-two percent of the neurotic series who had shown an almost complete lack of awareness of physical well-being throughout life and had never shown the slightest interest in sport, games, athletics or other physical activities. (p. 187)

There was an absence of neurotic markers in the life histories of the athletic patients, whereas the histories of the nonathletic patients were characterized by neurotic markers. In general, the athletic patients enjoyed excellent health throughout their lives, whereas the non-athletic patients had not. Of importance, however, was the observation that 72.5 percent of the athletic cases had neurotic breakdowns which were triggered by direct threats to the patient's physical well-being. This occurred in the form of an illness or injury in most cases. On the other hand, physical threats preceded the appearance of neurotic symptoms in the non-athletic patients in only 10.7 percent of the cases. This difference was statistically significant ($P < .001$). Also, while under treatment, the prognosis for the athletic group was generally less favorable. Although Little's paper does not necessarily challenge the efficacy of physical activity per se, it certainly does not support the view that physically active lifestyles prevent emotional illness, and, furthermore, it implies that such lifestyles inhibit recovery from a neurotic breakdown.

Little (1969, 1979) has reported that some individuals who require regular exercise develop a *deprivation crisis* if they are unable to exercise, and he has labeled these individuals fitness fanatics (1979).

Many specialists in sports medicine such as team physicians, orthopedists, podiatrists, psychiatrists, and psychologists have come to realize that a small proportion of those individuals who exercise appear to be (a) *addicted* to, (b) *committed* to, (c) *dependent* upon, (d) *obligated* to, and/or (e) *fanatical* about their personal exercise programs. Usage of various terms and jargon has a tendency to create semantic problems, and Sheehan (1983) interprets this particular situation by commenting that "we are divided by language" (p. 43).

These five terms obviously generate different emotional responses, and the choice of labels in this instance has a considerable value orientation reflecting personal preference. Unfortunately, authors who seem to agree that a particular behavioral syndrome exists are in disagreement about labeling the syndrome. Assume that a sedentary individual becomes interested in jogging and that he or she gradually progresses from running 1 mile, 3 days per week to 15 to 20 miles per day. Also assume that this person will not let anything interfere with the completion of 105 to 140 miles of running per week and that this includes fulfilling job requirements as well as maintaining relations with friends, spouse, and associates. Furthermore, assume that this runner is unwilling to reduce his or her training or to discontinue training even though a physician advises that continued running will result in permanent and irreversible physical damage. Finally, assume that this individual (a) loses his or her job, (b) is divorced or separated, (c) is hospitalized because of a chronic running injury, and (d) becomes clinically depressed. This hypothetical case may seem rather unusual, but similar cases have been reported by Katz (1986), Little (1969, 1979), Morgan (1979b), Peele (1981b), and Yates et al. (1983). Should this person be classified as addicted, committed, dependent, fanatical, or obligated with respect to exercise history? One might respond that it really does not matter what label is employed. It does matter, however, because commitments and obligations can be broken or modified and fanatical behavior can be redirected or changed, but dependencies and addictions are not easily broken or modified. Therefore, understanding whether individuals become addicted to or dependent upon exercise is important.

Possible resolution of the addiction–dependence debate is offered by Peele (1981b) who has proposed that "habits may be arranged in terms of a dimension of *addictivensss*" (p. 27). In this model addiction is viewed as existing on a continuum consisting of (a) daily routines, (b) dependencies, (c) compulsions, and (d) addictions. Peele points out that "an addiction exists when a person ceases to be able to make choices" (p. 27). Additional signs of an addictive experience are that (a) it eradicates awareness, (b) it hinders other involvements, (c) it lowers self-esteem, (d) it is not pleasurable, and (e) it is predictable. Each of these characteristics can be seen in the hard-core exercise addict, and examples of such individuals are presented by Morgan (1979b) and Peele (1981b). Agreement does not exist concerning the issue of withdrawal symptoms and addiction. Some authors think that addiction does not exist unless the individual who is presumed to be addicted experiences withdrawal symptoms when deprived of the substance or process. Peele (1981a, 1981b), on the other hand, maintains that withdrawal is a separate but related experience based upon the individual's overall involvement with a particular addictive experience.

Dependence and addiction may represent the same state, and the confusion surrounding the usage of these terms may be merely semantic. Another possibility is that dependence and addiction are both forms of addictiveness, but dependence is a less severe form (Peele, 1981a). The terms are not, however, interchangeable. Many runners would probably not object to being classified as dependent on running; however, they might resent being labeled exercise addicts. Furthermore, use of the term addiction has a tendency to generate illness and disease concepts for a given process.

Perhaps the most common misconception concerning drug addiction is the notion that an addict derives pleasure from the drug. Initially, drug taking eliminates pain and creates a loss of awareness. This is followed by drug intoxication and the inability to pay attention to or deal with problems, which results in damage to the addict's life (Peele, 1981b). The damage creates more problems and pain, which in turn lead to more drug taking to eliminate pain and awareness. Peele (1981b) reinforces this view by pointing out that ''a skid-row alcoholic who lies unconscious on the street is not enjoying himself in any conventional sense of the word'' (p. 5). The meaning of pleasure can be confusing. The alcoholic who loses consciousness, the heroin addict who nods out, and the barbiturate user who falls asleep all experience reduced pain, and the absence of cognition and affect leading to pain becomes pleasurable within the process. The process as a whole, however, is not pleasurable (Peele, 1981b).

Understanding addiction and dependence is complicated by the different but related sensory experiences associated with pain and pleasure. Solomon's (1980) opponent-process theory of acquired motivation deals with the costs of pleasure and the benefits of pain. The theory attempts to account for such diverse acquired motives as drug addiction, love, affection and social attachment, parachuting, jogging, marathoning, sauna bathing, and a variety of self-administered, aversive stimuli such as shock. In some of these cases the initial reinforcers are negative. Crucial variables in this theory include the quality, intensity, and duration of the stimulus. The theory also presents a plausible account of the development of addictive behaviors, and this applies to both those events that are initially pleasurable as well as those judged to be aversive. One simplistic interpretation of this theory would be that pain leads to pleasure and pleasure leads to pain. Solomon's theoretical formulations are particularly useful when one attempts to explain the running experience or exercise in general.

If addictions and/or dependencies develop in connection with exercise, it is important to develop basic information concerning how and why these states occur in some individuals. Adequate prevention or treatment of these conditions will not be possible, irrespective of the terminology employed, until we understand the nature of this syndrome. This volume deals with the enhancement of exercise adherence or compliance, behavior that preceeds exercise addiction/dependence; a reasonable objective would be to ensure exercise compliance without creating an addiction or dependence.

Several possible explanations account for the altered or euphoric state sometimes reported to accompany exercise. The endorphin hypothesis, for example, advanced by Katz (1986) represents a tenable explanation for the addictive, dependent, and compulsive behavior that occurs in some exercisers. This particular hypothesis will be evaluated in a later section.

Exercise–Mental Health Hypotheses

A number of hypotheses vie for attention as possible mechanisms responsible for improved mental health following the adoption of regular exercise. Most of these hypotheses fall in the reductionist category, and it is possible that the hypothesized mechanisms operate in an interactive or synergistic fashion. These hypotheses will be discussed independently, but it is possible that they are interactive, especially the monoamine, endorphin, and thermogenic hypotheses. Furthermore, although the fourth hypothesis is not reductionist in the traditional sense, the mechanism(s) underlying the distraction hypothesis may involve one or more of the reductionist hypotheses. The monoamine hypothesis will be discussed first, followed by the thermogenic, endorphin, and distraction hypotheses.

Monoamine Hypothesis

The monoamine hypothesis attempts to explain the improved affect associated with exercise by alteration in one or all of the major brain monoamines (i.e., dopamine, serotonin, and norepinephrine). Evidence for this idea originated from observations that psychoactive drugs, which alter affective states, also produce changes in brain amine levels in experimental animals (Schildkraut, Orsulak, Schatzberg, & Rosenbaum, 1983). These observations led to formulation of the catecholamine hypothesis of affective disorders (Schildkraut et al., 1983), which suggests that different types of affective disorders can be distinguished by differences in urinary metabolites of brain catecholamines. This hypothesis has had an important heuristic value and has stimulated considerable research involving the role of amines in affective disorders.

Because inactivity can be viewed as a component of affective disorder and an association exists between exercise and improved affect, several investigators have examined the relationship between activity and the monoamines. Studies involving activity and norepinephrine, or its major urinary metabolite 3-methoxy-4-hydroxyphenolglycol (MHPG), will be reviewed in this section. In an earlier review Ransford (1982) cautioned that "present statements that single out norepinephrine, dopamine or serotonin as the crucial amine may be premature and oversimplified" (p. 1). Nevertheless, most of the published research in this area has dealt with norepinephine.

Animal Studies.   Several studies have examined the effects of acute exercise on brain norepinephrine levels in the rat. Barchas and Freedman (1963) showed decreases in norepinephrine of 11%, 23%, and 10% compared to controls in the brains of rats who either swam for 15 to 30 minutes in water at 15° C, swam for 4 to 6 hours in water of 23° C, or ran on a treadmill for 3 hours at approximately 5.3 meters per minute. Gordon, Spector, Sjordsma, and Udenfriend (1966) examined the effects of exercise on the synthesis of rat brain norepinephrine. In the first part of the study they found marked decreases in brain norepinephrine in rats injected with a catecholamine inhibitor prior to 1 hour of treadmill running at the greatest speed the animals could run without losing their balance. In the second part of the study rats were injected with a radioactively labeled catecholamine precursor that is converted to catecholamines in direct proportion to the rate of synthesis. Exercise resulted in a 2- to 3-fold increase in precursor conversion to norepinephrine compared to controls. These experiments suggest that exercise *increased* the synaptic release of rat brain norepinephrine. Stone (1973) observed significant decreases in hypothalamic norepinephrine levels following 3 hours of treadmill running and an increased norepinephrine turnover during recovery from the exercise. These three studies suggest that acute exercise *decreases* brain norepinephrine levels in the rat. However, no attempt was made in any of these studies to disentangle the effects due to novel stressors (e.g., cold water or treadmill running).

Some evidence shows that chronic exercise may produce elevations in brain norepinephrine. For example, Brown and Van Huss (1973) found that rats that trained 5 days per week for 8 weeks by running on a treadmill at an intensity intended to simulate middle-distance interval training had significantly higher brain norepinephrine levels than did sedentary control animals. This work was replicated by Brown, Payne, Kim, Moore, Krebs, and Martin (1979); they found that rats running on a treadmill for 30 minutes a day, 5 days per week for 8 weeks had significantly higher brain norepinephrine levels than did sedentary controls. In a similar study deCastro and Duncan (1985) observed a 40% increase in norepinephrine in rats operantly conditioned to run for 2 hours a day, 5 days a week for 8 weeks. This elevation, however, was not significant because of small sample size in concert with high variability, and the elevation was computed by contrasting the exercised animals with yoked controls. Nevertheless these studies taken altogether suggest that chronic exercise produces an increase in brain norepinephrine levels in the rat.

Despite these consistent findings some question remains whether or not exercise per se produces changes in rat brain norepinephrine. For example, deCastro and Duncan (1985) question the validity of the typically employed rat model of human exercise for the following reasons: (a) exercise stress is confounded with other stressors when rats are forced to swim to total exhaustion or are forced to run on a treadmill to avoid foot shock, (b) exercise is confounded with the rat's lack of control over the intensity and duration of the exercise, and (c) the effects of exercise are confounded by the possible effects of inactivity when exercised animals are compared to extremely sedentary controls. The second point is particularly important because Weiss (1981) has shown that rats that had control over tail shocks had significantly higher locus coeruleus norepinephrine than yoked controls that received a shock of the same intensity but could not control it.

In addition, the validity of swim-training models of human exercise has recently been questioned by Harri and Kuusela (1986) because these experiments typically utilize cold water. Harri and Kuusela (1986) found that rats that trained in cold water had adaptive changes more closely resembling changes produced in rats acclimated to the cold than were found in a separate group of rats that trained by running on a treadmill. Some question remains regarding the validity of the rat models of human exercise that have been employed, and the findings regarding the effects of exercise per se on rat brain norepinephrine levels are perhaps best judged with caution. Nevertheless, animal studies are extremely important, and it is expected that continued refinements in animal models of human exercise as well as advances in animal models of psychopathology (Morgan, Olsen, & Peterson, 1982) will provide answers to questions that cannot otherwise be addressed in humans because of ethical considerations (Suomi, 1982).

Human Studies.   A number of investigators have attempted to explicate the relationship between physical activity and brain norepinephrine by assessing urinary levels of MHPG. Because brain norepinephrine does not cross the blood–brain barrier, investigators have relied on the metabolites of brain norepinephrine found in cerebrospinal fluid (CSF), blood, or urine. Although CSF assays possess the advantage of being most directly associated with brain levels, blood, and urine collections are safer and easier to obtain. Furthermore, because the methods used to detect the relatively small amounts of MHPG found in plasma are only a decade old and technically more demanding, the majority of work to date has utilized urine as the source for MHPG.

A critical issue in studies of this type has been the extent to which peripheral MHPG levels reflect brain norepinephrine activity. Estimates of the percentage of centrally derived MHPG found in the urine range from 20% to 60% (Schildkraut, Orsulak, Schatzberg, & Rosenbaum, 1983). However, increasing theoretical and empirical evidence shows that the central and peripheral adrenergic systems work as a linked unit. For example, Mass and Leckman (1983) cite four lines of evidence supporting this view: (a) recent findings of major projections from the locus coeruleus to the spinal cord; (b) 2- to 3-fold increases in plasma MHPG that are highly correlated to increases in CSF MHPG have been produced by stimulation of the rat locus coeruleus, and these increases can be significantly reduced by blockage of the sympathetic nervous system; (c) numerous studies involving human and nonhuman primates showing strong correlations between CSF and plasma norepinephrine; and (d) compelling studies linking central norepinephrine activity and blood pressure. Their work supports the notion that, regardless of the relative amounts of centrally derived MHPG in the periphery, changes in peripheral MHPG are related to central norepinephrine activity.

It is also important to realize that most of the studies regarding physical activity and peripheral MHPG have focused on absolute levels. However, Siever and Davis (1985) have argued that the activity of neurotransmitter systems in affective disorders is better understood as a function of the relative failure of regulation rather than as simple increases or decreases in the activity of the neurotransmitter system. This view has led to the reformulation of the original monoamine hypothesis into a testable dysregulation hypothesis (Siever & Davis, 1985). Whereas the usefulness of this hypothesis remains to be demonstrated, it suggests new ways of looking at the relationship between monoamines and affect.

Studies Involving Depressed Subjects. A number of studies involving acute increases in activity and urinary MHPG in depressed subjects have been conducted, and these investigations are summarized in Table 1. The results of these experiments are difficult to interpret primarily because of the variety of designs that have been employed. Two studies, for example, compared agitated and nonagitated patients. However, the well-known problems in quantifying agitation may limit this approach (Beckman, Ebert, Post, & Goodwin, 1979). The most common design has compared MHPG levels of patients on a day of increased activity to the levels found on a previous day of normal or limited activity. The results of these studies are equivocal. Some show significant increases in urinary MHPG with activity (Beckman, Ebert, Post, & Goodwin, 1979; Ebert, Post, & Goodwin, 1972; Post, Kotin, & Goodwin, 1973); others, however, show no effect of the increased activity (Sweeney, Leckman, Maas, Hattox, & Heninger, 1980; Sweeney, Maas, & Heninger, 1978). A major problem with these experiments has been the failure to adequately con-

Table 1 Studies Dealing With Acute Physical Activity and MHPG in Depressed Patients

Investigation	Subjects	Design	MHPG source	Findings
Ebert et al., 1972	6 depressives	Minimal activity day (reading & watching TV) compared to an increased activity day (outdoor walks, stair climbing and table tennis)	12-hour urine, 7 a.m. to 7 p.m.	Significant increase (.96 to 1.96 ug/12 hour).
Post et al., 1973	6 depressive females 19–75 years	Normal activity day compared to 4 hours of simulated mania (5 a.m. to 9 a.m.) consisting of physical and verbal hyperactivity	Two overnight urine, 9 a.m. separate days	Significant increase $(7.3 \pm 2.2$ to $14.2 \pm 3.4)$.
DeLeon-Jones, Maas, Dekirmenjian, and Sanchez, 1975	17 depressed females, mean age = 48 years	7 agitated patients (exhibited persistant pacing) compared to 10 retarded patients (who had minimal motor activity)	24-hour urine	No significant differences between agitated, retarded, and 21 normal controls.
Sweeney et al., 1978	14 unipolar, 4 bipolar, 4 schizophrenic, and 2 minor dysphoric females, mean age = 40 years	Pre- and postexperiment normal activity days compared with either restricted activity (bed rest, $N = 13$) or increased activity (brisk walking, cycle ergometry, table tennis, or shuffleboard, $N = 11$), state anxiety measured at 11:30 a.m. and 3:30 p.m.	Two 8-hour urine, 7:30 a.m. and 3:30 p.m.	No significant effect of activity on MHPG, significant correlation ($r = .71$) between change in state anxiety and change in MHPG.

(Cont.)

Table 1 (Cont.)

Investigation	Subjects	Design	MHPG source	Findings
Taube, Kirstein, Sweeney, Heninger, and Maas, 1978	14 depressive and 11 schizophrenic females	Agitated subjects ($N = 13$) compared to non-agitated subjects ($N = 12$)	24-hour urine	No significant differences between agitated and non-agitated subjects.
Beckman et al., 1979	11 depressives	Same design as pilot study reported by Ebert et al., 1972	12-hour urine, 7 a.m. and 7 p.m.	Activity increased 100% from control day, significant increase (.50 ± .14 to 1.54 ± .49 ug/12 hour).
Sweeney et al., 1980	7 depressives, 19–56 years	Normal activity days compared to a day of increased activity consisting of "a series of vigorous planned activities over the course of 8 hours on the ward"	Plasma and urine 7:30 a.m. and 7 p.m.	No effect of activity on MHPG or state anxiety.
Muscettola et al., 1984	15 depressives, 6 manics and 6 normals, 19–54 years	Spontaneous motor activity measured by a self-contained watch devise	24-hour urine	MHPG significantly correlated to activity in depressed group ($r = .46$).

trol for the intensity, duration, and/or mode of the increased activity. Consequently, interpreting the results of individual studies is difficult, and comparing results across studies is nearly impossible.

There have not apparently been any investigations that have assessed the effects of acute exercise on urinary MHPG in depressed patients by following standardized ergometric procedures. By controlling the mode, duration, and intensity of exercise, studies could be replicated by different groups, results could be compared with those from similar studies, and potential confounds, such as individual differences in level of physical fitness, could be minimized. Furthermore, no studies have been published that address the effects of chronic exercise on urinary MHPG in depressed subjects.

Studies Involving Nondepressed Individuals. Many investigators have considered the effects of acute exercise on MHPG levels in normal individuals, and these studies are summarized in Table 2. The variety of experimental designs employed make comparisons between studies difficult, and firm conclusions cannot be advanced. However, the designs of these experiments represent improvements over the studies involving depressed patients because the exercise is described in sufficient detail to permit replication. Also, in several of these investigations an attempt to relativize exercise intensity was made by having individuals exercise at a percentage of their estimated maximal oxygen uptake ($\dot{V}O_2$ max). An increase in MHPG was associated with acute exercise in the majority of these studies. Two studies (Goode, Dekirmenjian, Meltzer, & Maas, 1973; Tang, Stancer, Takahashi, Shephard, & Warsh, 1980) included MHPG measures of both urine and plasma, and each found significant increases in plasma but not urinary MHPG. In addition, two studies (Howlett & Jenner, 1978; Peryin & Pequignot, 1983) reported increases in MHPG subfractions, sulphate in one case and glucuronide in the other, but no significant difference in total urinary MHPG levels.

No studies have yet attempted to assess the effects of chronic exercise on urinary or plasma MHPG. However, the relationship between physical fitness and MHPG has been investigated in a series of related papers (Sothmann and Ismail, 1984, 1985; Sothmann, Ismail, and Chodko-Zajko, 1984). Early morning and postwork urinary MHPG levels were not significantly different for groups of subjects divided on the basis of estimated $\dot{V}O_2$max.

Cross-Species Studies. One rather novel approach to the study of exercise biochemistry and affect has involved a combined dog and human model (Stern & McDonald, 1965). It is recognized that depressed patients are characterized by physiological and psychomotor retardation and that this characteristic retardation is possibly due to central monoamine depletion, excess, or dysregulation. Furthermore, a biochemical factor found

Table 2 Studies Involving Acute Exercise and MHPG in Non-Depressed Individuals

Investigation	Subjects	Design	MHPG source	Findings
Goode et al., 1973	5 male students, 18–28 years	Subjects underwent 3 experimental conditions: 2 hours seated rest (control), 2 hours of isometric exercises (3 sets of a series of 10 seconds maximal isometric contractions using a variety of muscle groups), and isotonic bicycling exercise averaging 1-1/2 hours at a resistance equal to a "slight uphill grade." The experimental conditions were preceded and followed by 2 hours seated rest and the order of the conditions was randomized.	Plasma and urine measured at each 2 hour interval	No effect of exercise on urinary MHPG was found. Plasma MHPG increased significantly above preexercise levels for isotonic exercise, and preexercise MHPG levels were low in this condition; therefore the authors suggest a cautious interpretation.
Howlett and Jenner, 1978	1 high-fit and 4 low-fit teenage girls	The pilot study consisted of 15 minutes of intense cycle ergometry (17.5 kgm/second).	Pre- and postexercise urine	Unfit girls had a significantly larger increase in the sulphate and glucuronide MHPG subfractions than the fit girl.
	14 males, 16–17 years	Subjects were tested on two separate days under a rest or exercise condition. The order was randomized and the exercise consisted of a 5-minute step test followed by 50-minutes of cycle ergometry at an intensity of 8.33 kgm/second and a distance equal to an average of 15.3 kilometers.	Pre- and postexercise urine	A significant increase in the sulphate MHPG subfraction was found, and the sulphate subfraction was correlated to the kilometers cycled ($r = .55$).

(Cont.)

Table 2 (Cont.)

Investigation	Subjects	Design	MPHG source	Findings
Chodakowska, Wocial, Skorka, Nazar and Chwalbinska-Moneta, 1980	11 essential and 5 borderline male hypertensives and 9 normotensives, mean age = 27	Subjects rested for 3 hours, cycled for 30 minutes at a heart rate of 120 bpm, rested for 90 minutes, and cycled again for 30 minutes at a heart rate of 140 bpm.	Pre- and postexercise urine	All 3 groups exhibited an increase in MHPG, however, the hypertensives has a significantly smaller increase in MHPG than did the normotensives.
Tang et al., 1981	6 subjects, 18-47 years	Subjects walked on a treadmill for 30 minutes, rested for 2 1/2 hours then cycled for 30 minutes. Both exercise bouts were at an intensity of 40% of estimated $\dot{V}O_2$ max.	Postexercise plasma and urine	Both exercise bouts increased plasma but not urinary MHPG.
Peyrin and Pequignot, 1983	12 males, 25-70 years	Subjects cycled for 15 minutes at 80% of estimated $\dot{V}O_2$ max.	Pre- and postexercise urine	An increase of 25% in glucuronide MHPG subfraction and no change in free, sulphate or total MHPG were found.

outside the CNS may be responsible for the motor retardation. A study
described by Stern and McDonald (1965) supports this possibility. Dogs
were taught to run a maze and then were given an injection of centrifuged
blood serum from manic-depressive patients in the depressed phase.
These injections resulted in a mean slowing of 5.8 seconds in maze-
running time whereas injection of serum from normal controls had no
effect on running time. This suggests that the psychomotor retardation
seen in the depressed state is governed in part by a biochemical factor
or factors present in the circulating blood. This does not rule out a central influence, however, because the biochemical factor could be a metabolite of one or more central neurotransmitters. Perhaps the most important
feature of this study is the demonstration of an alternative, and novel,
approach to the study of the interaction between exercise, biochemical
factors, and mood state.

Thermogenic Hypothesis

Elevation of body temperature to produce a variety of therapeutic effects has been used for many centuries. This practice dates back to at least
800 A.D. in Finland. Residents of Finland and other countries take regular sauna baths for the alleged health benefits and the sensation of well-
being produced by this treatment. Objective evidence shows that muscle tension levels (i.e., somatic anxiety) are reduced following sauna
(deVries, Beckmann, Huber, & Dieckmeir, 1968).

During the 1930s and early 1940s pyrogens (i.e., fever producing sub-
stances) such as the malaria organism were injected into patients suffering from paresis. This treatment resulted in elevated temperatures lasting
for almost 2 weeks, and body temperatures in the range of 105°–106°F
were noted for periods of 30 to 50 hours during the so called fever therapy.
Bennett, Cash, and Hockstra (1941) reported that pyrogenic therapy improved the EEG of treated patients with an increase in alpha wave frequency immediately following treatment, and this normalized EEG was
found to persist at 3 years of follow-up. This procedure was eventually
discarded in favor of physical heating of patients that was found to be
equally effective and associated with a lower mortality (Bessemans, 1941).

Animal research carried out with cats, rats, and hamsters has revealed
that whole-body warming, as well as direct brain warming, has a profound effect on central and peripheral neuron activity (deVries et al., 1968;
von Euler & Soderberg, 1957). Gamma motor neuron activity is inversely related to hypothalamic temperature (von Euler & Soderberg, 1957),
and it also contributes significantly to tonic muscle activity (deVries,
Wiswell, Bulbulian, & Moritani, 1981).

An extensive literature demonstrates that deep body temperature is increased in proportion to the intensity of exercise an individual performs. Vigorous exercise, for example, produces an elevation in body temperature up to 40° C without thermal injury, and this elevation can persist for hours following an acute exercise bout (Haight & Keatinge, 1973). The increase in temperature during exercise is largely a function of the relative intensity of the exercise, but a number of factors can influence body temperature during and after exercise (Gisolfi & Wenger, 1984). Cannon and Kluger (1983), for example, reported that the rectal temperature of rats can be elevated by injecting them with plasma obtained from people who have just finished exercising. These findings led Cannon and Kluger to conclude that "endogenous pyrogen, a protein mediator of fever and trace metal metabolism during infection is released during exercise" (p. 617). They also reported that the pyrogenic component was heat-denaturable and incubation of human mononuclear leukocytes obtained postexercise "released a factor into the medium that also elevated body temperature in rats" (p. 617).

Krueger, Walter, Ginarello, Wolff, and Chedid (1984) reported that infusion of endogenous pyrogen directly into the lateral cerebral ventricles of rabbits produced a dose-dependent increase in slow wave sleep and that this response was associated with increasing body temperature. However, they also found that blocking the temperature increase by means of an antipyretic did not influence the sleep-promoting activity of the endogenous pyrogen. Thus the effects of endogenous pyrogens on sleep and temperature appear to be separable.

Decreasing muscle tension following both exercise and a sauna bath has been observed by deVries et al. (1981); measurement was taken electromyographically. In a somewhat related study Raglin and Morgan (1985) reported that a 5-minute shower at a water temperature of 38.5°C was associated with a significant decrease in state anxiety. Because gamma motor activity contributes significantly to muscle tone and because reductions in muscle tension and state anxiety occur following exercise and passive heating, the anxiolytic effects of exercise might be due to a reduction in muscle tension caused by an elevation in body temperature.

Another plausible explanation is that temperature elevations influence the release, synthesis, or uptake of certain brain monoamines. Thus the possible changes in brain monoamines discussed in the previous section may not occur as the result of exercise per se, but these changes may be due, rather, to the effects of increased brain temperature on the metabolism of these neurotransmitters.

Additional support for the thermogenic hypothesis is provided in a related paper by Horne and Staff (1983) who compared the effects of exercise and passive body heating on sleep. In this experiment 8 trained subjects underwent the following three conditions: (a) two 40-minute treadmill runs, separated by a 30-minute rest period, at 80% of $\dot{V}O_2$ max; (b) two 80-minute treadmill runs, separated by a 15-minute rest period, at 40% of $\dot{V}O_2$ max; and (c) two 40-minute sessions sitting in a hot bath, separated by a 30-minute rest period, in which the water temperature was set to elevate the subject's rectal temperature to the same rectal temperature produced during the high-intensity exercise condition. The results indicated that high-intensity exercise and passive heating produced similar increases in slow wave sleep. Horne and Staff (1983) concluded that "a high and sustained rate of body heating for 1 to 2 hours, particularly the inherernt rapid rates of core temperature increase and of body dehydration, may trigger a slow wave sleep, response, and that exercise may simply be a vehicle for these effects" (p. 36).

Holland, Sayers, Keatinge, Davis, and Peswani (1985) provide limited evidence refuting the thermogenic hypothesis. In their experiment subjects were immersed in warm or thermoneutral water and asked to perform memory and reasoning tasks. Mood was also assessed before and after the immersion sessions, and a significant increase in irritability was found in the heated versus the control condition. These results should be viewed with caution, however, because the memory and reasoning tasks themselves may have been a source of irritation and because the validity of the instrument used to measure mood has not been demonstrated.

It has recently been observed that some patients with affective disorders have abnormal temperature regulation. For example, Avery, Wildschiodtz, and Rafaelsen (1982) compared 9 drug-free patients with primary affective disorder to 12 normal control subjects and concluded that the depressed subjects had higher nocturnal temperatures than controls and that the nocturnal temperatures returned to normal with recovery. Furthermore, the amplitude of the 24 hour rectal temperature was significantly reduced in the depressed subjects versus controls, and the amplitude tended to increase with recovery. Thus evidence supports the notion that normal individuals experience a mood elevation concurrent with an elevation in body temperature, and some patients with mood disturbances suffer from temperature dysregulation that normalizes with an improvement in mood.

Discussions of this nature inevitably create problems relating to infinite regress, and this represents much of the basis for the anti-reductionistic movement in contemporary psychology (Peele, 1981b). At any rate, both somatic (e.g., EMG) and psychic (e.g., state anxiety), tension states are reduced following exercise, temperature is elevated when this takes place, rat brain catecholamines are altered, and a pyrogenic factor capable of altering body temperature is found in human plasma at the same time. Whether or not temperature effects per se produce the reduced anxiety and sensation of well-being remains to be demonstrated. The temperature hypothesis, however, is certainly tenable, and its confirmation (or refutation) awaits future research.

Endorphin Hypothesis

Despite the absence of compelling scientific evidence, it has become widely accepted that improved mood state following exercise is stimulated by the release of endorphins (Steinberg & Sykes, 1985). In some ways it was only natural that isolation of met-enkephalin and leu-enkephalin, because of the opiate agonist effect of these peptides, would lead to the proposal that exercise-induced euphoria was brought about by the release of endorphins. Indeed, in a recent paper Panksepp (1986) stated that "the recruitment of opioids during vigorous exercise may help diminish the general bodily consequences of accruing stress by stabilization of breathing rhythms and amplification of cardiovascular tone" (p. 95). In a recent review by Morgan (1985), however, it was concluded that the endorphin hypothesis of exercise-induced euphoria can be rejected or accepted on the basis of the investigations one chooses to cite or ignore. A similar view has been expressed by Steinberg and Sykes (1985) who state that the matter of exercise, elevated endorphin, and improved mood "is neither straightforward nor conclusive" (p. 850).

Because three recent reviews have dealt entirely or in part with the endorphin hypothesis of mood enhancement with exercise (Morgan, 1985; Panksepp, 1986; Steinberg & Sykes, 1985), this hypothesis will not be reviewed in detail in this chapter. The existing reviews are comprehensive and address the major methodological issues and concerns that exist in this area. Whereas further research is undoubtedly needed to explicate the biochemical mechanisms underlying exercise-induced alterations in affect, recent research by Farrell et al. (1986) questions the role of endorphins in this process, and a summary of their work follows.

In an effort to evaluate the influence of endogenous opioids on the tension reduction effects frequently observed following vigorous exercise, Farrell et al. (1986) administered a placebo or 50 mg naltrexone, a long lasting opioid antagonist, to 8 male subjects prior to 30 minutes of exercise performed on a bicycle ergometer at 70% of $\dot{V}O_2$ max. The Profile of Mood States was administered to these individuals before and after exercise under both conditions in order to evaluate the effect on tension. The subjects were asked to respond to the questionnaire by indicating how they felt "right now at this moment." Tension was decreased significantly following exercise under both conditions, and mood enhancement was therefore not influenced by the naltrexone treatment. These findings can be interpreted to mean that endogenous opioids are not involved in the tension reduction that customarily accompanies vigorous exercise.

Distraction Hypothesis

The distraction hypothesis is based on the observation that resting quietly in an area free of distractions for periods of time ranging in duration from 20 to 45 minutes is associated with significant reductions in state anxiety and blood pressure (Bahrke & Morgan, 1978; Raglin & Morgan, in press). This hypothesis, unlike the previous three, does not identify a specific mechanism to explain the improved affect known to follow exercise (Morgan, 1985). The process involved in the exercise response (e.g., reduced anxiety) can be operationalized in a generic manner without postulating specific mechanisms.

Exercise intervention involves at least one component that can occur in the absence of exercise—the passage of time (i.e., time-out). Furthermore, depending on the testing format employed, laboratory assessments can involve little or no external stimulation, and exercise outside of the laboratory can also involve restricted environmental stimulation. Therefore, it is important to distinguish between the psychological effects brought about by exercise per se and those due partly or completely to factors such as time-out and restricted sensory stimulation. The possibility is good, in other words, that psychological effects often attributed to exercise are actually caused by factors that covary with exercise. This proposal does not argue against the influence of peptides, neurotransmitters, or thermogenic effects; it simply does not rely on such mechanisms in explaining how affective benefits occur with exercise. It is simply possible that electroencephalographic alterations, or changes in brain temperature or biochemistry, occur with quiet rest as well as with exercise.

Bahrke and Morgan (1978), demonstrated that vigorous exercise performed at 70% of $\dot{V}O_2$ max for 20 minutes is associated with a signifcant decrease in state anxiety. The magnitude of this tension reduction, however, did not differ from that observed in test subjects who were randomly assigned to 20 minutes of meditation (Benson's procedure) or 20 minutes of rest in a sound-filtered room. Because exercise, meditation, and quiet rest were equally effective in reducing anxiety, Bahrke and Morgan (1978) postulated that reductions in state anxiety following vigorous exercise may be due in part to distraction from various stressors afforded by exercise. This general observation has been replicated in a series of experiments by Raglin and Morgan (1985).

More recent research by Raglin and Morgan (in press) has shown that blood pressure, as well as state anxiety, decreases significantly following either a 45-minute quiet rest or exercise. Unlike the earlier study by Bahrke and Morgan (1978) the participants in this research performed their usual form of aerobic exercise (e.g., jogging, cycling, or swimming) rather than being required to walk on the treadmill. Also, the subjects were evaluated psychobiologically for 3 hours following the exercise and time-out interventions. This research has shown that reductions in blood pressure and anxiety persist for a longer period of time following exercise. Exercise and quiet rest are apparently associated with similar quantitative but different qualitative effects.

The idea that exercise is no better than quiet rest in reducing anxiety and blood pressure could potentially discomfit many exercise enthusiasts. Although the observation that the two interventions may differ at a qualitative level may be attractive to the exercise enthusiast, these results must be viewed tentatively because they have not been replicated in a systematic manner.

Summary

A considerable body of literature attests to the affective benefits that are *associated* with long-term physical activity of a vigorous nature. Furthermore, whereas improved mood state has been observed both in patients with psychopathology as well as in nonhospitalized out-patients and normal individuals, the most consistent effects have been observed in those individuals with mild or moderate disturbances. On the other hand, normal individuals experience significant but transient effects on stress emotions such as anxiety following acute physical activity. In the cases of both acute and chronic physical activity, however, apparently no evidence supports the view that vigorous exercise *causes* the observed affective beneficence. A number of plausible explanations are presented in this chapter, but these proposed mechanisms are entertained within a hypothetical context. These hypotheses need to be systematically tested in order to explicate the reason or reasons for the altered mood as well as the conditions under which mood elevation can be maximized.

To suggest that adherence and dropout in exercise programs are governed by the extent to which positive psychological effects accompany exercise would certainly be premature for at least three reasons. First, and perhaps most important of all, no published evidence supports the contention that exercise actually causes an improvement in mood state. Second, although there is a substantial *descriptive* literature and a meager but compelling *predictive* literature dealing with exercise adherence, the volume of *explanatory* research is very small. Many investigators have described dropout and adherence patterns, and a few have even predicted these behaviors in advance. But very few workers in this field have made an effort to explain why people adhere or dropout. Third, to argue that people who feel good following exercise would be more likely to adhere than those who do not may be intuitively defensible, but such a view is simplistic because it is quite probable that many or most individuals who discontinue exercise programs may do so even though they too enjoy an improved mood state following exercise. This hypothesis could be tested empirically, but it is probably not necessary because roughly 80% to 90% of individuals in exercise programs report within 8–10 weeks that exercise makes them feel better, but 50% dropout within a few months.

The darker side of the exercise adherence problem must not be ignored. This involves what has been described by various authors as addictive, dependent, compulsive, committed, or obligatory behavior. The problem has been reviewed in the present chapter so that researchers and clinicians interested in the enhancement of exercise adherence might be aware of the potential for creating an undesired or unintended behavior (e.g., exercise addiction). Meanwhile, those who have been habitual exercisers for many years will continue addictive/dependent exercise patterns unless unanticipated, uncontrollable, and extraordinary forces prevent them from doing so—why is this so?

References

Avery, D.H., Wildschiodtz, G., & Rafaelsen, O. (1982). Nocturnal temperature in affective disorders. *Journal of Affective Disorders, 4*, 61–71.

Bahrke, M.S., & Morgan, W.P. (1978). Anxiety reduction following exercise and meditation. *Cognitive Therapy and Research, 2*, 323–333.

Barchas, J.D., & Freedman, D.X. (1963). Brain amines: Response to physiological stress. *Biochemistry and Pharmacology, 12*, 1232–1235.

Beckman, H., Ebert, M.H., Post, R., & Goodwin, E.K. (1979). Effects of moderate exercise on urinary MHPG in depressed patients. *Pharmakopsychiatry, 12*, 351–356.

Bennett, A.E., Cash, P.T., & Hoekstra, C.S. (1941). Artificial fever therapy in general paresis with electroencephalographic studies. *Psychiatric Quarterly, 15*, 750–771.

Brown, B.S., Payne, T., Kim, C., Moore, G., Krebs, P., & Martin, W. (1979). Chronic response of rat brain norepinephrine and serotonin levels to endurance training. *Journal of Applied Physiology, 46*, 19–23.

Brown, B.S., & Van Huss, W. (1973). Exercise and rat brain catechol-amines. *Journal of Applied Physiology, 34,* 664–669.

Cannon, J.G., & Kluger, M.J. (1983). Endogenous pyrogen activity in human plasma after exercise. *Science, 220,* 617–619.

Chodakowska, J., Wocial, B., Skorka, B., Nazar, K., & Chwalbinska-Moneta, J. (1980). Plasma and urinary catecholamines and metabolites during physical exercise in essential hypertension. *Acta Physiologica Polonica, 31,* 623–630.

Cureton, T.K. (1963). Improvement of psychological states by means of exercise-fitness programs. *Journal of the Association for Physical and Mental Rehabilitation, 17,* 14–25.

deCastro, J.M., & Duncan, G. (1985). Operantly conditioned running: Effects on brain catecholamine concentrations and receptor densities in the rat. *Pharmacology, Biochemistry & Behavior, 23,* 495–500.

DeLeon-Jones, F., Maas, J.W., Dekirmenjian, H., & Sanchez, J. (1975). Diagnostic subgroups of affective disorders and their urinary excretion of catecholamine metabolites. *American Journal of Psychiatry, 132,* 1141–1148.

deVries, H.A., Beckman, P., Huber, H., & Dieckmeir, L. (1968). Electromyographic evaluation of the effects of sauna on the neuromuscular system. *Journal of Sports Medicine and Physical Fitness, 8,* 1–11.

deVries, H.A., Wiswell, R.A., Bulbulian, R., & Moritani, T. (1981). Tranquilizer effect of exercise. *American Journal of Physical Medicine, 60,* 57–66.

Ebert, M.H., Post, R.M., & Goodwin, F.K. (1972). Effects of physical activity on urinary MHPG excretion in normal subjects. *Lancet, 11,* 766.

Epling, W.F., Pierce, W.D., & Stephan, L. (1983). A theory of activity-based anorexia. *International Journal of Eating Disorders, 3,* 27–46.

Farrell, P.A., Gustafson, A.B., Garthwaite, T.L., Kalkhoff, R.K., Cowley, A.W., Jr., & Morgan, W.P. (1986). Influence of endogenous opioids on the response of selected hormones to exercise in man. *Journal of Applied Physiology, 61*(3), 1051–1057.

Folkins, C.H., & Sime, W.E. (1981). Physical fitness training and mental health. *American Psychologist, 36,* 373–389.

Gisolfi, C.V., & Wenger, C.B. (1984). Temperature regulation during exercise: Old concepts, new ideas. In R. Terjung (Ed.), *Exercise and sports sciences reviews* (pp. 339–372). Lexington, MA: Collamore.

Goode, D.J., Dekirmenjian, H., Meltzer, H.Y., & Maas, J.W. (1973). Relation of exercise to MHPG excretion in normal subjects. *Archives of General Psychiatry, 29,* 391–396.

Gordon, R., Spector, S., Sjordsma, A., & Udenfriend, S. (1966). Increased synthesis of norepinephrine in the intact rat during exercise and exposure to cold. *Journal of Pharmacology and Experimental Therapy, 153*, 440–447.

Gruber, J.J. (1986). Physical activity and self-esteem development in children: A meta-analysis. In G.A. Stull & H.M. Eckert (Eds.), *Effects of physical activity on children* (pp. 30–48). Champaign, IL: Human Kinetics.

Haight, J.S.J., & Keatinge, W.R. (1973). Elevation in set point for body temperature regulation after prolonged exercise. *Journal of Physiology, 229*, 77–85.

Harri, M., & Kuusela, P. (1986). Is swimming exercise or cold exposure for rats? *Acta Physiologica Scandinavica, 126*, 189–197.

Holland, R.L., Sayers, J.A., Keatinge, W.R., Davis, H.M., & Peswani, R. (1985). Effects of raised body temperature on reasoning, memory and mood. *Journal of Applied Physiology, 59*, 1823–1827.

Horne, J.A., & Staff, C.H. (1983). Exercise and sleep: Body heating effects. *Sleep, 6*, 36–46.

Howlett, D.R., & Jenner, F.A. (1978). Studies relating to the clinical significance of urinary 3-methoxy-4-hydroxyphenylethylene glycol. *British Journal of Psychiatry, 132*, 49–54.

Katz, J.L. (1986). Long-distance running, anorexia nervosa, and bulima: A report of two case studies. *Comprehensive Psychiatry, 27*, 74–78.

Klissouras, V. (1970). Heritability of adaptive variation. *Journal of Applied Physiology, 29*, 358–367.

Krueger, J.M., Walter, J., Ginarello, C.A., Wolff, S.M., & Chedid, L. (1984). Sleep promoting effects of endogenous pyrogens (interleukin 1). *American Journal of Physiology, 246*, R994–R999.

Layman, E.M. (1960). Contributions of exercise and sports to mental health and social adjustment. In W.R. Johnson (Ed.), *Science and medicine of exercise and sports* (pp. 560–599). New York: Harper.

Layman, E.M. (1972). The contributions of play and sport to emotional health. In J.E. Kane (Ed.), *Psychological aspects of physical education and sport* (pp. 163–186). London: Routledge & Kegan Paul.

Little, J.C. (1969). The athlete's addiction in runners. *Acta Psychiatrica Scandinavica, 45*, 187–197.

Little, J.C. (1979). Neurotic illness in fitness fanatics. *Psychiatric Annals, 9*, 49–56.

Maas, J.W., & Leckman, J.F. (1983). Relationships between CNS noradrenergic function and urinary MHPG and other norepinephrine metabolites. In J.W. Maas (Ed.), *MHPG: Basic mechanisms and psychopathology* (pp. 33–42). New York: Academic.

Mihevic, P.M. (1981). Anxiety, depression and exercise. *Quest, 33*, 140–153.

Morgan, W.P. (1969). Physical fitness and emotional health: A review. *American Corrective Therapy Journal, 23*, 124–127.

Morgan, W.P. (1974). Exercise and mental disorders. In A.J. Ryan & F.L. Allman (Eds.), *Sports medicine* (pp. 671–678). New York: Academic.

Morgan, W.P. (1976). Psychological consequences of vigorous physical activity. In M.G. Scott (Ed.), *The academy papers* (pp. 15–30). Iowa City, IA: American Academy of Physical Education.

Morgan, W.P. (1979a). Anxiety reduction following acute physical activity. *Psychiatric Annals, 9*, 36–45.

Morgan, W.P. (1979b). Negative addiction in runners. *Physician and Sportsmedicine, 7*, 57–70.

Morgan, W.P. (1981). Psychological benefits of physical activity. In F.J. Nagle & H.J. Montoye (Eds.), *Exercise, health, and disease*. Springfield, IL: Charles C Thomas.

Morgan, W.P. (1982). Psychological effects of exercise. *Behavioral Medicine Update, 4*, 25–30.

Morgan, W.P. (1984). Physical activity and mental health. In H.M. Eckert & H.J. Montoye (Eds.), *Exercise and health*. Champaign, IL: Human Kinetics.

Morgan, W.P. (1985). Affective beneficence of vigorous physical activity. *Medicine and Science in Sports and Exercise, 17*, 94–100.

Morgan, W.P., & Goldston, S.E. (Eds.). (1987). *Exercise and mental health*. New York: Hemisphere.

Morgan, W.P., Olsen, E.B., & Pederson, N.P. (1982). A rat model of psychopathology for use in exercise science. *Medicine and Science in Sports and Exercise, 17*, 91–100.

Morgan, W.P., & Pollock, M.L. (1977). Psychological characterization of the elite distance runner. *Annals New York Academy of Science, 301*, 382–403.

Muscettola, G., Potter, W.Z., Pickor, D., & Goodwin, F.K. (1984). Urinary 3-methoxy-4-hydroxyphenyl glycol and major affective disorders. *Archives of General Psychiatry, 41*, 337–342.

Panksepp, J. (1986). The neurochemistry of behavior. *Annual Review of Psychology, 37*, 77–107.

Peele, S. (1981a). *How much is too much?* Englewood Cliffs, NJ: Prentice-Hall.

Peele, S. (1981b). Reductionism in the psychology of the eighties. *American Psychologist, 36*, 807–818.

Peyrin, L., & Pequignot, J.M. (1983). Free and conjugated 3-methoxy-4-hydroxyphenyl glycol in human urine: Peripheral origin of the glucuronide. *Psychopharmacology, 79*, 16–20.

Post, R.M., Kotin, J., & Goodwin, F.K. (1973). Psychomotor activity and cerebrospinal fluid amine metabolites in affective illness. *American Journal of Psychiatry, 130*, 67–72.

Raglin, J.S., & Morgan, W.P. (in press). Influence of acute exercise and distraction on state anxiety and blood pressure. *Medicine and Science in Sports and Exercise.*

Raglin, J.S., & Morgan, W.P. (1985). Influence of vigorous exercise on mood state. *Behavior Therapist, 8*, 179–183.

Ransford, C.P. (1982). A role for amines in the antidepressant effects of exercise: A review. *Medicine and Science in Sports and Exercise, 14*, 1–10.

Schildkraut, J.J., Orsulak, P.J., Schatzberg, A.F., & Rosenbaum, A.H. (1983). Relationship between psychiatric diagnostic groups of depressive disorders and MHPG. In J.W. Maas (Ed.), *MHPG: Basic mechanisms and psychopathology.* New York: Academic.

Sheehan, G. (1983). The best therapy. *Physician and Sportsmedicine, 11*, 43.

Siever, L.J., & Davis, K.L. (1985). Overview: Toward a dysregulation hypothesis of depression. *American Journal of Psychiatry, 142*, 1017–1031.

Solomen, R.L. (1980). The opponent-process theory of acquired motivation. *American Psychologist, 35*, 691–712.

Sonstroem, R.J. (1984). Exercise and self-esteem. In R.L. Terjung (Ed.), *Exercise and sports sciences reviews* (pp. 123–155). Lexington, MA: Collamore.

Sothmann, M.S., & Ismail, A.H. (1984). Relationships between urinary catecholamine metabolites, particularly MHPG, and selected personality and physical fitness characteristics in normal subjects. *Psychosomatic Medicine, 46*, 523–533.

Sothmann, M.S., & Ismail, A.H. (1985). Factor analytic derivation of the MHPG/NM ratio: Implications for studying the link between physical fitness and depression. *Biological Psychiatry, 20*, 570–583.

Sothmann, M.S., Ismail, A.H., & Chodko-Zajko, W.J. (1984). Influence of catecholamine activity on the hierarchical relationships among physical fitness conditions and selected personality characteristics. *Journal of Clinical Psychology, 40*, 1308–1317.

Steinberg, H., & Sykes, E.A. (1985). Introduction to symposium on endorphins and behavioral processes: Review of literature on endorphins and exercise. *Pharmacology Biochemistry and Behavior*, **23**, 857–862.

Stern, J.A., & McDonald, D.G. (1965). Physiological correlates of mental disease. In P.R. Farnsworth (Ed.), *Annual review of psychology*. Palo Alto, CA: Annual Reviews.

Stone, E.A. (1973). Accumulation and metabolism of norepinephrine in rat hypothalamines after exhaustive stress. *Journal of Neurochemistry*, **21**, 589–601.

Suomi, S.J. (1982). Relevance of animal models for clinical psychology. In P.C. Kendell & J.N. Butchner (Eds.), *Handbook of research methods in clinical psychology* (pp. 249–271). New York: John Wiley.

Sweeney, D.R., Leckman, J.F., Maas, J.W., Hattox, S., & Heninger, G.R. (1980). Plasma free and conjugated MHPG in psychiatric patients. *Archives of General Psychiatry*, **37**, 1100–1103.

Sweeney, D.R., Maas, J.W., & Heninger, G.R. (1978). State anxiety, physical activity and urinary 3-methoxy-4-hydroxyphenethylene glycol excretion. *Archives of General Psychiatry*, **35**, 1418–1425.

Tang, S.W., Stancer, H.C., Takahashi, S., Shephard, R.J., & Warsh, J.J. (1981). Controlled exercise elevates plasma but not urinary MHPG and VMA. *Psychiatry Research*, **4**, 13–20.

Taube, S.L., Kirstein, L.S., Sweeney, D.R., Heninger, G.R., & Maas, J.W. (1978). Urinary 3-methoxy-4-hydroxyphenylglycol and psychiatric diagnosis. *American Journal of Psychiatry*, **135**, 78–81.

vonEuler, C., & Soderberg, V. (1957). The influence of hypothalamic thermoreceptive structures on the electroencephalogram and gamma motor activity. *EEG Clinical Neurophysiology*, **9**, 391–408.

Yates, A., Leehey, K., & Slisslak, C.M. (1983). Running—An analogue of anorexia? *New England Journal of Medicine*, **308**, 251–255.

PART 2

Theoretical Models of Exercise Adherence: Understanding the Process

Despite a remarkable growth in applied interest about exercise adherence, the development of conceptual models leading toward a motivational theory of habitual physical activity has lagged behind. This section presents current thinking about available theory that is most relevant for understanding exercise adherence. Its purpose is to organize known correlates of exercise behavior within conceptually meaningful frameworks. This will foster hypothesis testing for future research, guide applied interventions by defining important psychological and behavioral targets, and set the stage for methods and strategies to facilitate adherence introduced in Part 3.

Chapter 5

''Psychological Models'' by Robert J. Sonstroem presents a unique social psychology integration of an exercise-specific model of habitual exercise with those derived from theories of general attitude, belief, and self-perception. Empirical support for the potential and delimitations of the models viewed separately and in unison is included. Particular attention is paid to the health belief model, health locus of control, self-motivation, self-efficacy theory, perceived competence, and reasoned-action. The chapter considers health beliefs about vulnerability and about the benefits of activity as they interact with reinforcements and barriers to influence behavior. It also addresses attitudes, beliefs, self-perceptions, and normative influences (including modeling) as they mediate exercise intentions and actual behavior. A goal is to outline plausible targets for exercise promotion strategies for adults and for those in the formative years of public education. The roles of health knowledge and exercise perceptions as targets for both mass persuasion and the private health care professional are highlighted.

Chapter 6

The public health outcomes and the behavioral determinants of physical activity and fitness are currently being investigated vigorously with adult populations. Less information has accumulated for children and youth. Exercise habits and fitness levels in the early years may influence adult activity or fitness or may alter the configuration of health risk factors among adults. The role of fitness and exercise in the health of children and youth is itself also important. These issues are discussed by Rod K. Dishman and Andrea L. Dunn in "Exercise Adherence in Children and Youth: Implications for Adulthood." First the scientific literature linking physical fitness and activity patterns with health outcomes and other health behaviors in children and youth is reviewed. Studies that suggest determinants of childhood physical activity are then presented. Next follows a survey of the existing health behavior models described in detail by Sonstroem in chapter 5 and the implications for research and interventions with children are noted. The chapter concludes with an interactive exercise adherence model and questions for future study.

CHAPTER 5

Psychological Models

Robert J. Sonstroem

Developing an understanding of exercise participation mechanisms poses an acute challenge for today's exercise scientists. An increasing amount of study over the past 10 years has failed to provide basic answers about who will exercise, why, or for how long (Cox, 1984; Dishman, 1982, 1985; Morgan, 1977). This lack of understanding hinders the delivery of exercise to those believed to be most in need of it (Dishman, 1982), precludes planning for optimal benefits for all within activity programs (Sonstroem, 1982), and most certainly contributes to the roughly 50% attrition rate experienced across organized group programs (Dishman, 1982). A majority of recent studies examining exercise participation have focused on adherence. Once enrolled in an activity program, who are the people who will remain in the program? Who will drop out and why? In general, these studies have been limited by a lack of standardization and by procedural shortcomings precluding the discovery of salient results replicated across settings. Most important for the purposes of this chapter, adherence research has evolved from applied and pragmatic questions and has been characteristically atheoretical in nature (Dishman, 1982). Although adherence research has tapped the discipline of psychology for its motivational relevance in predicting behavior, many of the psychological measures employed have been nonstandardized and administered ex post facto. Simply asking a dropout why he or she left the program can elicit an attribution dependent on the social desirability of the setting or the defensiveness of the subject. Relying on nonstandardized measures that vary from study to study prohibits an examination of response comparability, reliability, or validity (Dishman, 1982). The use of psychological variables in adherence research has been characterized by the lack of accompanying models and by single administrations. Evaluating an attitude measure only once, generally at the outset of a program, fails to consider how this variable will interact with other personal and setting variables during a process of change. Dishman (1982) and Dishman, Sallis, and Orenstein (1985) have suggested a need to develop models capable of guiding future exercise participation studies. Theoretical models are seen as furnishing a framework for the selection of variables that assist in developing a unified approach among investigators and provide heuristic advantages in the development of more complete theories (Hempel, 1977; Parcel, 1984).

The purpose of this chapter is to present several existent psychological models and associated variables that appear to be applicable to the study of exercise participation. These models or portions of them have been tested directly in exercise programs or more often have been used to examine other health promotion behaviors such as health screening, compliance to medical regimen, smoking cessation, or weight loss. Because recidivism rates for these behaviors are similar to exercise dropout rates, similar motivational constructs have been proposed (Dishman, 1982, 1987; Morgan, 1977). Models or variables that have been used in health behavior research include the health belief model (Becker & Maiman, 1975), the theory of reasoned action (Fishbein & Ajzen, 1975), and locus of control (Strickland, 1978; Wallston, Wallston, & DeVellis, 1978). Two models generated specifically for the prediction of exercise behavior include the psychological model for physical activity participation (Sonstroem, 1978) and the psychobiologic model (Dishman & Gettman, 1980). The potential for examining activity participation with other motivational variables such as self-esteem and self-efficacy are discussed. Evaluation of models is based on theoretical as well as limited research evidence. The guiding motivation for this chapter is to provide foundations leading to the use of more complete models and multivariate approaches in developing an understanding of exercise participation.

Psychological Model for Physical Activity Participation

The psychological model for physical activity participation (Sonstroem, 1978) is the first model developed specifically for the prediction of exercise involvement. This model is also concerned with the manner in which exercise and consequent physical fitness contribute to psychological benefit, which in this case is enhanced self-esteem. Paralleling the model's development, two logical scales, Estimation and Attraction, were constructed for adolescent boys and are contained in the Physical Estimation and Attraction Scales (PEAS) (Sonstroem, 1974). Estimation contains 33 items assessing self-perceptions of physical abilities (conceived as a component of global self-esteem). The 54 items of the Attraction scale measure interest in vigorous physical activity. The model has been uniformly successful in presenting correlational evidence associating physical activity and psychological health in adolescent males. Estimation has been related to physical fitness scores (Dishman, 1978; Morgan & Pollock, 1978; Neale, Sonstroem, & Metz, 1969; Sonstroem, 1974, 1976) and to global self-esteem (Fox, Corbin, & Couldry, 1985; Neale et al., 1969; Sonstroem, 1974, 1976). Estimation scores have also related positively and significantly to lack of personality disorder, neuroticism, or maladjustment (Sonstroem, 1976). In predicting exercise participation the model posits that self-perceptions of physical ability (Estimation) influence an individual's interest in physical activity (Attraction) and that Attraction provides the greater influence on exercise participation.

Adherence Research

The model has been less effective in predicting exercise behavior than in demonstrating positive correlates of exercise. Early associations were

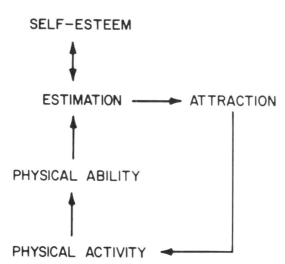

Figure 1   The psychological model for physical activity participation. *Note.*   From "Physical Estimation and Attraction Scales: Rationale and Research" by R.J. Sonstroem, 1978. *Medicine and Science in Sports,* 10, p. 101. Copyright 1978 by the American College of Sports Medicine. Reprinted by permission.

developed between Attraction and self-reports of physical activity (Neale et al., 1969; Sonstroem, 1978) and between Attraction and interscholastic athletic participation in high school boys (Sonstroem, 1974). However, using an adult form of the PEAS, Morgan and Pollock (1978) and Morgan (1976) failed to show a significant relationship between Attraction and exercise program adherence in prisoners and police officers respectively. Working with 45 healthy, nonrisk adults and 21 cardiac patients, Dishman and Gettman (1980) did not show a significant Attraction effect on adherence over a 20-week program. In a prospective study Sonstroem and Kampper (1980) were able to predict with 72% accuracy the interscholastic cross-country recruitment in junior high school males by Attraction first and Estimation second. However, these variables failed to significantly predict adherence over the entire season.

Critique of the Psychological Model for Physical Activity Participation

A summary of the preceeding research could conclude that the model is ineffective in predicting exercise adherence. This would mean that being interested in or attracted to exercise and believing oneself capable of success at exercise provides insufficient motivation for adhering to exercise (Dishman, 1982). Alternatively, failures of the model to predict adherence could be caused by the present form of PEAS items (Sonstroem & Kampper, 1980). The Attraction statements in particular, that were developed for adolescent males, contain a broad variety of interest objects. Wishing to belong to a white-water canoe club or preferring softball to poker would seem to bear minimal relationship to vigorous exercise behavior carried on over time. Additionally, newer attitude theory questions the effectiveness of measuring attitude toward a general object such as exercise. Ajzen and Fishbein (1977) have argued that attitude toward an object does not predict subsequent behavior with any degree of strength. Instead, an individual's attitude toward actually *performing* a specified referent behavior should be assessed. Exercise adherence literature has tended to discount the ability of attitudes to predict activity maintenance (Andrew & Parker, 1979; Dishman, 1982; Dishman et al., 1985). However, the summarized research has invariably employed broad attitudes posited by contemporary theory to bear only minimal association with behavior.

From a different perspective, the Attraction scale and attitude statements in general have been successful at predicting initial recruitment to exercise experiences (Dishman, 1978; Morgan, 1976; Morgan & Pollock, 1978; Sonstroem & Kampper, 1980). The previously cited studies also document relatively high Estimation scores for volunteers. Because most exercise programs are voluntary those people who initially enroll apparently are interested in physical activity and believe themselves capable of achieving success in exercise programs. It is concluded that the model is greatly limited by the present form of the PEAS scales. When the model was developed it was admittedly incomplete in explaining youth participation (Sonstroem, 1978). This condition becomes magnified when evaluated in terms of the complexities of predicting adult exercise adherence. Nevertheless, interest in vigorous physical activity and self-perceived ability at activity could become components of a future, more complex model explaining adult activity participation. Recent replicated data from college students have identified shortened PEAS scales that can provide for the development of more valid adult scales (Safrit, Wood, & Dishman, 1985).

Self-Motivation and the Psychobiologic Model

Dishman and Gettman (1980) proposed a psychobiologic screening model containing percent body fat, body weight, and self-motivation as predictor variables. "Self-motivation is conceptualized as a generalized, nonspecific tendency to persist in the absence of extrinsic reinforcement and is thus largely independent of situational influence" (Dishman & Gettman, 1980, p. 297). Self-motivation is most likely socially learned and dependent upon the individual's ability at self-reinforcement. This psychological construct has been developed and interpreted as a disposition to persevere in a task after the task has been started (Dishman, Ickes, & Morgan, 1980). The psychobiologic model was developed in a 20-week prospective study enrolling 21 male cardiac patients and 45 male healthy nonrisk subjects (Dishman & Gettman, 1980). Mean age was 39.6 years. Percent body fat, body weight, and self-motivation determined at program initiation were able to distinguish the 43 adherers and 23 dropouts with 78.8% accuracy at program termination. These same variables employed in a multiple regression analysis produced an $R^2 = .45$ with attendance values. These data were also reported in an additional study (Dishman et al., 1980) and indicate that, compared to dropouts, adherers tend to be leaner, lighter, and more self-motivated. This psychobiologic model was tested in recent research that used the exemplary procedure of predicting adherence at 10, 20, and 32 weeks into the program (Ward & Morgan, 1984). The equation developed by Dishman and Gettman (1980) was employed in testing classification accuracy of the male adherers (53%) and female adherers (54%). The psychobiologic model successfully predicted 88% of the adherers but failed to predict dropouts accurately (25% overall, only 5% accuracy in the female sample). Across the four testing occasions no significant univariate F differences were obtained between adherers and dropouts in percent body fat, body weight, or self-motivation. The authors were able to construct predictive discriminant function equations from other variables that differed for the different time periods and between sexes across the 32 weeks. Classification accuracies ranged from 75% to 81%. They concluded that factors influencing adherence differ between the sexes and that different factors affect adherence over time.

Self-Motivation

A separate section on the self-motivation variable is included because it has been used more frequently as a single predictor than as a model component. The 40-item Self-Motivation Inventory (SMI) developed from a large item pool via factor analysis and item-total correlations possesses high internal reliability (Cronbach alpha = .91) (Dishman & Ickes, 1981). SMI scores have correlated significantly (r = .23, $p < .001$) with self-reports of exercise frequency in college students (Dishman & Ickes, 1981). It successfully predicted length of adherence (r = .33, $p < .05$) in women crew members over an 8-month season (Dishman & Ickes, 1981) and adult male adherence (r = .44, $p < .01$) in the study discussed previously (Dishman & Gettman, 1980). Freedson, Mihevic, Loucks, and Girandola (1983) reported an SMI mean of 157.6 in competitive female bodybuilders as compared to a mean of 140.5 for college students (Dishman & Ickes, 1981). The results of Dishman and colleagues in obtaining salient SMI predictions of exercise and athletic adherence have been replicated by several investigators. Olson and Zanna (1982) found that the SMI significantly differentiated adult regular attenders (n = 19) and occasional attenders (n = 9) from dropouts (n = 32). Thompson, Wyatt, and Craighead (1984) and Wyatt and Craighhead (1984) predicted number of weeks adherence to aerobic exercise in 45 college students by means of the SMI. In a 12-week walk/run program for young adults self-motivation significantly predicted the number of sessions and minutes of participation (Dishman, 1983). Stone (1983) found that SMI scores and smoking behavior significantly separated corporate aerobic and recreational participants from dropouts with an accuracy of 82%. Low SMI scores predicted poor exercise adherence in a cardiac exercise therapy program (Snyder, Franklin, Foss, & Rubenfire, 1982). Self-motivation scores have also predicted adherence to training of Olympic speedskaters (Knapp, Gutmann, Foster, & Pollock, 1984).

Results of other investigations have been nonsignificant or equivocal, however. In 106 healthy adults self-motivation significantly differentiated early dropouts from occasional attenders and adherers in males but not in females (Gale, Eckhoff, Mogel, & Rodnick, 1984). In both sexes it failed to separate occasional attenders and nonadhereres from adherers. In summary, it did not predict male adherence beyond an early period in the program and was ineffectual in predicting female participation. SMI scores failed to predict number of pounds lost in a weight loss program emphasizing self-control techniques (Weinberg, Hughes, Critelli, England, & Jackson, 1984). Robinson and Carron (1982) found that the SMI failed to discriminate among starters, squad members, and dropouts in high school football squads. Previously, it was observed that SMI scores of adherers and dropouts were similar in the Ward and Morgan (1984) study. Two studies have examined the interaction of self-motivation, one investigating intervention factors of social support (Wankel & Yardley, 1982), and the other using a decision balance sheet (Wankel & Graham, 1980). The investigators hypothesized that low self-motivators would be influenced by external motivation whereas high self-motivators would be relatively unaffected by these psychological interventions. Subjects were adult females enrolled in a 10-week aerobic dance or a 5-week exercise program. Analyses of variance on attendance data failed to reveal either significant self-motivation main effects or interactions with intervention factors. In both studies the intervention variables were marginally significant ($p < .06$, $p < .10$ respectively).

Psychobiologic Model and SMI Critique

The small sample size ($n = 66$) employed in the model's development disallows confidence in the reliability or generalizability of predictive associations. In a replication Ward and Morgan (1984) were able to correctly classify 88% of adherers but only 25% of dropouts by means of the original discriminant equation. This lack of prediction in the case of dropouts quite possibly arose from the small sample size combined with the relatively small number of dropouts ($n = 23$) in the original sample. However, the primary negating data in the Ward and Morgan study reside in the very equivalent means for the two groups on all three model components. Research results have been extremely inconsistent for the unitary predictive capability of body weight and percent fat. Dishman (1981) analyzed data of 362 adult male patients referred to a University of Wisconsin exercise program over a 5-year period and found body weight and percent fat to be significantly associated with adherence. Although similar results were obtained by Massie and Shephard (1971), an amount of discounting evidence has been summarized by Morgan (1977) and Olson and Zanna (1982). In a multifactor model with many interactions between components, of course, a variable whose bivariate relationship with the dependent variable is negative can possibly make a positive predictive contribution in conjunction with other variables. Whether or not this is true in the case of the psychobiologic model awaits further testing.

The development of the self-motivation variable has been greeted with extreme enthusiasm by students of adherence. Its items reflect high face validity for adherence not only to exercise but for perseverence and the exhibition of willpower in meeting many life challenges. It offers the tantalizing prospect of a simple solution for the adherence dilemma. However, it was constructed as a stable trait measure and has exhibited an extremely high (for a psychological variable) test-retest reliability ($r = .86$) over a 20-week period (Dishman & Ickes, 1981). This implies that it is relatively resistant to change, which would reduce its effectiveness when used in process models of change to be discussed later. Whereas its early development included an examination of correlates such as ego strength, need achievement, locus of control, and social desirability, further convergent and discriminant validation efforts would provide a better understanding of the variable and would improve predictions of its manner of interacting with other personal and setting variables. Meanwhile, its use as a prediction and screening measure for exercise adherence is strongly recommended. Conceivably, its construction as a measure of perseverence should predict adherence to an exercise program once initiated. Subjects screened as low self-motivators would be provided with additional extrinsic reinforcement such as group support.

Health Belief Model

The health belief model (HBM) evolved from research conducted in the early 1950s by the U.S. Public Health Service in attempting to determine why people failed to utilize screening tests for the detection of asymptomatic disease (Rosentock, 1974). The formal model was developed by Rosenstock (1966) and Becker and Maiman (1975) and is presented in Figure 2. Research of the model has centered on its four major components. *Susceptibility* refers to an individual's perception of the likelihood of contracting a particular disease. By *Severity* is meant the evaluation of the consequences of developing this disease. The *benefits* component relates to an individual's beliefs regarding the effectiveness of taking a specific health action. *Barriers* represent beliefs regarding the potentially negative aspects, for example, pain, financial cost, embarrassment, or inconvenience of adopting the particular health behavior. These variables are influenced in turn by demographic and sociopsychological variables. In addition, a cue to action, such as perceived symptoms, media, or interpersonal communication, must be present if action is to be initiated. The

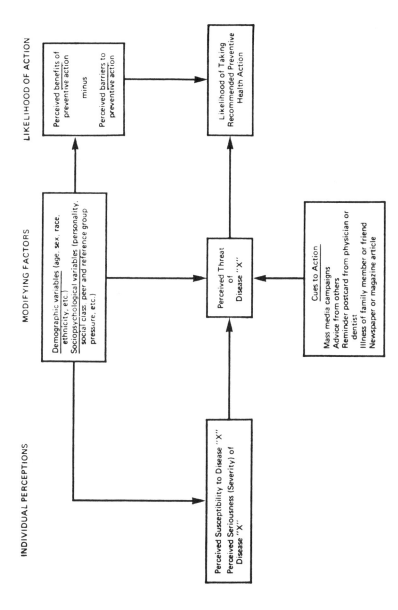

Figure 2 The health belief model. *Note.* From "Sociobehavioral Determinants of Compliance With Health and Medical Care Recommendations" by M.H. Becker and L.A. Maiman, 1975, *Medical Care,* **13,** p. 12. Copyright 1975 by J.B. Lippincott. Reprinted by permission.

utility of the HBM has been expanded since its inception to include investigation of sick-role behaviors and clinic visits.

Janz and Becker (1984) have critically reviewed 46 studies employing the HBM and report outstanding success of the model and most of its four major dimensions. Overall studies reporting significance levels, susceptibility, severity, benefits, and barriers have achieved predicted significance in 81%, 65%, 78%, and 89% of the cases respectively. Preventive health behavior studies (24) report increased percentages for susceptibility (86%) and barriers (93%) whereas severity has been effective in only 50% of these studies thus indicating a greater applicability for explaining sick-role behaviors.

Adherence Research

Limited use of the HBM in exercise settings has failed to replicate the previously cited positive results. Lindsay-Reid and Osborn (1980) induced 124 previously inactive members of the Toronto Fire Department to begin individual (3 times per week) exercise programs. Three study-developed scales were administered at program outset: a heart disease risk index, an illness probability index, and a benefits index. At 3 months, and contrary to prediction, 71% and 72% respectively of the 70 adherers had scores below the means of the entire group on two of the susceptibility measures ($p < .05$). Before initiating the program they had believed themselves less susceptible to heart disease and illness in general. A majority of these adherers also had lower belief scores in the benefits of preventive action.

Olson and Zanna (1982) studied 60 male and female subjects who began exercising at Vic Tanny and Nautilus centers. Adherers (19) were defined as those who attended at least once per week during the 3rd month of the study. Susceptibility and severity regarding heart, respiratory, blood pressure, and obesity problems and perceived benefits of exercising in preventing these problems were examined. Male adherers believed themselves more susceptible to heart, respiratory, and obesity problems which supported HBM predictions. However, an opposite, nonsignificant result occurred for females. Surprisingly, regular attenders had significantly lower severity scores than other subjects. Tirrell and Hart (1980) studied 30 coronary bypass patients and measured their knowledge about a prescribed heart-walk regimen, compliance to the regimen, and the use of pulse monitoring in daily activities. The four basic dimensions of the HBM plus general health motivation, a newer component introduced by Becker and Maiman (1975), served as predictors. Across the 15 correlations between behavior and model components, only 2 were significant in the predicted direction. Admittedly, all HBM components were not included in these studies, nor were standardized measures specific to exercise employed. The latter limitation has been addressed recently with the development of 49 HBM items specific to jogging (Slenker, Price, Roberts, & Jurs, 1984). Model variables correctly classified 92% of joggers and nonexercisers in an ex post facto discriminant function analysis.

Critique of the Health Belief Model

Calnan and Moss (1984) report that HBM support has been derived mainly from retrospective studies measuring belief and behavior concurrently. This may account for the lack of predictive efficiency in the already cited prospective studies. HBM variables may be ineffectual in anticipating later, ongoing compliant behaviors in healthy adults even though they associate with immediate actions (e.g., Slenker et al., 1984). The major deterrent to premier use of the HBM in gathering knowledge about exercise participation may reside in its theoretical foundations. It was developed essentially to predict a single instance of one specific behavior. Exercise adherence, however, encompasses a variety of behaviors carried on repeatedly over time. The HBM emphasizes a motivational orientation of illness avoidance; this precludes a careful analysis of the numerous motivations for exercise, of which many do not involve illness avoidance (Lindsay-Reid & Osborne, 1980; Olson & Zanna, 1982). The HBM could conceivably be employed with individuals concerned about health problems such as cardiac rehabilitation patients. The HBM has been used extensively in examining sick-role behaviors (Janz & Becker, 1984). Additionally, certain of its components, most notably barriers, have been associated with adherence or lack of it (Dishman, 1985) and warrant further individual study.

Theory of Reasoned Action

Fishbein and Ajzen (1975) have developed a model that predicts behavior (B) from a person's intention to actually perform the specific behavior in question. Behavioral intention (BI) in turn is influenced by the person's attitude toward performing the behavior (Aact) and by the subjective norm (SN) regarded as the perception of what generalized important others believe about the subject's performing the specific behavior. The model is represented by the following formula (Equation 1).

$$B \sim BI = w_1 \, Aact + w_2 \, SN$$

where w_1 and w_2 = weights developed by regression for the particular situation. As discussed earlier, attitude-behavior research has often been discounted because of the minimal relationships obtained (e.g., Wicker, 1969). Fishbein and Ajzen, however, believe that attitude can predict behavior via intention when the two measures of attitude and behavior are congruent in terms of action, target, context, and time. An impressive collection of research is cited to support this position (Ajzen & Fishbein, 1977). Their model has merit because it incorporates the contemporary psychological tenet of interactionism. By using narrow, situation-specific attitude and intention measures, interactions between personal determinants and the situation are promoted. Additionally, the model utilizes a particular situational variable, the subjective or social norm. Social support emanating from spouse, family, health professionals, and peers has been one of the better situational predictors of physical activity participation (Dishman et al., 1985; Heinzelmann & Bagley, 1970).

Whereas Equation 1 represents a direct measurement of attitude and subjective norm, these two components can also be measured indirectly. Attitudes may be reduced to a collection of beliefs (b_i) regarding the relevant behavior and to the evaluation of outcomes (e_i) associated with those respective beliefs. Subjective norm may be separated into a set of specific others (nb_i) in one's life and into motivation to comply (mc_i) with the wishes of each of these others. In Equation 2 attitude is measured indirectly by summing across products of all beliefs multiplied by respective outcome evaluations, and subjective norm is measured indirectly by summing across products of specific referents mutliplied by respective motivation to comply.

$$BI = \sum_{i=1}^{n} b_i e_i + \sum_{i=1}^{n} n b_i mc_i$$

Beliefs are regarded as cognitive components of attitudes. They measure specific attributes of an attitude object. By its reduction of components into more molecular elements, Equation 2 provides major heuristic benefits to the study of behaviors. As an example this section will later treat specific beliefs found to differentiate exercisers from nonexercisers. The theory of reasoned action has been applied successfully to a variety of health-related behaviors such as undergraduate intention of drinking alcohol (Budd & Spencer, 1984; Kilty, 1978), adolescent smoking intentions (Sherman et al., 1982), and weight loss behavior (Saltzer, 1982). For information on scale construction the reader is referred to Ajzen and Fishbein (1980), Riddle (1980), or Sonstroem (1982).

Adherence Research

In an incomplete test of the model, Olson and Zanna (1982) found that regular attenders as compared to occasional attenders and dropouts reported stronger intentions to exercise regularly ($p < .10$) and stronger motivations to comply with the wishes of significant others ($p < .05$). Inverse relationships held true for dropouts in comparison with the other groups. Riddle (1980) separated males and females who returned a questionnaire (86% rate) into 149 joggers and 147 nonexercisers. Subjects were telephoned 2 weeks later to determine interim jogging behavior. The correlation between intentions and actual behavior was established at .82. The combination of attitudes toward the behavior (Aact) and normative beliefs ($\Sigma nb_i\, mc_i$) explained 55% of the variance in intentions ($R = + .742$) with the standardized regression coefficient being approximately 4 times larger in the case of attitudes. The model was additionally supported in that indirect measures ($\Sigma b_i\, e_i$) and ($\Sigma n\, b_i\, mc_i$) of attitude and subjective norms correlated .76 and .73 with the respective direct measures. Results were replicated in a study of Japanese joggers and nonexercisers (Tokunaga, Tatano, Hashimoto, & Kanezaki, 1980, 1981). The superiority of attitude over subjective norm at predicting exercise intentions has been replicated by Godin, Cox, and Shephard (1983) and by Godin and Shephard (1985) in separate samples. A prominent result of the Riddle (1980) study was that 17 of the 19 employed beliefs significantly differentiated joggers from nonexercisers. Six items individually accounted for more than 20% of the variance between joggers and nonexercisers.

Sonstroem (1982) employed the same 19-item belief set in comparing high and low attenders in a faculty fitness program. The two attendance groups were saliently distinguished by 5 of the 19 items. All of these five were included in Riddle's set of six major differentiators, thus affording replication. Further unpublished research by the author and colleagues has identified four of these six beliefs as discriminating self-reports of recruits and adherers to exercise from those of nonexercisers. Those six belief items with full or partial replication across the three analyses include (all statements are in reference to attending a regular program of exercise): "take too much time," "require too much discipline," "make me feel too tired," "be unpleasant," "make me feel good mentally," "help me work off tensions and frustration." It is interesting that four of these six items refer to barriers (actual or perceived). Barriers have been mentioned repeatedly as major determinants of adherence (Andrew & Parker, 1979; Dishman, 1985; Shephard, chapter 11, this volume). Additional identified barriers have included work or schedule conflicts, program inaccessibility, and lack of proper facilities or exercise attire.

Critique of the Theory of Reasoned Action

Recent research has questioned the validity of predicting behavior by the simple additive model contained in the theory of reasoned action. Controversy clusters around the necessity of employing a mediating variable (BI) in explaining attitude-behavior associations (Bentler & Speckart, 1981; Liska, 1984) and on the nature of previous behavior's influence on present attitudes, intentions, and behavior (Fazio & Zanna, 1981; Sherman et al., 1982). In college students Bentler and Speckart (1981) found that attitudes rather than intentions provided a better prediction of exercise behavior but that the reverse held true for dating behavior. In general, however, behavioral intention "has been demonstrated to be one of the most important and one of the most consistently relevant predictors of continued participation in health improvement programs" (Davis, Jackson, Kronenfeld, & Blair, 1984, p. 362). Ajzen and Fishbein (1980) argue that attitudes based on experience are better predictors of future behavior because of greater stability. However, Fazio and Zanna (1981), state that "direct experience attitudes are more clearly defined, held with greater certainty, more stable over time, and more resistant to counter-influence" (p. 185). Additionally, they have been found to be more available and accessible (Sherman et al., 1982), hence more salient. Although the original Fishbein model is regarded as incomplete in explaining the nature of attitude formation and behavior associations, it remains the preferred model for exploring these complex interrelationships.

The model would appear to offer a variety of advantages in acquiring a greater understanding of exercise predictors. Its limited use has generally provided significant and at times sizeable predictions of immediate or subsequent short-term exercise. However, no direct examination of longer term activity adherence has been made to date. By its reliance on specific attitude and belief statements congruent to specified behaviors, the model has overcome criticisms of attitude theory occasioned by previously low attitude-behavior relationships. The same outcome may be anticipated in exercise research. Presence of the subjective norm (SN) component provides a mechanism for better interpreting the influence of social support, previously cited as an environmental determinant (Dishman et al., 1985). Separating attitudes into beliefs and evaluations of the consequences of acting on these beliefs provides prominent heuristic advantages to the study of exercise adherence. Salient belief differences between exercisers and nonexercisers leading to the implementation of behavior change strategies should be identifiable over replications. Harris (1970) found that beliefs of previously inactive exercisers changed in a positive fashion after a year of activity. Most important, the model possesses versatility because attitude and belief statements can be constructed to cover an almost limitless variety of suspected motivators, such as perceptions of susceptibility, benefits, barriers, fears, competence, and important others. The model is very capable of explaining the interaction of personal and environmental characteristics. This quality can be accentuated by employing a *process* approach, which will be discussed presently. Finally, it is possible to improve the predictive power of the model by incorporating nonattitudinal variables. The facilitative effect of previous experience on attitude strength and subsequent behavior was discussed earlier. Dishman et al. (1985) identify past program participation as "the most reliable correlate of current participation" (p. 162). Godin and Shephard (1985) used interaction terms (activity habits × spouses's intention to exercise and activity habits × socioeconomic status) to significantly improve the prediction of behavior intentions in men. Male activity habits in households where the wife intended to exercise or in households of lower socioeconomic status significantly predicted intentions to exercise. In separate research the addition of current physical activity habits to Aact and SN significantly increased the prediction of intention from a multiple R of .505 to one of .592 (Godin et al., 1983).

Locus of Control

Rotter's (1966) locus of control construct separated people into *internal* controllers, those who believe they can control the outcomes in their lives, and *external* controllers, those who believe their destinies are controlled by chance or powerful others. Because the construct was postulated as being more operative in important life events, it possesses a theoretical appeal for predicting health behavior. Internal controllers as opposed to external controllers would be expected to maintain more positive behaviors in the areas of preventive and corrective medicine. Sonstroem and Walker (1973) found that internal college males with positive attitudes toward exercise were more fit and more physically active than the remainder of the college male population. Weinberg et al. (1984) found that locus of control predicted weight loss ($r = .44$) in a program emphasizing self-control techniques. Whereas certain studies have associated internality and smoking cessation, results have been much more equivocal in the area of weight loss (Wallston & Wallston, 1978). Subsequent to Levinson's partitioning of external expectancies into Powerful Others and Chance components, Wallston et al. (1978) included these plus internality in a scale specific to health behavior, the Multidimensional Health Locus of Control (MHLC) Scale. However, the MHLC has been relatively unsuccessful in predicting health outcomes such as status of oral hygiene (Ludenia & Donham, 1983) or in predicting exercise program adherence (Dishman et al., 1980). Winefield's (1982) factor analysis of the

MHLC found four rather than three factors. Utilization of the original three components revealed a lack of relationship to health habits in medical and dental students and failed to predict compliance with medical advice. Lack of factor replication was also observed by Coelho (1985).

In fairness, the locus of control construct must be regarded as only one of a host of factors influencing health behaviors. Using an interactional model, Wallston, Wallston, Kaplan, and Maides (1976) found that internals in a self-directed program and externals in a group program tended to lose more weight and be better satisfied with the program than other subjects. Carrying the concept of specificity further, Saltzer (1982) developed a four-item Weight Locus of Control (WLOC) Scale. Over a 6-week weight loss program the correlation between behavioral intentions and actual behavior in WLOC internals with high values for physical appearance was .77. In WLOC externals, however, the correlation, developed with the same variables, was only .24. Of themselves none of the three MHLC scales significantly related to program completion. This research illustrates the prediction improvement that may be realized by examining interactions of several personal determinants. Use of the locus of control construct in physical activity research would imply the development of an exercise-specific control measure.

The Self in Exercise

The contemporary prominence of exercise has served to imbue it with therapeutic and beneficial properties. Exercise is "good," and many people enter it with the prospect of achieving personal growth, often of a psychological nature. Feelings of confidence, mastery, competence, and self-esteem are traditionally mentioned as anticipated outcomes of exercise participation (Sonstroem, 1984). Most important, these new-found attainments are expected to influence the person's entire behavior repertoire and to generalize to other important life situations.

Self-Esteem

Self-esteem and its kin, the ego, have been recognized as variables of the greatest consequence in psychotherapy (Freed, 1977; Gergen, 1971). What people think of themselves is apt to be the central process in their lives. Because of its intuitive appeal for defining anticipated psychological benefit, self-esteem has been regarded as the paramount variable in exercise-personality research (Folkins & Sime, 1981; Sonstroem, 1984). After reviewing 16 selected studies testing the hypothesis of enhanced self-esteem through exercise, Sonstroem (1984) concluded that significant increases in self-esteem are related to exercise participation. Unfortunately, experimental limitations and a lack of molecular analyses have barred an understanding of the mechanisms involved. Sonstroem has recommended the use of narrower scales containing stimuli more specific to the exercise setting. Body cathexis (Secord & Jourard, 1953) items such as physical stamina, weight, profile, muscle strength, and health would seem capable of reflecting outcomes of a training program. Repeated measurement could examine the degree to which changes in self-perception were associated with adherence. To date this type of paradigm, associating *changes* in *setting-relevant* self-perceptions with exercise maintenance, has not been used. Initial measures of ego strength predicted exercise adherence in one study (Blumenthal, Williams, Wallace, Williams & Needles, 1982). However, as indicated previously, initial use of the somewhat more setting-specific Estimation scale has failed to predict adherence. Other than Sonstroem's incomplete model, paradigms associating enhanced self-esteem and exercise are lacking. Additionally, self-esteem theory is itself so all-encompassing, so complex, and yet so vague that it provides acute conceptual and operational problems in the study of exercise participation.

Self-Efficacy

A more situation-specific self theory proposed by Bandura (1977) is that of perceived self-efficacy. Interaction of coping behavior and its persistence in particular situations is believed to be governed by individual perceptions of exerting or acquiring mastery in that particular area. As applied to exercise participation, an amount of parallelism with the Estimation scale and the psychological model for physical activity participation may be noted. The latter model, however, posits the additional variable of interest (Attraction) as better influencing participation. As well as having a directive function, mastery (self-efficacy) expectations "influence performance and are, in turn, altered by the cumulative effects of one's efforts" (Bandura, 1977, p. 194). Of additional importance is Bandura's concept that enhanced self-efficacy will generalize to a wide range of activities and situations including social interaction. A bridge with the traditionally suggested outcomes of exercise (sound body, sound mind and feeling of well-being) can be recognized. DiClemente (1981) found that self-efficacy for smoking avoidance significantly predicted ($p < .005$) maintenance versus recidivism at 5 months. Preprogram self-efficacy levels predicted weight loss, and subjects treated with self-efficacy enhancement methods lost more weight than subjects exposed only to the weight loss program (Weinberg et al., 1984). The motivational and responsive capabilities of self-efficacy are illustrated in a recent study with myocardial infarction patients (Ewart, Taylor, Reese, & DeBusk, 1983). Whereas peak treadmill heart rate correlated ($r = +.36$) with pretest self-efficacy, the relationship with posttest self-efficacy was higher ($r = +.50$), indicating the facilitative effect of performance feedback on self-efficacy levels. Self-efficacy was also associated with subsequent physical activity in the home, and it responded positively to counseling. Ryckman, Robbins, Thornton, and Cantrell (1982) have developed a *physical* self-efficacy scale generalizable to a wide variety of situations requiring physical skills. This scale, however, was unable to predict performance at any of four gymnastic events whereas four self-efficacy measures specific to each event were uniformly successful (McAuley & Gill, 1983). These results accentuate the common psychological difficulty of determining appropriate levels of specificity. Very general measures are incapable of predicting behavior in particular situations, but narrow, specific scales are able to do so. These latter scales, however, are somewhat limited in portraying major life adjustment changes. Safrit et al. (1985) administered the PEAS to several samples of college adults and identified a smaller factor of nine Estimation items that they label General Competence. Gender insensitive Estimation scales such as this appear to offer a reliable measure of self-efficacy or perceived physical competence in the young adult population. They have also obtained somewhat greater associations with self-esteem and fitness than that obtained by the larger Estimation scale (Fox, Corbin, & Couldry, 1985, April).

Perceived Competence

A construct roughly parallel to self-efficacy is that of *perceived competence*. Harter (1983) has developed a model for competence development in children with accompanying measurement procedures. Specific competence perceptions are developed from successful mastery experiences at particular skills. Her measurement scale has grouped these perceptions in the broader areas of cognitive competence, social or interpersonal competence, physical competence, and general sense of worth (self-esteem). The cognitive, physical, and general self-worth scales have discriminated youthful athletes from nonathletes (Roberts, Kleiber, & Duda, 1981), and physical competence has differentiated participants from dropouts in junior high school athletics (Feltz & Petlichkoff, 1983). Harter's theory includes the concept of *intrinsic* motivation, which is participation in an activity for the pleasure of the activity itself rather than for extrinsic rewards. Successful mastery attempts that are experienced under optimal degrees of challenge should result in satisfaction and enhanced intrinsic motivation. Vallerand and Reid (1984) used path analysis to show that increased self-competence led to an increase in intrinsic motivation. These considerations are immediately pertinent to exercise participation where the implicit goal of activity leaders is to cultivate satisfaction and pleasure in the performance of the activity itself.

Critique of Self Variables

Use of these self variables could offer several advantages to the study of exercise adherence. All are variables with strong theoretical and empirical links to total life adjustment. Changes recorded in these variables over the duration of an exercise program would serve to associate adherence rates and primary psychological functioning within a basic model predicating psychological benefit from exercise. This need not preclude the use of additional predictors such as barriers, setting variables, previous experience, and self-motivation in effecting a greater understanding of adherence. Also, because all of these self variables are proven motivators of behavior, they should be capable of reflecting exercise adherence. To date they have not been used in a systematic fashion to examine exercise adherence. The following section on adherence as a process is relevant to this discussion.

A major impediment to the immediate use of self variables is the lack of standardized measures applicable to middle-aged and elderly populations. The scales mentioned in this section have all been developed with either children or college students. Self-efficacy, perceived competence, or self-esteem scales should be constructed to contain content endemic to the exercise experiences of males and females over the age of 25. Items that refer to self-perceptions of flexibility, injury proneness, aerobic capacity, optimum weight, persistence at exercise, and fatigue would seem to be more relevant to adult cardiovascular conditioning classes than items tapping self-perceptions of athletic skills.

Toward More Complete Models: Adherence as a Process

Dishman (1985) aptly summarizes previous adherence research as incorporating static designs that focus on future behavior correlates of prescreening measures. The lack of notable results "may be largely due to transient interactions between the person and the exercise setting, and these may be best assessed as state measurements within the person, or trait changes, rather than static measures at program entry" (p. 19). Inherent in the idea of viewing exercise adoption as a process is the common assumption that people *change*. Today's positive attitude may incline toward the negative as the trainee interacts with barriers and regimens in the exercise setting. Delineating *how* change occurs is required of a process model, and this implies the initial use of a relatively complete model predicting relationships among background, personal, and situational variables. It also involves the use of repeated measures to examine changes in structure and magnitude of these associations over an intervention period. Ward and Morgan (1984) have documented the fact that different psychological and biological factors influence adherence over the course of a 32-week exercise program. Although improvement of health is often cited as a reason for beginning exercise (Olson & Zanna, 1982), factors such as choice of activities (Thompson & Wankel, 1980), goal attainment (Danielson & Wanzel, 1977), or previous program experience (Dishman et al., 1985) appear to relate better to adherence. Unfortunately, the use of static models has failed to provide reasons why or in whom these associations eventuate and the manner in which they may be regulated. The study of exercise adherence should deviate from a reliance on *predictive* designs characterized only by initial measures to *process* designs that examine the interplay of predictor and criterion variables in a process of growth or change.

Health psychology and psychotherapy have come to recognize that the behavior of people changes in distinct sequences rather than as an all-or-none phenomenon (Dishman, 1982; Horn, 1976; Prochaska & DiClemente, 1983). In studying smoking cessation Prochaska and DiClemente identified four change stages: precontemplation, contemplation (thinking of quitting), action (recent modification of habits), and maintenance (long-term abstinence). Utilizing a transtheoretical model encompassing both stages and processes of change, they found that process employment varied with particular stages. People in the precontemplative stage tended to use verbal strategies such as consciousness raising whereas action and maintenance subjects relied more on behavioral processes such as counter-conditioning and stimulus control. Of particular interest was a group of relapsers (196 of 872 subjects) who utilized those change processes most often employed by contemplators or action subjects. The authors argue that health behavior change may be better represented as a cyclical rather than a linear sequence. Many individuals are unable to effect lasting changes with the first attempt. After reverting to preintervention conduct they again attempt to travel the circuitous route from precontemplation to contemplation to action to maintenance. Recent exercise program results offer the challenging perspective that roughly 50% of program volunteers have experienced previous failures (Dishman, 1987; Fitness Ontario, 1982). Other research indicates that many dropouts from organized programs continue to exercise on their own (Wilhelmsen et al., 1975).

At the University of Rhode Island we have recently studied 4-year exercise behaviors of 220 men over the age of 30. Based on the change stages of Prochaska and DiClemente (1983), subjects were classified via self-report as immotives (precontemplators), contemplators, recruits (subjects who within the past 2 years had adopted a program of vigorous exercise for at least 20–30 minutes 3 times per week) and adherers (active at this type of program for at least 2 years). Utilizing the Fishbein model, we administered a pool of 69 belief statements regarding outcomes of regular participation in a program of exercise. One major discriminant function composed of nine belief statements produced a canonical r of .75 with stages of exercise adoption and a correct overall classification of 69.9%. Moreover, accuracy was consistent across stages ranging from 28.2% above baseline in the case of recruits to 46.3% above baseline for adherers. However, when 48 subjects reporting previous attrition from exercise were included in analyses, the overall classification accuracy decreased to 50.93%. Group centroids for contemplators and dropouts were not significantly different ($p < .11$) Further inspection revealed that 37 of these dropouts were again considering joining an exercise program. Categorizing these 37 as contemplators improved the overall accuracy to 60.3% and obtained significant differences ($p < .001$) between the centroids of contemplators and dropouts.

These considerations indicate that exercise maintenance may be best studied as other than an all-or-none phenomenon. Dropouts appear to represent several subsets of people, of whom some intend to and do return to exercise.

Summary

The empirical results of adherence research provide little guidance in recommending superior models for the study of exercise participation. Certainly, human exercise involvement can now be seen to be so complex as to negate a reliance on broad or global predictors. Nonstandardized inventories and procedures, diverse populations, and the employment of incomplete models have led to a proliferation of nonreplicated results. Even though this chapter has advocated the use of certain models in preference to others, these suggestions have been based on methodological or theoretical considerations rather than on substantive research results. The Ajzen and Fishbein methodology has been recommended because it appears capable of initiating an understanding of the beliefs and attitudes of exercise participants at a molecular level. The methodology is versatile in that it can incorporate a variety of predictors such as barriers, susceptibility, social support and background variables. Alternatively, the use of self-efficacy or perceived competence paradigms is recommended for those wishing to study participation from the standpoint of derived psychological benefits. Whatever model is employed, however, it should be implemented in its theoretical entirety. The use of frequently repeated measures should develop an understanding of the processes leading to adherence. Moreover, ongoing measurement can assist in defining the stages a person passes through in becoming an exercise adherent. It is hoped that future research will forsake dichotomizing exercise adherence as an all-or-none phenomenon. Developing the ability to categorize people into various stages of exercise adoption and then to follow these people over time promises assistance in developing a greater understanding of physical activity participation.

References

Ajzen, I., & Fishbein, M. (1977). Attitude-behavior relations: A theoretical analysis and review of empirical research. *Psychological Bulletin, 84,* 888–918.

Ajzen, I., & Fishbein, M. (1980). *Understanding attitudes and predicting social behavior.* Englewood Cliffs, NJ: Prentice-Hall.

Andrew, G.M., & Parker, J.O. (1979). Factors related to dropout of post myocardial infarction patients from exercise programs. *Medicine and Science in Sports and Exercise, 11,* 376–378.

Bandura, A. (1977). Self-efficacy: Towards a unifying theory of behavioral change. *Psychological Review, 84,* 192–215.

Becker, M.H., & Maiman, L.A. (1975). Sociobehavioral determinants of compliance with health care and medical care recommendations. *Medical Care, 13,* 10–24.

Bentler, P.M., & Speckart, G. (1981). Attitudes "cause" behaviors: A structural equation analysis. *Journal of Personality and Social Psychology, 40,* 226–238.

Blumenthal, J.A., Williams, R.S., Wallace, A.G., Williams, R.B., & Needles, T.I. (1982). Physiological and psychological variables predict compliance to prescribed exercise therapy in patients recovering from myocardial infarction. *Psychosomatic Medicine, 44,* 519–527.

Bowers, K.S. (1973). Situationism in psychology: An analysis and a critique. *Psychological Review, 80,* 307–336.

Budd, R., & Spencer, C. (1984). Latitude of rejection, centrality, and certainty: Variables affecting the relationship between attitudes, names and behavioral intentions. *British Journal of Social Psychology*, **23**, 1–8.

Calnan, M.W., & Moss, S. (1984). The health belief model and compliance with education given at a class in breast self-examination. *Journal of Health and Social Behavior*, **25**, 198–210.

Coelho, R.J. (1985). A psychometric investigation of the multidimensional health locus of control scales with cigarette smokers. *Journal of Clinical Psychology*, **41**, 372–376.

Cox, M.H. (1984). Fitness and life-style programs for business and industry: Problems in recruitment and retention. *Journal of Cardiac Rehabilitation*, **4**, 136–142.

Danielson, R.R., & Wanzel, R.S. (1977). Exercise objectives of fitness program dropouts. In D.M. Landers & R.W. Christina (Eds.), *Psychology of motor behavior and sport*. Champaign, IL: Human Kinetics.

Davis, K.E., Jackson, K.L., Kronenfeld, J.J., & Blair, S.N. (1984). Intent to participate in worksite health promotion activities: A model of risk factors and psychosocial variables. *Health Education Quarterly*, **11**, 361–377.

DiClemente, C.C. (1981). Self-efficacy and smoking cessation maintenance: A preliminary report. *Cognitive Therapy and Research*, **5**, 175–187.

Dishman, R.K. (1978). Aerobic power, estimation of physical ability, and attraction to physical activity. *Research Quarterly for Exercise and Sport*, **49**, 285–292.

Dishman, R.K. (1981). Biologic influences on exercise adherence. *Research Quarterly for Exercise and Sport*, **52**, 143–159.

Dishman, R.K. (1982). Compliance/adherence in health-related exercise. *Health Psychology*, **1**, 237–267.

Dishman, R.K. (1983). Predicting exercise compliance using psychometric and behavioral measures of commitment. *Medicine and Science in Sports and Exercise* (abstract), **15**, 118.

Dishman, R.K. (1985). Medical psychology in exercise and sport. *Medical Clinics of North America*, **69**(1), 123–143.

Dishman, R.K. (1986). Exercise adherence. In W.P. Morgan & S.N. Goldston (Eds.), *Exercise and mental health* (pp. 57–83). Washington, DC: Hemisphere.

Dishman, R.K., & Gettman, L.R. (1980). Psychobiologic influences in exercise adherence. *Journal of Sport Psychology, 2,* 295–310.

Dishman, R.K., & Ickes, W.D. (1981). Self-motivation and adherence to therapeutic exercise. *Journal of Behavioral Medicine, 4,* 421–438.

Dishman, R.K., Ickes, W.J., & Morgan, W.P. (1980). Self-motivation and adherence to habitual physical activity. *Journal of Applied Social Psychology, 10,* 115–131.

Dishman, R.K., Sallis, J.F., & Ornstein, D.R. (1985). The determinants of physical activity and exercise. *Public Health Reports, 100,* 158–171.

Ewart, C.K., Taylor, C.B., Reese, L.B., & DeBusk, R.F. (1983). Effects of early postmyocardial infarction exercise testing on self-perception and subsequent physical activity. *The American Journal of Cardiology, 51,* 1076–1080.

Fazio, R.H., & Zanna, M.P. (1981). Direct experience and attitude-behavior consistency. *Advances in Experimental Social Psychology, 14,* 161–202.

Fishbein, M., & Ajzen, I. (1975). *Belief, attitude, intention, and behavior: An introduction to theory and research.* Reading, MA: Addison-Wesley.

Fitness Ontario (1982). *The relationship between physical activity and other health-related lifestyle behaviors.* Toronto: Government of Ontario, Ministry of Culture and Recreation, Sports and Fitness Branch.

Folkins, C.H., & Sime, W.E. (1981). Physical fitness training and mental health. *American Psychologist, 36,* 383–389.

Fox, K., Corbin, C., & Couldry, W. (1985, April). *Validity and reliability of shortened physical estimation scales.* Paper presented at the national convention, American Alliance for Health, Physical Education, Recreation and Dance, Atlanta, GA.

Fox, K.R., Corbin, C.B., & Couldry, W.H. (1985). Female physical estimation and attraction to physical activity. *Journal of Sport Psychology, 7,* 125–136.

Freed, A. (1977). Social case work: More than a modality. *Social Case Work, 20,* 214–223.

Freedson, P.S., Mihevic, P.M., Loucks, A.B., & Girandola, R.N. (1983). Physique, body composition, and psychological characteristics of competitive female body builders. *The Physician and Sportsmedicine, 11*(5), 85–93.

Feltz, D.L., & Petlichkoff, L. (1983). Perceived competence among interscholastic sport participants and dropouts. *Canadian Journal of Applied Sport Sciences, 8,* 231–235.

Gale, J.B., Eckhoff, W.T., Mogel, S.F., & Rodnick, J.E. (1984). Factors related to adherence to an exercise program for healthy adults. *Medicine and Science in Sports and Exercise, 16,* 544–549.

Gergen, K.J. (1971). *The concept of self.* New York: Holt.

Godin, G., Cox, M.H., & Shephard, R.J. (1983). The impact of physical fitness evaluation on behavioral intentions towards regular exercise. *Canadian Journal of Applied Sport Science, 8,* 240–245.

Godin, G., & Shephard, R.J. (1985). Psycho-social predictors of exercise intentions among spouses. *Canadian Journal of Applied Sport Science, 10,* 36–43.

Harter, S. (1983). Developmental perspectives on the self system. In E.M. Hetherington (Ed.), *Handbook of child psychology* (Vol. 4, pp. 275–385). New York: John Wiley.

Harris, D. (1970). Physical activity history and attitudes of middle-aged men. *Medicine and Science in Sports, 2,* 203–208.

Heinzelmann, F., & Bagley, R.W. (1970). Response to physical activity programs and their effects on health behavior. *Public Health Reports, 85,* 905–911.

Hempel, C. (1977). Formulation and formation of scientific theories. In F. Suppe (Ed.), *The structure of scientific theories* (pp. 244–265). Urbana, IL.: University of Illinois Press.

Horn, D. (1976). A model for the study of personal choice health behaviors. *International Journal of Health Education, 19,* 89–98.

Janz, N.K., & Becker, M.H. (1984). *Health Education Quarterly, 11,* 1–47.

Kilty, K.M. (1978). Attitudinal and normative variables as predictors of drinking behavior. *Journal of Studies on Alcohol, 39,* 1178–1194.

Knapp, D., Gutmann, M., Foster, C., & Pollock, M. (1984). Self-motivation among 1984 Olympic speedskating hopefuls and emotional response and adherence to training. *Medicine and Science in Sports and Exercise* (abstract), *16,* 114.

Lindsay-Reid, E., & Osborn, R.W. (1980). Readiness for exercise adoption. *Social Science and Medicine, 14A,* 139–146.

Liska, A.E. (1984). A critical examination of the causal structure of the Fishbein/Ajzen attitude-behavior model. *Social Psychology Quarterly, 47,* 61–74.

Ludenia, K., & Donham, G. (1983). Dental outpatients: Health locus of control correlates. *Journal of Clinical Psychology, 39,* 854–857.

Massie, J.F., & Shephard, R.J. (1971). Physiological and psychological effects of training—A comparison of individual and gymnasium programs, with a characterization of the exercise "dropout." *Medicine and Science in Sports, 3,* 110–117.

McAuley, E., & Gill, D. (1983). Reliability and validity of the physical self-efficacy scale in a competitive sport setting. *Journal of Sport Psychology, 5,* 410–418.

Morgan, W.P. (1976). *Influence of chronic physical activity on selected psychological states and traits of police officers.* Gaithersburg, MD: International Association of Chiefs of Police, Inc.

Morgan, W.P. (1977). Involvement in vigorous physical activity with special reference to adherences. In L.I. Gedvillas & M.E. Kneer (Eds.), *National College Physical Education Association Proceedings* (pp. 235–246). Chicago: University of Illinois-Chicago.

Morgan, W.P., & Pollock, M.L. (1978). Physical activity and cardiovascular health: Psychological aspects. In F. Laundry & Orban (Eds.), *Physical activity and human well-being* (pp. 163–181). Miami: Symposium Specialists.

Neale, D.C., Sonstroem, R.J., & Metz, K.F. (1969). Physical fitness, self-esteem, and attitudes towards physical activity. *Research Quarterly, 40,* 743–749.

Olson, J.M., & Zanna, M.P. (1982). *Predicting adherence to a program of physical exercise: An empirical study.* Toronto: Government of Ontario, Ministry of Tourism and Recreation.

Parcel, G.S. (1984). Theoretical models for application in school health education research. *Journal of School Health, 54,* 39–49.

Prochaska, J.O., & DiClemente, C.C. (1983). Stages and processes of self-change of smoking: Toward an integrative model of change. *Journal of Consulting and Clinical Psychology, 51,* 390–395.

Riddle, P.K. (1980). Attitudes, beliefs, behavioral intentions, and behaviors of men and women toward regular jogging. *Research Quarterly for Exercise and Sport, 51,* 663–674.

Roberts, G.C., Kleiber, D.A., & Duda, J.L. (1981). An analysis of motivation in children's sport: The role of perceived competence in participation. *Journal of Sport Psychology, 3,* 206–216.

Robinson, T.T., & Carron, A.V. (1982). Personal and situational factors associated with dropping out versus maintaining participation in competitive sport. *Journal of Sport Psychology, 4,* 364–378.

Rosenstock, I.M. (1966). Why people use health services. *Millbank Memorial Fund Quarterly, 44,* 94–124.

Rosenstock, I.M. (1974). Historical origins of the health belief model. *Health Education Monographs*, **2**, 328–335.

Rotter, J.B. (1966). Generalized expectancies for internal versus external control of reinforcement. *Psychological Monographs*, **80** (Whole No. 609).

Ryckman, R.M., Robbins, M.A., Thornton, B., & Cantrell, P. (1982). Development and validation of a physical self-efficacy scale. *Journal of Personality and Social Psychology*, **42**, 891–900.

Safrit, M.J., Wood, T.M., & Dishman, R.K. (1985). The factorial validity of the physical estimation and attraction scales for adults. *Journal of Sport Psychology*, **7**, 166–190.

Saltzer, E.B. (1982). The weight locus of control (WLOC) scale: A specific measure for obesity research. *Journal of Personality Assessment*, **46**, 620–628.

Secord, P.F., & Jourard, S.M. (1953). The appraisal of body cathexis: Body cathexis and the self. *Journal of Consulting Psychology*, **17**, 343–347.

Sherman, S.J., Presson, C.C., Chassin, L., Bensenberg, M., Corty, E., & Olshavsky, R.W. (1982). Smoking intentions in adolescents: Direct experience and predictability. *Personality and Social Psychology Bulletin*, **8**, 376–383.

Slenker, S.E., Price, J.H., Roberts, S.M., & Jurs, S.G. (1984). Joggers versus non-exercisers. *Research Quarterly for Exercise and Sport*, **55**, 371–378.

Snyder, G., Franklin, B., Foss, M., & Rubenfire, M. (1982). Characteristics of compliers and non-compliers to cardiac exercise therapy programs. *Medicine and Science in Sports and Exercise* (abstract), **14**, 179.

Sonstroem, R.J. (1974). Attitude testing examining certain psychological correlates of physical activity. *Research Quarterly*, **45**, 93–103.

Sonstroem, R.J. (1976). The validity of self-perceptions regarding physical and athletic ability. *Medicine and Science in Sports*, **8**, 126–132.

Sonstroem, R.J. (1978). Physical estimation and attraction scales: Rationale and research. *Medicine and Science in Sports*, **10**, 97–102.

Sonstroem, R.J. (1982). Attitudes and beliefs in the prediction of exercise participation. In R.C. Cantu (Ed.), *Sports medicine, sports science: Bridging the gap* (pp. 3–16). Lexington, MA: Collomore Press.

Sonstroem, R.J. (1984). Self-esteem and physical activity. In R.L. Terjung (Ed.), *Exercise and sport sciences reviews* (Vol. 12, pp. 123–155). Lexington, MA: Collomore Press.

Sonstroem, R.J., & Kampper, K.P. (1980). Prediction of athletic participation in middle school males. *Research Quarterly for Exercise and Sport,* **51,** 685–694.

Sonstroem, R.J., & Walker, M.I. (1973). Relationship of attitudes and locus of control to exercise and physical fitness. *Perceptual and Motor Skills,* **36,** 1031–1034.

Stone, W.J. (1983, August–September). Predicting who will drop out. *Corporate Fitness and Recreation,* pp. 31–36.

Strickland, B.R. (1978). Internal-external expectancies and health related behaviors. *Journal of Clinical Psychology,* **46,** 1192–1211.

Thompson, C.E., & Wankel, L.M. (1980). The effects of perceived activity choice upon frequency of exercise behavior. *Journal of Applied Social Psychology,* **10,** 436–443.

Thompson, J., Wyatt, J.T.B., & Craighead, L.W. (1984). Three theoretically based interventions to increase exercise adherence in a health-promotion regimen. *Psychosomatic Medicine* (abstract), **46**(1), 80.

Tirrell, B.E., & Hart, L.K. (1980). Patient perceptions in critical care: The relationship of health beliefs and knowledge to exercise compliance in patients after coronary bypass. *Heart and Lung,* **9,** 487–493.

Tokunaga, M., Tantano, H., Hashimoto, K., & Kanezaki, R. (1980, 1981). Behavioral intentions, attitudes and beliefs as factors for predicting sport behavior. *Japanese Journal of Physical Education,* 1980, **25,** 179–190. (Abstract from *Journal of Sport Psychology,* 1981, **3,** 178)

Vallerand, R.J., & Reid, G. (1984). On the causal effects of perceived competence on intrinsic motivation: A test of cognitive evaluation theory. *Journal of Sport Psychology,* **6,** 94–102.

Wallston, B.S., & Wallston, K.A. (1978). Locus of control and health: A review of the literature. *Health Education Monographs,* **6,** 107–117.

Wallston, K.A., Wallston, B.S., & DeVellis, R. (1978). Development of the multidimensional health locus of control (MHLC) scales. *Health Education Monographs,* **6,** 160–170.

Wallston, B.S., Wallston, K.A., Kaplan, G.D., & Maides, S.A. (1976). Development and validation of the health locus of control (HLC) scales. *Journal of Consulting Clinical Psychology,* **44,** 580–585.

Wankel, L.M. & Graham, J. (1980). *The effects of a decision balance sheet intervention upon exercise adherence of high and low self-motivated females.* Paper presented at the Canadian Psycho-Motor Learning and Sport Psychology Symposium, Vancouver, BC.

Wankel, L.M., & Yardley, J.K. (1982). An investigation of the effectiveness of a structured social support program for increasing exercise adherence of high and low self-motivated adults. In D. Ng (Ed.), *Proceedings of the Leisure Research Section.* Saskatoon, Saskatchewan: Canadian Parks/Recreation Association Conferences.

Ward, A., & Morgan, W.P. (1984). Adherence patterns of healthy men and women enrolled in an adult exercise program. *Journal of Cardiac Rehabilitation,* **4**, 143–152.

Weinberg, R.S., Hughes, H.H., Critelli, J.W., England, R., & Jackson, A. (1984). Effects of preexisting and manipulated self-efficacy on weight loss in a self-control program. *Journal of Research in Personality,* **18**, 352—358.

Wicker, A.W. (1969). Attitudes versus actions: The relationship of verbal and overt behavioral responses to attitude objects. *Journal of Social Issues,* **25**, 41–78.

Wilhelmsen, L., Sanne, H., Elmfeldt, D., Grimby, G., Tibblin, G., & Wedel, H. (1975). A controlled trial of physical training after myocardial infarction. *Preventive Medicine,* **4**, 471–508.

Winefield, H.R. (1982). Reliability and validity of the health locus of control scale. *Journal of Personality Assessment,* **46**, 614–619.

CHAPTER 6

Exercise Adherence in Children and Youth: Implications for Adulthood

Rod K. Dishman and
Andrea L. Dunn

"Train up a child in the way he should go; and
when he is old, he will not depart from it."

Holy Bible
Book of Proverbs
Chapter 22, verse 6
(cf. Stull, 1986, p. 1)

The impact of habitual exercise and physical fitness on behavioral health (on health outcomes or risks, and on other health behaviors) is currently being studied in adults. Less attention is being paid to these concerns in children and youth. Because the welfare of younger age groups is equally important and because behavioral patterns in children and youth may exert influences on both health and behavior in adulthood, exercise and fitness in childhood is an area of concern for public health. Much remains to be learned about health-related outcomes associated with childhood exercise and fitness. A principal contribution by fields that study public health problems (e.g., behavioral epidemiology, behavioral medicine, health psychology, and exercise science) will most likely come from research on determinants of physical activity patterns during early years and how these patterns and determinants might later impact exercise, fitness, health behaviors, and health outcomes in adult years. Targets for behavioral interventions during early development might thus be identified.

Our purpose in this chapter is (a) to review what is currently known about the relationship of exercise and fitness to health risk factors in children, (b) to review the existing research on determinants of physical activity in children and to examine how childhood determinants might impact adult exercise and health, (c) to summarize prominent theoretical models used to describe or predict exercise behavior and examine their suitability for children and youth, (d) to propose an interactive model that might be used to guide future research/interventions for exercise behavior and its outcomes with children and across the life span and (e) to pose key questions to challenge the several disciplines that articulate public health concerns to study exercise adherence in children and youth.

A Rationale

Little is known about the determinants and health outcomes of physical activity patterns among school-age children and youth. This is perplexing because it has become increasingly clear that the roles of habitual physical activity, exercise, and physical fitness in public health cannot be understood or facilitated unless research and program interventions with school-age groups are accelerated (Takanishi, DeLeon, & Pallak, 1984). Previous reviews have examined the roles of medical psychology (Melamed, 1980) and exercise (Bar-Or, 1985) for rehabilitation or secondary prevention of chronic disease in children. Our focus, however, will be on primary prevention and health promotion. From this perspective an understanding of exercise determinants and outcomes during the early years of life is important for public health for two major reasons.

First, it is well established that the prevalence rates of known risk factors for chronic disease, including coronary artery disease (CAD), and mortality in adults are alarmingly high in childhood. Several risk factors linked to behavior such as smoking, obesity, hypertension, hyperlipidemia, diabetes mellitus, stress emotions, and Type A behavior are seen in children and youth 7 to 17 years of age (Berenson, 1980; Frerichs, Srinivasan, Webber, & Berenson, 1976; Gilliam, Katch, Thorland, & Weltman, 1977; Khoury, Morrison, Kelly, Mellies, Horuitz, & Glueck, 1980; Lauer, Connor, Leaverton, Reiter, & Clarke, 1975; Matthews & Siegel, 1985; Siegel, 1984; Wilmore & McNamara, 1974). Studies also show that high-risk profiles can be detected in preschool-age children (Hunter et al., 1982; Lundberg, 1983; Murray & Bruhn, 1983; Wolf, Sklov, Wenzl, Hunter, & Berenson, 1982). Among adults these factors are believed to respond favorably in many cases to increased physical activity (see chapters 1 and 2; Haskell, Montoye, & Orenstein, 1985; Siscovick, Laporte, & Newman, 1985). Cross-sectional, correlational, and experimental studies also show that mental health in adults and children is associated with fitness and physical activity (see chapter 4; Dishman, 1985; Taylor, Sallis, & Needle, 1985). However, available studies indicate the typical American child of school age demonstrates fitness and physical activity profiles below the levels believed necessary to significantly lower health risk. In fact, the current participation rate for ages 10 to 17 is 66% (Centers for Disease Control, 1985). This is well below the Public Health Service 1990 objective of 90% for these ages.

The consensus of public health officials is that the likelihood of reaching the 1990 exercise and fitness objectives for children is poor (Centers for Disease Control, 1985) and that behavioral interventions will be required if participation rates are to be increased. Though physical activity profiles are beginning to be known, their trends and reliable determinants for children and youth are empirically unknown (Dishman, Sallis, & Orenstein, 1985; Stephens, Jacobs, & White, 1985). As a result, the information needed to guide effective interventions to increase physical activity and exercise in these age groups is not available.

Second, it is commonly assumed that patterns of exercise and health habits for adulthood are established during early years. However, the influence of childhood fitness or physical activity history on adult fitness or physical activity patterns remains unstudied. This is a significant concern because the determinants of exercise and physical activity in the adult population are also not understood (Dishman et al., 1985). The Public Health Service Objectives call for 60% of 18- to 65-year-olds to be regular participants in vigorous exercise by 1990, but just 10–20% are currently active at this level (Centers for Disease Control, 1985). For these reasons, approximating the exercise participation goals for adults may also require a better understanding of exercise determinants among children and youth.

In their recent review of physical activity patterns in North America, Stephens et al. (1985) suggest that the most remarkable decrease in participation across the age-span occurs in late adolescence. This presumably occurs, in part, as activity patterns in school environments change or end. Despite the apparent trend toward inactivity in adolescence, the determinants of physical activity at these ages or the carryover influence of activity habits from previous years, as well as their impact in later years, are unknown. Our lack of knowledge in this area is particularly noteworthy because adolescents (e.g., 12 to 17 years) who are sedentary demonstrate the greatest biological potential for fitness improvements, and perhaps health improvements, from exercise training (Haskell et al., 1985). It is important to understand childhood physical activity for early welfare, but useful insights may also be gained about facilitating later exercise and healthy activity habits in adults. Early activity histories and their determinants can help identify and interpret barriers and reinforcements for later activity.

These observations point to the importance of developing a systematic view of the determinants of exercise that encompasses relationships with risk factors for chronic disease. More important, these relationships must be understood within a framework that takes into account age and developmental stages within the population as well as the social, historical context (Leventhal, Prohaska, & Hirschman, 1985) of both preventive and promotive health behaviors.

Relationship of Exercise to Risk Factors in Children

Although studies with adults implicate that a lifetime of habitual exercise can reduce overall risk for premature mortality and specific risk for several chronic diseases, available evidence on children comes largely from studies relating to adult risk factors for coronary heart disease (Binkhorst, Kemper, & Saris, 1985).

Current statistics indicate that an American child has 1 chance in 5 of developing clinical symptoms of coronary heart disease before the age of 16 (Varni, 1983). Linder and DuRant (1982) have proposed that nine risk factors of cardiovascular disease should be identified during childhood. These are: (a) a first-degree relative with heart disease before age 55; (b) a first-degree relative with hypertension, diabetes, stroke, or obesity before age 55; (c) elevated levels of serum cholesterol, triglycerides, and total cholesterol; (d) elevated blood pressure; (e) smoking; (f) obesity; (g) sedentary lifestyles; (h) Type A Behavior or inability to cope with stress; and (i) overeating of saturated fat, sodium, sugar, and total Calories.

It has been reasoned that early prevention and treatment will result from this identification process so that the onset of cardiovascular disease will be mitigated. Early prevention and treatment has focused on use of behavior modification strategies; changing exercise, eating and diet patterns, and stress coping skills have been of central interest. Although there is reliable research that provides evidence for these methods of treatment, few experimental studies with children demonstrate the direct effect of exercise on risk factors or the interaction of exercise with other risk factor interventions. Montoye (1986) has provided a comprehensive review of this literature, so our summary will be limited to a few representative studies.

A longitudinal study by Williams, Carter, Arnold and Wynder (1979) illustrates a public health approach. In this program for children ages 10–15, entitled "Know Your Body," screening for relevant risk factors such as total cholesterol, blood pressure, and skinfold thickness was combined with a behaviorally oriented health education curriculum that emphasized lifestyle habits such as better nutrition, daily exercise, and weight/cholesterol control. Initial findings from the 2nd year showed that risk factors were reduced in the intervention schools compared to control schools. Although this study will provide valuable information, the effect of exercise on specific risk factors remains cloudy. A few studies have reported significant weight loss among obese children following short-term (10 weeks to 5 months) school-based interventions that combine behavior modification or psychological support with nutrition education and exercise (Brownell & Kaye, 1982). However, these studies have not quantified physical activity in the school setting or spontaneous non-school activity, and they do not specify the extent to which exercise contributed to the weight loss.

The few studies that have looked at the direct effects of exercise on specific risk factors have yielded mixed results (Dwyer, Coonan, Leitch, Hetzel, & Baghurst, 1983). Much of this research has been conducted to determine the effects of exercise on serum cholesterol levels in normal children, on resting blood pressures in hypertensive adolescents, and on weight loss in obese children. The bulk of evidence from clinical studies confirms that both fitness-producing exercise and increased activity in daily routines have potential for weight control among obese children (Brownell & Stunkard, 1980; Epstein, Wing, Koeske, Ossip, & Beck, 1982; Epstein, Koeske, & Wing, 1984). However, evidence on blood lipids and blood pressures following exercise is largely equivocal.

Linder, DuRant, and Gray (1979) reported that after a 4-week moderate exercise program, serum lipid levels of black children and adolescents did not differ significantly from controls participating in normal activity. A randomized study of 7- to 9-year-old students participating for 12 weeks in aerobic classes showed no lipid changes compared with regular physical education (Gilliam & Freedson, 1980); a more recent study by Linder, DuRant, and Mahoney (1983) also showed no significant difference in lipid levels after an 8-week walk-jog program for adolescent males. On the other hand, 3 weeks of exercise training and diet decreased total cholesterol and weight in 11- to 13-year-old boys and girls compared with nonrandomized controls (Widhalm, Maxa, & Zynam, 1978). An uncontrolled 6-week program of games, calisthenics, and running among 8- to 10-year-old girls increased high density lipoprotein-cholesterol (HDL-C) and HDL-C/total cholesterol ratio, but total cholesterol was unchanged

(Gilliam & Burke, 1978). Cross-sectional studies have also demonstrated that habitual physical activity in normal children was predictive of serum lipid levels. For instance, Thorland and Gilliam (1981) found that active preadolescent males had significantly lower levels of triglycerides, higher HDL-C/total cholesterol, and consumed more Calories than less active subjects.

The effects of exercise conditioning on hypertension in children is equally unclear. Six months of thrice weekly running at 60–65% of aerobic capacity has been accompanied by reductions in systolic and diastolic resting pressures in hypertensive adolescents (Hagberg et al., 1983), but the control comparison group was self-selected. Similarly, Fisher and Brown (1982) reported a reduction in diastolic pressure compared with control subjects when 7th graders increased their treadmill endurance following 12 weeks of training for 30 minutes daily, 5 days per week. Studies using weight training have shown that decreased blood pressure can be maintained (Hagberg et al., 1984) but not reliably reduced (Laird, Fixler, & Swanbom, 1979). Other studies of similar design have not, however, shown reductions in blood pressures following exercise training and increased fitness (e.g., Dwyer et al., 1983; Linder et al., 1983).

When conflicting results in this literature have appeared, they might be due to a number of reasons: (a) studies may contain selection bias and differing initial fitness values of subjects; (b) the level of physical activity necessary for fitness is unclear; (c) determinants of exercise patterns and other influences on the health outcomes studied are not specified, measured, or controlled; and (d) stage of development of the subjects is sometimes not taken into account or may not be comparable.

The first concern is selection bias and initial values. As Gillum, Prineas, Gomez-Marin, Finn, and Chang (1985) pointed out in The Minneapolis Children's Blood Pressure Study, black adolescents generally have higher blood pressures than whites.

> Although the reasons for these racial differences are not known, black children as a group may be considered to be at high risk for hypertension as adults. Low socioeconomic status is associated with higher blood pressure levels and greater hypertension prevalence in U.S. adults accounting for some of the racial differences. (p. 187)

In addition, many of the above studies do not indicate whether change or no change is related to the exercise per se or the initial level of fitness (including body fatness) of the child (Bar-Or, 1985). This has relevance for the second possible reason for conflicting results.

The level of physical activity necessary for fitness and health in children is not well known (LaPorte et al., 1982). Considering adult requirements, however, available studies converge in showing that few children spontaneously participate in activity with enough intensity (e.g., to elevate heart rate to 160 bpm), duration (20 to 60 minutes), or frequency (3 to 5 days per week) to maintain cardiorespiratory fitness (Gilliam, Freedson, Geener, & Shabraray, 1981). Moreover, it remains unclear what portion of daily Caloric expenditure among children is due to activity from vigorous or fitness-producing play (Waxman & Stunkard, 1980) or daily routines (Epstein et al., 1982). This lack of quantification of physical activity has been a major problem in studies investigating the relationship between exercise and cardiovascular disease (Linder & DuRant, 1982). The study by Linder et al. (1983) and a study by Gilliam and Freedson (1980) monitored activity level at 80–85% of maximum heart rate 4 times per week for 8 and 12 weeks respectively. No changes were reported in lipid or lipoprotein profiles in either study. As Bar-Or (1985) points out, studies/ interventions of longer duration are now needed.

In addition to determining effective physical activity levels, studies need to take into account determinants of physical activity. Children classified as sedentary may be so due to health problems associated with chronic disease or due to other factors that predispose them to both inactivity and disease. Whether the increased risk for morbidity/mortality is due to the sedentary lifestyle or to the health problems responsible for the sedentary lifestyle or to other factors producing both health risk and inactivity is unknown. Specifying determinants of physical activity/ inactivity could help identify this methodological and practical problem. Among adults, for example, dropping out of supervised exercise programs (Oldridge, 1982) and inactivity in the population base (Dishman et al., 1985) are generally associated with higher risk factors for chronic disease. Smokers, blue-collar workers, the overweight, Type As, and those who show atypical stress emotion profiles are seen in many studies to leave, or sporadically attend, supervised programs or to choose a sedentary lifestyle. Determining in adults whether these health-risk factors precede or follow inactivity has not been possible. The degree to which health risks other than inactivity may interact with healthful exercise adaptations in children is also unstudied. For example, body weight and stress emotions are implicated in essential hypertension among children (Matthews, Weiss, & Detre, 1984), but their impacts on blood pressure outcomes with exercise has not been studied in children (Martin & Dubbert, 1985). Similar issues seem relevant for studies of hyperlipidemia, diabetes, and smoking. Cross-sectional and longitudinal studies with children and restrospective studies with adults can clarify these critical questions.

Another possible reason for the equivocal results on exercise and risk factors in children and youth is the age range or stage of development of the subjects studied. For example, DuRant, Linder, Harkess, and Gray (1983) found that active adolescent blacks had significantly lower levels of triglycerides and very low density lipoprotein cholesterol than those less active. However, this relationship did not hold for preadolescent blacks.

These studies illustrate the importance of quantifying the level of physical activity and accounting for the stage of development of the child. They underscore the importance of understanding the determinants of physical activity/inactivity and their relationship with other health habits if more effective interventions can be designed to determine and mitigate risk factors of cardiovascular disease.

Exercise and Mental Stress in Children

In addition to prescribing exercise to prevent the physical symptoms of cardiovascular disease, exercise has also been an adjunctive treatment for behavioral and psychological risk factors such as Type A behavior or the inability to cope with stress.

As Morgan and O'Connor note in chapter 4, studies with adults show that vigorous exercise is associated with reductions in anxiety, tension, and moderate depression, and both quasiexperimental and experimental clinical trials show reductions in Type A behavior assessed by self-report and structured interview (Dishman, 1985; Morgan & Goldston, 1987). Convincing exercise studies of these variables in children and youth have not been conducted, but increases in self-esteem and perceived physical competence following fitness training is a reliable result among obese and physically impaired children (Gruber, 1986; Sonstroem, 1984). These findings could have important implications for behavioral health because self-esteem and perceived competence are viewed as mediators for coping with mental stress. Longitudinal epidemiological studies with adults that show an impact by mental health on physical health (e.g., Vaillant, 1979) have not considered exercise patterns, but cross-sectional (Kobasa, Maddi, & Puccetti, 1982) and retrospective (Morgan, 1986) evidence suggests that exercise can augment mental coping skills for managing stress. The development of such skills in childhood should be studied.

In a review of physical activity and mental health in children, Brown (1982) summarizes equivocal results for the effects of exercise on mental health (Dishman, 1986b). The reasons for these mixed results are similar to those previously cited for hypertension and serum cholesterol levels; these levels and the determinants of physical activity and fitness in available studies are not clearly specified. Developmental stages are also frequently neglected when measuring psychological and physical characteristics. Brown (1982) concludes that although

the generally accepted belief in the psychological benefits of exercise for children has very little documentation by well controlled studies, the risk: Benefit ratio nonetheless tends to favor exercise when competition is sensibly controlled. The field is a fertile one for longitudinal and developmental investigations employing more sophisticated psychological measures and appropriate physiological assessment. (pp. 524–525)

In summary, our review clearly indicates the importance of specifying levels of physical activity and their determinants within an age/developmental framework if the origins and health significance of exercise and fitness outcomes are to be identified. It seems likely that more effective interventions could be implemented with both children and adults if this base of knowledge were developed. However, knowledge about determinants of exercise and physical activity in children is unclear at present. In the following section we examine what is known about determinants of childhood exercise and how they might impact adult exercise patterns and fitness.

Determinants of Physical Activity in Children

Studies suggest that exercise program interventions in the school can be effective in increasing fitness and leisure activity. Gilliam and co-workers (Gilliam et al., 1981; MacConnie, Gilliam, Geener, & Pels, 1982) describe an 8-month program for 6- and 7-year-old boys and girls consisting of aerobic dances, running, rhythmic activity, and rope jumping 4 days per week, 25 minutes per day at heart rates greater than 150 beats per min. This activity reinforced a once-per-week, 20 minute, classroom session on the relationships between exercise and nutrition and CAD. Compared with controls who maintained normal weekly activities, including a single 40-minute physical education class, experimental children spent more time in high-level activity (> 160 bpm) and less time in low level activity (< 110 bpm). Notably, this increase appeared to include more high-intensity exercise during leisure time as well. The maintenance of this increased activity after the study period was not examined.

Although a few small-sample reports indicate that controlled behavioral interventions in school settings can be associated with increased frequency, intensity, and duration of physical activity, and in some cases desirable health outcomes (Brownell & Kaye, 1982; Dwyer et al., 1983), they do not specify the determinants of the increases observed. Thus their effectiveness in other settings cannot be predicted. The critical components of the interventions or their target behavioral variables have not been identified and assessed. This prevents a standardized evaluation or application of the results. The studies also fail to address the impact of the interventions or the increased activity on activity at later time periods. Furthermore, because subjects are sampled for convenience rather than representativeness, the generalizability of results across school settings, gender, grade level, race, and socioeconomic status is unknown.

A 3-year, community-based exercise and education program recently completed in Jackson County, Michigan, (Kuntzleman, 1985) suggests that school interventions are *capable* of increasing fitness and reducing known cardiovascular risk factors among many child population segments. However, the degree to which typical school systems are doing so is unclear. Moreover, the available research in this area again reveals little about determinants of existing school-age activity patterns or how early habits relate to activity in later years (Coates, Jeffrey, & Slinkard, 1981; Dwyer et al., 1983; Walter, Hofman, Connelly, Barrett, & Kost, 1986).

In their recent review of physical activity promotion programs in the United States, Iverson, Fielding, Crow, and Christenson (1985) conclude:

> It appears that a major opportunity to influence favorable physical activity in the United States is being missed in schools. A large majority of students are enrolled in physical education classes, but the classes appear to have little effect on the current physical fitness levels of children and, furthermore, have little impact on developing lifelong physical activity skills. (p. 212)

Montoye (1986) concurred: "Can physical educators influence children to remain active in later life, and if so, how? As far as I know, this question has not been studied with an appropriate research design" (p. 144). These views seem supported by the controlled, small-sample studies described previously and also by cross-sectional population surveys of children and adults.

Population-Based Studies of Children

The National Children and Youth Fitness Study (NCYFS) conducted by the School Health Initiative of the Public Health Service (Department of Health and Human Services, 1985) shows that of the national random sample of 8,800 boys and girls from grades 5 through 12, 80% are now enrolled in physical education, with a weekly average of 3.6 class meetings of 46.7 minutes duration each. However, only 36.3% of students take physical education daily, and although an average of 11.8 different activities are engaged in during a year, less than half of the curriculum is based on lifetime activities believed to have health significance. The 1990 Public Health Service goal calls for 60% daily participation in health-related physical education activity in the school (Department of Health and Human Services, 1980).

The typical student reports that over 80% of total physical activity comes from leisure or sport activities outside the physical education class. The five most popular activities for boys are, in order, bicycling, basketball, American football, baseball/softball, and swimming; for girls, swimming, bicycling, popular dance, rollerskating, and brisk walking are most popular. The average girl devotes 70.7% of nonschool activity to what can be regarded as lifetime physical activities compared to 55.7% for the typical boy.

The degree to which this involvement reflects sufficient intensity and regularity for cardiorespiratory fitness and health is not encouraging. If activity appropriate for health and fitness is defined by minimum standards of dynamic, large-muscle movements for 20 minutes duration three or more times weekly at an intensity of 60% of cardiorespiratory capacity, about half of boys and girls appear active enough to benefit. According to self-report, 58.9% are appropriately active year-round; 46.9% use a lifetime activity to achieve this level, but only 41.0% state that they regularly exert themselves during exercise so that they breathe hard and sweat. The 1990 Public Health Service goals call for more than a 90% rate of regular participation among 10- to 17-year-olds. Much of the physical activity involvement of children and youth appears to be in team sports or recreational pursuits where fitness gains are negligible and health benefits are unknown.

Health-related fitness in the NCYFS sample was associated with (a) greater participation in high-intensity physical activity during nonsummer months, (b) enrollment in physical education classes with frequent weekly meetings and a variety of activities, and (c) the number and variety of nonschool activities during the past year. The cross-sectional design of this survey cannot, however, address the degree to which these factors lead to greater fitness or, conversely, the degree to which higher initial fitness levels (and other behavioral or environmental factors) selectively dispose children to more and varied activity. Also, the year-round behavioral differences noted appeared only when extreme fitness groups were contrasted (i.e., students at or above the 75th percentile vs. students below the 40th percentile). This further obscures the origins and meaning of the fitness and activity relationship.

These results hint at other activity trends that are also disturbing for public health. First, the portion of the active student population drops substantially during fall and winter months and then rises in spring and summer. The authors of the NCYFS report surmise that this may set an unhealthy precedent for adult activity patterns, where consistent participation is desirable. Second, although enrollment in physical education is at a rate of 97% at grades 5 and 6, only 50% of 11th and 12th grade students are enrolled. This corresponds with the rapid decrease in exercise patterns seen later as children leave school and enter the work force (Stephens et al., 1985). Finally, when contrasted with a comparable sample of American children from the 1960s, the NCYFS sample appeared significantly fatter (2 to 3 mm) as indicated by triceps brachii skinfold assessment. This finding suggests that current activity levels in school-age children and youth do not adequately offset dietary habits. A recent study (Dietz & Gortmaker, 1985) attributes much of this gain in body fat to excessive television watching and inadequate exercise habits. Safrit (1986), however, notes that methodological and measurement questions surrounding the NCYF study may render the apparent increase in childhood fatness insignificant from a practical or epidemiological view (Brandt & McGinnis, 1985).

Very few controlled studies of self-selected leisure activity in children have been reported, and these have involved descriptions of small samples. Observation, questionnaires, diaries kept by parents, heart rate monitors, estimates of energy expenditure or caloric balance, and changes in fitness (Baranowski et al., 1984; Bradfield, Chan, Bradfield, & Payne, 1971; Campaigne, Gilliam, Spencer, & Gold, 1984; Epstein, McGowen, & Woodall, 1984; Gilliam et al., 1981; Ilmarinen & Rutenfranz, 1980; Lussier & Buskirk, 1977; Spady, 1980; Waxman & Stunkard, 1980) have been used to estimate activity during the school year, during recess periods, and during summer months when school is not in session (Gilliam et al., 1981; Hovell, Bursick, Sharkey, & McClure, 1978; LaPorte et al., 1982; Saris, Binkhorst, Cramwinckel, van Waesberghe, & van der Veen-Hezemans, 1980; Wallace, McKenzie, & Nader, 1985).

Daily exercise dairies, weight loss, and fitness changes have also been contrasted as estimates of exercise compliance among children outpatients undergoing supervised treatment for obesity (Epstein, Koeske, & Wing, 1984; Epstein, Woodall, Goreczny, Wing, & Robertson, 1984). Although exercise and physical activity are effective adjuncts to weight loss therapy, both fitness changes and weight loss are poor estimates of activity patterns in obese children. Behavioristic techniques have been used to increase activity in mentally retarded children (Allen & Iwata, 1980), but fitness and health outcomes were not reported. Follow-up after treatment was also not reported, but based on adult studies (Leventhal et al., 1985; Martin et al., 1984), activity will very likely return to previous levels when this type of intervention is removed. None of these studies specify reliable determinants of childhood activity or their potential impact on adult activity.

Available evidence on the relationship between childhood and adulthood exercise patterns is not compelling; it comes exclusively from cross-sectional and retrospective surveys with adults and is limited to sport and physical education experiences.

Population-Based Retrospective Surveys in Adults

A 1972 National Adult Fitness Survey (Clarke, 1973) estimated that just 36% of Americans had taken physical education or gym classes in elementary school whereas 42% had such classes in junior high school and 57% in senior high school. Nearly all of the 76 million Americans who had school physical education felt their experience was good for them, but 1.1 million felt it was a bad experience, and 9.8 million were neutral in their opinion. However, the impact of physical education or school sports on adult activity patterns was unclear in this survey. Although 90% to 91% of the total public felt children should have physical education at all education levels from elementary school through college, 45% of those surveyed were themselves completely sedentary. In addition, while former participants in more than one school sport reported they were twice as likely to be active than inactive in adulthood, former participants in just one sport or adults with no school sport background were each equally likely to be inactive or to be active.

The meaning of early population surveys is cloudy. In the 1984 Annual Gallup Poll of the Public's Attitudes Toward the Public Schools (Gallup, 1984b) only 43% to 44% of American adults stated physical education should be required for high school students, regardless of their plans for college. This rate has not changed from the 1981 and 1983 Gallup surveys. Physical education was ranked directly behind health education as the eighth most important subject matter.

Yet, it is likely that large numbers of adults are uninformed about the types and amounts of physical activity needed for fitness and health. In the Perrier Fitness in America Survey of 1978 (Harris, 1979), in which general health was perceived as the top benefit of exercise, 33% of adults 18 years or older stated that bowling or golf three times a week for 1 hour is enough exercise for fitness, and 57% stated this belief for baseball. The widely known consensus in exercise science for many years has been that the impact of these activities on fitness and health is generally minimal. Despite this misinformation among the public, only 3% stated that more information on the benefits of exercise would motivate them to more activity.

Although the 1983 Miller-Lite report (Research and Forecasts, Inc., 1983) estimates more than one-half of Americans over 14 years of age have played organized sport as a child and although 42% say their interest in sports participation is high or somewhat high, only 19% report they are vigorously involved in sport and physical activity as a participant. This rate is inversely proportional to age. It ranges from 66% among 14- to 17-year-olds to 6% of 50- to 64-year-olds to 2% of those 65 and older. The biggest drop in sport and physical activity appears to occur as youth leave school; activity falls abruptly from 66% to 29% in the 18- to 24-year-old age group. This finding is consistent with other national surveys of physical activity patterns across age groups (Stephens et al., 1985).

In their recent review Powell and Dysinger (1986) located only six research articles on childhood participation in sport and physical education as antecedents to adult activity patterns. They conclude that available data are equivocal and that future studies must standardize definitions/measures and control confounding variables, recall bias, selection bias, and the content and quality of sport and physical education programs.

There is a growing literature on participation motivation and determinants of dropout in organized youth sport (e.g., Feltz & Petlichkoff, 1983; Gould & Horn, 1984; Robinson & Carron, 1982; Sonstroem & Kampper, 1980; Wankel & Kreisel, 1985a, 1985b) that parallels public health concerns about childhood activity patterns. However, interpretation is also difficult because studies have largely involved cross-sectional and correlational comparisons of static groups, and the validity of the self-reports used to assess determinants has not been confirmed. Because the available data are descriptive rather than predictive or experimental, guidelines for interventions to increase youth sport participation are not available. Moreover, the influences of participation motivation or dropping out of youth sport upon adult physical activity have not been studied either prospectively or retrospectively.

These sparse and inconclusive findings highlight the need to search for effective interventions that can be implemented for children and adolescents, and it is again disturbing that knowledge about the determinants of physical activity and exercise in these ages is absent. Our search of the scientific literature reveals a single abstracted report (Ho et al., 1981) of a direct predictive relationship, in a self-selected group of 48 men, between voluntary jogging mileage and a retrospective measure of a perceived positive elementary school experience in physical education.

The findings collectively challenge the current effectiveness of American education and public health agencies to make a positive impact on physical activity, exercise, and health-related physical fitness in children. More important, they signal a challenge to fields of study concerned with public health problems to advance knowledge about the determinants of physical activity patterns among children and youth and about how these determinants and activity patterns might relate to the determinants and activity patterns of adults.

Theories of Health Behavior as Models for Physical Activity and Exercise Across Age Groups

From the perspective of public health, it is important to determine the degree to which fitness, physical activity, and exercise are similar or different in origins or patterns when compared to other health behaviors and risk factors. Exercise or fitness might augment or diminish the impact of other health risk factors, and exercise might reinforce or create barriers for other health behaviors. Collectively, if models unique to exercise and physical activity are required to account for habitual participation, successful interventions will need to focus on determinants that are different from, or may complement, those encompassed by existing health education and promotion principles and techniques. However, this important issue has received little study in adults, and information on children is essentially nonexistent (Dishman et al., 1985). Past behavioral studies of physical activity and exercise reflect a pragmatic rather than theoretical approach. Although the behavior-modification and cognitive behavior-modification techniques described by Knapp in chapter 7 have shown some promise with adults, the determinants of physical activity and exercise that have been studied are seldom standardized in either concept or measurement technology across diverse settings and populations. As a result, comparing the origins of exercise and physical activities in general with those of other health behaviors is difficult.

To clarify possible similarities and differences, it is instructive to view existing exercise and physical activity studies within the most prominent generalized health behavior models. These models and relevant exercise studies have been fully described in chapter 5 by Sonstroem, but they are briefly summarized here with a focus on implications for children and youth. Although nearly all exercise studies have exclusively examined adults, the theoretical models have implications for physical activity relationships and behavioral impact from childhood to adulthood. These health behavior models and related studies are summarized in Table 1.

The models summarized are limited to accounting for the variability in health behaviors due to attitudes, beliefs, and self-perceptions. These factors are important for public health interventions because they provide targets for mass information or persuasion campaigns and education. However additional forces obviously influence some health actions. Additional forces that appear important for determining health-related exercise are (a) exertion, (b) age or developmental stage, and (c) the role of the individual and/or the role of social forces in determining exercise behavior. Because these three factors should be an integral part of any

Table 1 Summary of Health Behavior Models for Exercise

Health behavior model and summary statement	Results of studies	General conclusions	Implications for children
A. Models that have generated research			
1. *Health Belief Model* (Rosenstock, 1974). Compliance with any health behavior depends on perceived vulnerability to a disorder, belief that health risk is increased by noncompliance, and belief that health effectiveness of the behavior outweighs barriers.	a. Not valid for all health behaviors, e.g., health-related vs. health-directed (Janz & Becker, 1984). b. Validity for exercise has been mixed (Dishman, 1986a), but most studies have not tested the total model (Lindsay-Reid & Osborn, 1980; Morgan, Shephard, & Finucane, 1984; Noland & Feldman, 1984; Oldridge & Spencer, 1985; Slenker, Price, Roberts, & Jurs, 1984). Valid and reliable measures for perceived exercise benefits and barriers not available.	a. Failure to predict may be due to the positive view of health behaviors held by the general public or the wide range in behavioral demands. b. Active individuals often perceive their health as good, not vulnerable to disease. Time, convenience, and exertion are viewed as barriers, but equally so by the already active.	a. Do not know how health beliefs about exercise are formed in children or if they predict exercise patterns. b. Do not know how health beliefs from childhood affect later adult beliefs and habits (Dielman, Leech, Becker, Rosenstock, Horvath, & Radius, 1982; Green, Heit, Iverson, Kolbe, & Kreuter, 1980; Holcomb, Carbonari, Ingersoll, Luce, & Melson, 1984).

(Cont.)

Table 1 (Cont.)

Health behavior model and summary statement	Results of studies	General conclusions	Implications for children
2. *Theory of Reasoned Action* (Ajzen & Fishbein, 1977). Attitudes about a specific exercise prescription (i.e., time, place, and type of exercise) can predict behavior through its interaction with social norms. Both influence exercise intention.	a. No studies show social desirability of activity can predict exercise patterns (Dishman & Ickes, 1981). Spouse impact is reliable but personal attitudes are not. Few tests of theory are available. b. Available data from supervised and community settings suggests that only 25% to 54% of intentions to begin and maintain an exercise program translate to sustained action (Dishman, 1986a; Godin, Shephard, & Colantonio, 1986; Godin et al., 1985; Mackeen et al., 1983). Model predicts less than half of exercise intentions in children (Godin & Shephard, 1986).	Intentions seem largely necessary but not sufficient to predict physical activity. The extent to which the active plan their exercise routines and the impact of interventions on intentions and subsequent exercise remains unknown.	a. Extent to which physical activity patterns in children stem from reasoned action and how exercise intentions interact with other activity influences is not known. b. Contrasts between general and specific exercise attitudes as predictors across time, settings, activities, and age groups are needed.

(Cont.)

Table 1 (Cont.)

Health behavior model and summary statement	Results of studies	General conclusions	Implications for children
3. *Self-Efficacy* (Bandura, 1977). To attempt and persist at a behavior change, one must perceive a personal ability to carry out the behavior when the outcome is known. Self-efficacy develops by (a) actual mastery, (b) modeling, (c) verbal persuasion, and (d) emotional signs of coping ability.	a. Among post-MI patients beliefs about ability to exercise can increase following fitness testing or training (Ewart et al., 1983, 1984; Sanne, 1973). b. Self-efficacy beliefs: distinguish patients who exceed or do not attain their exercise intensity prescription (Gilliam et al., 1984); are better predictors of exercise compliance than health control beliefs for chronic obstructive-lung patients (Kaplan, Atkins, & Reinsch, 1984); relate to adoption of vigorous activity in men and adoption and maintenance of moderate activity for men and women in unsupervised settings (Sallis et al., 1986).	a. Feelings of self-efficacy most accurately predict when they are specific to a narrow range of behavior and time. b. Self-efficacy is influenced by actual experience and subjective signs of inability. Therefore need to take into account past experience and perceived exertional strain. c. Self-efficacy does not predict persistence of behavior change when incentives are not present. d. General feelings of physical ability might be a better predictor of overall exercise patterns across time, settings, and activities than specific self-efficacy beliefs, but this has not been tested.	a. Because past experience seems to mediate self-efficacy, studies with children are needed. b. Need to understand incentives to engage in health-related exercise during childhood and how they change and/or remain in adulthood. c. Feelings of general physical ability vs. specific self-efficacy needs to be studied with children across activities, time, and settings.

(Cont.)

Table 1 (Cont.)

Health behavior model and summary statement	Results of studies	General conclusions	Implications for children
	c. Dropouts and compliers have been equally likely to perceive the major benefit of exercise as increased ability for safe exertion (Sanne, 1973). Low self-efficacy has been related to intention to begin a corporate exercise program (Davis, Jackson, Kronenfeld, & Blair, 1984).		
4. *Physical Activity Model* (Sonstroem, 1978). Attraction to physical activity is reinforced by increased self-esteem; mediated by perceived increases in physical ability and fitness due to increased activity.	Studies of adult fitness programs show a weak relationship with sustained participation (Dishman, 1982; Morgan, 1977), but suggest an influence on initial adoption.	Attractive model because it provides a link between past activity history, fitness self-perceptions and attitude. The model is recursive and permits an empirical contrast with other models of attitude (e.g., Ajzen & Fishbein, 1977) and perceived ability (e.g., Bandura, 1977).	Model has not been experimentally tested, but cross-sectional evidence supports its validity for spontaneous exercise in children. Only available model designed specifically for youth physical activity patterns.

(Cont.)

Table 1 (Cont.)

Health behavior model and summary statement	Results of studies	General conclusions	Implications for children
5. *Health Locus of Control* (Wallston, Wallston, & DeVellis, 1978). This is also concerned with perceived competence but extends the concept to the source of control over health and behavior reinforcements.	Studies with adults have yielded mixed results. Cross-sectional comparisons show exercisers more internal whereas prospective studies show inconsistent relationships with adherence (Dishman & Ickes, 1981; Long & Haney, 1986; Noland & Feldman, 1984; Noland & Feldman, 1985; Oldridge & Streiner, 1985; Slenker, Price, & O'Connell, 1985). Exercise specific measures and reinforcement value have received little attention (Dishman & Gettman, 1980; McCready & Long, 1985; Noland & Feldman, 1985). No studies on children's exercise have employed locus of control models.		Because this model and the ones that follow (perceived competence, personal investment, and subjective expected utility) encompass a developmental or social learning perspective and offer targets for social psychology interventions with exercise, they should be contrasted among children and youth.

(Cont.)

Table 1 (Cont.)

B. Unresearched Models

1. *Perceived Competence* (Harter, 1982). The focus of this model is on goal directed behavior and is similar to Sonstroem's (1978) model.	No studies related to exercise behavior in adults or children although the model has been tested in youth sport settings (Feltz & Petlichkoff, 1983); it has not been examined in exercise adherence studies.	These models share common or related elements but have different measurement technologies, were designed for different behaviors and populations, and have not been contrasted in exercise and physical activity settings.	Same as above.
2. *Personal Investment* (Maehr, 1984). Based on congruence between beliefs, attitudes, values, intentions, perceived competence, and behavior. Emphasis on goal setting.	No studies related to exercise behavior in adults or children.		Same as above.
3. *Subjective Expected Utility* (SEU) (Edwards, 1961). SEU theory views attitude as a function of self-expectations of an object's characteristics or the consequences of a behavior and the evaluation of these characteristics and consequences. Of note, SEU is essentially an attitude toward an alternative action.	Unpublished report that SEU predicts interest in, but not adherence to, an exercise program by young adults (Kendzierski & LaMastro, in press). Some promise for examining attitudes toward *not* exercising on adherence.		Same as above.

health behavior model for exercise, issues related to each will be discussed in the following sections.

The Role of Exertion in a Health Behavior Model

Consideration of the role of exertion is important for two reasons. First, it is fundamental to exercise behavior. Studies suggest that individual differences in both biological and subjective indicators of exertional strain with exercise (Dishman, 1982; Hughes, Crow, Jacobs, Mittlemark, & Leon, 1984; Oldridge, 1982) are associated with dropout in preventive and rehabilitative exercise (where health behavior is emphasized as a motive). Behavior models that exclude considerations about biological and exertional (both perceived and preferred) aspects of exercise are unlikely to be sufficient to explain exercise behavior. This is consistent with multidimensional scaling of health attitudes and behavioral self-report among college students, teachers, and nurses (Turk, Rudy, & Salovey, 1984). Compared with 29 other health-protective actions, getting enough exercise was viewed as an effective practice, but it was also perceived as one that requires a great deal of effort. Reported frequency of exercise paralleled this attitudinal distinction for teachers and nurses; actual practices were in general those that were viewed as effective but required little effort. Activity frequencies for college students corresponded with perceived effectiveness and were not influenced by perceived effort. Similar studies with children and youth have not been conducted.

Although these results were cross-sectional, based on unvalidated self-report of behavior, they are consistent with an effort-behavior hypothesis for physical activity participation. They reinforce the importance of considering exertional properties of exercise as they may interact with health beliefs, exercise attitudes, and actual physical activity patterns across age groups. This hypothesis has not been tested, but several studies suggest that exercise is indeed unique from other health behaviors and that exertion may help explain this uniqueness (Dishman et al., 1985). How and when exertion perceptions and preferences develop across the age-span has not been studied.

Existing models of health behavior do not place an emphasis on biological aspects that may distinguish physical activity and exercise from other health behaviors. Nevertheless, it is commonly recognized that other health behaviors are not homogenous in origin. Differences in determinants and health outcomes make it useful to regard most health behaviors as either illness reducing or health promoting. Janz and Becker (1984) recently distinguished between preventive health behavior, sick role behavior, and clinic utilization. Also, a distinction between health-related and health-directed behavior is an illustrative contrast. It is recognized that actions may be initiated purposely for health or that health outcomes may result from behaviors motivated by nonhealth reasons. In addition, many health behaviors may occur due to predisposition or environmental bias that is independent of conscious decisions. This is evidenced by the prevailing main effects that age, sex, and socioeconomic status exert on many health behaviors and their associated morbidity and mortality rates.

Despite these meaningful distinctions, physical activity and exercise have apparently been viewed generically by various investigators, at different times, as either health related or as health directed. Moreover, nonspecific health behavior models have been applied without regard for this important distinction or for how this might confound or limit the predictive utility of generalized models. This poses potential problems for the use of general behavior principles with physical activity because existing social psychology approaches, which have appeal for broad-based social promotions, or cognitive-behavioral and behavioristic approaches, which have high validity for self-regulation among some individuals, currently cannot account for the biological and exertional aspects of physical activity. Behavior modification studies that have shown increases in chronic exercise behavior have not shown or been designed to show increases in exercise intensity (Dishman, 1987).

When physical activity is viewed as a goal-directed behavior, any of a number of exertional factors could interact with goal setting and goal attainment to influence reinforcement for participation. This possibility, coupled with the promotion of high-intensity, fitness-related exercise as the health norm, may explain why large portions of the adult population remain sedentary even though they accept and endorse the publically known, abstract benefits of physical activity. They may not yet have experienced personally known, tangible benefits. This may also explain why many who intend to be active are unable to act on their intentions (Godin, Shephard, & Colantonio, 1986). If so, knowledge, beliefs, attitudes, and intentions might well be overridden by exertion barriers. Indeed, Sallis et al. (1986) report that community adults are twice as likely to maintain a program of moderate daily routines (e.g., walking) than a program of vigorous conditioning. Conversely, the key to regular participation may well lie in concrete feelings of exertional vigor, well-being, or intrinsic enjoyment rather than abstract fears about poor health or promises of longevity. This may be particularly the case for children and youth, for whom health concerns are often remote.

Despite this possibility, the most prominent general models of health behavior do not include a principle role for concrete reinforcements from activity among healthy, asymptomatic individuals. Because of the comparatively extreme behavioral challenge imposed by physical activity and exercise, exclusion of the biological basis of physical activity appears to be a major shortcoming of existing behavioral models as sufficient estimates of physical activity patterns among large segments of child, youth, and adult populations. For example, initial declines in activity levels in adolescence could be influenced by social changes (e.g., changes in school environments or entry into the work force), and failures to maintain attempts at a later return to activity may signal self-regulatory problems of balancing other work and leisure reinforcements against the exertional barriers of fatigue that stem from reduced fitness. This might occur despite positive exercise attitudes and health beliefs. In this instance, factors such as past activity and fitness history or perceived competence might well be more useful than health beliefs in overcoming subjective exertion barriers. Past studies that show that beliefs and attitudes about exercise or health predict adoption but not maintenance of exercise or physical activity routines have failed to consider exertion as a behavioral variable (Dishman, 1982).

Findings collectively suggest that factors other than abstract beliefs are necessary to reinforce participation and that the behavioral impact of these reinforcements may be proportional to the demands on time and effort inherent in the activity in question (e.g., Dishman, 1986a; Godin et al., 1986). Beliefs in eventual health gains may sustain an involvement with a small time and exertional requirement, but more tangible and immediate reinforcements that are inherent in the activity or the setting in which it occurs may be required for a more vigorous, time-consuming involvement. When social and exertional reinforcements and perceptible gains in personal competence receive appropriate attention and importance, an active and vigorous lifestyle can become a self-motivated and intrinsically rewarding decision (Dishman, 1987). Exercise may then become a time-management priority and a personal investment; but this likely process is now poorly described and cannot be understood without studies of children and youth and an understanding of the role of exertion.

The Role of Age or Developmental Stage in a Health Behavior Model

The role of age or developmental stage is another important component that needs to be taken into account to guide research and interventions with health beliefs, attitudes, and behaviors (Leventhal et al., 1985). As Roberts, Maddux, and Wright (1984) point out, children are different from adults in their ability to understand health issues and to assume personal responsibility for their health. What's more, the rapid changes that occur in childhood may call for different strategies for questions of determinants and effective interventions.

Among the seven health and risk behaviors studied by Breslow and associates in the Human Population Laboratory (Belloc & Breslow, 1972), a few studies have tried to assess differences by age. For example, Glynn (1983) studied health and illness behaviors in 2nd to 10th graders in the Milwaukee, Wisconsin, school system. A gradual and consistent decline in health behaviors from 2nd to 10th grade was found, with the decline being somewhat greater for females than for males. The majority of the decline was due to changes in regular sleeping and eating patterns. Other factors that contributed to this decline were cigarette smoking, consumption of alcoholic beverages, and a decline in physical activity.

Other investigators have found that this decline begins to reverse itself during young adulthood (Belloc & Breslow, 1972; Breslow & Enstrom, 1980; Prohaska, Keller, Leventhal, & Leventhal, 1983; Wilson & Elinson, 1981). The reversal of this trend is seen for all health behaviors except exercise. As Leventhal et al. (1985) point out, this is unfortunate because Palmore (1970) indicated that lack of exercise showed a higher association with illness and mortality in the aged than any of the other health behaviors studied. Moreover, the behavioral risk factors among the aged appear to be different from those affecting mortality in ages 45 to 65 (Branch & Jette, 1984). Similarly, we might expect adult risk profiles to be altered by changes in preadult risk patterns including exercise and fitness.

Health behaviors seem to change differentially across the life span, but the issue may be further complicated. Determinants of exercise may be different from other health behaviors. Indeed, a number of studies (Harris & Guten, 1979; Langlie, 1977, 1979; Steel, Gutmann, Leventhal, & Easterling, 1983; Zimmerman, 1983) indicate very low intercorrelations (e.g., .20 to .30) among several health promotive and risk behaviors. However, as Leventhal et al. (1985) point out, when social, psychological, and biological mechanisms are examined, low correlations should be expected.

> The regularities or order sought by behavioral scientists will be found in the mechanisms controlling health behaviors and not in the surface associations among the behaviors themselves. Furthermore, we may expect little temporal consistency across the lifespan (e.g., Mechanic, 1979) since the mechanisms controlling these behaviors are likely to change with age. (p. 8)

The impact of exercise and its patterning on surface measures of health status and health behaviors in children seems to be an important link in expanding our understanding of underlying behavioral mechanisms of health promotion and disease prevention.

Community (Fitness Ontario, 1982) and national (Gallup, 1984a) surveys show that adults *perceive* a strong relationship between their activity level and other health related behavior such as diet, smoking, substance abuse, and stress management. Nevertheless, recent reviews of objective evidence (Blair, Jacobs, and Powell, 1985; Norman, 1986; see chapter 3 in this volume) show that activity and weight control are closely related, but little correspondence appears between exercise and other health habits. Intervention results from a regional sample of 347 coronary bypass patients given medical instructions (Miller, Johnson, Wikoff, McMahan, & Garrett, 1983) and from a combined media and medical education and instruction campaign in Northern California communities (Meyer, Nash, McAlister, Maccoby, & Farquhar, 1980) provide evidence that diet, smoking, stress management, and medication compliance are amenable to change through increasing knowledge or attitudes about health behavior, but physical activity levels are not. Despite positive attitudes or increased knowledge, exercise patterns remained unchanged or unrelated to other health habits.

Studies that examine cross-sectional relationships between exercise or physical activity and other health behaviors among adults show little overlap. Exercise-related variables tend to group alone, although dietary behavior is frequently correlated with activity patterns. A recent study with high school students shows a similar pattern (Hays, Stacy, & DiMatteo, 1984). Exercise habits were unlinked to meal regularity, to drug, alcohol, or cigarette use, and to hours of sleep. In one of the most convincing studies with young adults, Mechanic (1979) has reported that leisure physical activity (measured as blocks walked and other exercise during the past 24 hours and a preference for using stairs over an elevator) was correlated only with enjoyment of physical activity, perceived physical health, and perceived control over illness. Using seat belts, smoking, risk taking, illness coping, practicing preventive health care, and drinking alcohol were each unrelated to physical activity. The correspondence among surface health behavior attitudes across a 16-year period from childhood to young adulthood was low in these subjects. Stage of development and the link between health behaviors across the lifespan are clearly important factors for a health behavior model of exercise.

The Roles of the Individual and Social Forces in a Health Behavior Model

At the present time our understanding of how health-related knowledge, beliefs, attitudes, and intentions about exercise and fitness are formed or function in children is incomplete. Whether increases in activity levels across age will most reliably result from socially-based public intervention or from self-initiated regulation by the individual remains unclear. This must be determined before effective interventions can be designed and implemented. The targets and methods of public promotions can necessarily be quite different from those geared toward behavior change and maintenance in individuals. Only a handful of exercise studies that bear on these fundamental issues are available, and they exclusively involve adults (e.g., Wankel, Yardley, & Graham, 1985). The behavioral skills that enable knowledge, beliefs, attitudes, and intentions to promote the adoption and maintenance of health-related exercise and fitness are essentially unstudied among children. These gaps in our knowledge must be filled if interventions based on contemporary principles and methods from health psychology and behavioral fitness are to be effectively used in exercise settings.

Studies Bearing on Socially Based Interventions in Children.   A cross-sectional randomized survey of 3,106 Finnish school children 11 to 19 years of age (Telama & Silvennoinen, 1979) illustrates methodological and conceptual concerns for socially based interventions and research. Across age, near-linear shifts in self-perceived motivation for exercise occurred. Performance-oriented, competitive motivation and a normative emphasis on health (e.g., fitness exercise is everybody's duty, exercise is one of the healthy habits of life, physical activity is useful at a later age) decreased with age whereas recreation for relaxation increased. Most important, the motives most strongly linked to frequency and intensity of volitional physical activity were perceived fitness and physical competence, recreation for relaxation, and functional health (e.g., maintaining one's health, improving endurance). These factors increased with age. According to the authors of this report,

> health can be broken into a normative and functional health motive. . . . Functional health was primarily related to . . . physical activity whereas normative motivation was mainly related to age, and not at all to manifest activity. . . . In speaking of the promotion of health as a motive for physical activity it is thus adviseable to make a distinction between an opinion learned from health propaganda and a more personal internalized motive. (p. 27)

Noteworthy gender differences in activity motivation were also found. Boys, particularly the younger ages, tended to endorse competition and fitness motivation whereas girls, particularly older ages, endorsed recreation.

These results are largely consistent with findings from studies of 1,752 and 1,895 boys and girls in grades 4 through 7 and 11th grade in the state of Washington and British Columbia province, Canada (Schutz, Smoll,

& Wood, 1981). These studies compared the psychometric form of physical activity attitudes in children and youth with a previously validated structure for adults. Although similarities were seen, two key differences from the original attitude structure were noted. An original social domain emerged as two independent factors: social growth (meeting new people through physical activity) and social continuation (perpetuating existing interpersonal relationships through physical activity). Although an original health and fitness domain remained intact (i.e., both children and adults appear to view "taking part in physical activities to make your health better" and "to get your body in better shape" as the same), a distinction was made between endorsing this concept as a value or as enjoyment. This finding is consistent with the Finnish results, and it reinforces the significance of distinguishing between abstract value endorsements and concrete, personal rewards or personal investment when physical activity attitudes are assessed. The implications of this distinction for predicting actual behavior are clear because the reinforcement properties implied by enjoyment are greater than those implied by value. The psychometric overlap between health and fitness is also significant because it may signal a barrier to later activity among those who view fitness as the key to health but do not enjoy heavy exertion.

Other studies with children in the United States and Canada are also consistent with the Finnish observations in suggesting that health and exercise beliefs differ in stability, form, and gender across age. When over 300 young adults from Madison, Wisconsin, who had been tested as children in 1961 were followed up 16 years later in 1977, Mechanic (1979) observed a limited degree of stability in perceived health and illness over time. Factors related to health care utilization appeared very pliable across age. Communication of illness feelings to others and feeling at ease with seeing a doctor were unrelated from childhood to adulthood. However, factors related to self-monitoring and self-regulating health showed moderate stability. Denial of pain, risk taking, and perceived illness susceptibility were the most predictable from childhood to adulthood. Young children who did not pay attention to pain seemed more likely to become adults who deny pain, maintain normal activities when ill, do not discuss illness symptoms, and take health risks. The reporting of exercise among the Wisconsin adults was related to enjoyment of exercise and to feelings of physical health and personal control over health but not to illness symptoms or health care utilization. These data may have relevance for understanding which part of exercise and health behaviors remains stable or self-regulated across age.

Data on exercise attitudes show similar results. Smoll and Schutz (1980) report a small-sample, longitudinal study across grades 4, 5, and 6 among 2 birth cohorts of boys and girls from Bellevue, Washington. Repeated measurements of perceived values of physical activity for social exchange, health and fitness, risk taking, aesthetics, tension release, and ascetics revealed that attitudes were stable across grade levels but not within individuals. Also, only the factors of aesthetics and risk-taking showed some stability of precision across grades. Collectively, these studies have several implications for socially based interventions designed to increase physical activity.

It is very important to increase one's intention to be active. National surveys suggest that 25–65% of the population segment who are physically inactive have no intention to begin an exercise program in the coming year (Dishman et al., 1985). Socially based interventions will most likely exert their greatest impact by increasing intentions to adopt an exercise program. However, recent data indicate that just 30% to 60% of those who intend to be active will sustain habitual participation (Godin, Valois, Shephard, & Desharnais, 1985; Mackeen, Franklin, & Nicholas, 1984); other behavioral targets and interventions, therefore, appear equally important for reinforcing continued participation (Dishman, 1987). Mechanic (1979) has observed factors relating to self-regulation that showed moderate stability over time, and these may have important implications for maintenance of exercise behavior. For example, interventions are best targeted at determinants sensitive to change agents while planning for or accommodating those more resistive.

Studies Bearing on Self-Regulation of Exercise in Children. Recent studies in the area of self-regulation research provide some evidence that it is important to target interventions to existing cognitive influences on health behavior (see chapter 7 by Knapp and chapter 10 by Oldridge). First, in a study conducted by Prohaska et al., (1983), it was found that older respondents attempted to avoid anger, anxiety, depression, and stress by learning to take things as they come. A passive coping strategy was adopted. This study also found that emotional control was more valued as a preventive strategy among older persons although vigorous exercise was perceived to be an effective preventive strategy for younger respondents for several chronic illnesses. A greater understanding of changes with age in cognitive-emotional control mechanisms is important for understanding determinants of physical activity.

Second, it is also important to understand how self-regulatory processes are acquired. Harter (1982) has proposed a framework for understanding how self-regulatory health behaviors can come about. The framework hypothesizes that the order of self-regulatory component processes in children occurs in the reverse order of how self-regulation is thought to operate in adulthood. In other words, self-regulation in adulthood is thought to operate sequentially through the processes of (a) self-monitoring, (b) self-evaluation, and (c) self-reinforcement. However, children first learn to imitate verbal approval. This is applied before they learn the processes of self-evaluation. In turn, self-evaluation must be learned before they can apply it to situations where it is necessary to self-monitor. Although few studies provide support or disaffirm this developmental model, some research on rule forming and rule using (Mischel & Mischel, 1976) supplies initial confirming evidence. In addition, other researchers (Magrab, 1978; Matthews & Angulo, 1980; Melamed & Siegel, 1980) have advocated the use of interventions designed to enhance self-regulatory skills, particularly for children who have difficulty complying with a health regime or who show early signs of Type A behavior.

In summary, the lack of information (a) about what constitutes healthful physical activity from childhood to adulthood; (b) on how social, psychological, and biological mechanisms interact to promote self-regulatory behaviors across the life span; (c) concerning which self-regulatory skills most facilitate execise adherence in children and adults; and (d) about how self-regulatory behaviors are acquired in the developmental process indicates that a need exists for a conceptual framework to guide future research and interventions. The next section will summarize and raise questions concerning present theoretical models of health behavior as models for physical activity and exercise.

An Interaction Model and Implications for Future Research

As we have noted elsewhere (Dishman et al., 1985), it seems worthwhile to view habitual physical activity and exercise as a dynamic process in which adoption and sustained participation are each targets for interventions in both supervised settings and in the population base. Personal intentions, physical and behavioral skills for activity change, willingness and commitment to change, and social, psychological, or biological reinforcements surface as reliable influences across many populations, settings, and types of activity. Perceived needs, values, or abilities and expected or real outcomes combine with biomedical traits and personality, feelings, lifestyle habits, and perceived or real environments and barriers to shape a person's disposition to start, sustain, or increase an activity routine. This disposition may also be shaped by activity history; social norms; modeling and reinforcement by family, peers, educators, and medical or health care providers; by prompts to action from the environment; by accessibility of facilities; and by activity type, frequency, duration, and intensity.

Any of these factors have the practical potential to influence exercise under certain conditions, but the predictability of exercise decisions and actions seems hampered by complex interactions within and between variations in personal, environmental, and physical activity characteristics. Models that fail to consider this breadth of influence on exercise, as well as its complexity, may have little chance of explaining physical activity and exercise patterns. Few factors seem to be strong enough to produce main effects sufficient to offset the complex interactions of the many influences on activity from childhood to the adult years. A focus on single factors or single changes shows little promise. Moreover, influences may operate in more than one direction, and their relative importance may change over time and age. A model that encompasses these interactions across the age-span is beginning to be tested for adults (Dishman, 1987), but it will remain theoretically and practically incomplete without descriptions and interventions with children and youth (see Figure 1). This is the present challenge for the allied public health sciences and professions.

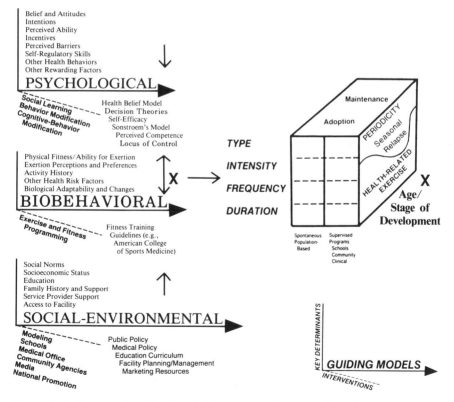

Figure 1 A lifespan interactional model for exercise adherence. Considered are psychological, biobehavioral and social-environmental determinants and interventions; type, intensity, frequency, duration, setting, and periodicity of activity; and the age or developmental stage of the individual.

We do not know how attitudes, beliefs, intentions, and self-perceptions interact with exertional preferences or outcomes and self-regulatory skills to reinforce a decision to adopt or maintain physical activity and exercise. How these interactions are formed or may change across the age-span has not been described. Neither do we know how each independent factor may differ in magnitude or in form at different ages. Because exertional preferences and perceptions may create motivational barriers to effective interventions aimed at attitudes and beliefs about health and fitness or may interact with self-regulatory skills, these issues appear critical for understanding activity patterns and determinants across the age-span.

Conclusions

Any study that examines determinants of physical activity and exercise across age groups must address several concerns if it is to have implications for interventions. First, naturally occurring relationships between activity patterns and behavioral variables must be described for children and youth. This provides the necessary baseline conditions against which the impact of future interventions can be compared. Second, the variables chosen to describe these relationships must be based on theory in order to increase standardization and the likelihood of generalizability. They must also, however, represent feasible targets for interventions; they will most likely be characteristics of children, environments, or physical activity and exercise that are stable enough to predict future behavior or outcomes but are accessible and responsive to public or personal intervention and change. Variables that are naturally unstable and transient or appear resistive to intervention must also be identified, so intervention plans can omit them or take their impact into consideration.

A review of existing data on the determinants of physical activity and exercise, in both supervised exercise programs and spontaneous activity in the population, indicates that advancing age and elapsed time after initial adoption of an activity routine are among the most consistent predictors of inactivity (Dishman et al., 1985; Stephens et al., 1985). This time factor suggests that past activity environments and experiences may be strong influences on present and future participation. Because little is known in these areas, several questions appear answerable and fundamentally critical if effective interventions are to be planned and implemented with school-age children and youth in a way that may also favorably impact our understanding of physical activity in the adult years.

1. When and how do preferences for activity types and intensities develop, and how do they correspond with activity patterns in children and youth and later in adults?
2. What determinants of physical activity and exercise in children or youth can guide interventions to increase the likelihood of activity in childhood and later in adulthood?
3. Are certain types of individuals predisposed to activity or inactivity? If so, does this change at definable stages in the life span (e.g., from childhood to adolescence to the college years to middle age)? Do parental profiles on known correlates of adult inactivity (e.g., education, socioeconomic level, and activity history) correlate with children's activity patterns and preferences? Do youth experiences in sport and physical education influence adult activity patterns or their determinants?
4. How do abstract incentives, such as health knowledge and beliefs, or tangible exercise outcomes, such as exertional sensations and perceived competence or social reinforcement, interact to influence both the intention to adopt activity and reinforcement for sustained participation? Does their relative importance vary reliably across age groups so that different interventions may be required for different physical activity and exercise behaviors for different ages? What is the relative behavioral impact of socially based interventions designed to increase children's knowledge, attitudes, or beliefs about exercise when compared with the impact of interventions designed to develop self-regulatory skills for exercise?
5. How do exercise patterns and fitness relate to other health behaviors in children and youth? Is there continuity in these relationships from childhood to adulthood? Will childhood exercise or fitness influence known adult risk factors for disease or premature mortality? Might changes in childhood exercise and fitness alter the constellations of factors that constitute present day risk for morbidity and mortality? Are the known health risk factors that relate to inactivity in adults similarly related to inactivity in children and youth? If so, do they predispose, or result from, inactivity?

Although these questions reflect the programmatic concerns of public health initiatives, they must be conceptualized and assessed in a standardized manner if their answers can impact public health decision making. For this purpose it is necessary to view them within the frameworks of theoretical models for health behavior and habitual physical activity. It is from this perspective that hypotheses for descriptive and intervention-based research on physical activity and exercise determinants can be operationalized for various age groups. This objective represents a key challenge for the study of exercise adherence and public health.

Acknowledgment

Thanks go to Donna Smith for preparing the manuscript.

References

Allen, C.D., & Iwata, B.A. (1980). Reinforcing exercise maintenance: Using existing high rate activities. *Behavior Modification, 4*, 337–354.

Ajzen, I., & Fishbein, M. (1977). Attitude-behavior relations: A theoretical analysis and review of empirical research. *Psychological Bulletin, 84*, 888–918.

Bandura, A. (1977). Self-efficacy: Toward a unifying theory of behavioral change. *Psychological Review, 84*(2), 191–215.

Baranowski, T., Dworkin, R.J., Cieslik, C.J., Hooks, P., Clearman, D.R., Ray, L., Dunn, J.K., & Nader P.R. (1984). Reliability and validity of self-report of aerobic activity: Family health project. *Research Quarterly for Exercise and Sport, 55*(4), 309–317.

Bar-Or, O. (1985). Physical conditioning in children with cardiorespiratory disease. *Exercise and Sport Sciences Reviews, 13*, 305–334.

Belloc, N.B., & Breslow, L. (1972). Relationship of physical health status and family practices. *Preventive Medicine, 1*, 409–421.

Berenson, G.S. (1980). *Cardiovascular risk factors in children.* Oxford University Press.

Binkhorst, R.A., Kemper, H.C.G., & Saris, W.H.M. (Eds.). (1985). *Children and exercise XI.* Champaign, IL: Human Kinetics.

Blair, S.N., Jacobs, D.R., & Powell, K.E. (1985). Relationships between exercise or physical activity and other health behaviors. *Public Health Reports, 100*(2), 172–180.

Bradfield, R.B., Chan, H., Bradfield, N.E., & Payne, P.R. (1971). Energy expenditures and heart rates of Cambridge boys at school. *American Journal of Clinical Nutrition, 24*, 1461–1466.

Branch, L.G., & Jette, A.M. (1984). Personal health practices and mortality among the elderly. *American Journal of Public Health, 74*(10), 1126–1129.

Breslow, C., & Enstrom, J.E. (1980). Persistence of health habits and their relationship to mortality. *Preventive Medicine, 9*, 469–483.

Brown, R.S. (1982). Exercise and mental health in the pediatric population. *Clinics in Sports Medicine, 1*(3), 515–527.

Brownell, K.D., & Kaye, F.S. (1982). A school-based behavior modification, nutrition education, and physical activity program for obese children. *The American Journal of Clinical Nutrition, 35*, 277–283.

Brownell, K., & Stunkard, A.J. (1980). Physical activity in the development and control of obesity. In A.J. Stunkard (Ed.), *Obesity* (pp. 112–138). Philadelphia: W.B. Saunders.

Campaigne, B.N., Gilliam, T.B., Spencer, M.L., & Gold, E.R. (1984). Heart rate holter monitoring of 6- and 7-year-old children with insulin dependent diabetes mellitus, cardiovascular and short term metabolic response to exercise: A pilot study. *Research Quarterly for Exercise and Sport, 55*, 69–73.

Centers for Disease Control. (1985). Status of the 1990 physical fitness and exercise objectives. *Morbidity and Mortality Weekly Report, 34*(34), 521–524, 529–531.

Clarke, H.H. (1973, May). National adult physical fitness survey [Special edition]. *Newsletter, Presidents Council on Physical Fitness and Sports.*

Coates, J.R., Jeffrey, R.W., & Slinkard, L. (1981). Heart healthy eating and exercise: Introducting and maintaining changes in health behaviors. *American Journal of Public Health, 71*, 15–23.

Davis, K.E., Jackson, K.L., Kronenfeld, J.J., & Blair, S.N. (1984). Intent to participate in worksite health promotion activities: A model of risk factors and psychosocial variables. *Health Education Quarterly, 11*(4), 361–377.

Department of Health and Human Services. (1980). *Promoting health/ preventing disease: Objectives for the nation.* Washington, DC: U.S. Government Printing Office.

Department of Health and Human Services. (1985). National Children and Youth Fitness Study. *Journal of Physical Education, Recreation and Dance, 56*(1), 44–90.

Dielman, T.E., Leech, S., Becker, M.H., Rosenstock, I.M., Horvath, W.J., Radius, S.M. (1982). Parental and child health beliefs and behavior. *Health Education Quarterly, 9*(2 & 3), 60–77.

Dietz, W.H., & Gortmaker, S.L. (1985). Do we fatten our children at the television set? Obesity and television viewing in children and adolescents. *Pediatrics, 75*(5), 807–812.

Dishman, R.K. (1982). Compliance/adherence in health-related exercise. *Health Psychology, 1*(3), 237–267.

Dishman, R.K. (1985). Medical psychology in exercise and sport. *Medical Clinics of North America*, **69**(1), 123–143.

Dishman, R.K. (1986a). Exercise compliance: A new view for public health. *The Physician and Sportsmedicine*, **14**(5), 127–145.

Dishman, R.K. (1986b). Mental health. In V. Seefeldt (Ed.), *Physical activity and well being* (pp. 304–341). Reston, VA: American Alliance for Health, Physical Education, Recreation, and Dance.

Dishman, R.K. (1987). Exercise adherence and habitual physical activity. In W.P. Morgan & S.N. Goldston (Eds.), *Exercise and mental health* (pp. 57–83). Washington, DC: Hemisphere.

Dishman, R.K., & Gettman, L.R. (1980). Psychobiologic influences on exercise adherence. *Journal of Sport Psychology*, **2**, 295–310.

Dishman, R.K., & Ickes, W. (1981). Self-motivation and adherence to therapeutic exercise. *Journal of Behavioral Medicine*, **4**, 421–438.

Dishman, R.K., Sallis, J.F., & Orenstein, D. (1985). The determinants of physical activity and exercise. *Public Health Reports*, **100**(2), 158–171.

DuRant, R.H., Linder, C.W., Harkess, J.W., & Gray, R.G. (1983). The relationship between physical activity and serumlipids and lipoproteins in black children and adolescents. *Journal of Adolescent Health Care*, **4**, 55–60.

Dwyer, T., Coonan, W.E., Leitch, D.R., Hetzel, B.S., & Baghurst, R.A. (1983). An investigation of the effects of daily physical activity on the health of primary school students in South Australia. *International Journal of Epidemiology*, **12**, 308–313.

Edwards, W. (1961). Behavioral decision theory. *Annual Review of Psychology*, **12**, 473–498.

Epstein, L.H., Koeske, R., & Wing, R. (1984). Adherence to exercise in obese children. *Journal of Cardiac Rehabilitation*, **4**, 185–195.

Epstein, L.H., McGowan, C., & Woodall, K. (1985). The development and validation of a behavioral observation system for free play activity in young overweight female children. *Research Quarterly for Exercise and Sport*, **55**, 180–183.

Epstein, L.H., Wing, R.R., Koeske, R., Ossip, D., & Beck, S. (1983). A comparison of lifestyle change and programmed aerobic exercise on weight and fitness changes in children. *Behavior Therapy*, **13**, 651–665.

Epstein, L.H, Woodall, K., Goreczny, A.J., Wing, R., & Robertson, R.J. (1984). The modification of activity patterns and energy expenditure in obese young girls. *Behavior Therapy*, **15**, 101–108.

Ewart, C.K., Stewart, K.J., Keleman, M.H., Gillilan, R.E., Valenti, S.A., Manley, J.D., & Keleman, M.D. (1984). Psychologic impact of circuit weight testing and training in cardiac patients. *Medicine and Science in Sports and Exercise* (abstract), **16**(2), 139.

Ewart, C.K., Taylor, C.B., Reese, L.B., & DeBusk, R.F. (1983). Effects of early post-myocardial infarction exercise testing on self-perception and subsequent physical activity. *American Journal of Cardiology,* **51,** 1076–1080.

Feltz, D.L., & Petlichkoff, L. (1983). Perceived competence among inter-scholastic sport participants and dropouts. *Canadian Journal of Applied Sport Sciences,* **8,** 231–235.

Fisher, H.G., & Brown, M. (1982). The effects of diet and exercise on selected coronary risk factors in children. *Medicine and Science in Sports and Exercise* (abstract), **14,** 171.

Fitness Ontario (1982). *The relationship between physical activity and other health-related lifestyle behaviors.* Toronto: Government of Ontario, Ministry of Culture and Recreation, Sports and Fitness Branch.

Frerichs, R.R., Srinivasan, S.R., Webber, L.S., & Berenson, G.S. (1976). Serum cholesterol and triglyceride levels in 3,446 children from a bi-racial community: The Bogalusa heart study. *Circulation,* **54,** 302–309.

Gallup, G. (1984a). American Health Magazine Survey. New York City.

Gallup, G. (1984b, September). The 16th annual Gallup poll of the public's attitudes toward the public schools. *Phi Delta Kappan,* pp. 23–28.

General Mills. (1979). *The American family report, 1978–1979: Family health in an era of stress.* New York: Yankelovich, Skelly, and White.

Gilliam, T.B., & Burke, M.B. (1978). Effects of exercise on serum lipids and lipoproteins in girls, ages 8 to 10 years. *Artery,* **4,** 203–213.

Gilliam, R.E., Chopra, A.K., Keleman, M.H., Stewart, K.J., Ewart, C.K., Keleman, M.D., Valenti, S.A., & Manley, J.D. (1984). Prediction of compliance to target heart rate during walk-job exercise in cardiac patients by a self-efficacy scale. *Medicine and Science in Sports and Exercise* (abstract), **16**(2), 115.

Gilliam, T.B., & Freedson, P.S. (1980). Effects of a 12-week school physical fitness program on peak $\dot{V}O_2$, body composition, and blood lipids in 7- to 9-year-old children. *International Journal of Sports Medicine,* **1,** 73–78.

Gilliam, T.B., Freedson, P.S., Geener, D.L., & Shabraray, B. (1981). Physical activity patterns determined by heart rate monitoring in 6-7 year old children. *Medicine and Science in Sports and Exercise,* **13**(1), 65–67.

Gilliam, T.B., Katch, V.L., Thorland, W., & Weltman, A. (1977). Prevalence of coronary heart disease risk factors in active children 7 to 12 years of age. *Medicine and Science in Sports, 9*(1), 21–25.

Gillum, R.F., Prineas, R.J., Gomez-Marin, O., Finn, S., & Chang, P.N. (1985). Personality, behavior, family environment, family social status, and hypertension risk factors in children. *Journal of Chronic Diseases, 38*(2), 187–194.

Glynn, K. (1983). *Juvenile illness behavior: Effect of age, sex, personality, and distress.* Unpublished doctoral dissertation, University of Wisconsin, Madison.

Godin, G., & Shephard, R.J. (1986). Psychosocial factors influencing intentions to exercise of young students from grades 7 to 9. *Research Quarterly for Exercise and Sport, 57*, 41–52.

Godin, G., Shephard, R.J., & Colantonio, A. (1986). The cognitive profile of those who intend to exercise but do not. *Public Health Reports, 101*(5), 521–526.

Godin, G., Valois, P., Shephard, R.J., & Desharnais, R. (1985). The direction of causality between attitude, past behavior, intention and future behavior. *Canadian Journal of Applied Sport Sciences* (abstract), *9*, 152.

Gould, D., & Horn, T. (1984). Participation motivation in young athletes. In J. Silva & R. Weinberg (Eds.), *Psychological foundations of sport* (pp. 359–370). Champaign, IL: Human Kinetics.

Green, L.W., Heit, P., Iverson, D.C., Kolbe, L.J., & Kreuter, M. (1980). The school health curriculum project: Its theory, practice, and measurement experience. *Health Education Quarterly, 7*(1), 14–34.

Gruber, J.J. (1986). Physical activity and self-esteem development in children: A meta-analysis. In G.A. Stull & H.M. Eckert (Eds.), *Effects of physical activity on children: American Academy of Physical Education papers, 19*, 30–48. Champaign, IL: Human Kinetics.

Hagberg, J.M., Ehsani, A.A., Goldring, D., Hernandez, A., Sinacore, D.R., & Holloszy, J.O. (1984). Effect of weight training on blood pressure and hemodynamics in hypertensive adolescents. *Journal of Pediatrics, 104*, 147–151.

Hagberg, J.M., Goldring, D., Ehsani, A.A., Heath, G.W., Hernandez, A., Schechtman, K., & Holloszy, J.O. (1983). Effect of exercise training on the blood pressure and hemodynamic features of hypertensive adolescents. *American Journal of Cardiology, 52*, 763–768.

Harris, D.M., & Guten, S. (1979). Health-protective behavior: An exploratory study. *Journal of Health and Social Behavior, 20*, 17–29.

Harris, L. (1979). *The Perrier Study: Fitness in America.* New York: Perrier-Great Waters of France.

Harter, S. (1982). A developmental perspective on some parameters of self-regulation in children. In P. Karoly & F.H. Kanfer (Eds.), *Self-management and behavior change: From theory to practice* (pp. 172–188). New York: Pergamon.

Haskell, W.L., Montoye, H.J., & Orenstein, D. (1985). Physical activity and exercise to achieve health-related physical fitness components. *Public Health Reports*, **100**(2), 202–212.

Hays, R., Stacy, A.W., & DiMatteo, M.R. (1984). Covariation among health related behaviors. *Addictive Behaviors*, **9**, 315–318.

Ho, P., Graham, L., Blair, S., Wood, P., Haskell, W., Williams, P., Terry, R., & Farquhan. (1981). Adherence prediction and psychological/behavioral changes following one-year randomized exercise programs. In *Abstracts of the Pan American Congress and International Course on Sports Medicine and Exercise Science (p. 9)*.

Holcomb, J.D., Carbonari, J.P., Ingersoll, R.V., Luce, W.M., & Nelson, J. (1984). The long-term impact of a cardiovascular school health curriculum. *Health Education*, 19–23.

Hovell, M.F., Bursick, J.H., Sharkey, B., & McClure, J. (1978). An evaluation of elementary students' voluntary physical activity during recess. *Research Quarterly for Exercise and Sport*, **49**(4), 460–474.

Hughes, J.R., Crow, R.S., Jacobs, D.R., Mittlemark, M.B., & Leon, A.S. (1984). Physical activity, smoking, and exercise-induced fatigue. *Journal of Behavioral Medicine*, **7**, 217–230.

Hunter, S.M., Wolf, T.M., Sklov, M.C., Webber, L.S., Watson, R.M., & Berenson, G.S. (1982). Type A coronary-prone behavior pattern and cardiovascular risk factors variables in children and adolescents: The Bogalusa heart study. *Journal of Chronic Disease*, **35**, 613–621.

Ilmarinen, J., & Rutenfranz (1980). Longitudinal studies of the changes in habitual physical activity of school children and working adolescents. In K. Berg & B.O. Eriksson (Eds.), *Children and exercise IX* (pp. 149–159). Baltimore: University Park Press.

Iverson, D.C., Fielding, J.E., Crow, R.S., & Christenson, G.M. (1985). The promotion of physical activity in the United States population: The status of programs in medical, worksite, community, and school settings. *Public Health Reports*, **100**(2), 212–224.

Janz, N.K., & Becker, M.H. (1984). The health belief model: A decade later. *Health Education Quarterly*, **11**(1), 1–47.

Kaplan, R.M., Atkins, C.J., & Reinsch, S. (1984). Specific efficacy expectations mediate exercise compliance in patients with COPD. *Health Psychology*, **3**(3), 223–242.

Kendzierski, D., & LaMastro, V.D. (in press). Reconsidering the role of attitudes in exercise behavior: A decision theoretic approach. *Journal of Applied Social Psychology.*

Khoury, P., Morrison, J.A., Kelly, K., Mellies, M., Horuitz, R., & Glueck, C.J. (1980). Clustering interrelationships of coronary heart disease risk factors in school children, ages 6–19. *American Journal of Epidemiology,* **112**(4), 524–538.

Kobasa, S.L., Maddi, S.R., & Puccetti, M.C. (1982). Personality and exercise as buffers in the stress-illness relationship. *Journal of Behavioral Medicine,* **5**, 391–404.

Kuntzleman, C.T. (1985). *W.K. Kellogg Feeling Good Project.* Spring Arbor, MI: Fitness Finders.

Laird, W.P., Fixler, D.E., & Swanbom, C.D. (1979). Effect of chronic weight lifting on the blood pressure in hypertensive adolescents. *Preventive Medicine* (abstract), **3**, 184.

Langlie, J. (1977). Social networks, health beliefs, and preventive health behavior. *Journal of Health and Social Behavior,* **18**, 244–260.

Langlie, J.K. (1979). Interrelationships among preventive health behaviors: A test of competing hypotheses. *Public Health Reports,* **94**, 216–225.

LaPorte, R.E., Cauley, J.A., Kinsey, C.M., Corbett, W., Robertson, R., Black-Sandler, R., Kuller, C.H., & Falkel, J. (1982). The epidemiology of physical activity in children, college students, middle-aged men, menopausal females, and monkeys. *Journal of Chronic Diseases,* **35**, 787–795.

Lauer, R.M., Conner, W.E., Leaverton, P.E., Reiter, M.A., & Clarke, W.R. (1975). Coronary heart disease risk factors in school children: The Muscatine Study. *Journal of Pediatrics,* **86**(5), 697–706.

Leventhal, H., Prohaska, T.R., & Hirschman, R.S. (1985). Preventive health behavior across the life span. In J.C. Rosen & L.J. Solomon (Eds.), *Prevention in health psychology.* Hanover, NH: University Press of New England.

Linder, C.W., & DuRant, R.H. (1982). Exercise, serum lipids, and cardiovascular disease—risk factors in children. *Pediatric Clinics of North America,* **29**(6), 1341–1354.

Linder, C.W., DuRant, R.H., Gray, R.H., (1979). The effects of exercise on serum lipid levels in children. *Clinical Research,* **27**, 797.

Linder, C.W., DuRant, R.H., & Mahoney, O.M. (1983). The effects of exercise on serum lipid levels and lipoproteins in white male adolescents. *Medicine and Science in Sports and Exercise,* **15**, 232–236.

Lindsay-Reid, E., & Osborn, R.W. (1980). Readiness for exercise adoption. *Social Science and Medicine, 14,* 139–146.

Long, B.L., & Haney, C.J. (1986). Enhancing physical activity in sedentary women: Information, locus of control, and attitudes. *Journal of Sport Psychology, 8,* 8–24.

Lundberg, U. (1983). Note on Type A behavior and cardiovascular responses to challenge in 3–6 year old children. *Journal of Psychosomatic Research, 27*(1), 39–42.

Lussier, L., & Buskirk, E.R. (1977). Effects of an endurance training regimen on assessment of work capacity in prepubertal children. *Annals of the New York Academy of Sciences, 301,* 743–747.

MacConnie, S.E., Gilliam, T.B., Geenen, D.L., & Pels, A.E. (1982). Daily physical activity patterns of prepubertal children involved in a vigorous exercise program. *International Journal of Sports Medicine, 3,* 202–207.

Mackeen, P.C., Franklin, B.A., & Nicholas, W.C. (1983). Body composition, physical work capacity and physical activity habits at 18-month follow-up of middle-aged women participating in an exercise intervention program. *International Journal of Obesity, 7,* 61–71.

Maehr, M. (1984). Meaning and motivation: Toward a theory of personal investment. *Research on Motivation in Education: Student Motivation, 1,* 115–144.

Magrab, P.R. (Ed.). (1978). *Psychological management of pediatric problems* (Vol. 1). Baltimore: University Park Press.

Martin, J.E., & Dubbert, P.M. (1985). Exercise in hypertension. *Annals of Behavioral Medicine, 7*(1), 13–18.

Martin, J.E., Dubbert, P.M., Katell, A.D., Thompson, J.K., Raczynski, J.R., Lake, M., Smith, P.O., Webster, J.S., Sikora, T., & Cohen, R.E. (1984). The behavioral control of exercise in sedentary adults: Studies 1 through 6. *Journal of Consulting and Clinical Psychology, 52,* 600–612.

Matthews, K.A., & Angulo, J. (1980). Measurement of Type A behavior pattern in children: Assessment of children's competitiveness, impatience-anger, and aggression. *Child Development, 51,* 466–475.

Matthews, K.A., & Siegel, J.M. (1985). The Type A behavior pattern in children and adolescents: Assessment, development, and associated coronary risk. In A.R. Baum & J.E. Singer (Eds.), *Handbook of health and medical psychology* (Vol. 2, pp. 205–235). Hillsdale, NJ: Lawrence Erlbaum Associates.

Matthews, K.A., Weiss, S.M., & Detre, T. (1984). Status of and prospects for stress, reactivity, and cardiovascular disease: Themes from the

NHLBI–University of Pittsburgh Working Conference. *Behavioral Medicine Update*, **6**(3), 7–9.

McCready, M.L., & Long, B.L. (1985). Locus of control, attitudes toward physical activity, and exercise adherence. *Journal of Sport Psychology*, **7**, 346–359.

Mechanic, D. (1979). The stability of health and illness behavior: Results from a 16-year follow-up. *American Journal of Public Health*, **69**, 1142–1145.

Melamed, B.G. (1980). Behavioral psychology in pediatrics. In S. Rachman (Ed.), *Contributions to medical psychology* (Vol. 2, pp. 255–288). Oxford, England: Pergamon Press.

Melamed, B.G., & Seigel, L.J. (1980). *Behavioral medicine: Practical applications in health care.* New York: Springer.

Meyer, A., Nash, J., McAlister, A., Maccoby, N., & Farquhar, J. (1980). Skills training in a cardiovascular health education campaign. *Journal of Consulting and Clinical Psychology*, **48**, 129–142.

Miller, P., Johnson, N.C., Wikoff, R., McMahan, M.F., & Garrett, M.J. (1983). Attitudes and regimen adherence of myocardial infarction and cardiac by-pass patients. *Journal of Cardiac Rehabilitation*, **3**, 541–548.

Mischel, W., & Mischel, H.N. (1976). A cognitive social-learning approach to morality and self-regulation. In T. Lickona (Eds.), *Moral development and behavior*. New York: Holt, Rinehart & Winston.

Montoye, H.J. (1986). Physical activity, physical fitness and heart disease risk factors in children. In G.A. Stull & H.M. Eckert (Eds.), *Effects of physical activity on children: American Academy of Physical Education papers*, **19**, 127–152. Champaign, IL: Human Kinetics.

Morgan, P.P., Shephard, R.J., & Finucane, R. (1984). Health beliefs and exercise habits in an employee fitness programme. *Canadian Journal of Applied Sport Sciences*, **9**(2), 87–93.

Morgan, W.P. (1977). Involvement in vigorous physical activity with special reference to adherence. In G.I. Gedvilas & M.E. Kneer (Eds.), *National College of Physical Education Association proceedings* (pp. 235–246). Chicago: University of Illinois Press.

Morgan, W.P. (1986). Athletes and nonathletes in the middle years of life. In B.D. McPherson (Ed.), *Sport and aging* (pp. 167–186). Champaign, IL: Human Kinetics.

Morgan, W.P., & Goldston, S.N. (Eds.). (1987). *Exercise and mental health.* Washington, DC: Hemisphere.

Murray, J.L., & Bruhn, J.G. (1983). Reliability of the MYTH scale in assessing Type A behavior in preschool children. *Journal of Human Stress*, 9(4), 23–28.

Natapoff, J.N. (1982). A developmental analysis of children's ideas of health. *Health Education Quarterly*, 9(2&3), 35–45.

Noland, M.P., & Feldman, R. (1984). Factors related to the leisure exercise behavior of "returning" women college students. *Health Education*, 15, 32–36.

Noland, M.P., & Feldman, R. (1985). An empirical investigation of leisure exercise behavior in adult women. *Health Education*, 16, 29–34.

Norman, R.M.G. (1986). *The nature and correlates of health behavior.* Health Promotion Studies Series No. 2. Health and Welfare, Ottawa, Canada.

Oldridge, N.B. (1982). Compliance and exercise in primary and secondary prevention of coronary heart disease: A review. *Preventive Medicine*, 11, 56–70.

Oldridge, N.B., & Spencer, J. (1985). Exercise habits and perceptions before and after graduation or dropout from supervised cardiac exercise rehabilitation. *Journal of Cardiopulmonary Rehabilitation*, 5, 313–319.

Oldridge, N.B., & Streiner, D.L. (1985). Health locus of control and compliance with cardiac exercise rehabilitation. *Medicine and Science in Sports and Exercise* (abstract), 17(2), 181.

Palmore, E. (1970). Health practices and illness among the aged. *The Gerontologist*, 1, 313–316.

Powell, K.E., & Dysinger, W. (1986). *Childhood sports and physical education as precursors of adult physical activity.* Unpublished manuscript, the Behavioral Epidemiology and Evaluation Branch, Centers for Disease Control, Atlanta, GA.

Prohaska, T., Keller, M., Leventhal, E., & Leventhal, H. (1983). *Health behaviors and beliefs across the adult lifespan.* Unpublished manuscript.

Research and Forecasts, Inc., (1983). *The Miller Lite report on American attitudes toward sports.* Milwaukee, WI: Miller Brewing Company.

Roberts, C.C., Maddux, J.E., & Wright, L. (1984). Developmental perspectives in behavioral health. In J.D. Matarazzo, S.M. Weiss, J.A. Herd, N.E. Miller, & S.M. Weiss (Eds.), *Behavioral health* (pp. 56–68). New York: Wiley Interscience.

Robinson, T., & Carron, A. (1982). Personal and situational factors associated with dropping out versus maintaining participation in competitive sport. *Journal of Sport Psychology*, 4, 364–378.

Rosenstock, I.M. (1974). Historical origins of the health belief model. *Health Education Monographs*, **2**(4), 1–9.

Safrit, M.J. (1986). Health-related fitness levels of American youth. In G.A. Stull & H.M. Eckert (Eds.), *Effects of physical activity on children: American Academy of Physical Education papers*, **19**, 153–166. Champaign, IL: Human Kinetics.

Sallis, J.F., Haskell, W.L., Fortmann, S.P., Vranizan, K.M., Taylor, C.B., & Solomon, D.S. (1986). Predictors of adoption and maintenance of physical activity in a community sample. *Preventive Medicine*, **15**, 331–341.

Sanne, H.M. (1973). Exercise tolerance and physical training of non-selected patients after myocardial infarction. *Acta Medica Scandinavica* (Suppl.), **551**, 1–124.

Saris, W.H.M., Binkhorst, R.A., Carmwinckel, A.B., van Waesberghe, F., & van der Veen-Hezemans, A.M. (1980). The relationship between working performance, daily physical activity, fatness, blood lipids and nutrition in school children. In K. Berg & B.O. Eriksson (Eds.), *Children and exercise IX* (pp. 166–174). Baltimore: University Park Press.

Schutz, R.W., Smoll, F.L., & Wood, T.M. (1981). A psychometric analysis of an inventory for assessing children's attitudes toward physical activity. *Journal of Sport Psychology*, **4**, 321–344.

Siegel, J.M. (1984). Anger and cardiovascular risk in adolescents. *Health Psychology*, **3**(4), 293–313.

Siscovick, D.S., LaPorte, R.E., & Newman, J.M. (1985). The disease specific benefits and risks of physical activity and exercise. *Public Health Reports*, **100**(2), 180–188.

Slenker, S.E., Price, J.H., & O'Connell, J.K. (1985). Health locus of control of joggers and nonexercisers. *Perceptual and Motor Skills*, **61**, 323–328.

Slenker, S.E., Price, J.H., Roberts, S.M., & Jurs, S.G. (1984). Joggers versus nonexercisers: An analysis of knowledge, attitudes and beliefs about jogging. *Research Quarterly for Exercise and Sport*, **4**, 371–378.

Smoll, F., & Schutz, R.W. (1980). Children's attitudes toward physical activity: A longitudinal analysis. *Journal of Sport Psychology*, **2**, 137–147.

Sonstroem, R.J. (1978). Physical estimation and attraction scales: Rationale and research. *Medicine and Science in Sports*, **10**, 97–102.

Sonstroem, R.J. (1984). Exercise and self-esteem. *Exercise and Sport Sciences Reviews*, **12**, 100–130.

Sonstroem, R.J., & Kampper, K.P. (1980). Prediction of athletic participation in middle school males. *Research Quarterly for Exercise and Sport*, **51**, 685–694.

Spady, D.W. (1980). Total daily energy expenditure of healthy, free ranging school children. *The American Journal of Clinical Nutrition,* **33,**
766–775.

Steele, D.J., Gutmann, M., Leventhal, H., & Easterling, D. (1983).
Symptoms and attributions of health behavior. Unpublished manuscript,
University of Wisconsin, Madison.

Stephens, T., Jacobs, D.R., & White, C.C. (1985). A descriptive epidemiology of leisure-time physical activity. *Public Health Reports,* **100**(2),
147–158.

Stull, G.A. (1986). Introduction. In G.A. Stull & H.M. Eckert (Eds.), *Effects
of physical activity on children: American Academy of Physical Education
papers,* **19,** 1. Champaign, IL: Human Kinetics.

Takanishi, R., DeLeon, P.H., & Pallak, M.S. (1984). Child health policy.
American Psychologist, **39,** 894–895.

Taylor, C.B., Sallis, J.F., & Needle, R. (1985). The relation of physical
activity and exercise to mental health. *Public Health Reports,* **100**(2),
195–202.

Telama, R., & Silvennoinen, M. (1979). Structure and development of
11- to 19-year-olds' motivation for physical activity. *Scandinavian Journal of Sports Science,* **1,** 23–31.

Thorland, W.G., & Gilliam, T.B. (1981). Comparison of serum lipids between habitually high and low active pre-adolescent males. *Medicine
and Science in Sports and Exercise,* **13,** 316–321.

Turk, D.C., Rudy, T.E., & Salovey, P. (1984). Health protection: Attitudes
and behaviors of LPNs, teachers, and college students. *Health Psychology,* **3**(3), 189–210.

Vaillant, G.E. (1979). Natural history of male psychologic health: Effects of
mental health on physical health. *New England Journal of Medicine,* **301,**
1249–1254.

Varni, J.W. (1983). *Clinical behavioral pediatrics, an interdisciplinary biobehavioral approach.* New York: Pergamon.

Wallace, J.P., McKenzie, T.L., & Nader, P.R. (1985). Observed vs. recalled
exercise behavior: A validation of a seven day exercise recall for boys
11 to 13 years old. *Research Quarterly for Exercise and Sport,* **56,** 161–165.

Wallston, K.A., Wallston, B.S., & DeVellis, M.R. (1978). Development of
a multi-dimensional health locus of control (MHLC) scale. *Health Education Monographs,* **6,** 160–170.

Walter, H.J., Hofman, A., Connelly, P.A., Barrett, L.T., & Kost, K.L.
(1986). Coronary heart disease prevention: One-year results of a ran-

domized intervention study. *American Journal of Preventive Medicine,* **2**(4), 239–245.

Wankel, L.M., & Kreisel, S.J. (1985a). Factors underlying enjoyment of youth sports: Sport and age group comparisons. *Journal of Sport Psychology,* **7**, 51–64.

Wankel, L.M., & Kreisel, S.J. (1985b). Methodological considerations in youth sport motivation research: A comparison of open-ended and paired comparison approaches. *Journal of Sport Psychology,* **7**, 65–74.

Wankel, L.M., Yardley, J.K., & Graham, J. (1985). The effects of motivational interventions upon the exercise adherence of high and low self-motivated adults. *Canadian Journal of Applied Sport Sciences,* **10**, 147–156.

Waxman, M., & Stunkard, A.J. (1980). Caloric intake and expenditure of obese boys. *The Journal of Pediatrics,* **96**(2), 187–193.

Widhalm, K., Maxa, E., & Zyman, H. (1978). Effect of diet and exercise upon the cholesterol and triglyceride content of plasma lipoproteins in overweight children. *European Journal of Pediatrics,* **127**, 121–126.

Williams, C.L., Carter, B.J., Arnold, C.B., & Wynder, E.L. (1979). Chronic disease risk factors among children: The "Know Your Body" study. *Journal of Chronic Diseases,* **32**, 505–513.

Wilmore, J.H., & McNamara, J.J. (1974). Prevalence of coronary heart disease risk factors in boys, 8 to 12 years of age. *Journal of Pediatrics,* **84**(4), 527–533.

Wilson, R.W., & Elinson, J. (1981). National survey of personal health practices and consequences: Background, conceptual issues, and selected findings. *Public Health Reports,* **96**, 213–225.

Wolf, T.M., Sklov, M.C., Wenzl, P.A., Hunter, S.M., & Berenson, G.S. (1982). Validation of a measure of Type A behavior pattern in children: Bogalusa heart study. *Child Development,* **53**, 126–135.

Zimmerman, R. (1983). *Preventive health attitudes and behaviors: A test of three models.* Unpublished doctoral dissertation, University of Wisconsin, Madison.

PART 3

Methods and Strategies for Behavior Intervention and Fitness Programming

Whereas Part 2 helped define psychological and behavioral targets that can be effectively changed to facilitate exercise adherence, this section outlines technologies for inducing, enabling, or supporting change. The papers describe various plans for practical intervention that may be best directed at behavioral deficiencies in factors such as knowledge, attitude, intentions, exercise skills, commitment, goal setting, environmental engineering, self-monitoring, and normative and self-reinforcement. Exercise-tested strategies as well as those based in principles from behavioral science are discussed.

Chapter 7

''Behavioral Management Techniques and Exercise Promotion'' by Dorothy N. Knapp provides a theoretically based beginning for a series of practical papers that outline feasible interventions for increasing exercise adherence. The paper discusses principles of behavior management and promotion programs applicable to clinical, worksite, and community exercise programs. Evidence from available exercise studies is examined, and the usefulness of the techniques for group settings and for personal exercise programs is explored. Both behavior modification and cognitive-behavior modification approaches are reviewed, including recent work on relapse prevention planning in health behavior change. Practical examples illustrate the uniqueness of these approaches in helping to explain and control habitual exercise behavior among previously sedentary and low-active individuals. The potential for generalizing across clinical, corporate, community, and personal exercise programs is described.

Chapter 8

"Program Factors That Influence Exercise Adherence: Practical Adherence Skills for the Clinical Staff" by Barry A. Franklin augments chapter 7. It describes the skills an exercise specialist must possess to facilitate exercise adherence in a way that complements standard clinical exercise physiology skills to ensure a safe and biologically effective plan for exercise. In this regard the chapter provides an overview of newly established American College of Sports Medicine certification categories against a background of sound fitness and safety principles. This information is augmented by a discussion of common educational-exercise skill development packages and staff-originated reinforcement strategies that appear to be clinically effective for increasing adherence.

Chapter 9

Although exercise guidelines are well established for ensuring safe and substantial gains in fitness, much less is known about the type, intensity, frequency, and duration that promotes health and fitness but also optimizes behavioral adherence. "Prescribing Exercise for Fitness and Adherence" by Michael L. Pollock discusses the likely impact of training dosage and activity forms on adherence. It specifically considers the clinical use of perceived exertion as a training variable that can assist exercise planners in tailoring intensity to the biomedical needs and behavioral preferences of participants.

CHAPTER 7

Behavioral Management Techniques and Exercise Promotion

Dorothy N. Knapp

This chapter presents strategies for the promotion of exercise derived from psychological research, theory and experience in behavior change, as well as available studies of exercise. Although a relatively powerful and flexible technology for behavior change has been developed, the application of many techniques to the area of exercise promotion is not yet adequately tested.

The acquisition of habits of increased physical activity is viewed as a process with three stages: (a) the decision to start exercising, (b) the early stages of behavior change, and (c) maintenance of the new behavior. Strategies deriving from different theoretical models will be described.

Decision to Initiate Exercise

In 1978 it was estimated that only about one-third of adults in the United States exercised regularly (Harris, 1979). Data on adherence suggest that many of these individuals subsequently failed to adhere to their exercise (Dishman, 1987). Regular exercise is not a normative expectation in the way that other aspects of personal hygiene are (e.g., taking regular baths, brushing one's hair, etc.). Naturally occurring social and material contingencies are not sufficient to shape and maintain regular exercise. Therefore, in order for most individuals to increase their physical activity, either mass change is needed concerning normative expectations, social and material contingencies, and developmental experiences with exercise or the individual must make a conscious decision to increase physical activity despite unfavorable socioenvironmental influences.

Mass change has been attempted through media campaigns, and so forth, with disappointing results, probably due to emphasis upon educational approaches rather than behavior change (Godin & Shephard, 1983). One exception may be the Pawtuckett Heart Health Program currently in progress, which incorporates sound behavioral and social psychological principles in an attempt to alter the health behavior of the community (Lasater et al., 1984; Lefebvre, in press; Lefebvre, Lasater, Carleton, & Peterson, 1986). Until effective mass change strategies are validated, however, strategies aimed at individuals and small groups must attempt to fill the gap. The process begins with facilitating the decision to increase physical activity.

A common strategy used in attempting to facilitate such a decision is to educate individuals and groups about the health benefits of exercise, particularly the reduced risk of cardiovascular disease. Many individuals who begin an exercise regimen state that they do so for health reasons (e.g., Mann, Garrett, Farhi, Murray, & Murray, 1969; Martin et al., 1984). This may simply be a learned response that is socially acceptable and reinforced but that may not reflect the actual influences that lead to the decision to exercise. For example, exercise may be undertaken for cosmetic or social reasons, as in health clubs serving as singles meeting places (Becker, 1984; "Perfect! Coed Health," 1983). Furthermore, belief in the health benefits of exercise is very common among exercisers and nonexercisers alike, with little apparent impact on behavior (Andrew & Parker, 1979). Nonetheless, some individuals may be assisted to decide to increase their physical activity for health reasons. The health beliefs model (Becker, 1976) and the self-regulatory model of health behavior and beliefs (Leventhal, Meyer, & Gutmann, 1980; Leventhal, Meyer, & Nerenz, 1980; Leventhal, Zimmerman, & Gutmann, 1984; Meyer, Leventhal, & Gutmann, 1985) have implications for how this might be accomplished.

Health Belief Model

The health belief model states that readiness to undertake a regimen such as exercise depends upon motivations (e.g., concern about health, willingness to accept direction), evaluation of the illness threat (e.g., subjective estimates of susceptibility, possible bodily harm and interference with social role, symptoms), and subjective estimates of the probability that compliance will reduce the threat (based on perceived safety and efficacy of the regimen.) Various other factors modify or enable compliance, including demographic factors (e.g., age), structural factors (e.g., cost, complexity, side effects), attitudes (e.g., satisfaction with visit), interaction factors (e.g., mutuality of expectations and agreement between professional and client), and enabling factors (e.g., previous experience with regimen, social pressure).

Self-Regulatory Model

The self-regulatory model of health behavior and beliefs assumes that individuals respond to communications and problems related to their health according to their commonsense understanding of the nature, causes, and treatment of the problem. Their understanding is based not only on abstract, intellectual information such as the increase in statistical risk for cardiac disease with inactivity but also, and what's more important, on concrete inputs such as symptoms and previous experience with the health problem. Ensuing self-regulation involves following two areas that occur simultaneously and are at times in conflict: (a) regulation of disease, health, or physical state; and (b) regulation of affect (e.g., fear).

To give an example, an aspiring exercise promoter might tell a middle-aged, sedentary man that his physical inactivity increases his risk of heart attack. The promoter hopes and expects that the man will respond to the message by increasing his exercise (regulating his physical state). The sedentary man, on the other hand, might reflect on his and his peers' past and current apparent good health and fail to perceive himself as vulnerable. Any affect aroused by the mention of risk might be dealt with by avoidance of any further discussion of the topic. Unless some other influence can be brought to bear, this gentleman is likely to remain sedentary. One implication of the self-regulatory model is that fear and/or personal vulnerability messages must be titrated carefully, so that the affect induced is sufficient to motivate response without overwhelming the individual such that the message is turned off. One method by which this may be accomplished is to simultaneously offer a response that the individual may use to decrease risk, such as joining a program "for individuals like you who wish to reduce their cardiac risk," or recommending a specific home exercise regimen.

Implications

Individuals will be more likely to decide to comply with a recommended regimen if the following conditions apply:

- They feel vulnerable to the condition targeted for prevention (personal vulnerability)
- They believe that the consequences of the condition would be bad and so wish to avoid that condition (reinforcement salience or efficacy)
- They believe that the recommended regimen will be effective (response efficacy)
- They believe the side effects (risks and disadvantages) of the regimen do not outweigh its benefits (favorable cost-benefit analysis)
- They believe they can perform the regimen (self-efficacy)

The common health educational approach to exercise promotion attempts to educate individuals about exercise's efficacy in reducing cardiovascular risk. However, none of the following are addressed: individuals' perceived personal vulnerability to cardiovascular or other health problems, their motivation to avoid the health problems to which they feel vulnerable, their analysis of the advantages and disadvantages of exercise, or their self-efficacy with regard to exercise. Education alone regarding potential health benefits is thus generally ineffective.

Furthermore, perceived personal vulnerability may be a key factor limiting the utility of health benefits arguments in the general public even when such arguments are modified to appropriately address other important aspects of the decision to comply with recommendations to exercise. Belief in the health benefits of exercise, as well as education designed to engender such beliefs, has not been consistently associated with behavior change except in individuals where there is evidence of a health deficiency or correctable disability, such as cardiac patients (Andrew et al., 1981; Dishman, 1982). Most individuals think of themselves as relatively invulnerable to major health problems. It may be neither possible nor desirable to increase the collective sense of personal vulnerability suffi-ciently to increase exercise through arguments for its preventive health benefits alone.

Decision-Making Model

The model of health behavior and beliefs may be viewed as a special case of a broader self-regulatory or decision-making model of behavior change similar to that proposed by Bandura (1977). This model considers situations where the anticipated reinforcing consequences of behavior change are not limited to, and may not even involve, avoidance or allevia-tion of ill health. For example, individuals may anticipate that exercise participation may lead to fun interactions with other exercisers, increased ability to participate in desired activities such as sports, and increased mobility. They may also expect that exercise will result in improved ap-pearance, maintenance of a successful image, and opportunities to inter-act with individuals who may significantly affect one's career. Exercise may also decrease tension and provide time-out from stressful or un-pleasant situations. In addition, individuals may look forward to the op-portunity to compete, the opportunity to participate in postgame beer drinking, facilitation of fantasies of sexual desirability and prowess, or any number of other outcomes unrelated to health. This broader model of decision making and behavior change states that individuals will be more likely to attempt a behavior change such as increasing physical ac-tivity if they desire the promised outcome, believe that the proposed be-havior change will accomplish it, and perceive no easier or more attractive way to achieve the desired outcome. Other factors previously discussed, notably self-efficacy, also apply.

The discussion implies that the promotion of exercise will be more effectively accomplished through realistic emphasis of a variety of desir-able outcomes as opposed to health benefits alone. Education will also be more effective to the degree that it can be individually tailored to em-phasize outcomes that the individual desires, and, perhaps, to enhance personal vulnerability as appropriate.

Strategies to Facilitate Decisions to Initiate Exercise

In addition to education, decision-making procedures and strategies to promote self-efficacy may facilitate the decision to increase physical activity. They include the decision balance sheet and decision matrix, modeling, and behavior rehearsal.

Decision-Making Procedures.   The use of a decision balance sheet procedure (Hoyt & Janis, 1975; Wankel, 1984) has been studied in relation to exercise decisions and participation, with results suggesting its utility in improving participation in exercise clubs or classes. The procedure may promote awareness of potential benefits and costs that are salient to the individual and reveal other factors of importance such as personal vulnerability. The procedure involves asking the individual to write down the anticipated consequences of exercise participation in terms of (a) gains to self, (b) losses to self, (c) gains to important others, (d) losses to important others, (e) approval from others, (f) disapproval from others, (g) self-approval, and (h) self-disapproval.

No studies were found in which this technique was used to facilitate a decision to increase physical activity by sedentary individuals who had not already volunteered for an exercise class albeit one study used new members of such a class (Hoyt & Janis, 1975).

A similar procedure, the decision matrix, is described by Marlatt and Gordon (1985) for use with clients attempting to change health-related behaviors such as smoking. In this procedure the individual is asked to list anticipated consequences of both undertaking and adhering to the desired behavior change (exercise) and of failing to achieve the desired behavior change (remaining sedentary). Individuals are asked to generate responses to short- and long-term, positive and negative consequences of (a) regular participation in exercise and (b) not participating in or dropping out of regular exercise. The therapist and client discuss the responses, and the therapist assists the client in devising ways to avoid or cope with the negative consequences of the desired behavior change and reducing positive outcomes of failure or providing alternate means of attaining such outcomes. Although Marlatt's decision matrix procedure has not been studied with regard to exercise promotion or adherence, it has the advantages of differentiating between short- and long-term consequences as well as making the individual consider the consequences of failure to initiate or adhere to desired behavior change.

The open and nonjudgmental use of such techniques allows aspects of the individual's decision making to be more explicit and available for education and intervention and provides valuable information for facilitating behavior change. The decision matrix is also a useful tool for relapse prevention, which will be discussed later.

Self-Efficacy Enhancement Strategies.   Self-efficacy (Bandura, 1977), the belief that one can perform a particular response, is a function of past learning and perceptions of the response required. Although giving a clear, specific, and realistic description of the physical activity expected and correcting misperceptions are helpful approaches, effective modeling and behavioral rehearsal are two especially powerful techniques for enhancing self-efficacy.

Modeling is most effective when the model is similar to the individual and successfully performs the activity. The deconditioned 65-year-old cardiac patient will find the sight of other senior cardiac patients exercising more reassuring than observing the young, fit, and trim exercise leaders demonstrating the expected activity. Other examples are obese housewives in their 40s who feel they cannot keep up with the slender, athletic 20-year-olds and busy Type A executives who feel that the demands of their position do not allow the time for exercise that people in less prestigious positions might have.

In behavioral rehearsal the individual performs the exercise in a manner that maximizes success and allows reinforcing feedback. Ewart, Taylor, Reese, and DeBusk (1983) found that exercise testing performed early in the postmyocardial infarction period led to increased perceived self-efficacy with regard to similar physical activities (e.g., walking, running, stair climbing) and that exercise intensity and duration at home were more highly correlated with self-efficacy than with peak heart rate. Among individuals with low pretest self-efficacy scores, those who performed well on the exercise test had larger increases in self-efficacy than those who did less well, and individuals with high pretest self-efficacy who performed less well on the test tended to have decreased self-efficacy. These results illustrate the importance of assuring a successful experience with the sample exercise.

Behavior Change and Habit Acquisition

Neither intention, willpower, commitment, nor knowledge will be adequate by themselves to change a sedentary lifestyle to an active one. Exercise, like other behaviors, is influenced by biological factors (e.g., cardiorespiratory fitness, percent fat, disease states), psychological factors (e.g., emotional status, problem-solving skills, attitudes), and the environment. Of these three, the environment is usually the most amenable to manipulation.

Enduring behavior patterns are sustained because they are cued and reinforced by aspects of the environment: antecedent → behavior → consequence. The basic strategy in successfully modifying one's habits is to make environmental changes to support the desired behavior and to weaken competing behaviors. Three places in the behavior chain to make changes are (a) the behavioral antecedents or cues, using stimulus control techniques; (b) the behavior itself, using, for example, skill training (or an exercise prescription); and (c) the behavioral consequences, using contingency management, contracting, and so forth.

Behavioral Antecedents

Habitual behaviors are cued by aspects of the mental, social, and/or physical environment. The sight and smell of food is a powerful cue to eat for most people. Hearing the alarm clock may be a cue to go running for a habitual morning runner. The sight of the television after work is a cue for many to sit for the rest of the evening. Differentiating between cues for desired behaviors and those for competing behaviors is important for changing behavior. In promoting exercise the goal is to increase a low-frequency behavior. Therefore, although there may be many cues for competing behaviors, there are few effective cues for exercise in the lives of sedentary individuals. An appropriate strategy is to build on and increase such cues.

Increasing Exercise Cues.   The more often and consistently a behavior such as exercise occurs in a particular stimulus situation, the more powerful a cue the stimulus situation will become. Keefe and Blumenthal (1980) instructed their subjects who had chronic problems with exercise maintenance to exercise at the same time and in a similar location each day and to engage in a consistent warm-up before exercise. All 3 subjects were still exercising consistently at a high level at the 2 year follow-up. Undergraduate females who performed a low-frequency activity prior to working out increased their exercise more than controls who did not pair exercise with another activity but also more than subjects who performed a high-frequency activity prior to the workout or either kind of activity after (Nelson, Haynes, Spong, Jarrett, & McKnight, 1983). Nelson and her colleagues interpret this finding in terms of cuing; low-frequency activities were more powerful cues because they were more salient than high-frequency activities.

Self-monitoring, the keeping of records of one's exercise, may also serve a cuing function particularly when such records are posted in a visible place or encountered regularly. Nelson et al. (1983) found that subjects who simply self-monitored their exercise increased their exercise more than all other groups except those who did low-frequency activities prior to exercise.

In another study using stimulus control techniques (Lipsker, 1983) adults in a community exercise program who were instructed to prepare for the class the night before, post printed reminders, and enlist the aid of a significant person in providing additional reminders increased their attendance over baseline. They also attended more frequently and regularly than their nonstudy counterparts although whether or not the latter were randomly assigned to be control subjects is not clear.

The time, place, and people involved in an exercise program will come to be cues for exercise for those who adhere to the program. Unfortunately, when the program is over most of the exercise cues are withdrawn. To expect people to continue to exercise following sudden withdrawal of their cues for exercise is naive; nevertheless, a frequent strategy for increasing physical activity is to involve individuals in an exercise class or program of finite duration. One way to deal with this problem is to build into the program strategies to generalize stimulus control of exercise to other settings prior to cessation of the program. Martin et al. (1984) attempted this by meeting for exercise with their subjects twice weekly and requiring a third-day, outside-of-class run, which was self-monitored and potentially verifiable by a third person. Other approaches that avoid this problem altogether are shaping exercise on one's own (Atkins, Kaplan, Timms, Reinsch, & Lofback, 1984; Keefe & Blumenthal, 1980; King & Frederiksen, 1984) and/or encouraging participation in an ongoing exercise facility, such as the YMCA. One may also make more informal lifestyle changes in physical activity instead of formal programmatic exercise (Epstein, Koeske, & Wing, 1984; Epstein, Wing, Koeske, Ossip, & Beck, 1982).

Decreasing Cues for Competing Behaviors.   Another aspect of stimulus control is decreasing cues for competing or problematic behaviors. This is a crucial part of efforts to reduce or eliminate high frequency problematic behaviors such as smoking and alcohol/drug abuse. Its role in increasing exercise may be somewhat less but should be considered. Examples of this strategy include choosing an exercise time and place in which one is less likely to be tempted by cues of other behaviors. A morning exercise time has the advantage for many people that social and work activities rarely compete. This might be an especially helpful time for Type A individuals with high job commitment, who might be vulnerable to cues to continue working rather than taking the time to exercise. For individuals who exercise after work, it may be helpful to carry exercise clothing in the car rather than planning to pick it up at home, where one might be distracted by the television, one's family, or the easy chair, and to plan a route that does not pass such competing cues as one's favorite bar or restaurant.

Behavioral Consequences

Behavior is determined predominantly, at least during the habit acquisition stage, by its immediate consequences. But even though many positive consequences may eventually occur with regular exercise and many negative consequences are attendant upon inactivity, these are not effective in shaping or maintaining exercise. Consequences that occur during or closely following a behavior will be much more powerful influences than those that do not occur until sometime in the distant future.

Two kinds of behavioral consequences are reinforcers and punishers. Reinforcers *increase* the likelihood that the behavior will be repeated in similar circumstances. Punishers, on the other hand, *decrease* the likelihood that the behavior will be repeated in similar circumstances. Note that the kind of consequence is determined by its actual effect on the behavior it follows, not whether it appears desirable or undesirable. For example, negative attention given to punish and eliminate an undesired behavior may actually serve to reinforce it, particularly in an individual who receives little attention for any other behavior.

Punishment. In general, punishment alone, without simultaneous reward for alternate behavior, is ineffective in eliminating a high-frequency, undesired behavior although it can be very effective in sabotaging attempts to build a new, desired habit. The elimination or reduction of naturally-occurring punishing consequences of increased physical activity will be essential.

Punishing consequences of increased physical activity certainly occur. In fact, exercise itself has been used effectively as a punishing consequence (Luce, Delquadri, & Hall, 1980). New exercisers are subject to boredom, discomfort, fatigue, muscle soreness, and injuries; to shame and embarrassment at bodily exposure; to anxiety about time taken away from work or family; to foregoing pleasurable activities; to real and imagined negative attention from those more fit than they; to ridicule, harassment, hostility, and even fears for their personal safety. Those who most need to increase their physical activity and who may be most subject to such punishing consequences are (a) the very unfit, (b) the obese, (c) older individuals, and (d) Type A individuals (Dishman & Gettman, 1980; Oldridge, 1982).

Intervention at the level of the behavior itself in the form of an individualized exercise prescription and education regarding appropriate exercise may be helpful in reducing discomfort, muscle soreness, fatigue, and injuries. Cognitive restructuring to eliminate maladaptive self-talk (e.g., "I wish I wasn't doing this! I'm so tired! Why does exercise have to feel bad?") (Atkins et al., 1984) and training in cognitive strategies such as dissociation (Martin et al., 1984) are likely to reduce perceived discomfort during exercise, and both strategies have been found to improve adherence. Dissociative strategies (the use of coping thoughts and distraction through focusing on the external environment rather than bodily sensations and the exercise itself) have also been associated with improved maintenance of exercise after the termination of a formal exercise class (Martin et al., 1984).

Flexibility in available exercise times and care in the choice of a regular exercise time may serve to reduce conflicts with family and work time and pleasure activities. Improved availability of attractive exercise clothing in larger sizes, exercising with others of similar fitness levels, body size, age, and so on, and consistent adoption by exercise leaders of that quality which in psychotherapy is referred to as unconditional positive regard may all help to reduce shame, embarrassment, and perceived negative attention. Choosing and making available exercise locations that are reasonably safe and that avoid contact with animal and human harassment and hostility are also important.

Reinforcement.   Two kinds of reinforcers exist, positive and negative. Both increase the probability that the behavior they follow will be repeated. Positive reinforcers involve the presentation of a stimulus or event during or following a behavior. These are also sometimes called rewards. Negative reinforcers are ongoing stimuli or events that are withdrawn during or following the behavior.

Negative reinforcement is not the same as punishment although the terms are often confused. An example of a behavior that is negatively reinforced is turning off an alarm clock; the reinforcement is the cessation of the noise. Negative reinforcement commonly involves escape from an aversive or unpleasant situation or stimulus and when it is repeated it may lead to learning avoidance behavior.

Examples from everyday human interactions include critical remarks, suggestions, threats, and reminders that the potential exerciser experiences as aversive nagging. Unfortunately, such strategies seldom produce exercise adherence because an easy way to escape the nagging is simply to avoid the person who is doing it.

Positive reinforcement, on the other hand, is absolutely crucial. Many repetitions of physical activity in the presence of a new cue are required, as previously discussed, before that cue will be effective in the absence of reinforcement. In order for the necessary number of repetitions to occur, the behavior must be reinforced (i.e., the person must get something out of it now).

Furthermore, behaviors such as exercise frequently involve a series or chain of individual behaviors (e.g., traveling to the exercise location, entering the locker room, putting on exercise clothing, warming up, exercising, cooling down, etc.). In general, the longer the chain of behaviors prior to reinforcement, the less likely it is for reinforcement to occur. Reinforcement for individual parts of the behavior chain will thus be needed initially, and longer behavior chains will require more shaping.

The forms that positive reinforcement takes vary considerably and often do not look especially like rewards. Simple feedback may serve as a reinforcer. Watching the miles mount on an odometer or pedometer may result in an individual biking or walking more. Keeping a cumulative chart of exercise behavior and having a goal against which the record may be favorably compared may make this feedback a more powerful reinforcer. Goal-setting and self-monitoring can thus be important aspects of reinforcement of exercise either directly or by eliciting reinforcing cognitions in the exerciser and (if posted) favorable attention from others.

To be most helpful, goals need to be specific and behavioral and must state what one actually needs to do to achieve them. For example, "I'm going to be more active" and "I'm going to reduce my resting heart rate to 60 beats per minute" are not helpful goals; the first is not specific and the second is not behavioral. "I'm going to take three 30-minute walks this week" and "I'm going to ride 20 miles this week" are more helpful, assuming they are also realistic and achievable. Keefe and Blumenthal (1980) had their subjects set distance goals for the week that were not more than a 10% increase in the distance walked the previous week, so goals would be specific and achievable.

Although self-monitoring is frequently described as a reactive measure for its effect of producing behavior change in a desired direction (e.g., reduced food intake in the obese, reduced smoking) and even though it is commonly included in studies of behavioral interventions to increase exercise, no study was found of the effects on physical activity of goal-setting and self-monitoring or of self-monitoring alone. Oldridge and Jones (1983) studied the effect of a written agreement and self-monitoring on compliance in cardiac exercise rehabilitation. Experimental subjects were asked to sign a written agreement to participate in the program for 6 months (76% signed) and were given graphs for plotting heart rates obtained in submaximal exercise testing performed once per month. They were also asked to complete a 24-hour recall questionnaire of daily activities on 6 randomly chosen days each month. This procedure differs from the more usual behavioral self-monitoring in which behavior itself, rather than physiological indices, is consistently recorded. Therefore, the procedure of Oldridge and Jones may be more useful for plotting physiological progress than behavioral achievements. Experimental and control subjects did not differ in attendance.

The results of two studies indicate that the effects of self-monitoring on exercise behavior can be improved upon by the addition of other behavioral strategies. Nelson et al. (1983) found that self-monitoring subjects who cued their exercise by performing another salient activity first did more exercise than those utilizing self-monitoring alone. Keefe and Blumenthal (1980) found that adding goal-setting, stimulus control procedures, and self-reinforcement to the baseline self-monitoring of their subjects led to substantially increased and sustained exercise over a follow-up period of 2 years.

Both of these studies purported to use self-reinforcement, but the procedures differed significantly. Nelson et al. instructed subjects in their self-reinforcement group to engage in a high-frequency, enjoyed behavior after exercise. This procedure resulted in the group doing *less* exercise than any of the other groups. Keefe and Blumenthal had their subjects complete the Reinforcement Survey Schedule (Cautela & Kastenbaum, 1967) and then list 10 potentially rewarding stimuli to use as self-reinforcement. Subjects were encouraged to select physical and material rewards relevant to exercise, such as running shoes, and then instructed to set exercise criterion levels for self-administration of the rewards. The investigators report that the subjects relied heavily upon these rewards initially but that the self-reinforcement procedure appeared less important as time went on. By the 2-year follow-up, subjects reported no longer using the procedure ''because they found exercise itself to be rewarding'' (Keefe & Blumenthal, 1980, p. 33). In addition to receiving more intrinsic or natural reinforcing consequences from their exercise and fewer punishing consequences as a function of greater fitness, exercise time and setting and other frequently encountered stimuli may have become strong cues for exercise.

Material reinforcement strategies can also be administered by the staff. This has the advantage that the reinforcement may be more likely to be administered when earned, with the bonus of social attention and praise that may serve as further reinforcement. However, it has the potential disadvantage of being less individually tailored. Some people may just not like T-shirts with road-runners on them. Exercise investigators (e.g., Epstein, Wing, Thompson, & Griffin, 1980) have found that an attendance lottery improves exercise attendance when compared with a control group. However, if exercise is already richly reinforced, attendance lotteries may not provide further improvement. Martin et al. (1984) found that an attendance lottery did not improve attendance in an exercise program already rich in social reinforcement in the form of personal feedback. Controlled studies of the impact on physical activity of material reinforcement contingencies alone, other than attendance lotteries, were not found.

Either self-reinforcement or staff administered reinforcement contingencies may be specified in a written contract. Behavioral contracts typically specify the behavior expected and may also specify stimulus control strategies to be implemented as well as consequences. A behavioral contract should make behavioral goals and any contingencies explicit and is typically signed by a witness in addition to the client.

Several studies have used behavioral contracts as part of interventions to increase exercise behavior (Atkins et al., 1984; Epstein et al., 1982; Epstein et al., 1980; Kau & Fischer, 1974; Wysocki, Hall, Iwata, & Riordan, 1979). For example, Epstein et al. (1980) found that weekly attendance contracts ($1 deposit return) significantly improved attendance, and Wysocki et al. (1979) found that contracting for aerobic points to earn back deposited personal items led 7 of 12 subjects to greatly increase aerobic points earned. In general, results tend to be encouraging for initial attendance or adherence but less so in terms of longer term improvement. Nonetheless, as Dishman (1987) points out, strategies that enhance initial involvement may be important if they help to provide the time and necessary behavioral repetitions for other strategies and factors to work.

A disadvantage of formal written contracts and staff-administered material reinforcement strategies is that they are dependent upon someone who will not always be there. Although clients can continue to contract with themselves or with family or friends, no study has attempted to teach this, and how long such a behavior would be maintained by the majority of clients is questionable. Further, individuals may be inclined to attribute their continuing exercise to the reinforcement, the staff, the contract, or the program rather than to themselves. Such attributions can be detrimental to the maintenance of positive behavior change after an intervention is over. In addition, material reinforcement that goes beyond what is necessary to maintain a behavior (as when behavior is already adequately sustained by other contingencies such as social enjoyment) may be counterproductive. Such manipulations may turn what was play into work, which is discontinued when the formerly unnecessary material reinforcers are withdrawn (Barnett, 1980; Halliwell, 1979; Kleiber, 1981; Parkhouse, 1980; Watson, 1976). Nonetheless, material reinforcement contingencies have been shown to be very helpful in the early stages of health behavior change, including exercise. Using such strategies only when needed (as they frequently are initially), gradual fading of the material reinforcement, and efforts toward promoting more natural reinforcements that will be more likely to continue are strategies for avoiding these problems.

One very important natural reinforcer is social reinforcement, which may take the form of verbal feedback, praise and encouragement, attention, or simply the opportunity for interaction. However, social interactions that are intended as positive can sometimes function as punishment. For example, obese persons can be exquisitely sensitive to simply being seen by slender, athletic, and attractive exercisers, let alone being selected for attention, and encouragements such as "that's okay, you're doing the best you can" are seldom helpful.

The concept of social support is related to but not identical with social reinforcement. Social support usually refers to a favorable attitude on the part of significant others (especially the spouse) toward an individual's exercise program. Spouse support is frequently associated with better compliance with exercise programs (Andrew et al., 1981; Erling & Oldridge, 1985; Knapp, Gutmann, Squires, & Pollock, 1983), which leads some to experiment with involving the spouse in cardiac rehabilitation programs (Erling & Oldridge, 1985). On the other hand, a recent national survey indicated that only about one-third of regular exercisers had an active spouse. In a related finding (Shephard & Cox, 1980) men with a high number of recent stressful life events in their personal and family life were *more* likely to continue their participation in an industrial fitness program, suggesting that a high need for adjustment to home and family changes was associated with high exercise participation. Shephard and Cox suggested, among other possibilities, that exercise may serve as an escape from domestic problems.

Social and family interactions may influence physical activity in many different ways. Spouses, family members, and friends may cue exercise through verbal reminders. Those who are themselves exercisers may model and cue physical activity by their behavior as well as (potentially) reinforce it by providing companionship during the exercise. They may alter the family routine and give tacit permission for the individual to take time away from family activities to exercise. They may also give practical assistance such as providing transportation, measuring exercise routes, providing exercise clothing and equipment, and so on. Effective social support may thus include stimulus cuing and reduction of punishing consequences as well as provision of social reinforcement. Many families of cardiac patients will attempt to provide these kinds of positive social support to help reduce the likelihood of another cardiac event. Families of nonpatients may be less likely to make such changes to support an individual's attempts to increase physical activity.

In a study of interventions to promote exercise adherence, King and Frederiksen (1984) used strategies designed to increase social support in half of their subjects. These subjects were assigned to jogging groups of 3 or 4 members, instructed to jog with at least 1 group member throughout the study, and took part in team-building exercises to increase group cohesiveness. These strategies (without the relapse prevention training received by half the subjects, to be described later) resulted in increased exercise during the 5-week study period compared with controls although this effect was not sustained in the follow-up period. Such strategies may be useful in the early stages of an exercise program.

Martin et al. (1984) encouraged their subjects to run in pairs or small groups and had instructors run with the subjects and converse with them. They further increased the social reinforcement available to half of the subjects in their first study by giving them personalized, immediate feedback about their running and praise for adherence during the run whereas the other half of the subjects received feedback and praise directed at the group after all had completed their exercise for the day. Personalized, immediate feedback, rather than group feedback, was associated with better class attendance and better maintenance of exercise at 3-month follow-up.

Summary of Behavior Change Strategies

Several basic strategies for achieving behavior change have been discussed, and examples have been given. It is recommended that two basic strategies, negative reinforcement and punishment, be avoided. Further, decreasing or removing punishment for the desired behavior is important. Basic strategies that are recommended are stimulus control and positive reinforcement. Stimulus control involves (a) increasing cues for desired behaviors and (b) decreasing cues for undesired or competing behaviors. Self-monitoring is an example. Effective reinforcement for behavior change involves (a) increasing positive reinforcement for desired behavior and (b) decreasing positive reinforcement for undesired or competing behaviors. Techniques to increase positive reinforcement include goal setting, self-monitoring, material rewards, self-reinforcement, and social support.

Maintenance of Exercise

In discussing the maintenance of a new habit of exercise or some other form of increased physical activity, four general areas include (a) prevention of extinction of behavior, (b) attribution of change and self-control strategies, (c) the concept of self-motivation, and (d) Marlatt's relapse model and prevention strategies.

Prevention of Extinction

Learning theory indicates that extinction of a new behavior occurs when the behavior is punished or when the reinforcements and cues maintaining the behavior are withdrawn, as when the program is over. Behavior may also decrease in frequency, at least temporarily, when the individual is satiated by the reinforcement. Therefore, punishing consequences must be reduced and reinforcing consequences continued for physical activity to be maintained.

Experimental studies of learning have also shown that certain kinds of reinforcement schedules, called lean, variable ratio reinforcement schedules, will render behavior more resistant to extinction in the face of lack of reinforcement. The procedure for accomplishing this is to start shaping the behavior with a rich schedule of reinforcement and then, after the behavior is established, *gradually* to reduce the frequency and regularity of reinforcement while maintaining stimulus cuing. Phenomenologically, the individual continues to perform the desired behavior at a high rate; he or she knows that reinforcement is forthcoming but not when. Such a fading strategy is likely to be a useful way to deal with reinforcers that are needed initially but cannot be continued at the same high rate. Gambling addiction provides a good example of the effectiveness of variable ratio reinforcement. The individual graduates from frequent wins at the nickel slot machines to fewer wins at other games, but the high rate of gambling behavior is sustained.

Attribution and Self-Control Strategies

Attribution of positive change in physical activity to things outside of oneself (e.g., the exercise class, the staff) is detrimental to maintenance of behavior after such external influences are withdrawn. One strategy for dealing with this problem is to teach the individual self-control strategies. This involves teaching individuals to self-apply behavior modification strategies such as self-monitoring, goal setting, self-reinforcement, stimulus control, social engineering, problem solving, and so on.

A self-control approach does not obviate the need for external cuing and reinforcement—indeed, the individual is likely to need coaching and reinforcement in the process of learning to effectively apply self-control strategies. Rather, the individual learns to arrange for external cuing and reinforcement as well as for self-cuing and self-reinforcement. In the process, the individual learns skills and strategies that will remain after the formal intervention is over. Such individuals are less dependent upon an external program, or, more accurately, they become more effective and flexible relative to their dependency upon external supports and capable of arranging new environmental supports when old ones terminate.

Self-Motivation

Constructs such as motivation or self-motivation are too often invoked in a circular manner (e.g., "Subjects did not comply with the exercise program because they lacked motivation." "How do you know they lacked motivation?" "They didn't stick with the program."). In contrast, Dishman and his colleagues have devised an instrument to measure self-motivation that is conceived as a relatively enduring, trait-like "behavioral tendency to persevere independent of situational reinforcements" (Dishman & Ickes, 1981, p. 421). Self-motivation, as assessed by Dishman's Self-Report Questionnaire, has been found to relate to adherence to exercise or sport training in several studies although the relationship is sometimes weak (Dishman & Ickes, 1981; Dishman, Ickes, & Morgan, 1980; Gale, Eckhoff, Mogel, & Rodnick, 1984; Knapp, Gutmann, Foster, & Pollock, 1984, 1985; Snyder, Franklin, Foss, & Rubenfire, 1982; Ward & Morgan, 1984). A comprehensive discussion of this topic is provided by Sonstroem in chapter 5. However, a few comments seem in order at this point.

The exact nature of the behavioral tendency to persevere and of what is being measured by Dishman's questionnaire is not yet clearly defined. To be consistent with the data, however, it may be useful to hypothesize that self-motivation is a learned set of skills and habitual responses that function to assist individuals to adhere to activities that are not adequately cued and reinforced by the environment or that may even be punished. The influence of self-motivation is thus more likely to be observed in situations where cuing and reinforcement are not sufficient by themselves to maintain a behavior to which an individual is committed.

The specific skills and habits that may be involved are not yet known, but they may include problem solving, skills in self-reinforcement, or simply the propensity to plan behavior in a regular schedule in order to strengthen stimulus control. Verbal commitments for such individuals may more strongly cue the relevant behavior (i.e., the person may not have had repeated failure experiences or encountered models that would weaken verbal commitments as a cue to behavior). Perhaps persons scoring high in self-motivation have not yet learned how to state intentions for the social reinforcement they receive but not to follow through with behavior, a propensity that seems reflected in high scores on the Sociable Style scale of Millon's Behavioral Health Inventory. High scores on this scale have been found to be associated with early dropout from an exercise program (Knapp, 1986). Individuals high in self-motivation may have a greater desire for closure—incompletion of intention leads to tension that is relieved by following through. They may also lack negative emotional response and self-blame for lapses. Such hypotheses are intriguing, but they remain speculative.

Future research findings may have implications for intervention, and for when and under what conditions self-motivation scores will be predictive of adherence. Self-motivation scores are resistant to change (Dishman & Ickes, 1981; Knapp et al., 1984), which indicates that whatever is being measured is relatively enduring. This does not imply that an intervention cannot be found to promote self-motivated adherence once the process is better understood. However, given both the stability of the measure and recent findings suggesting it is better at predicting adherence than dropout (Ward & Morgan, 1984), its most immediate clinical usefulness may be in identifying individuals who will need less assistance to adhere.

Relapse Model

Marlatt's model of the phenomenon of relapse and the derived strategies for relapse prevention (Figure 1) (Marlatt, 1985) have elicited interest in their potential application to the problem of exercise adherence (King & Frederiksen, 1984; Martin & Dubbert, 1984; Martin et al., 1984). However, the basic model has not yet been tested in the area of exercise relapse. The model was derived from observations of relapse in alcohol problems, smoking, and drug abuse. In these areas the goal is to reduce a high-frequency, undesired behavior whereas in the promotion of physical activity the goal is to increase a low-frequency, desired behavior. This basic behavioral difference may lead to the need to modify the relapse model as applied to exercise adherence.

The reader is strongly encouraged to refer to the more comprehensive presentation of the relapse model by Marlatt and Gordon (1985). The model applies to relapse in *voluntary* behavioral self-control efforts rather than to relapse by individuals who have had behavior change thrust upon them, such as military personnel who are no longer required to exercise after their basic training is complete.

Positive Scenario. In voluntary behavior change the relapse process begins with a *high-risk situation*, defined as a situation that challenges one's perceived self-control relative to the behavior change regimen. An example would be a recent lunchtime exerciser who is assigned an important deadline project requiring extra work time. The positive scenario for

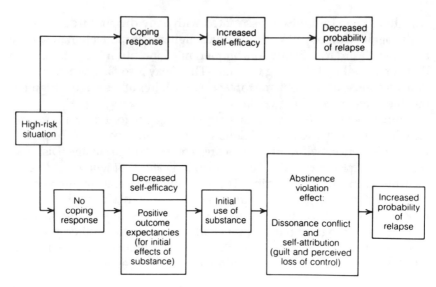

Figure 1   A cognitive-behavioral model of the relapse process. *Note.*   From "Relapse Prevention: Theoretical Rationale and Overview of the Model" by G.A. Marlatt, 1985. In G.A. Marlatt and J.R. Gordon (Eds.), *Relapse Prevention* (p. 38). New York: Guilford Press. Copyright 1985 by Guilford Press. Reprinted by permission.

what may ensue is that the individual responds to the high-risk situation with an *adequate coping response* (e.g., time management, delegating other projects) that deals with the situation while maintaining the desired behavioral self-control (the exercise regimen). Such positive responding leads to *increased self-efficacy*, an internal, upbeat "I *can* do it!" response, and *decreased probability of relapse*.

Negative Scenario.   The negative scenario also begins with a high-risk situation, but this time the individual's *coping response is inadequate or lacking.* The individual then experiences *decreased self-efficacy*, the feeling that "I don't think I can do this!" (i.e., continue the exercise program), and at the same time may have *positive outcome expectancies* for the anticipated "slip." For example, the individual may expect to finish the project more quickly, please the boss, and take off the pressure by skipping the exercise only once. The combination of lowered self-efficacy and positive outcome expectancies can be very powerful and often leads to the initial slip or violation of the individual's self-imposed behavioral rule. The more rigid the rule, the more perceptible the slip and the more likely it is to lead to phenomena such as the *abstinence violation effect.*

The abstinence violation effect is so called because it is most readily observed in the case of violations of an abstinence resolve or rule (e.g., the first drink by an abstaining alcoholic). Such violations lead to dissonance conflict and self-attribution of failure. The dissonance conflict is the cognitive or mental aspect of the abstinence violation effect and involves perceiving the behavior (the slip) as in conflict with the new self-concept as a successful abstainer (or adherent exerciser). The thinking can be quite all or nothing; just as one cannot be a little bit pregnant, one cannot be a little bit nonabstinent. The dissonance conflict is all too often resolved by deciding that, in fact, one is not successfully controlling one's behavior.

The second aspect of the abstinence violation effect is the emotional response. The cause of the failure is attributed to the self, to personal weakness ("I just don't have any willpower. I don't have what it takes."). This leads to further self-blame, lowered self-esteem, guilt, perceived loss of control, *increased probability of relapse,* and often simply giving up.

Slips in a self-control regimen may be more discreet, easily defined events (the first drink, cigarette, drug use, etc.) in the areas of alcohol, drug abuse, and smoking than they are in exercise adherence. Because nobody is expected to exercise continually, at what point does the failure to exercise become a perceptible slip that elicits dissonance conflict? Further, the first drink or cigarette by an abstainer may be a more visible sign of weakness and less socially acceptable than failure to exercise, thus eliciting more "catastrophizing." Considerations such as this lead to questions regarding whether and to what degree the abstinence violation effect is involved in exercise relapse. Although King and Frederiksen (1984) gave their subjects a description of a runner's relapse effect based on the abstinence violation effect, no research yet documents this phenomenon. Nonetheless, the observation that rigid, all-or-nothing rules lead to all-or-nothing behavior is valuable, and other aspects of Marlatt's relapse model may also be useful as applied to exercise adherence.

Covert Antecedents.   Marlatt also describes the process that predisposes individuals to encounter difficult, high-risk situations. Marlatt observes that a particular kind of *lifestyle imbalance* in which shoulds exceed wants is the starting point. Shoulds refers to activities that one does because one should—frequently such activities are to some degree externally imposed or perceived to be so. Wants refers to activities that one does out of desire—they are the activities an individual will choose when under no real or perceived pressure either to choose or to avoid them. An over-balance of shoulds in daily life leads to *desire for indulgence or self-gratification* (e.g., "I owe myself a drink" or "I deserve a break" or "I've done enough.'') This, in turn, leads to *urges or cravings* that are mediated by positive expectancies for immediate effects of the forbidden substance or of skipping exercise. These urges and cravings are accompanied by *rationalization, denial, and apparently irrelevant decisions.*

Apparently irrelevant decisions are decisions that, although they appear on the surface to be unrelated to the self-control resolution, function to put the individual in a *high-risk situation.* Examples include a recent exsmoker selecting a seat in the smoking section on an airplane because that's the safest section or a new exerciser choosing to do volunteer work just before exercise class to save trips and gas even though this will lead to continuing difficulty making it to the class on time.

Relapse Prevention

A variety of relapse prevention strategies derive from the model, and they are useful both for identifying and dealing with high-risk situations and the ensuing relapse process (see Figure 2) and for altering the covert antecedents of high-risk situations (see Figure 3).

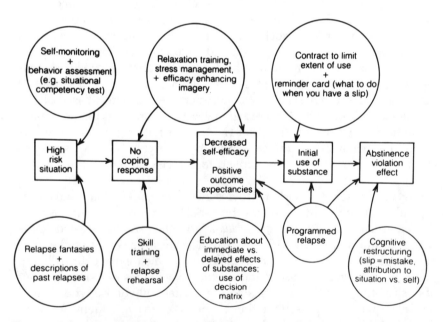

Figure 2 Relapse Prevention: Specific intervention strategies. *Note.* From ''Relapse Prevention: Theoretical Rationale and Overview of the Model'' by G.A. Marlatt, 1985. In G.A. Marlatt and J.R. Gordon (Eds.), *Relapse Prevention* (p. 54). New York: Guilford Press. Copyright 1985 by Guilford Press. Reprinted by permission.

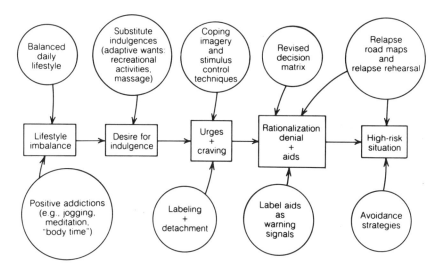

Figure 3   Relapse Prevention: Global self-control strategies. *Note.*   From "Relapse Prevention: Theoretical Rationale and Overview of the Model" by G.A. Marlatt, 1985. In G.A. Marlatt and J.R. Gordon (Eds.), *Relapse Prevention* (p. 61). New York: Guilford Press. Copyright 1985 by Guilford Press. Reprinted by permission.

Relapse prevention begins with educating the individual regarding the process of relapse and enlisting the individual's active cooperation and participation in its prevention. This will require emphasizing the importance of reporting the inevitable difficulties as well as successes and greeting these reports in a nonjudgmental manner (i.e., what can be learned from this experience?).

Identifying High-Risk Situations.   The next step is to identify, define, and predict high-risk situations for relapse. Means for accomplishing this include self-monitoring in which the individual records not only exercise behavior but also time of day, place, people involved, mood, and other potentially relevant aspects of the situation (e.g., "just had fight with wife about her nagging me to exercise"). Another form of behavioral assessment is a situational competency test (Chaney, O'Leary, & Marlatt, 1978; Marlatt & Gordon, 1985; Shiffman, Read, Maltese, Rapkin, & Jarvik, 1985) in which individuals describe or role-play their responses to presumed high-risk situations that are either verbally presented or enacted. Individuals may also be asked to describe their fantasies regarding what would occur to lead them to discontinue exercise or to describe actual past relapses.

Improving Coping Responses.   Once high-risk situations are identified, it may be possible to avoid them or to plan coping responses. If individuals do not cope adequately, they may simply lack the behavioral skill required (e.g., assertiveness, time management). In this case skill training and relapse rehearsal (role-played and/or in real situations) to practice the newly learned responses are recommended. On the other hand, individuals may already have the needed skills but be inhibited, often by anxiety, in performing them. In this instance relaxation training, stress management, rehearsal, and/or efficacy-enhancing imagery (e.g., having the persons visualize themselves dealing competently and successfully with the situation) may be helpful. These same strategies may also be useful in dealing with decreased self-efficacy regarding adhering to the exercise program in difficult situations.

Correcting Positive Outcome Expectancies.   Another aspect of relapse prevention is dealing with positive expectancies for slipping. This is an especially important aspect of relapse prevention in substance abuse; individuals may expect very positive effects from the substance. Similar expectancies may influence exercise adherence. For example, individuals who feel too tired to exercise when they are bored may expect that they will feel better if they skip the exercise. In fact, rest is unlikely to reduce their feelings of fatigue but rather may add guilt and lowered self-esteem whereas exercise may possibly have improved their energy and their mood. Identifying the positive expectancies an individual may have for skipping exercise and providing education regarding the actual immediate and delayed effects may be useful. Marlatt proposes building in a controlled programmed relapse or slip as a way of changing unrealistic and unhelpful positive expectancies. The decision matrix, described earlier, is a technique that is especially well-suited to eliciting expectancies for short-term and long-term consequences of both continuing to exercise and stopping exercise, and it may be used in a manner that provides good opportunity for corrective education as well as problem solving. Rereading a pocket-size copy of the decision matrix, particularly if a contract is drawn up, may be helpful when tempted to skip a planned exercise session.

Planning for Slips.   A particularly practical aspect of Marlatt's recommendations is planning for and dealing with inevitable lapses. Lapses are seen as critical incidents that can lead to full-blown relapse but that can also be dealt with in a manner to prevent relapse. This can be done by contracting to limit the extent of the lapse and by training the individual very specifically about what to do when a lapse occurs. Such plans may be written on a reminder card carried by the individual and may be rehearsed in a programmed relapse. King and Frederiksen (1984) trained their subjects to employ appropriate cognitive restructuring and promptly to reschedule the missed exercise session. Subjects given this training and instructed to jog alone were twice as likely as other subjects to report continued jogging at 3-month follow-up. Individuals may also be assisted to plan specific alternate times, places, and/or types of exercise to use if they miss their class, get injured, and so forth.

Minimizing the Abstinence Violation Effect.   The other aspect of dealing with a lapse is preventing, reducing, and minimizing damage caused by the maladaptive mental and emotional fallout from lapses. Flexible goal setting and cognitive restructuring are appropriate strategies.

One aspect of preventing phenomena such as the abstinence violation effect is avoiding excessively rigid rules while simultaneously utilizing behavioral goals and guidelines that are sufficiently clear to be helpful. Martin et al. (1984) found that setting flexible behavioral exercise goals rather than fixed goals was associated with less dropout, better attendance, and better maintenance at 3-month follow-up (except when the flexible goals were introduced after a period in which fixed goals were set). They also found that setting goals to be achieved in 5 weeks led to marginally better exercise adherence during the program ($p < .07$) and significantly better maintenance of exercise at 3-month follow-up than setting goals to be achieved that week (67% vs. 33%). They hypothesize that this may be due to increased flexibility in daily and weekly performance with more distant goals and less opportunity to experience failure when faltering (abstinence violation effects) than would be the case with weekly goals.

Another intervention to reduce the abstinence violation effect is cognitive restructuring, in which the slip is seen as a mistake from which one can learn, not a disaster or a sign of inevitable relapse. Individuals are taught to attribute the slip to the situation rather than to personal weakness and to respond by analyzing the situation and planning how to deal with it in the future without having a lapse in their self-control efforts.

Correcting Lifestyle Imbalance.   Relapse prevention strategies also address covert antecedents of high risk situations such as lifestyle imbalance in which shoulds outnumber wants. Correcting this imbalance is recommended as shown in Figure 3. Attempting to build an exercise habit is all too often adding another should to many others when far too few wants are being gratified. To the degree that increasing physical activity can be done in such a way that it rapidly becomes a gratifying want, probability of relapse will be greatly reduced. It may be helpful to have alternate forms of exercise that can be especially enjoyable or indulgent in some way, which can be used at times when one is feeling deprived. Another helpful strategy would be to plan a special indulgence to follow and reinforce the exercise, such as arranging for a massage after the workout. Similarly, building gratifications into daily life such as personal time, pleasure reading, or perhaps meditation may help to prevent the sense of deprivation and desire for indulgence that can contribute to increasing risk of relapse. Ironically, Marlatt recommended that abstaining substance abusers use jogging, a positive addiction, as a substitute indulgence. Although running can clearly become an addiction for some people (i.e., a high frequency behavior that is difficult to eliminate), achieving this outcome appears to be approximately as difficult as eliminating and preventing relapse in substance abuse (Dishman, 1982).

Preventing and Coping With Urges to Lapse.   Urges and cravings may be sudden, impulsive, and almost automatic or they may take the form of persistent, nagging thoughts and mental images of skipping the exercise and of the benefits of doing so. Avoiding cues for competing behaviors at the exercise time will reduce the frequency of urges to skip. Two strategies that may be helpful when experiencing such urges are (a) thought-stopping combined with coping imagery and (b) labeling and detachment.

Thought-stopping is a technique designed to interrupt undesired but persistent thoughts and mental images by internally (or sometimes, if feasible, out loud) shouting the word "Stop!" The interrupted thoughts can then be deliberately replaced with coping imagery, such as vividly imagining oneself energetically and enthusiastically involved in a desired physical activity performed with strength, competence, and vigor to the admiration of onlookers and fellow participants.

Teaching individuals to expect to have urges to skip exercise and to label them intellectually as urges with which they can cope rather than irresistible forces and to observe them in a more emotionally detached and objective manner can also be helpful. Would-be exercisers also have a great advantage over exsmokers or individuals attempting to reduce or eliminate other high-frequency behaviors in that the former can turn off the urges to lapse, at least for that day, by actually doing the exercise. The more exercise becomes habitual and automatically elicited by stimulus cues such as exercise time, the less frequently the individual is likely to experience urges to skip.

Rationalization, Denial, and Apparently Irrelevant Decisions.   Having individuals refer to their decision matrix and expand or revise it as needed may be a useful way to deal with rationalization and denial. Teaching individuals about the role of apparently irrelevant decisions in relapse and helping them to identify and label them as warning signals is also advised. It can be useful to draw upon an individual's relapse fantasies, past relapse descriptions, and current lapse situations and to ask pertinent questions such as "If you wanted to start skipping your exercise, how could you arrange things to make that more likely?" "What sort of situations might you run into that might make it more difficult to stick with your exercise?'' ''What could you do or how could you arrange things so that you would be most likely to stick with your exercise?'' Information gained can be used to generate a relapse road map in which choice points and potential high-risk situations are anticipated, which allows alternate decisions and appropriate coping strategies to be planned and practiced in a relapse rehearsal.

Research on Relapse Prevention in Exercise

As of this writing, only two studies (King & Frederiksen, 1984; Martin et al., 1984) have attempted to test portions of relapse prevention strategies for effectiveness in improving exercise maintenance, and one of these was, by its authors' own report, seriously though inadvertently flawed (Martin et al., 1984). Martin and his colleagues taught their relapse prevention subjects about the realistic likelihood of adherence slips, apparently irrelevant decisions and other factors that would increase the likelihood of slips, and the abstinence violation effect. Examples were elicited and group members were encouraged to solve problems together. Subjects were also urged to have a planned relapse of 1 week, after which they were to start running again on a nonclass day using procedures they had been taught. Thus the investigators used many, though not all, of the relapse prevention strategies previously described. Their results were unfortunately confounded when a course assistant continued to arrange exercise meeting times for several of the nonrelapse subjects, and other procedural drift occurred. No differences in exercise maintenance were observed between groups. Interested readers are encouraged to refer to Martin et al. (1984) for a fuller discussion of their experience.

King and Frederiksen (1984) gave their relapse prevention subjects a description of a runner's relapse effect modeled on the abstinence violation effect and vignettes of situations in which skipping exercise sessions would be likely. Subjects were instructed in coping strategies for modifying self-defeating thoughts and for promptly rescheduling the session. Subjects given relapse training and instructed to run alone did significantly more exercise than controls during the 5-week jogging period and at the 3-month follow-up whereas those given relapse training but instructed to jog with other team members did no better than controls at either time point.

More research on the potential of relapse prevention strategies for reducing exercise dropout is clearly needed. King and Frederiksen's results, though limited in scope in terms of strategies used and duration of the study, nonetheless provide encouragement although cautioning that differing adherence strategies may not always work well together without appropriate adaptation. Moreover, further research on the nature of the process of relapse in exercise may be useful given the basic differences between the behavioral task involved in building an exercise habit versus reducing a problematic addictive behavior.

Summary and Concluding Comments

The acquisition of habits of increased physical activity has been described as a three stage process: (a) the decision to initiate exercise, (b) early habit acquisition, and (c) maintenance of the new behavior. Behavioral and cognitive strategies for the promotion of exercise were provided for each of the three phases. Strategies for facilitating a decision to exercise, drawn from health beliefs, self-regulatory, and decision-making models, have been delineated, which emphasize potential reinforcement beyond preventive health benefits and enhance self-efficacy. For habit acquisition stimulus control measures, reduction of punishing contingencies, and the provision of social, material, and other forms of reinforcement are recommended. Continuing exercise cues and reinforcement, avoidance of punishment, and self-attribution of positive change appear necessary for maintenance. The relationship of self-motivation to maintenance, the relapse model, and derived relapse prevention strategies have been discussed with respect to their potential applicability to enhancing exercise maintenance.

The strategies have been described as they would apply to exercise promotion with individuals or small groups. When applied comprehensively in this manner, they can be costly (in terms of professional time and expertise) and effortful, and they reach relatively few individuals. But they are needed to assist individuals in counteracting and perhaps to some extent in changing the stream of environmental influences that militate against adequate physical activity. However, if the goal of significantly increasing the exercise participation of the United States population as a whole is to be achieved, mass change in social norms and contingencies is needed. The effectiveness of mass change strategies will depend in part on the degree to which these behavioral principles are effectively applied. Effective mass change strategies will have the potential to reach more people but will probably have less ability to respond to and tailor interventions to individuals. The people not reached by such strategies may then be appropriate targets for more intensive intervention. Thus mass change and small group applications are complementary rather than competing approaches, and both are needed in the effort to promote healthful physical activity.

References

Andrew, G.M., Oldridge, N.B., Parker, J.O., Cunningham, D.A., Rechnitzer, P.A., Jones, N.L., Buck, C., Kavanaugh, T., Shephard, R.J., Sutton, J.R., & McDonald, W. (1981). Reasons for dropout from exercise programs in post coronary patients. *Medicine and Science in Sports and Exercise, 13*, 164–168.

Andrew, G.M., & Parker, J.O. (1979). Factors related to dropout of post myocardial infarction patients from exercise programs. *Medicine and Science in Sports and Exercise, 11*, 376–378.

Atkins, C.J., Kaplan, R.M., Timms, R.M., Reinsch, S., & Lofback, K. (1984). Behavioral exercise programs in the management of chronic obstructive pulmonary disease. *Journal of Consulting and Clinical Psychology, 52*, 591–603.

Bandura, A. (1977). Self-efficacy: Toward a unifying theory of behavioral change. *Psychological Review, 84*, 191–215.

Barnett, L.A. (1980). The social psychology of children's play: Effects of extrinsic rewards on free play and intrinsic motivation. In S.E. Iso-Ahola (Ed.), *Social psychological perspectives on leisure and recreation* (pp. 138–170). Springfield, IL: Charles C Thomas.

Becker, A. (1984, March). Fitness vacation. *Single Life*, pp. 41–44.

Becker, M.H. (1976). Sociobehavioral determinants of compliance. In D.L. Sackett & R.B. Haynes (Eds.), *Compliance with therapeutic regimens* (pp. 40–50). Baltimore: The John Hopkins University Press.

Cautela, J.R., & Kastenbaum, R.A. (1967). A reinforcement survey schedule for use in therapy, training and research. *Psychological Reports, 20*, 1115–1130.

Chaney, E.F., O'Leary, M.R., & Marlatt, G.A. (1978). Skill training with alcoholics. *Journal of Consulting and Clinical Psychology, 46*, 1092–1104.

Dishman, R.K. (1982). Compliance/adherence in health-related exercise. *Health Psychology, 1*, 237–267.

Dishman, R.K. (1987). Exercise adherence. In W.P. Morgan & S.N. Goldston (Eds.), *Exercise and mental health* (pp. 57–83). New York: Hemisphere.

Dishman, R.K., & Gettman, L.R. (1980). Psychobiologic influences on exercise adherence. *Journal of Sport Psychology, 2*, 295–310.

Dishman, R., & Ickes, W. (1981). Self-motivation and adherence to therapeutic exercise. *Journal of Behavioral Medicine, 4*, 421–438.

Dishman, R.K., Ickes, W., & Morgan, W.P. (1980). Self-motivation and adherence to habitual physical activity. *Journal of Applied Social Psychology*, **10**, 115–132.

Epstein, L.H., Koeske, R., & Wing, R.R. (1984). Adherence to exercise in obese children. *Journal of Cardiac Rehabilitation*, **4**, 185–195.

Epstein, L.H., Wing, R.R., Koeske, R., Ossip, D., & Beck, S. (1982). A comparison of lifestyle change and programmed aerobic exercise on weight and fitness changes in obese children. *Behavior Therapy*, **13**, 651–665.

Epstein, L.H., Wing, R.R., Thompson, J.K., & Griffin, W. (1980). Attendance and fitness in aerobics exercise. *Behavior Modification*, **4**, 465–479.

Erling, J., & Oldridge, N.B. (1985). Effect of a spousal-support program on compliance with cardiac rehabilitation. *Medicine and Science in Sports and Exercise*, **17**, 284.

Ewart, C.K., Taylor, B., Reese, L.B., & DeBusk, R.F. (1983). Effects of early postmyocardial infarction exercise testing on self-perception and subsequent physical activity. *The American Journal of Cardiology*, **51**, 1076–1080.

Gale, J.B., Eckhoff, W.T., Mogel, S.F., & Rodnick, J.E. (1984). Factors related to adherence to an exercise program for healthy adults. *Medicine and Science in Sports and Exercise*, **16**, 544–549.

Godin, G., & Shephard, R.J. (1983). Physical fitness promotion programmes: Effectiveness in modifying exercise behavior. *Canadian Journal of Applied Sport Sciences*, **8**, 104–113.

Halliwell, W.R. (1979). Toward an interactionist approach to the study of intrinsic motivation. In G.C. Roberts & K.M. Newell (Eds.), *Psychology of motor behavior and sport, 1978* (pp. 72–78). Champaign, IL: Human Kinetics.

Harris, L. (1979). *The Perrier Study: Fitness in America.* Perrier-Great Waters of France.

Hoyt, M.F., & Janis, I.L. (1975). Increasing adherence to a stressful decision via a motivational balance-sheet procedure: A field experiment. *Journal of Personality and Social Psychology*, **31**, 833–839.

Kau, M.L., & Fischer, J. (1974). Self-modification of exercise behavior. *Journal of Behavior Therapy and Experimental Psychiatry*, **5**, 213–214.

Keefe, F.J., & Blumenthal, J.A. (1980). The life fitness program: A behavioral approach to making exercise a habit. *Journal of Behavior Therapy and Experimental Psychiatry*, **11**, 31–34.

King, A.C., & Frederiksen, L.W. (1984). Low-cost strategies for increasing exercise behavior: Relapse preparation training and social support. *Behavior Modification, 8*, 3–21.

Kleiber, D.A. (1981). Searching for enjoyment in children's sports. *The Physical Educator, 38*, 77–84.

Knapp, D. (1986). [Psychological determinants of dropout from exercise in apparently healthy individuals]. Unpublished raw data.

Knapp, D., Gutmann, M., Foster, C., & Pollock, M. (1984). Self-motivation among 1984 Olympic speedskating hopefuls and emotional response and adherence to training. *Medicine and Science in Sports and Exercise, 16*, 114–115.

Knapp, D., Gutmann, M., Foster, C., & Pollock, M. (1985). Olympic speedskating training and trials: Effects of self-motivation on emotional response and adherence. *Medicine and Science in Sports and Exercise, 17*, 287.

Knapp, D., Gutmann, M., Squires, R., & Pollock, M. (1983). Exercise adherence among coronary artery bypass surgery (CABS) patients. *Medicine and Science in Sports and Exercise, 15*, 120.

Lasater, T., Abrams, D., Artz, L., Beaudin, P., Cabrera, L., Elder, J., Ferreira, A., Knisley, P., Peterson, G., Rodrigues, A., Rosenberg, P., Snow, R., & Carleton, R. (1984). Lay volunteer delivery of a community-based cardiovascular risk factor change program: The Pawtuckett experiment. In J.D. Matarazzo, S.M. Weiss, J.A. Herd, N.E. Miller, & S.M. Weiss (Eds.), *Behavioral health: A handbook of health enhancement and disease prevention* (pp. 1166–1170). New York: Wiley.

Lefebvre, R.C. (in press). Primary prevention of coronary heart disease: A review of multifactor prevention trials. In M. Hersen, R.M. Eisler, & P.M. Miller (Eds.), *Progress in behavior modification* (Vol. 21). New York: Academic.

Lefebvre, R.C., Lasater, T.M., Carleton, R.A., & Peterson, G. (1986). *Theory and delivery of health programming in the community: The Pawtuckett heart health program.* Manuscript submitted for publication.

Leventhal, H., Meyer, D., & Gutmann, M. (1980). The role of theory in the study of compliance to high blood pressure regimens. In R.B. Haynes & M.E. Mattson (Eds.), *Patient compliance to prescribed antihypertensive medication regimens* (NIH Publication No. 81-2102, pp. 1–58). Bethesda, MD: National Institutes of Health.

Leventhal, H., Meyer, D., & Nerenz, D. (1980). The common sense representation of illness danger. In S. Rachman (Ed.), *Contributions to medical psychology* (Vol. 2, pp. 7–30). New York: Pergamon.

Leventhal, H., Zimmerman, R., & Gutmann, M. (1984). Compliance: A self-regulatory perspective. In D. Gentry (Ed.), *The handbook of behavioral medicine* (pp. 369–436). New York: Guilford.

Lipsker, L.E. (1983). An investigation of variables affecting exercise adherence. *Dissertation Abstracts International, 44,* 1222.

Luce, S.C., Delquadri, J., & Hall, R.V. (1980). Contingent exercise: A mild but powerful procedure for suppressing inappropriate verbal and aggressive behavior. *Journal of Applied Behavior Analysis, 13,* 583–594.

Mann, G.V., Garrett, H.L., Farhi, A., Murray, H., & Murray, H. (1969). Exercise to prevent coronary heart disease. An experimental study of the effects of training on risk factors for coronary heart disease in men. *American Journal of Medicine, 46,* 12–27.

Marlatt, G.A. (1986). Relapse prevention: Theoretical rationale and overview of the model. In G.A. Marlatt and J.R. Gordon (Eds.), *Relapse prevention: Maintenance strategies in the treatment of addictive behaviors.* New York: Guilford.

Marlatt, G.A., & Gordon, J.R. (Eds.). (1985). *Relapse prevention: Maintenance strategies in the treatment of addictive behaviors.* New York: Guilford.

Martin, J.E., & Dubbert, P.M. (1984). Behavioral management strategies for improving health and fitness. *Journal of Cardiac Rehabilitation, 4,* 200–208.

Martin, J.E., Dubbert, P.M., Katell, A.D., Thompson, J.K., Raczynski, J.R., Lake, M., Smith, P.O., Webster, J.S., Sikora, T., & Cohen, R.E. (1984). Behavioral control of exercise in sedentary adults: Studies 1 through 6. *Journal of Consulting and Clinical Psychology, 52,* 795–811.

Meyer, D., Leventhal, H., & Gutmann, M. (1985). Common-sense models of illness: The example of hypertension. *Health Psychology, 4,* 115–135.

Nelson, R.O., Haynes, S.C., Spong, R.T., Jarrett, R.B., & McKnight, D.L. (1983). Self-reinforcement: Appealing misnomer or effective mechanism? *Behavior Research and Therapy, 21,* 557–566.

Oldridge, N.B. (1982). Compliance and exercise in primary and secondary prevention of coronary heart disease: A review. *Preventive Medicine, 11,* 56–70.

Oldridge, N.B., & Jones, N.L. (1983). Improving patient compliance in cardiac rehabilitation: Effects of written agreement and self-monitoring. *Journal of Cardiac Rehabilitation, 3,* 257–262.

Parkhouse, B.L. (1980). Let's melt down all that gold and silver and put it to better use. *Journal of Physical Education and Recreation, 51*(8), 29–30.

Perfect! Coed health clubs are the singles' bars of the eighties. (1983, June 9). *Rolling Stone*, p. 20.

Shephard, R.J., & Cox, M. (1980, June). Some characteristics of participants in an industrial fitness programme. *Canadian Journal of Applied Sport Sciences*, 69–76.

Shiffman, S., Read, L., Maltese, J., Rapkin, D., & Jarvik, M.E. (1985). Preventing relapse in ex-smokers: A self-management approach. In G.A. Marlatt & J.R. Gordon (Eds.), *Relapse prevention: Maintenance strategies in the treatment of addictive behaviors* (pp. 472–520). New York: Guilford.

Snyder, G., Franklin, B., Foss, M., & Rubenfire, M. (1982). Characteristics of compliers and non-compliers to cardiac exercise therapy programs. *Medicine and Science in Sports and Exercise*, **14**, 179.

Wankel, L.M. (1984). Decision-making and social support strategies for increasing exercise involvement. *Journal of Cardiac Rehabilitation*, **4**, 124–135.

Ward, A., & Morgan, W.P. (1984). Adherence patterns of healthy men and women enrolled in an adult exercise program. *Journal of Cardiac Rehabilitation*, **4**, 143–152.

Watson, G.G. (1976). Reward systems in children's games: The attraction of game interaction in Little League baseball. *Review of Sport and Leisure*, **1**, 93–121.

Wysocki, T., Hall, G., Iwata, B., & Riordan, M. (1979). Behavioral management of exercise: Contracting for aerobic points. *Journal of Applied Behavior Analysis*, **12**, 55–64.

CHAPTER 8

Program Factors That Influence Exercise Adherence: Practical Adherence Skills for the Clinical Staff

Barry A. Franklin

Adult fitness and cardiac exercise programs have reported considerable variability in dropout rates, 9% to 87% ($\bar{x}$ = 44%–46%), which indicates substantial noncompliance among those individuals who voluntarily enter physical conditioning programs (Figure 1) (Andrew et al., 1981; Blumenthal, Williams, Wallace, Williams, & Needles, 1982; Bruce, Frederick, Bruce, & Fisher, 1976; DeBusk, Haskell, Miller, Berra, & Taylor, 1985; Gale, Eckhoff, Mogel, & Rodnick, 1984; Gottheiner, 1968; Hellerstein, 1968; Kavanagh, Shephard, Doney, & Pandit, 1973; Kentala, 1972; Mann, Garrett, Farhi, Murray, & Billings, 1969; Massie & Shephard, 1971; Nye & Poulsen, 1974; Oja, Teraslinna, Partanen, & Karava, 1974; Oldridge, 1974, 1979; Oldridge, Wicks, Hanley, Sutton & Jones, 1978; Palatsi, 1976; Shaw, 1981; Taylor, Buskirk, & Remington, 1973; Ward & Morgan, 1984; Wilhelmsen, Sanne, Elmfeldt, Grimby, Tibblin, & Wedel, 1975). Although widely differing definitions of ''exercise dropout'' in these studies may

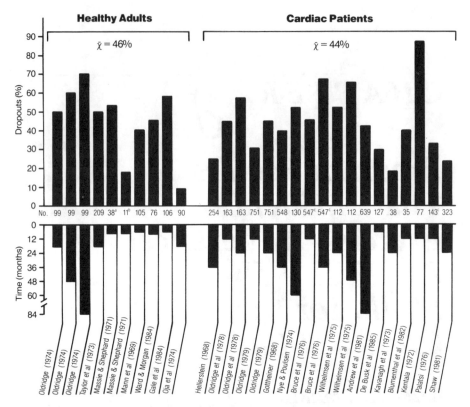

Figure 1 Relationship between the dropout rate (%) and the duration of exercise training (months) in studies of healthy adults and cardiac patients. *Note.* The number (no.) of participants in each study is designated: [a] = assigned to individual exercise program; [b] = assigned to YMCA group exercise program; [c] = men only.

have contributed to the variability in results, endurance exercise regimens are apparently similar to other health-related behaviors (e.g., medication compliance, smoking cessation, weight reduction) in that typically half of those who initiate the behavior will continue regardless of cardiovascular status or the duration of training.

Although numerous variables are related to and predictive of exercise dropout (Table 1), the exercise leader appears to be the single most important variable affecting exercise compliance (Franklin, 1984; Oldridge, 1977). Oldridge (1977) considers the exercise leader as "the pivot on which the success or failure of a program will depend" (p. 86). Although he acknowledges that motivation for participation is health-related in most instances, "the stimulus for continuing or adhering to the program grows from the participants' response to the environment set up by the exercise leader" (p. 86).

Table 1   Variables Predicting the Exercise Dropout

Personal factors	Program factors	Other factors
Smoker	Inconvenient time/location	Lack of spouse support
Inactive leisure time	Excessive cost	Inclement weather
Inactive occupation	High intensity exercise	Excessive job travel
Blue-collar worker	Lack of exercise variety,	Injury
Type A personality	e.g., running only	Medical problems
Increased physical strength	Exercises alone	Job change/move
Extroverted	Lack of positive feedback	
Poor credit rating	or reinforcement	
Overweight and/or overfat	Inflexible exercise goals	
Poor self-image	Low enjoyability ratings	
Depressed	for running programs	
Hypochondriacal	Poor exercise leadership	
Anxious		
Introverted		
Low ego strength		

Knowledgeable and trained exercise leaders play a critical role in the development and implementation of adult fitness or cardiac exercise programs. Moreover, exercise leaders are responsible for (a) educating participants *why* and *how* they should be physically active and (b) motivating them to follow through with a personal exercise program (Wilmore, 1974).

The purposes of this chapter are (a) to present pragmatic educational and motivational ideas to the exercise leader or fitness program director who is interested in stimulating interest, enthusiasm, and adherence among program participants and (b) to review the knowledge and proficiency requirements, responsibilities, and behavioral strategies of the good exercise leader, with specific reference to continuing education through workshops and American College of Sports Medicine (ACSM) certification programs.

Educating and Motivating Program Participants

Unfortunately, the education and motivation components of an exercise program are often underemphasized (Franklin, 1978). Consequently, negative variables may outweigh the positive variables affecting sustained participant interest and enthusiasm (Figure 2). Such imbalance leads to poor adherence and a decline in program effectiveness.

Exercise programs for adults should include an educational component and selected motivational strategies (Franklin, 1986).

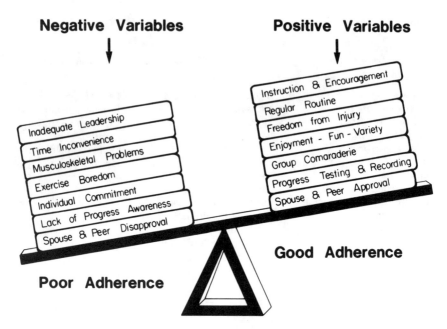

Figure 2 Programmatic and related variables affecting adherence to an exercise training program. Oftentimes, the negative variables outweigh the positive variables causing poor adherence.

Education Component

Education of participants should serve as an integral part of a physical fitness program and include substantive information on biomechanics, caloric expenditure, appropriate exercise intensity, frequency, duration, and modes of training (Franklin, 1986), the concept of perceived exertion (Borg, 1970), the importance of warm-up and cool-down, exercise myths and misconceptions, suitable exercise clothing and shoes, nutrition, and the effects of environmental conditions on performance. Participants should also be cautioned against certain proscriptions that counteract the benefits of exercise and/or may be potentially hazardous, such as exercise during illness, cigarette smoking, alcohol consumption, and spasmodic, high-intensity exercise (Hellerstein & Franklin, 1984).

Several programmatic variables, which include films, booklets, and lectures, can be used to promote the educational component. Such aids can help give participants a better understanding of the health benefits of regular physical activity. Bulletin boards, murals, and a physical fitness newsletter (Figure 3) can also be used to provide useful information to participants. Finally, periodic individual or group meetings for par-

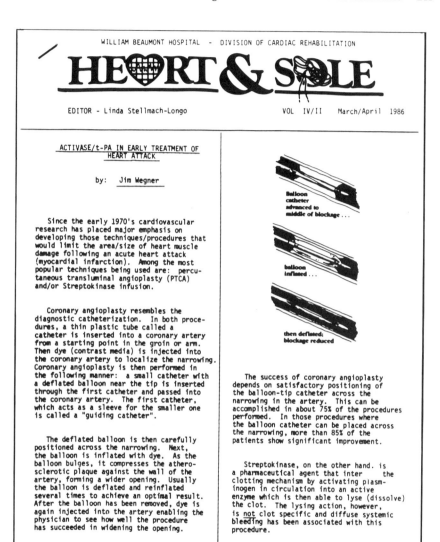

Figure 3 Bimonthly health-fitness newsletter published by the William Beaumont Hospital Cardiac Rehabilitation Program. Newsletter topics include information for participants on exercise, weight control, heart disease, stress, and nutrition.

ticipants and spouses allow for the discussion of topics such as exercise prescription, diet, and weight control.

In addition to educating participants, motivating them to initiate and continue exercise training programs is necessary.

Motivational Strategies

Motivation is a critical factor in exercise program effectiveness, safety, and long-term compliance (McHenry, 1974; Stoedefalke, 1974). Research and empirical observation suggest that the following selected exercise program modifications and motivational strategies may enhance participant interest, enthusiasm, and long-term compliance.

- *Minimize musculoskeletal injuries with a moderate exercise prescription.* Excessive frequency ($\geq$ 5 days/week) or duration ($\geq$ 45 minutes/session) of training offer the exerciser little additional gain in aerobic capacity ($\dot{V}O_2max$), and the incidence of orthopedic injury increases disproportionately (Figure 4) (Pollock, Gettman, Milesis, Bah, Durstine,

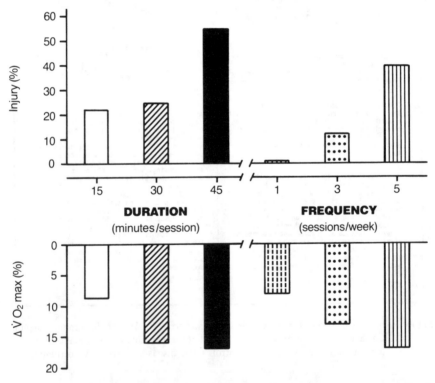

Figure 4 Relationships among exercise frequency and duration, improvement in maximal oxygen consumption, and the incidence of orthopedic injury. Above an exercise duration of 30 minutes/session or a frequency of 3 sessions/week, additional improvement in $\dot{V}O_2max$ is small, and the injury rate increases disproportionately. *Note.* Adapted from "Effects of Frequency and Duration of Training on Attrition and Incidence of Injury" by M. Pollock, L. Gettman, C. Milesis, M.P. Durstine, and R.B. Johnson, 1977, *Medicine and Science in Sports, 9,* 31–37.

& Johnson, 1977). High-intensity exercise ($\geq$ 90% $\dot{V}O_2$max) is similarly associated with an injury rate of at least 50% (Kilbom, Hartley, Saltin, Bjure, Grimby, & Astrand, 1969; Mann et al., 1969) although it provides little or no additional cardiorespiratory improvements. A recommended program for the previously sedentary adult is to exercise 20 to 30 minutes, 3 days per week, at an intensity level of 50% to 70% $\dot{V}O_2$max (Figure 5). Attention to warm-up, using proper walking or running shoes, and training on appropriate terrain (avoiding hard and uneven surfaces) should aid in decreasing attrition due to injury.

- *Encourage group participation.* Poorer exercise compliance has been observed in individual programs than in those incorporating group dynamics (Massie & Shephard, 1971; Wilhelmsen et al., 1975). Approximately 90% of adult exercisers prefer group programs to those in which one exercises alone (Heinzelman & Bagley, 1970). The social reinforcement and comaraderie and companionship associated with a group program apparently may facilitate increased exercise compliance.

Figure 5 Previously sedentary adults can minimize the potential for injury with a moderate exercise prescription.

comaraderie and companionship associated with a group program apparently may facilitate increased exercise compliance.

• *Emphasize variety and enjoyment in the physical activity program.* The type of exercise program has also been shown to influence long-term compliance (Massie & Shephard, 1971). Regimented calisthenics often become monotonous and boring, which leads to poor exercise adherence. Programs that are most successful are those that are pleasurable and offer the greatest diversification to the physical conditioning program (Figure 6). The "Games-As-Aerobics" approach provides

Figure 6 Exercise training facility at William Beaumont Hospital, Barnum Health Center, Birmingham, Michigan. Participants have access to sophisticated exercise equipment, including a variety of arm and leg ergometers, treadmills, rowing machine, combined arm-leg ergometers (Schwinn Air-Dyne), the Nordic Track cross-country skiing device, and progressive resistance weight training equipment. A swimming pool program serves as an added option.

a physical activity format that stresses fun, pleasure, and repeated success as opposed to the pain and discomfort associated with many traditional programs. Stretching and flexibility exercises and endurance activities are camouflaged as individual or group games or relays that incorporate ball passing and other movement skills for variety (Figure 7). Game modifications that minimize athletic ability

Figure 7 The "Games-As-Aerobics" approach to exercise. Calisthenics are modified to incorporate ball passing and other movement skills for fun and variety.

and competition and that maximize participant success are particularly important. For example, playing volleyball but allowing one bounce of the ball per side facilitates longer rallies, provides additional fun, and decreases the skill level required to appreciate the game (Figure 8). Through such modifications the exercise leader is better able to emphasize the primary goal of the activity—enjoyment of the game itself.

- *Incorporate effective behavioral and programmatic techniques into the physical conditioning regimen.* Personal goal setting (i.e., established by the exerciser) provides the greatest potential for long-term exercise success (Martin, 1981). Research has also demonstrated the effectiveness of self-management strategies, including contracting, in improving exercise adherence (Epstein, Thompson, & Wing, 1980; Oldridge & Jones, 1981).
- *Employ periodic testing to assess the participant's response to the training program.* Favorable physiological adaptations to chronic endurance exercise include a decreased heart rate and systolic blood pressure

Figure 8 Volleyball is an excellent recreational game to complement an adult fitness or cardiac exercise program. Modification of game rules, for example, allowing one bounce of the ball per side, permits successful participation by less skilled players.

at rest and at submaximal workloads, increased work capacity and $\dot{V}O_2$max, reduced body weight and fat stores, and an improved serum lipid profile. Such changes are powerful motivators that produce renewed enthusiasm and dedication.

We have employed both submaximal and maximal exercise testing to assess serial changes in cardiovascular fitness (Figure 9). Submaximal testing is particularly easy to administer and requires no physician supervision. The baseline exercise test protocol is followed, facilitating a comparison of the heart rate, blood pressure, and rating of perceived exertion at standard submaximal work loads (Franklin, 1984). The endpoint of the test is that work load at which the peak target or training heart rate has been achieved. Aerobic capacity can be estimated by plotting the submaximal or minitest heart rate versus work load relationship; the latter is expressed in metabolic equivalents (METs) (1 MET = 3.5 ml O_2/kg body weight/min) extrapolated to the maximum heart rate attained on initial exercise testing (Figure 10). These data and other test results can be trans-

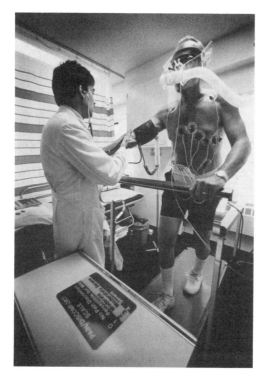

Figure 9 Periodic exercise testing can be used to assess the participants' response to chronic endurance exercise training.

formed into a participant report card to provide additional positive reinforcement.

- *Recruit spouse support of the exercise program.* Exercise leaders should focus attention not only on the participant but on those with whom the person relates most directly. The importance of this influence became evident in one study that showed that the husband's adherence to the exercise program was directly related to the wife's attitude toward the program (Figure 11) (Heinzelman & Bagley, 1970). Of those men whose spouses had a positive attitude toward the program, 80% demonstrated good to excellent adherence and only 20% exhibited fair to poor adherence. When the spouse was neutral or negative, in contrast, 40% showed good to excellent adherence and 60% exhibited fair to poor adherence. These data suggest that program counseling and educational meetings including participants and spouses will help to create and maintain positive attitudes that support exercise adherence.

Workloads	Mini-Test			Initial Test (Pre-conditioning)		
	Heart Rate	Blood Pressure	RPE	Heart Rate	Blood Pressure	RPE
Rest	64	106/74		59	120/78	
2.0 mph 0% grade	68	122/70	6	94	130/78	11
3.0 mph 0% grade	76	132/74	7	113	158/78	14
3.0 mph 2.5% grade	80	136/80	9	120	170/78	15-16
3.0 mph 5.0% grade	86	142/78	9-10	125	182/78	17
3.0 mph 7.5% grade	98	146/82	12			
3.0 mph 10% grade	106	148/80	13-14			

**Estimated Peak Mets After Phase II
Exercise Program - From mini test results**

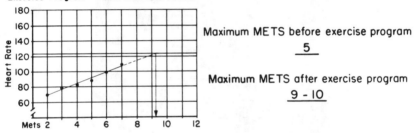

Maximum METS before exercise program

5

Maximum METS after exercise program

9 - 10

Figure 10 Comparison of heart rate, blood pressure, and rating of perceived exertion (RPE) at standard submaximal work loads during minitesting versus initial exercise testing. Extrapolation of the minitest heart rate/work load (METs) relationship facilitates estimation of the maximal oxygen consumption, expressed in METs.

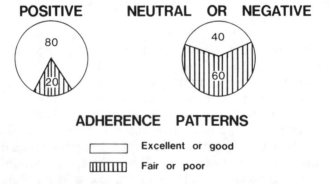

POSITIVE   NEUTRAL   OR   NEGATIVE

ADHERENCE   PATTERNS

☐ Excellent or good

▥ Fair or poor

Figure 11 Relation of wives' attitudes to husbands' adherence in a physical conditioning program. *Note.*   Adapted from "Response to Physical Activity Programs and Their Effects on Health Behavior" by F. Heinzelman and R. Bagley, 1970, *Public Health Reports, 85,* 905-911.

- *Provide progress charts to document exercise achievements.* Research substantiates the importance of immediate, positive feedback on reinforcement of health-related behaviors (Heinzelman, 1973). A progress chart that permits participants to record daily and cumulative exercise achievements can facilitate this objective.
- *Play music during exercise sessions.* Appropriate background music may mask general fatigue and stimulate participants to exercise more energetically. This belief was substantiated in a survey in which 99 out of 114 joggers (87%) indicated a preference for background music during their training (Franklin, 1978). Many felt that inspiring music aided their workout and noted a reduction in the rating of perceived exertion at any given pace.
- *Recognize participant accomplishments through a system of rewards.* Peer recognition of fitness accomplishments provides another motivational technique. Recognition of lifestyle, health, or exercise achievements can be made in the form of inexpensive trophies, plaques, ribbons, or certificates. To this end, an annual health and physical fitness award ceremony is recommended.
- *Provide qualified, enthusiastic exercise leaders.* Although numerous variables affect participant exercise compliance, perhaps the most important is the exercise leader (Franklin, 1984; Oldridge, 1977). Exercise leaders should be well-trained, highly motivated, innovative, and enthusiastic. Selected responsibilities of the exercise specialist, as designated by the American College of Sports Medicine (ACSM), are outlined in Table 2. Recommended behavioral strategies of the good exercise leader are shown in Table 3.

Table 2 Selected Competencies of the Preventive and Rehabilitative Exercise Specialist

1. Meet the requirements of the exercise test technologist.
2. Interpret metabolic data obtained on the participant.
3. Execute the exercise prescription under guidelines established by the physician and the program director.
4. Educate the participant concerning exercise.
5. Evaluate the participant's response to exercise.
6. Interact and communicate with all personnel involved in the exercise program.

Note. For a complete listing of required competencies, see *American College of Sports Medicine Guidelines for Exercise Testing and Prescription* (pp. 131–137), 1986, Philadelphia: Lea and Febiger.

Table 3   Behavioral Strategies of the Good Exercise Leader

1. Show a sincere interest in the participant.
2. Be enthusiastic in your instruction and guidance.
3. Develop a personal association and relationship with each participant and learn their names.
4. Consider the various reasons why adults exercise (i.e., health, recreation, weight loss, social, personal appearance) and allow for individual differences.
5. Initiate participant follow-up (e.g., written notes or telephone calls) when several unexplained absences occur in succession.
6. Participate in the exercise session yourself.
7. Honor special days (e.g., birthdays) or exercise accomplishments with extrinsic rewards such as t-shirts, ribbons, or certificates.
8. Attend to orthopedic and musculoskeletal problems.
9. Counsel participants on proper foot apparel and exercise clothing.
10. Motivate participants to make a long-term exercise commitment.

Continuing Education and Training for Exercise Program Personnel

The emergence of exercise as an accepted intervention or therapeutic modality in preventive and rehabilitative programs has created the need for educating and training allied health personnel, including nurses, physical and health educators, exercise physiologists, and physical therapists. Numerous professional organizations including the American Heart Association; the American College of Cardiology; the American Medical Association; the American Alliance for Health, Physical Education, Recreation, and Dance; the Aerobics and Fitness Association of America; and the National YMCAs have responded through the sponsorship of conferences, establishment of committees, and development of educational materials. However, perhaps the most significant efforts within this area have been through the American College of Sports Medicine (ACSM).

The ACSM has published a "position statement" concerning the recommended quantity and quality of exercise for developing and maintaining fitness in healthy adults (American College of Sports Medicine, 1979). In addition, it has developed guidelines for exercise testing and prescription for apparently healthy adults and patients with coronary artery disease (American College of Sports Medicine, 1986). Paralleling the evolution of the guidelines has been the development of workshops (Figure 12) held at selected sites throughout the country and a certification

Figure 12 Exercise specialist workshops and certification examinations are sponsored by selected sites each year.

process incorporating both written and practical examinations for individuals involved in the administration of graded exercise testing and physical conditioning programs. These workshop and certification offerings have served admirably to fill a void in the continuing education and training of an increasing number of individuals who aspire to conduct preventive and rehabilitative exercise and health promotion programs.

The ACSM Certification Process

Candidates for the varied certification levels (i.e., exercise test technologist, fitness leader, health fitness instructor, exercise specialist, health fitness director, and exercise program director) must apply directly to the ACSM, completing the appropriate forms and submitting evidence of practical experience, letters of reference, and current certification in cardiopulmonary resuscitation. This material is reviewed by the ACSM Director of Certifications and/or by members of the ACSM Preventive and Rehabilitative Exercise Programs Committee. If accepted, the candidate must pass a written test as a prerequisite to participation in the practical examination. Practical examinations are generally administered in conjunction with ACSM workshops and certifying faculties.

The practical portion of the certification may include an oral examination and a hands-on demonstration of knowledge and competency in one or more of the following areas: (a) conduct and administration of graded exercise testing; (b) evaluation of case studies including the interpretation of clinical data and graded exercise test results for the formulation of an exercise prescription (intensity, frequency, duration, and mode of exercise training); (c) conduct of gymnasium exercise sessions including the demonstration of leadership, enthusiasm, and creativity with appropriate activity selection; (d) capability to effectively respond to simulated, untoward events (cardiovascular or musculoskeletal) during exercise testing or training; (e) modification of the exercise prescription for patients with specific limitations; (f) competency in program organization and administration; and (g) teaching ability. The areas tested would depend on the particular certification.

To successfully complete the written and practical examinations, candidates must have knowledge or understanding of many or all of the following areas, depending on the level of certification: functional anatomy, exercise physiology, pathophysiology, electrocardiography, human behavior, psychology, gerontology, nutrition, health promotion, cardiac pharmacology, principles and practices of graded exercise testing, exercise prescription, exercise leadership skills, and emergency procedures. These areas are outlined as general and specific behavioral learning objectives in the *American College of Sports Medicine Guidelines for Exercise Testing and Prescription* (1986), a valuable guide to assist the candidate in study preparation. Additional information, study guidelines, and the requirements for certification can be obtained directly from the ACSM, P.O. Box 1440, Indianapolis, IN 46206.

Categories of Certification

The ACSM has developed two major categories of certification for personnel involved in preventive and rehabilitative exercise programs: the Preventive and Rehabilitative Tracts (American College of Sports Medicine Guidelines, 1986). The former is designed primarily for persons working in programs of a preventive nature (i.e., for healthy individuals or those with controlled disease). In contrast, the Rehabilitative Tract is for professionals who are primarily responsible for working with diseased individuals, particularly those with cardiovascular or pulmonary problems. However, these specialists are also authorized to provide similar leadership in programs of a preventive nature.

Preventive Tract. There are progressive degrees of knowledges, skills, and competencies within each of the preventive certification levels. Moreover, individuals certified at a given level are responsible for the knowledge and proficiency requirements of the level(s) below theirs. Three levels of certification are currently offered.

Fitness Leader/Specialty. Individuals certified at this level are considered to be entry level personnel whose primary responsibility is exercise leadership. Such persons serve under the direction of a health fitness instructor and/or health fitness director. Although no special educational prerequisites are required for this level, fitness leaders must have knowledge and skills in a particular area of specialization such as dance exercise, military, or law enforcement.

Health Fitness Instructor. Certification at the level of health fitness instructor requires a depth and breadth of knowledge greater than that for the fitness leader. Such individuals must demonstrate competence in exercise testing, designing and implementing a physical conditioning program, leading activity, and organizing and operating exercise facilities for healthy individuals or those with controlled diseases. The health fitness instructor may also be responsible for the training and/or supervision of fitness leaders and the health counseling of participants who may require multiple intervention strategies for lifestyle change. The minimum educational requirement for this level is a baccalaureate degree in an allied health field.

Health Fitness Director. The individual certified at this highest preventive level is required to have a postgraduate degree in an allied health field, at least a 1-year internship or equivalent practical experience, and, in addition to the qualifications of the two previous levels, competence in preventive program administration, supervision of staff, and program evaluation.

Rehabilitative Tract. Similar to the hierarchical order of the Preventive Tract, the Rehabilitative Tract includes progressive levels of knowledges, skills, and competencies. Individuals certified at a given level are responsible for the knowledge and proficiency requirements of the level(s) below theirs. Three levels of certification are currently offered:

Exercise Test Technologist. This individual must demonstrate competence in the exercise testing of individuals with or without disease. Specific responsibilities include preparing the laboratory for administration of the test, preliminary screening of the participant, administering tests and recording data, implementing necessary emergency procedures, summarizing test data, and communicating the test results to exercise program personnel and physicians. The technologist must also be able to delineate contraindications to exercise testing, to recognize abnormal responses during or after the exercise test, and to respond appropriately. No special experience or educational prerequisites are required for this level.

Preventive and Rehabilitative Exercise Specialist. In addition to the competencies expected of the exercise test technologist and health fitness instructor, the exercise specialist must be able to design an exercise prescription based on the results of an exercise test, lead exercise for healthy individuals or those with medical limitations (especially cardiorespiratory or metabolic diseases), evaluate participants' responses to exercise training, and assist in the education of patients. An internship of 6 or more months (approximately 800 hours) in a clinical setting is a prerequisite for this certification.

Exercise Program Director. In addition to the competencies expected of the exercise test technologist, health fitness instructor, preventive and rehabilitative exercise specialist, and health fitness director, the exercise program director must demonstrate competence in administering preventive and rehabilitative programs, designing and implementing exercise programs, educating staff and community, and conducting research. Such individuals generally possess an advanced degree in fields such as exercise physiology, physiology, health education, nursing, medicine, or physical education.

Conclusion

Individuals who attain ACSM certification have demonstrated the competency to participate in the design and implementation of exercise programs for healthy adults or those with medical limitations, particularly those with cardiovascular, pulmonary, or related metabolic diseases. This achievement involves a strong personal commitment to continuing education and the candidate's willingness to submit to a rigorous examination process. The certifications, although formidable, are important to the promotion of quality control and knowledge and proficiency standards among preventive and rehabilitative exercise program personnel (Franklin, 1981).

References

American College of Sports Medicine. (1986). *Guidelines for exercise testing and prescription* (3rd ed.). Philadelphia: Lea and Febiger.

American College of Sports Medicine Position Statement. (1979). The recommended quantity and quality of exercise for developing and maintaining fitness in healthy adults. *Medicine and Science in Sports,* **10**, 7-9.

Andrew, G.M., Oldridge, N.B., Parker, J.O., Cunningham, D.A., Rechnitzer, P.A., Jones, N.L., Buck, C., Kavanagh, T., Shephard, R.J., & Sutton, J.R. (1981). Reasons for dropout from exercise programs in post-coronary patients. *Medicine and Science in Sports and Exercise,* **13**, 164-168.

Blumenthal, J.A., Williams, R.S., Wallace, A.G., Williams, R.B., & Needles, T.L. (1982). Physiological and psychological variables predict compliance to prescribed exercise therapy in patients recovering from myocardial infarction. *Psychosomatic Medicine,* **44**(6), 519-527.

Borg, G. (1970). Perceived exertion as an indicator of somatic stress. *Scandinavian Journal of Rehabilitative Medicine,* **2**, 92-98.

Bruce, E.H., Frederick, R., Bruce, R.A., & Fisher, L.D. (1976). Comparison of active participants and dropouts in CAPRI cardiopulmonary rehabilitation programs. *American Journal of Cardiology,* **37**, 53-60.

DeBusk, R.F., Haskell, W.L., Miller, N.H., Berra, K., & Taylor, C.B. (1985). Medically directed at-home rehabilitation soon after clinically uncomplicated acute myocardial infarction: A new model for patient care. *American Journal of Cardiology,* **55**, 251-257.

Epstein, L., Thompson, J., & Wing, R. (1980). The effects of contract and lottery procedures on attendance and fitness in aerobic exercise. *Behavior Modification,* **4**, 465-479.

Franklin, B. (1978). Motivating and educating adults to exercise. *Journal of Physical Education and Recreation,* **49**(6), 13-17.

Franklin, B. (1981). Meeting manpower and training needs in cardiac rehabilitation [Editorial]. *Journal of Cardiovascular and Pulmonary Technique,* **9**, 12-66.

Franklin, B. (1984). Exercise program compliance: Improvement strategies. In J. Storlie & H. Jordan (Eds.), *Behavioral management of obesity* (pp. 105-135). New York: Spectrum.

Franklin, B. (1986). Clinical components of a successful adult fitness program. *American Journal of Health Promotion, 1*, 6–13.

Franklin, B., Hellerstein, H., Gordon, S., & Timmis, G.C. (1986). Exercise prescription for the myocardial infarction patient. *Journal of Cardiopulmonary Rehabilitation, 6*, 62–79.

Gale, J.B., Eckhoff, W.T., Mogel, S.F., & Rodnick, J.E. (1984). Factors related to adherence to an exercise program for healthy adults. *Medicine and Science in Sports and Exercise, 16*, 544–549.

Gottheiner, V. (1968). Long-range strenuous sports training for cardiac reconditioning and rehabilitation. *American Journal of Cardiology, 22*, 426–435.

Heinzelman, F. (1973). Social and psychological factors that influence the effectiveness of exercise programs. In J. Naughton & H. Hellerstein (Eds.), *Exercise testing and exercise training in coronary heart disease* (pp. 275–287). New York: Academic.

Heinzelman, F., & Bagley, R. (1970). Response to physical activity programs and their effects on health behavior. *Public Health Reports, 85*, 905–911.

Hellerstein, H.K. (1968). Exercise therapy in coronary disease. *Bulletin of the New York Academy of Medicine, 44*, 1028–1047.

Hellerstein, H., & Franklin, B. (1984). Exercise testing and prescription. In N. Wenger & H. Hellerstein (Eds.), *Rehabilitation of the coronary patient* (2nd ed., pp. 197–284). New York: John Wiley.

Kavanagh, T., Shephard, R.J., Doney, H., & Pandit, V. (1973). Intensive exercise in coronary rehabilitation. *Medicine and Science in Sports, 5*, 34–39.

Kentala, E. (1972). Physical fitness and feasibility of physical rehabilitation after myocardial infarction in men of working age. *Annals of Clinical Research, 4*(Suppl. 9), 1–84.

Kilbom, A., Hartley, L., Saltin, B., Bjure, J., Grimby, G., & Astrand, I. (1969). Physical training in sedentary middle-aged and older men. I. Medical evaluation. *Scandinavian Journal of Clinical and Laboratory Investigation, 24*, 315–322.

Mann, G.V., Garrett, H.L., Farhi, A., Murray, H., & Billings, F.T. (1969). Exercise to prevent coronary heart disease: An experimental study of the effects of training on risk factors for coronary disease in men. *American Journal of Medicine, 46*, 12–27.

Martin, J. (1981). *I. The effects of feedback, reinforcement and goal selection on exercise adherence. II. Self-control and exercise maintenance: The effects of proximal and distal goal setting.* Papers presented at the 15th Annual Convention of the Association for Advancement of Behavior Therapy, Toronto, Canada.

Massie, J.F., & Shephard, R.J. (1971). Physiological and psychological effects of training—A comparison of individual and gymnasium programs, with a characterization of the exercise "drop-out." *Medicine and Science in Sports, 3,* 110–117.

McHenry, M. (1974). Medical screening of patients with coronary artery disease: Criteria for entrance into exercise conditioning programs. *American Journal of Cardiology, 33,* 752–756.

Nye, E.R., & Poulsen, W.T. (1974). An activity programme for coronary patients: A review of morbidity, mortality and adherence after five years. *New Zealand Medical Journal, 79,* 1010–1013.

Oja, P., Teraslinna, P., Partanen, T., & Karava, R. (1974). Feasibility of an 18 months' physical training program for middle-aged men and its effect on physical fitness. *American Journal of Public Health, 64,* 459–465.

Oldridge, N. (1974). *A program of physical activity for the coronary-prone individual—A seven-year follow-up.* Paper presented at the Human Kinetic Symposium, University of Guelph, Ontario, Canada.

Oldridge, N. (1977). What to look for in an exercise class leader. *The Physician and Sportsmedicine, 5,* 85–88.

Oldridge, N.B. (1979). Compliance of post myocardial infarction patients to exercise programs. *Medicine and Science in Sports, 11,* 373–375.

Oldridge, N., & Jones, N. (1981). Contracting as a strategy to reduce drop out in exercise rehabilitation. *Medicine and Science in Sports, 13,* 125–126.

Oldridge, N.B., Wicks, J.R., Hanley, C., Sutton, J.R., & Jones, N.L. (1978). Noncompliance in an exercise rehabilitation program for men who have suffered a myocardial infarction. *Canadian Medical Association Journal, 118,* 361–364.

Palatsi, I. (1976). Feasibility of physical training after myocardial infarction and its effect on return to work, morbidity and mortality. *Acta Medica Scandinavica,* (Suppl. 559), 7–84.

Pollock, M., Gettman, L., Milesis, C., Bah, M.D., Durstine, L., & Johnson, R.B. (1977). Effects of frequency and duration of training on attrition and incidence of injury. *Medicine and Science in Sports, 9,* 31–36.

Shaw, L.W. (1981). Effects of a prescribed supervised exercise program on mortality and cardiovascular morbidity in patients after a myocardial infarction. *American Journal of Cardiology, 48,* 39–46.

Stoedefalke, K. (1974). Physical fitness programs for adults. *American Journal of Cardiology, 33*, 787–790.

Taylor, H.L., Buskirk, E.R., & Remington, R.D. (1973). Exercise in controlled trials of the prevention of coronary heart disease. *Federation Proceedings, 32*, 1623–1627.

Ward, A., & Morgan, W.P. (1984). Adherence patterns of healthy men and women enrolled in an adult exercise program. *Journal of Cardiac Rehabilitation, 4*, 143–152.

Wilhelmsen, L., Sanne, H., Elmfeldt, D., Grimby, G., Tibblin, G., & Wedel, H. (1975). A controlled trial of physical training after myoardial infarction: Effects on risk factors, nonfatal reinfarction, and death. *Preventive Medicine, 4*, 491–508.

Wilmore, J.H. (1974). Individual exercise prescription. *American Journal of Cardiology, 33*, 757–759.

CHAPTER 9

Prescribing Exercise for Fitness and Adherence

Michael L. Pollock

The guidelines and recommendations for exercise prescription have been well documented (American College of Sports Medicine, 1978; Åstrand & Rodahl, 1986; Cureton, 1969; Kasch & Boyer, 1968; Pollock, Wilmore, & Fox, 1984). The guidelines recommended by most include the following: frequency of training, 3 to 5 days per week; intensity of training, 60 to 90% of maximum heart rate reserve (HR max reserve) or 50 to 85% of maximum oxygen uptake ($\dot{V}O_2$max); duration of training, 20 to 50 minutes; and mode of activity, aerobic activities such as running, walking, bicycling, swimming, cross-country skiing, vigorous dancing, and various endurance sport activities. These guidelines were designed to give an average participant the amount of stimulation necessary to develop and maintain an optimal level of cardiorespiratory endurance and body composition. A well-rounded program would also include strength conditioning of the major muscle groups and flexibility exercises (American College of Sports Medicine, 1978; Pollock et al., 1984). The exercise prescription is designed to expend a certain amount of energy per exercise session (approximately 250 to 300 kilocalories [kcal] for a 70 kg person) that is reflected in the energy cost of the activity (Cooper, 1977; Cureton, 1969; Olree, Corbin, Penrod, & Smith, 1969; Pollock et al., 1984).

Intensity and duration of exercise are interrelated; thus if intensity is maintained at the lower end of the training zone, the duration should be increased. If the increased duration is enough to offset the decrease in kcal of the reduced intensity, similar training effects can be attained (Burke & Franks, 1975; Pollock et al., 1972). In contrast, if the intensity is at the higher end of the training zone, the duration can be lessened. In general, jogging programs are conducted between 80 and 90% of HR max reserve, and fast walking and other activities of similar intensity are performed at 60 to 75% of HR max reserve (Leon, Conrad, Hunninghake, & Serfass, 1979; Pollock et al., 1971; Pollock et al., 1984). Therefore, the high-intensity program would be conducted for approximately 20 to 30 minutes per exercise session, and the more moderate intensity program for 30 to 50 minutes per session.

An adequate program stressing the various components of physical fitness can be designed for a 60-minute period. For most individuals a program lasting more than 60 minutes may become a deterrent for long-term continuation. The four main components of an exercise program would include periods of warm-up, muscle conditioning, aerobics, and cool-down. Table 1 gives a suggested time frame for each component. The variability of each time frame—in particular, the muscle-conditioning and aerobic periods—depends on health and fitness status and individual needs and goals. For example, if the program was being designed for police officers or fire fighters, the muscle-conditioning component would become more important, and a minimum of 20 minutes would be recommended. Depending on intensity, the aerobic period would be 20 to 30 minutes in duration. In contrast, a healthy but overweight 48-year-old

Table 1 Components of a Training Program

Component	Activities	Recommended time (min)
Warm-up	Stretching, low-level calisthenics, walking	10
Muscular conditioning	Calisthenics, weight training, pulley weights	10 to 20
Aerobics	Fast walk, jog/run, swim, bicycle, cross-country skiing vigorous games, dancing	20 to 40
Cool-down	Walking, stretching	5 to 10

Note. From *Exercise in Health and Disease—Evaluation and Prescription for Prevention and Rehabilitation* (p. 247) by M.L. Pollock, J.H. Wilmore, and S.M. Fox, 1984, Philadelphia: W.B. Saunders. Copyright 1984 by W.B. Saunders. Reprinted by permission.

executive would probably start out with 5 to 10 minutes of strength activities and an aerobic period of 30 to 45 minutes. Initially, the sedentary executive will emphasize stretching and low-level muscle-conditioning exercises. The aerobic activity would be of low-to-moderate intensity, probably of an interval type stressing a combination of walking and jogging or slow and fast walking. More details concerning an exercise prescription for both healthy adults and cardiac patients are available (Pollock et al., 1984; Pollock, Pels, Foster, & Ward, 1986).

Adherence to Exercise Programs

Exercise programs should be designed not only to develop optimal fitness but also to enhance long-term adherence to training. The focus of this chapter is on the major components of the exercise prescription and how they affect adherence. Data from a series of exercise training studies conducted by Pollock and associates are presented to identify factors affecting adherence. Use of the perceived exertion scale to prescribe and monitor exercise is discussed as a strategy to increase adherence to training programs.

Factors Affecting Adherence to Training

As described earlier in this text, many factors may affect adherence to exercise training programs. Attitude toward physical activity, personality, type of exercise program (frequency, intensity, and duration of training and mode of activity), body weight and composition, medical problems (injuries, level of fitness, group supervision), staff, spouse influence, age, sex, socioeconomic status, cost/method of payment, and time-related factors are most often mentioned (Andrew et al., 1981; Bruce, Frederick, Bruce, & Fisher, 1976; Dishman, 1981; Dishman, Sallis, & Orenstein, 1985; Oldridge, 1982, 1984a, 1984b; Pollock, Foster, Salisbury, & Smith, 1982). Self-motivation (Dishman, Ickes, & Morgan, 1980) and whether one is a smoker or a blue-collar worker have also been shown to be significant in depicting the exercise program dropout (Oldridge, 1984a).

Adherence to exercise regimens has been shown to average from 50 to 80% for the first 5 to 6 months of a program (Dishman et al., 1985; Oldridge, 1982, 1984a, 1984b; Ward & Morgan, 1984). Programs conducted for 1 year or longer show adherence to be less than 50% and significantly less thereafter (Dishman et al., 1985; Oldridge, 1982; Ward & Morgan, 1984). Most data show that the largest percent dropout in an exercise program occurs during the first 12 weeks. In the three university study Taylor, Buskirk, and Remington (1973) found a 50% dropout during the first 6 months of training with attendance becoming stable for the next 9 to 15 months.

Adherence to Training Programs: Results From Pollock and Associates, 1968–1985

Because of inherent differences and methods of exercise, prescription techniques, and program management, comparing adherence figures among investigators is often difficult. The following sections show adherence data from studies conducted and reported by Pollock and associates from 1968 to 1985. These studies were primarily designed to add information to the literature concerning the exercise prescription and not necessarily designed to evaluate adherence. Even so, it is hoped that the summary of information from a large, collated sample of studies conducted by one primary investigator helps to provide insight into prescribing exercise for better program adherence.

Subjects.   The subjects from exercise training studies conducted by Pollock and associates included 679 men ranging from 21 to 71 years of age (Table 2). (The 73 subjects of Pels et al., in press, were analyzed too late to be included in this summary of studies.) The subjects were participants of 17 training studies conducted by Pollock and colleagues over an 18 year period (Foster et al., 1984; Gettman, Ayres, & Pollock, 1978; Gettman et al., 1976; Gettman, Pollock, Ayres, Durstine, & Graham, 1979; Gettman, Pollock, & Ward, 1983; Milesis et al., 1976; Pels, Pollock, Dohmeier, Lemberger, & Oehrlein, in press; Pollock, Broida, Kendrick et al., 1972; Pollock, Cureton, & Greniger, 1969; Pollock, Demmick, Miller, Kendrick, & Linnerud, 1975; Pollock et al., 1971, 1974, 1976; Pollock, Gettman, Janeway, Lofland, & Tiffany, 1969; Pollock, Gettman, Raven, Bah, & Ward, 1978; Pollock, Ward, & Ayres, 1977; Price, Pollock, Gettman, & Dent, 1977). All subjects were volunteers and except for one cardiac group (Foster et al., 1984) were healthy and free from overt signs or symptoms of disease and orthopedic problems. Most were professionally employed in white-collar jobs.

The control subjects were either randomized or were from an overflow of volunteer subjects wanting to participate in the exercise program. In all cases controls were promised an exercise program when their control period was completed. The control–no treatment group differed from the control–placebo group in that the control–no treatment group only attended testing sessions. The control-placebo group took tests plus attended class on a regular basis. Classes include nonendurance type activities.

Design of Training Protocols.   Fourteen of the 17 training studies were carried out over a 20-week period; one was for 16 weeks (Pollock, Gettman, et al., 1969) and two for 24 weeks (Foster et al., 1984; Gettman et al., 1979). The experiments were conducted at a frequency of from 1 to 5 days per week for a duration of 15 to 45 minutes per day and at an intensity of 60 to 95% of HR max reserve. The HR max reserve was first described by Karvonen, Kentala, and Mustala (1957) and is calculated as a percentage of the difference between maximum and resting heart rate and added back to the resting heart rate.

For the most part similar techniques were used to monitor the exercise training regimens. Exercise leaders were either graduate students in physical education or full-time staff with a BS or MS in physical education with a special emphasis in adult fitness/cardiac rehabilitation. The study with cardiac patients included supervision by cardiac rehabilitation nurses. The author was directly involved in the organization and supervision of all studies and was present for most training sessions. Supervision usually included no more than 7 or 8 subjects per staff member. The study with cardiac patients had a 2 or 3:1 patient to staff ratio.

Subjects were given an exercise prescription based on the results of a symptom-limited graded exercise test. When appropriate, a cardiovascular physical examination (American College of Sports Medicine Guidelines, 1986) and evaluation of health status for cardiovascular disease was administered. All studies included the determination of maximum aerobic capacity and body composition.

In all cases training was quantified by time-motion analysis (Consolazio, Johnson, & Pecora, 1963) and by heart rate response to the exercise. After each training session the subjects recorded pace/resistance and time spent in each activity. To estimate energy expenditure, recorded values were converted to kcal. Heart rate (beats/10 sec) was determined at the middle and end of each training session by the palpation technique. This method has been validated and described elsewhere (Pollock, Broida, & Kendrick, 1972).

Most studies included a combination of jogging/walking, walking, or stationary cycling. Two studies included circuit weight training as an activity. The cardiac group did a combination of walking, walking-jogging, and stationary cycling.

Dropouts included subjects who stopped attending class or who had a poor attendance record (less than 80%). If subjects missed an exercise session, they were given ample time to make it up. When possible, reasons for dropping out were obtained.

Overall Adherence to Exercise Programs.   The overall adherence rate for the 679 subjects studied are shown in Table 2. The 70% adherence rate shown for the exercise group is higher than the average of 50 to 60% summarized by Oldridge (1984b) for healthy adults over a similar time span. The reason for the better than average adherence to exercise in our studies compared to the average reported in the literature is only speculative. Most of the groups studied were tested at the beginning, middle (8 to 12 weeks), and end of the training period, had a small participant to instructor ratio (less than 8:1), and were in total groups of less than 50 subjects. All of these factors have been suggested as giving participants a more individualized program with greater feedback (reinforcement) and personal attention (Dishman et al., 1985; Massie & Shepherd, 1971; Oldridge, 1982, 1984a, 1984b; Taylor et al., 1973).

Table 2   Overall Adherence to Exercise Programs Conducted by Pollock et al., 1966–1985

Group	Started (n)	Finished (n)	Adherence (%)
Exercise	501	349	70
Control–no treatment	151	112	74
Control-placebo	27	23	85

In the analysis of our data it would first appear that the total size of a group studied was an important factor in adherence to exercise. Participants in studies conducted with fewer than 50 subjects had an adherence rate of 74% (180/244), and studies having more than 50 subjects had an adherence rate of 60.5% (190/314). The latter group includes some recent data from 73 subjects trained by Pels et al., (in press). These data were not analyzed in time to be included in Table 2 or other aspects of this summary of studies. Further analysis of the groups who had more than 50 participants revealed that distance traveled to the exercise center may have been the factor related to adherence. Of the 314 subjects in the more-than-50-participants group, 101/187 (54%) adhered when they had to travel to a downtown, centralized location, and 89/127 (70%) adhered when the training facility was closer to home. Distance traveled to a training site has been well established as a significant factor related to exercise adherence (Andrew et al., 1981; Bruce et al., 1976; Hanson, 1976; Price et al., 1977). Because the instructor to subject ratios and other factors related to the testing and training were consistent among all study groups, it appears that, in our hands, the total size of the group per se was less of a factor than distance traveled to the training site.

The non-treatment control group had an adherence rate similar to the exercise groups, and there was a nonsignificant trend for the placebo-control groups to have a higher adherence (Table 2). Both control groups took all the same preliminary tests and orientation as the exercise groups as well as the final tests. They did not usually take any mid-term tests or receive feedback information in the interim between initial and final testing.

Frequency of Training.   The effect of frequency of training on exercise adherence is shown in Table 3. The data show no significant differences among groups when training from 1 to 5 days per week. Although injuries increased significantly when frequency of training was greater than 3 days per week, these were mainly associated with jogging/running type of regimens (Pollock, Gettman, et al., 1977). The one walking study that had a frequency of 4 days per week (data not included in Table 3) had one of the lowest injury rates (16 of 19 adhered, 84%) of all the studies conducted (Pollock et al., 1971). Mode of training and its effect on adherence will be discussed later. Short-term stationary cycling was sometimes substituted for jogging/running when injuries prevented subjects from continuing jogging/running training. This allowed time for injuries to heal and thus improved adherence for the 4 to 5 days per week programs.

Table 3   Effect of Frequency of Training on Adherence to Exercise

Group days/week	Started (n)	Finished (n)	Adherence (%)
1	15	11	73
2	52	40	77
3	306	197	64
4	34	23	68
5	18	13	72

Intensity of Training.   The effect of high intensity interval training and continuous jogging on adherence to exercise is shown in Table 4. The combination group alternated between days of continous jogging and interval training. The purpose of the study was to determine the physiological and body composition effects of aerobic and anaerobic training. The results showed similar improvements in aerobic capacity for all three groups. The energy expenditure was estimated each week for all groups and programs were modified to keep the kcal relatively equal among training groups.

Table 4   Effect of High Intensity Interval Training and Continuous Jogging on Adherence to Exercise

Group (run)	Started (n)	Finished (n)	Adherence (%)
Continous	26	16	62
Interval	25	10	40
Combination	26	11	42

High-intensity interval training caused more injuries and dropouts than the continuous training program (Pollock et al., 1978; Price et al., 1977). At the completion of the study the combination group was asked which program they preferred. The combination group preferred continous jogging over high-intensity interval training at a rate of 90%.

These data on high-intensity training compared to more moderate intensity training have important implications for the recommendation of exercise programs to average participants. High-intensity exercise appears to be neither enjoyable nor well tolerated by the nonathlete who is training for general health and fitness. High-intensity exercise may also be contraindicated for low-fit, overweight, older populations and individuals with cardiovascular disease (Pollock et al., 1986).

Although intensity of training is an important ingredient of the exercise prescription, the program does not have to be exhausting or of very high intensity to be optimally beneficial for fitness development and maintenance. For example, Pollock, Broida, Kendrick, et al., (1972) trained middle-aged men by jogging/running at either 90 or 80% of HR max reserve for a 20-week period. The 90% group perceived their training as difficult, and the 80% group as moderate. Frequency of training was the same for both groups, but the 80% intensity group trained 4 to 5 minutes longer per exercise session. The additional training minutes equalized the kcal expenditure per training session for both groups, and both groups showed similar improvements in aerobic capacity. Thus, for long-term adherence to training, intensity should be sufficient to elicit and maintain a training effect but not so extreme as to be a deterrent (Pollock et al., 1984).

Duration of Training.   The effect of duration of training on adherence to exercise is shown in Table 5. Duration of training did have an effect on adherence to training. The two factors contributed greatly here were, first, the time component (commitment) and, second, injuries. (Milesis et al., 1976; Pollock et al., 1984; Pollock, Gettman, et al., 1977).

Table 5 Effect of Duration of Training on Adherence to Exercise

Group (min)	Started (n)	Finished (n)	Adherence (%)
15	20	15	75
30	25	17	68
45	24	13	54

"It takes too much time" has been shown to be an important reason why many participants drop out of exercise programs (Dishman et al., 1985; Oldridge, 1982, 1984a, 1984b; Price et al., 1977). As a result of the time factor's relation to adherence, Pollock et al., (1984) have recommended that exercise programs be designed to be no longer than 60 minutes. The 60-minute period should include all the components of the program: warm-up, muscle conditioning, aerobic phase, and cool-down. The program should be at a convenient time of day and close to work or home.

The training programs shown in Table 5 included jogging/running as the major mode of activity; thus the reference to injuries may not be related to activities that do not include a running component. The injury rate increased from 22 to 53% when participants trained for 45 minutes compared to 30 minutes per exercise session.

Mode of Training.   To determine the effect of mode of training on physiological function and change in body composition, running, walking, and stationary cycling were compared (Pollock et al., 1975). Frequency (3 days per week), intensity (85% HR max reserve), and duration (30 minutes) were standardized among groups. After 20 weeks of training all groups improved similarly in aerobic capacity and body weight and fat loss. As shown in Table 6, no differences among groups in adherence to training were found.

Table 6   Effect of Different Modes of Training on Adherence to Exercise

Group (mode)	Started (n)	Finished (n)	Adherence (%)
Run	12	9	75
Walk	12	9	75
Bicycle	12	8	67

Although the walking study mentioned earlier (Pollock et al., 1971) had an adherence rate of 84% after 20 weeks of training, it was conducted at a lower intensity (70 to 75% of HR max reserve). Thus the mode of activity in itself may not affect adherence to training as much as other factors such as intensity and duration of training.

Jogging/running, aerobic dance, and other activities that have a jogging component cause a significant number of debilitating injuries (Oja, Teraslinna, Partanen, & Karava, 1975; Pollock et al., 1984; Richie, Felso, & Bellucci, 1985). When participants have a bad experience, such as an injury, while participating in an exercise program, the likelihood of good adherence is significantly reduced. Because most dropouts occur early in the program (Oldridge, 1982; Taylor et al., 1973; Ward & Morgan, 1984), it appears that beginners should be prescribed programs that start gradually and progress at a slow pace (Pollock et al., 1984; Pollock, Gettman, et al., 1977). Thus the manner in which the program is introduced and progresses appears to reduce injuries (Pollock, Gettman, et al., 1977). For example, the two studies that were conducted that introduced the aerobic phase of training by walking produced the fewest injuries and had the best adherence rates of all our studies (Foster et al., 1984; Pollock et al., 1971). The results of the Foster et al. (1984) study conducted with cardiac patients over a 24-week period showed an adherence rate of 81% (see Table 7). The walking study described earlier had an adherence rate of 84% over a

Table 7   Adherence of Cardiac Patients to Six Months of Rehabilitation

Group	Started (n)	Finished (n)	Adherence (%)
Exercise	26	21	81
Control-placebo	14	11	77

20-week period. One other study that had a low injury rate began with an 8-week circuit weight training program prior to 8 to 16 weeks of jogging/running (Gettman et al., 1979).

Rating of Perceived Exertion

Because heart rate and oxygen cost have a linear relationship at submaximal exercise, heart rate has been traditionally used as the standard for estimating the energy cost or intensity of the activity (Åstrand & Rodahl, 1986). More recently the rating of perceived exertion scale (RPE), described by Borg (1962, 1978, 1982), has been used in conjunction with heart rate to estimate the intensity of effort and to prescribe exercise in both cardiac patients and noncardiac participants (Dishman, Patton, Smith, Weinberg, & Jackson, in press; Noble, 1982; Pollock et al., 1984, 1986). A recent report describes in more detail the validity and use of the RPE scale for use in prescribing exercise (Pollock, Jackson, & Foster, in press).

The RPE scale, as shown in Figure 1, is a 15-point category scale ranging from 6 to 20. The scale has descriptive, verbal anchor points at every odd number. The RPE and heart rate are linearly related to each other and to work intensity across a variety of exercise modalities and conditions (Skinner, Hutsler, Bergsteinova, & Buskirk, 1973a, 1973b; Sargeant & Davies, 1973; Pandolf, 1982; Borg, 1982). RPE also relates well to various physiological factors: A multiple correlation of 84 was found between pulmonary ventilation, heart rate, lactate and oxygen consumption (Morgan & Pollock, 1977).

The original concept of the RPE scale was developed from young adults; addition of a zero to each of the points on the scale would reflect the heart rate value under various levels of exercise intensity. For example, 6 would become 60 and represent heart rate at rest, and 19 and 20 would represent HR max (190 to 200 beats/min). When the scale was applied

6	
7	Very, very light
8	
9	Very light
10	
11	Fairly light
12	
13	Somewhat hard
14	
15	Hard
16	
17	Very hard
18	
19	Very, very hard
20	

Figure 1   The rating of perceived exertion scale (RPE) developed by Borg. *Note.* From "Subjective Effort in Relation to Physical Performance and Working Capacity" by G. Borg, 1978. In H.L. Pick (Ed.), *Psychology: From Research to Practice* (p. 44). New York: Plenum. Copyright 1978 by Plenum. Reprinted by permission.

to persons of various ages, the same linear relationship with work intensity was found to exist at all ages, but the heart rate was consistently lower at each older age increment used (Borg, 1978). When subjects were placed on atropine or practolol, the heart rate was significantly increased or decreased in relation to the control test, but the heart rate values under these conditions remained linear and parallel with increased intensity of exercise (Davies & Sargeant, 1979). Another study using propranolol showed the same results as practolol (Pollock, Foster, Rod, Stoiber, 1982). In all cases (age differences, drug effects on heart rate, arm versus leg exercise, obese versus lean subjects), when RPE was expressed in terms of relative work (percent of $\dot{V}O_2$max or percent of HR max reserve), the RPE values were similar (Borg, 1978, 1982; Davies & Sargent, 1979; Pollock & Foster, 1983; Pollock, Foster, & Hare, 1983; Pollock, Foster, Rod, Stoiber, et al., 1982; Sargent & Davies, 1973; Skinner et al., 1973a, 1973b).

Because RPE is related to the heart rate response at submaximal levels, it can be used as an important adjunct to heart rate in prescribing and monitoring an exercise program. Heart rate is still to be considered the primary physiological variable for estimating intensity (% of $\dot{V}O_2$max), but the RPE assists in adjusting the intensity to a level that is both suitable for eliciting a training effect and psychologically tolerable. Knowing the individual's heart rate to RPE relationship allows participants to monitor and adjust their program without having to stop and count their heart rate. Also, knowing how participants perceive their training intensity assists the professional in adjusting and refining the exercise prescription. The training zone of 60 to 90% of HR max reserve as described earlier shows a training zone of somewhat hard (RPE 12 to 13) to hard (RPE 15 to 16) that is recommended for both low-risk cardiac patients and healthy adults (Pollock et al., 1984, 1986; Pollock, Foster, Rod, & Wible, 1982).

From a practical standpoint knowledge of both heart rate and RPE will allow the exerciser to develop a more precise individual relationship between the two indicators. Once this individual relationship is determined, the participant can usually estimate training heart rate rather accurately by knowing the RPE (Dishman et al., in press). An important point is that knowledge of RPE informs the exercise leader of how the participant is adjusting to the exercise program and when further progression in training should occur.

Although the previous discussion shows the value of the RPE scale in determining the exercise prescription and monitoring training, it must be interpreted in the proper context. There are under- and over-raters, and it has been estimated that approximately 10% of the population cannot use the scale with any accuracy (Morgan, 1981). Because the RPE appears to remain consistent over time, persons who under- and over-rate may still find the scale of value as long as the tester, exercise leader, and participant are aware of this fact.

It is advisable to remind participants to focus not on any one cue but rather on general fatigue. For patients with angina pectoris, claudication, orthopedic problems, and weak musculature in the legs, rating their specific problems or weakness separately may be helpful. Reminding the participant of the various anchor points listed on the scale is also useful: 6 to 7 is resting, 13 to 15 is moderately difficult, and most persons rate maximum between 17 and 20 (Pollock, Foster, Rod, et al., 1982). When the RPE scale is introduced, written instructions should be used first and then followed by verbal reinforcement.

Final Comments

Exercise programs should be designed not only to develop optimal fitness but also for enhancing long-term adherence. Two important factors that are considered a deterrent to both short- and long-term adherence to an exercise program are excessive duration (longer than one hour) and a high proportion of high-intensity exercise (Price et al., 1978; Pollock et al., 1984). In our experience, programs that can be completed within

1 hour and at moderate intensity will enhance both fitness and adherence to training. The use of the RPE scale should help the participant as well as the exercise leader adjust the intensity of training to a level that will both elicit and maintain fitness and that is at a tolerable perceptual level.

Special attention should be given to participants when initiating their training program. Programs that start at a low intensity, progress at a moderate rate, and give the participant a more pleasant early experience should help avoid injury and the high rate of early dropouts. The use of walking rather than jogging/running may be best for participants who have been shown to be at a higher risk for injury and dropout. Finally, give participants a sufficient amount of rest between workout days. This is true particularly for jogging/running types of activities.

References

American College of Sports Medicine (1978). Position statement on the recommended quantity and quality of exercise for developing and maintaining fitness in healthy adults. *Medicine and Science in Sports,* **10**, vii–x.

American College of Sports Medicine. (1986). *Guidelines for exercise testing and exercise prescription* (3rd ed.). Philadelphia: Lea & Febiger.

Andrew, G.M., Oldridge, N.B., Parker, J.O., Cunningham, D.A., Rechnitzer, P.A., Jones, N.L., Buck, C., Kavanagh, T., Shephard, R.J., & Sutton, J.R. (1981). Reasons for dropout from exercise programs for the post coronary patients. *Medicine and Science in Sports and Exercise,* **13**, 164–168.

Åstrand, P.O., & Rodahl, K. (1986). *Textbook of work physiology* (3rd ed.). New York: McGraw-Hill.

Borg, G. (1962). *Physical performance and perceived exertion.* Lund, Sweden: Gleerup.

Borg, G. (1978). Subjective effort in relation to physical performance and working capacity. In H.L. Pick, Jr. (Ed.), *Psychology: From research to practice* (pp. 333–361). New York: Plenum.

Borg, G. (1982). Psychophysical bases of perceived exertion. *Medicine and Science in Sports and Exercise,* **14**, 337–381.

Bruce, E.G., Frederick, R., Bruce, R.A., & Fisher, L.D. (1976). Comparison of active participants and dropouts in CAPRI cardiopulmonary rehabilitation programs. *American Journal of Cardiology,* **37**, 53–60.

Burke, E.J., & Franks, B.D. (1975). Changes in $\dot{V}O_2$max resulting from bicycle training at different intensities holding total mechanical work constant. *Research Quarterly for Exercise and Sport, 46,* 31–37.

Consolazio, D., Johnson, R.E., & Pecora, A. (1963). *Physiological measurements of metabolic methods in man.* New York: McGraw-Hill.

Cooper, K.H. (1977). *The aerobics way.* New York: M. Evans.

Cureton, T.K. (1969). *The physiological effects of exercise programs upon adults.* Springfield, IL: Charles C Thomas.

Davies, C.T.M., & Sargeant, A.J. (1979). The effects of atropine and practolol on the perception of exertion during treadmill exercise. *Ergonomics, 22,* 1141–1146.

Dishman, R.K. (1981). Biologic influences on exercise adherence. *Research Quarterly for Exercise and Sport, 52,* 143–159.

Dishman, R.K., Ickes, W., & Morgan, W.P. (1980). Self-motivation and adherence to habitual physical activity. *Journal of Applied Social Psychology, 2,* 115–132.

Dishman, R.K., Patton, R., Smith, J., Weinberg, R., & Jackson, A.W. (in press). Using perceived exertion to prescribe and monitor exercise training heart rate. *International Journal of Sports Medicine.*

Dishman, R.K., Sallis, J.F., & Orenstein, D.R. (1985). The determinants of physical activity and exercise. *Public Health Reports, 100,* 158–171.

Foster, C., Pollock, M.L., Anholm, J.D., Squires, R.W., Ward, A., Rod, J.K., Johnson, W.D., Saicheck, R., & Schmidt, D.H. (1984). Work capacity and left ventricular function during rehabilitation after myocardial revascularization surgery. *Circulation, 69,* 748–755.

Gettman, L.R., Ayres, J., and Pollock, M.L. (1978). The effect of circuit weight training on strength, cardiorespiratory function and body composition of adult men. *Medicine and Science in Sports, 10,* 171–176.

Gettman, L.R., Pollock, M.L., Ayres, J., Durstine, L., & Gratham, W. (1979). Physiological effects on adult men of circuit strength training and jogging. *Archives of Physical Medicine and Rehabilitation, 60,* 115–120.

Gettman, L.R., Pollock, M.L., Ayers, J., Durstine, L., Ward, A., & Linnerud, A. (1976). Physiological responses of men to 1, 3, and 5 day per week training programs. *Research Quarterly, 47,* 638–646.

Gettman, L.R., Pollock, M.L., & Ward, A. (1983). Effects of supervised and unsupervised endurance exercise on middle-aged men. *Physician and Sportsmedicine, 11,* 56–66.

Hanson, M.G. (1976). *Coronary heart disease, exercise and motivation in middle-aged males.* Unpublished doctoral dissertation, University of Wisconsin.

Karvonen, M., Kentala, K., & Mustala, O. (1957). The effects of training heart rate: A longitudinal study. *Annales Medicinae Experimentalis Et Biologiae Fenniae,* **35,** 307–315.

Kasch, F.W., & Boyer, J.L. (1968). *Adult fitness principles and practices.* San Diego: San Diego State College.

Leon, A.L., Conrad, J., Hunninghake, D.B., & Serfass, R. (1979). Effects of a vigorous walking program on body composition and carbohydrate and lipid metabolism of obese young men. *American Journal of Clinical Nutrition,* **32,** 1776–1787.

Massie, J.F., & Shephard, R.J. (1971). Physiological and psychological effects of training—A comparison of individualized and gymnasium programs, with a characterization of the exercise "dropout." *Medicine and Science in Sports,* **3,** 110–117.

Milesis, C., Pollock, M.L., Ayres, J., Bah, M., Ward, A., & Linnerud, A. (1976). Effects of different durations of training on cardiovascular function, body composition and serum lipids. *Research Quarterly,* **47,** 716–725.

Morgan, W.P. (1981). Psychophysiology of self-awareness during vigorous physical activity. *Research Quarterly for Exercise and Sport,* **52,** 385–427.

Morgan, W.P., & Pollock, M.L. (1977). Psychologic characterization of the elite distance runner. *Annals of the New York Academy of Science,* **301,** 382–403.

Noble, B.J. (1982). Clinical applications of perceived exertion. *Medicine and Science in Sports and Exercise,* **14,** 406–411.

Oja, P., Teraslinna, P., Partanen, T., & Karava, R. (1975). Feasibility of an 18 months' physical training program for middle-aged men and its effect on physical fitness. *American Journal of Public Health,* **64,** 459–465.

Oldridge, N.B. (1982). Compliance and exercise in primary and secondary prevention of coronary heart disease: A review. *Preventive Medicine,* **11,** 56–70.

Oldridge, N.B. (1984a). Compliance and drop-out in cardiac exercise rehabilitation. *Journal of Cardiac Rehabilitation,* **4,** 166–177.

Oldridge, N.B. (1984b). Adherence to adult exercise fitness programs. In T.D. Matarazzo, S.M. Weiss, J.A. Herd, N.E. Miller, & S.M. Weiss. (Eds.), *Behavior health: A handbook of health enhancement and disease prevention* (pp. 467–487). New York: John Wiley.

Olree, H.D., Corbin, B., Penrod, J., & Smith, C. (1969). *Methods of achieving and maintaining physical fitness for prolonged space flight* (Final Progress Report to NASA, Grant No. NGR-04-002-004).

Pandolf, K.B. (1982). Differentiated ratings of perceived exertion during physical exercise. *Medicine and Science in Sports and Exercise, 14,* 397–405.

Pels, A.E., Pollock, M.L., Dohmeier, T.E., Lemberger, K.A., & Oehrlein, B.F. (in press). Effects of leg press training on cycling, leg press, and running peak cardiorespiratory measures. *Medicine and Science in Sports and Exercise.*

Pollock, M.L., Broida, J., & Kendrick, Z. (1972). Validation of the palpation technique of heart rate determination and its estimation of training heart rate. *Research Quarterly, 43,* 77–81.

Pollock, M.L., Broida, J., Kendrick, Z., Miller, H.S., Janeway, R., & Linnerud, A. (1972). Effects of training two days per week at different intensities on middle-aged men. *Medicine and Science in Sports, 4,* 192–197.

Pollock, M.L., Cureton, T.K., & Greniger, L. (1969). Effects of frequency of training on working capacity, cardiovascular function and body composition of adult men. *Medicine and Science in Sports, 1,* 70–74.

Pollock, M.L., Dawson, G., Miller, H., Ward, A., Cooper, D., Headley, W., Linnerud, A., & Nomeir, A. (1976). Physiologic responses of men 49 to 65 years of age to endurance training. *Journal of the American Geriatric Society, 24,* 97–104.

Pollock, M.L., Dimmick, J., Miller, H.S., Kendrick, Z., & Linnerud, A.C. (1975). Effects of mode of training on cardiovascular function and body composition of middle-aged men. *Medicine and Science in Sports, 7,* 139–145.

Pollock, M.L., & Foster, C. (1983). Exercise prescription for participants on propranolol. *Journal of the American College of Cardiology* (abstract), 2, 624.

Pollock, M.L., Foster, C., & Hare, J. (1983). Metabolic and perceptual responses to arm and leg exercise. *Medicine and Science in Sports and Exercise* (abstract), 15, 140.

Pollock, M.L., Foster, C., Rod, J., Stoiber, J., Hare, J., & Schmidt, D.H. (1982). Effects of propranolol dosage on the response to submaximal and maximal exercise. *American Journal of Cardiology* (abstract), 49, 1000.

Pollock, M.L., Foster, C., Rod, J.L., & Wible, G. (1982). Comparison of methods for determining exercise training intensity for cardiac patients and healthy adults. In J.J. Kellermann (Ed.), *Comprehensive cardiac rehabilitation* (pp. 129-133). Basel, Switzerland: S. Karger.

Pollock, M.L., Foster, C., Salisbury, R., & Smith, R. (1982). Effects of a YMCA starter fitness program. *Physician and Sportsmedicine, 10*, 89-100.

Pollock, M.L., Gettman, L., Janeway, R., Lofland, H.B., & Tiffany, J. (1969). Effects of frequency of training on serum lipids, cardiovascular function and body composition. In B.D. Franks (Ed.), *Exercise and fitness: 1969* (pp. 161-178). Chicago: The Athletic Institute.

Pollock, M.L., Gettman, L.R., Milesis, C.A., Bah, M.D., Durstine, J.L., & Johnson, R.B. (1977). Effects of frequency and duration of training on attrition and incidence of injury. *Medicine and Science in Sports, 9*, 31-36.

Pollock, M.L., Gettman, L.R., Raven, P.B., Bah, M., & Ward, A. (1978, May). *Physiological comparisons of the effects of aerobic and anaerobic training.* Paper presented to the American College of Sports Medicine, Washington, DC.

Pollock, M.L., Jackson, A.S., & Foster, C. (in press). The use of the perception scale for exercise prescription. In G. Borg (Ed.), *Proceedings International Symposium on Perception of Exertion in Physical Exercise.* Stockholm, Sweden: October 3-5, 1985.

Pollock, M.L., Miller, H.S., Janeway, R., Linnerud, A.C., Robertson, R., & Valentino, R. (1971). Effects of walking on body composition and cardiovascular function of middle-aged men. *Journal of Applied Physiology, 30*, 126-130.

Pollock, M.L., Miller, H.S., Linnerud, A., Coleman, E. Laughridge, E., & Ward, A. (1974). Follow-up study on the effects of conditioning four days per week on the physical fitness of adult men. *American Correctional Therapy Journal, 28*, 135-139.

Pollock, M.L., Pels, A.E., Foster, C., & Ward, A. (1986). Exercise prescription for rehabilitation of the cardiac patient. In M.L. Pollock & D.H. Schmidt (Eds.), *Heart disease and rehabilitation* (2nd ed., pp. 477-516). New York: John Wiley.

Pollock, M.L., Ward, A., & Ayres, J. (1977). Cardiorespiratory fitness: Response to differing intensities and durations of training. *Archives of Physical Medicine and Rehabilitation, 58*, 467-473.

Pollock, M.L., Wilmore, J.H., & Fox, S.M. (1984). *Exercise in health and disease—Evaluation and prescription for prevention and rehabilitation.* Philadelphia: W.B. Saunders.

Price, C.S., Pollock, M.L., Gettman, L.R., & Dent, D.A. (1977). *Physical fitness programs for law enforcement officers: A manual for police administrators* (Final report prepared for the Law Enforcement Assistance Administration, U.S. Department of Justice, Grant No. 76-NI-99-0011, March). Washington, DC: U.S. Government Printing Office.

Richie, D.H., Felso, S.F., & Bellucci, P.A. (1985). Aerobic dance injuries: A retrospective study of instructors and participants. *Physician and Sportsmedicine*, **13**, 114–120.

Sargent, A.J., & Davies, C.T.M. (1973). Perceived exertion during rhythmic exercise involving different muscle masses. *Journal of Human Ergology*, **2**, 3–11.

Skinner, J.S., Hutsler, R., Bergsteinova, V., & Buskirk, E.R. (1973a). The validity and reliability of a rating scale of perceived exertion. *Medicine and Science in Sports*, **5**, 94–96.

Skinner, J.S., Hutsler, R., Bergsteinova, V., & Buskirk, E.R. (1973b). Perception of effort during different types of exercise and under different environmental conditions. *Medicine and Science in Sports*, **5**, 110–115.

Taylor, H.L., Buskirk, E.R., & Remington, R.D. (1973). Exercise in controlled trials of the prevention of coronary heart disease. *Federation Proceedings*, **32**, 1623–1627.

Ward, A., & Morgan, W.P. (1984). Adherence patterns of healthy men and women enrolled in an adult exercise program. *Journal of Cardiac Rehabilitation*, **4**, 143–152.

4

Exercise Adherence in Clinical, Corporate, and Community Settings

This section has been included on the assumption that, although exercise adherence is a generalized problem, specific environments and population segments deserve distinct attention. Cardiopulmonary rehabilitation is an area of particular concern for public health due to the prevalence of the associated disorders and the unique outcome goals of treatments. Thus the methods for pursuing adherence and the standards by which success is gauged may be somewhat distinctive. Because many health care professionals focus their efforts in primary or secondary preventive medicine, a topical treatment of adherence for clinical settings is informative. Similarly, unique reasons exist for providing special coverage for presumably healthy populations in worksite and community leisure settings. These are equally prevalent and distinct areas of exercise concern where unique problems of adherence are found and where unique health and behavior outcomes are desirable. Whether or not the impact of exercise adherence within public health can be defined is doubtful without separate attention to these areas. In fact, the inability of several other health care agencies to promote exercise adherence may well be buffered by accelerated efforts in worksite and community leisure environments.

Chapter 10

Coronary heart disease is a major cause of morbidity and mortality in North America, and exercise is commonly used as a method of primary and secondary prevention. "Compliance With Exercise in Cardiac Rehabilitation" by Neil B. Oldridge is a particularly important inclusion. It serves two principal purposes. Personal and programmatic factors associated with dropping out of clinical exercise programs are described, and the impact of exercise compliance on identifying coronary health outcomes from exercise is discussed. Self-regulation principles and theory introduced by Dorothy Knapp in chapter 7 are integrated with current understanding of exercise compliance in medical settings.

Chapter 11

Only recently have studies examined factors associated with recruitment and retention in worksite exercise programs. "Exercise Adherence in Corporate Settings: Personal Traits and Program Barriers" by Roy J. Shephard is an important contribution because of the continued increase in companies that provide exercise facilities and resources for employees and the U.S. Government's commitment to facilitate this in the future. One of the Public Health Service's fitness and exercise objectives states that by 1990 the proportion of companies with more than 500 employees that offer employer-sponsored fitness programs should be greater than 25 percent. In this chapter rates of activity among eligible employees are described, behavioral correlates originating in both the program and the individual are outlined, and similarities and contrasts with clinical and community programs are drawn when possible. Research-based suggestions for increasing corporate adherence are also advanced.

Chapter 12

In "Who Are Corporate Exercisers and What Motivates Them?" William B. Baun and Edward J. Bernacki describe in detail the activity patterns of a single corporate population and discuss the promotional techniques used to maintain involvement and to recruit new participants. Empirically derived profiles of exercisers as they relate to corporate performance are also presented. The chapter is unique in addressing practical corporate-based concerns about exercise adherence (i.e., how to promote program involvement, what adherence may reveal about employees, and the feasibility of allocating company resources to promote exercise adherence). One of the largest corporate programs in America is featured; it has committed an investment in exercise and is accumulating a systematic data base on adherence. Whether the patterns and approaches described can extend to other corporate settings is unknown. However, the paper provides an informative account for examination by exercise program planners in worksite environments.

Chapter 13

"Occupation-Related Fitness and Exercise Adherence" by Larry R. Gettman reports the results from several studies of job-related fitness among high-risk occupational groups. Although the principal focus of this volume is on health-related outcomes of being active, safe, and effective, performance in several high-risk occupations depends on adequate fitness that may be suited to particular on-the-job demands. For many of these hazardous occupations (e.g., fire, police, oil field workers, etc.) fitness is a prerequisite for personnel safety and job execution. These populations also present unique behavioral problems for implementing exercise programs that will be followed by employees. The feasibility of implementing and perpetuating such programs also depends on acceptance by management that they are cost-effective. A cost-benefit analysis is included, and a pragmatic view of promoting exercise adherence is provided.

Chapter 14

"Exercise Adherence and Leisure Activity: Patterns of Involvement and Interventions to Facilitate Regular Activity" by Leonard M. Wankel describes the patterns and determinants of leisure-time sport and physical activity around the world. Intervention approaches in commercial and community exercise programs are discussed and existing factors that motivate leisure-time physical activity are highlighted. Finally, the important potential impact of using leisure sport involvement to increase activity levels toward a health advantage for certain populations is entertained.

CHAPTER *10*

Compliance With Exercise in Cardiac Rehabilitation

Neil B. Oldridge

Coronary heart disease (CHD) is the number one cause of death in many industrialized countries. In the United States, approximately one male in five by the age of 60–65 years will have developed one or another form of this disease, usually documented as angina pectoris, coronary insufficiency, myocardial infarction, sudden death, or non-sudden death coronary heart disease (Castelli, 1984). At the same time, evidence suggests that it is perhaps possible to control CHD. Mortality from CHD has decreased in the U.S. by approximately 30% since 1968; this trend has also been observed in other countries, most notably Australia and Canada (Stamler, 1985). Although there is little solid evidence of change in the incidence of CHD in the U.S., a recent report by Pell and Fayerweather (1985) indicated that the incidence of first major coronary events in males had decreased by 28% over 27 years in a large group of male employees. When the observed decline in CHD mortality is paralleled by the decline in CHD incidence, the interpretation is that risk factor reduction or primary prevention must be considered a major factor in the lower CHD mortality.

The decline in mortality is perhaps greatest in the more affluent and younger age groups and is associated with improvements in related risk factors and lifestyles such as better control of blood pressure, better diets with less serum cholesterol, lower smoking, and increased exercise habits (American Health Association [AHA] Committee, 1980; Stamler, 1985). No one factor can be assumed to be the cause of the development of CHD; the concept of synergism must be considered central to the preventive management of CHD. The impact of interactive yet reversible risk factors develops over extended periods of time; the effectiveness of risk factor reduction management programs is directly related to compliance with the intervention strategies. The intervention strategies generally mean life-long behaviors such as not smoking; maintaining control of hypertension, blood lipids, and stress; and participating in regular physical activity. Compliance with management interventions such as these is not overly encouraging particularly (a) when there is considerable disability, (b) if existing habits need to be changed extensively, (c) if the treatment is complex, and (d) if it needs to be carried out over extended periods of time (Haynes, 1979).

There is considerably less evidence for the effectiveness of either risk factor reduction or control in secondary prevention of CHD than there is in primary prevention of CHD. Although there has been an increased awareness of the need for secondary preventive efforts over the last 20 years, a recent report from the Mayo Clinic suggests that five-year survivorship after myocardial infarction (MI) was essentially the same at 71% over the periods of 1965–1969 and 1970–1975 (Elveback, Connolly, & Kurland, 1981). Despite this, an AHA Medical and Community Program Committee report (1980) states "Nevertheless, the logic for secondary prevention is reasonable and . . . it seems warranted that cigarette smoking be discouraged, that overweight be corrected, that high blood cholesterol be controlled by dietary means, and that prudent exercise under supervision be prescribed" (p. 454A). In the last 10–15 years the number of cardiac rehabilitation programs designed for persons with documented heart disease in North America has increased considerably from a few generally research-oriented programs in the late 1960s and early 1970s to a large number of hospital-, university-, company-, and community-based clinical programs in the 1980s. Despite the continued and increasing enthusiasm for exercise rehabilitation programs, a critical review of the pertinent literature reveals equivocal scientific evidence with respect to whether these programs are of significant long-term benefit to patients after documentation of CHD.

Exercise Rehabilitation

Randomized clinical trials of physical activity after myocardial infarction have focused on the morbidity and mortality issue. The question usually asked in these trials was, "Does appropriate exercise reduce the rate of recurrent myocardial infarction?'' (Wilhelmsen, Sanne, Elmfeldt, Grimby, Tibblin, & Wedel, 1978; Shaw, 1981; Carson et al., 1982, Rechnitzer et al., 1983). Posed another way the same question would be: "Is exercise after myocardial infarction safe or hazardous?''. Although the confirmation of the original exercise hypothesis has not been unequivocally provided by the randomized trials (probably because the dropout rates were high), the trend is for lower, but not statistically significant, reinfarction in exercising subjects (Wilhelmsen et al., 1978; Shaw, 1981; Carson et al., 1982; Rechnitzer et al., 1983). With appropriate statistical analysis, combining the trials to increase sample size reveals clinically and statistically significant reductions in all cause-death and cardiovascular mortality rates but not in non-fatal recurrent myocardial infarction (Oldridge & Guyatt, 1986). The answer to the alternative question is that appropriately prescribed, moderate- or low-intensity exercise is safe in large populations of selected patients after myocardial infarction (Naughton, 1985).

Outcomes of exercise-focused rehabilitation, other than morbidity and mortality, have been investigated and documented with varying degrees of rigor. These include: (a) the various clinical benefits that are associated with regular surveillance; (b) physiological benefits such as increases in exercise tolerance and decreases in submaximum myocardial oxygen demand; and (c) the associated behavioral benefits such as reduced depression, increased self-esteem, and increased self-efficacy. Each of these is associated with compliance, which can be defined as the degree to which the advice of a health professional is addressed or followed (Haynes, 1979).

The Stanford group (DeBusk, Houston, Haskell, Fry, & Parker, 1979; DeBusk et al., 1985) has demonstrated that some 50% of the improvement seen in exercise tolerance from 3 to 11 weeks after myocardial infarction occurs spontaneously with counseling and without any specific exercise prescription. The statistically significant 0.7 metabolic equivalents (METs) increase in functional capacity reported at 11 and 26 weeks in the training compared to the no-training groups may have relatively little real biological, clinical, or practical significance. What were the submaximal physiological improvements? What were the behavioral differences? Short-term behavioral improvements such as a reduction in depression (Stern & Cleary, 1981), better morale (Prosser et al., 1978; Mayou, MacMahon, Sleight, & Florencio, 1981), enhanced psychosocial functioning, (Roviaro, Holmes, & Holmes, 1984), and an improved self-report of decreased employment stress and improved attitude toward employment (Roviaro et al., 1984; Oldridge & Spencer, 1985) have been demonstrated in a training group. Unfortunately, these psychosocial benefits do not appear to be maintained over an extended period of time (Stern & Cleary, 1982; Mayou et al., 1981, Mayou, 1983). Haynes (1979) has aptly stated that the term *compliance* is strictly utilitarian and further that the definition of the term implies no fault even though in some situations the therapist, patient or circumstances may be appropriately blamed for noncompliance. It may be useful in the context of long-term health behavior change to conceptually differentiate between compliance and adherence. Compliance is more appropriate with reference to immediate or short-term health and medical advice, and direct prescription to relieve symptomatology. Adherence is more appropriate with reference to long-term behavior changes made initially while complying with medical or health advice either given to relieve symptomatology, or developed over time in order to prevent symptomatology.

Compliance With Exercise Rehabilitation

Dropout is a major problem in trials of exercise and CHD (Wilhelmsen et al., 1975; Stern & Cleary, 1981, 1982; Oldridge et al., 1983). Kuller (1984) has concluded that "the results of secondary prevention trials [of exercise and CHD] have been equivocal primarily due to the high dropout rate for treatment" (p. 10). Even in short-term studies there has been a considerable dropout rate: DeBusk et al. (1985) report a 15% dropout over the first 8 weeks of exercise which doubled over the next 15 weeks. The larger and longer trials of exercise demonstrate that the dropout rate by 18–24 months is 40% but that this tends to remain relatively constant with a 50% dropout rate reported at 36–48 months (Oldridge, 1982, 1984). A major problem in interpreting the published compliance literature is the lack of a consistent definition of exercise compliance (Oldridge, 1982, 1984). Compliance has been reported variously as: the percentage of possible sessions actually attended; the number of sessions or weeks missed; the meeting of certain physiological or other kinds of objectives; and even a retest. Despite this, the reported compliance rates are surprisingly consistent across exercise rehabilitation trials and most studies even though they were carried out in different cultures and during different decades (Oldridge, 1982, 1984).

The characteristics of the typical dropout from exercise rehabilitation programs after myocardial infarction have been identified by various authors. Dropouts tend to be middle-class rather than upper-class (Stern & Cleary, 1981), to be blue-collar rather than white-collar workers (Oldridge et al., 1983), to have angina (Shephard, Corey, & Kavanagh, 1981; Oldridge et al., 1983), to smoke (Nye & Poulsen, 1974; Oldridge et al., 1983), to have fewer infarctions, to be more anxious and more depressed (Stern & Cleary, 1981), and to be less physically active (Oldridge et al., 1983). These factors suggest that the dropout is probably physiologically and psychologically at greater risk for a recurrence and therefore needs special attention to keep the individual adhering to the exercise prescription and the rehabilitation program (Shephard et al., 1981; Stern & Cleary, 1981; Oldridge et al., 1983). Neither the exercise dropout nor the complier, however, can be predicted consistently with more than a 75% accuracy (Oldridge & Spencer, 1985). This is not a high enough hit rate to exclude persons from the opportunity to participate in a rehabilitation program, even if the concept of exclusion on an a priori basis were philosophically acceptable.

The real issue then is neither who is at risk of dropout nor who is likely to comply, but rather what can be done to decrease dropout from rehabilitation to a minimum or alternatively to increase compliance to a maximum. Dishman (1982) has been critical of the atheoretical nature of research into compliance with exercise rehabilitation. However correct he may be from a theoretical standpoint, the first steps in exploring the compliance phenomenon are descriptive: Was there a dropout or compliance problem? Could the characteristics of the most likely dropout or complier be identified? The next steps are more experimental and need to be pursued from a sound theoretical basis: Are compliance-enhancing strategies appropriate? Are they feasible? Which of the strategies is likely to be effective? Under what circumstances are specific strategies most likely to be effective? What do compliers do that is different from dropouts? This permits development and testing of models and investigation of the effectiveness of the intervention.

Our experience is that many patients are willing to consider changing behaviors in the period of time soon after their infarction; reinforcement of behavior change therefore should begin while the patient is still in the cardiac care unit and be continued as long as is necessary. A small minority of patients are able to effect behavior change with no necessary overt reinforcement; another minority, probably equal in number, will never change their behaviors; a large, uncommitted majority, with minimal input, probably can be persuaded to consider changing behaviors to alter their risk factors for heart disease.

At McMaster University, we initially approached the compliance phenomenon in cardiac rehabilitation from a predominantly descriptive, practical, and atheoretical perspective (Oldridge, Wicks, Hanley, Sutton, & Jones, 1978; Oldridge et al., 1983). We have since attempted to incorporate and study strategies that reinforce self-responsibility and involvement in decision-making as part of our management approach. The strategies include simple behavioral contracting, reinforcement control such as self-monitoring, and spouse support as well as cognitive strategies such as goal setting (Oldridge & Jones, 1983; Oldridge & Spencer, 1985; Erling & Oldridge, 1985). The overall compliance rate in the McMaster Cardiac Rehabilitation Program (see Figure 1) has shown a gradual but consistent upward trend since the mid 1970s (Oldridge & Jones, 1986). Whereas the important role of exercise leadership has not

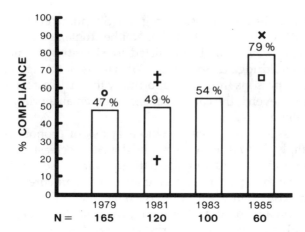

Figure 1   Mean program compliance rates at McMaster University (1978–1985). *Note.* The symbols represent compliance with experimental strategies: 0 = committed to a 4 year randomized trial (57%); ‡ = signed agreement to comply (65%); + = would not sign (20%); × = spouses participate with patients (90%); □ = patients without spouse participation (66%).

been evaluated as a factor in compliance with cardiac rehabilitation (Oldridge & Stoedefalke, 1984), we believe the improved compliance is due to increased experience with and utilization of various compliance-enhancing strategies. The process of communication between the patient and the health professional is probably essential for long-term adherence to prescriptions such as medications and to lifestyle behavior changes, but it may not be feasible to expect an overall compliance rate of more than 75% in programs where there is freedom of choice.

Our philosophical approach to cardiac rehabilitation at McMaster University has always essentially been: I am *not* my brother's keeper; rather we are support agents. In other words, the relationship is one of collegiality rather than teacher and student or provider and patient. We do not encourage patients to join programs of rehabilitation soon after myocardial infarction because it will make them fitter. Rather, we believe that participation in a rehabilitation program, preferably with spouses and in some instances children, will result in a reduced cardiovascular risk factor profile, an improved outlook, an improved cardiac performance and exercise tolerance, and therefore an improved quality of life with perhaps a reduction in the likelihood of an early fatal reinfarction (Oldridge & Jones, 1986). These benefits, however, will never be achieved if the patient (a) does not consider the behaviors to be of value, (b) does not adopt them, and (c) does not comply with or adhere to them for long enough to gain the perceived or actual benefit.

Enhancing Compliance With
Exercise Rehabilitation

The first issue that needs to be addressed when considering compliance-enhancing strategies in exercise rehabilitation is that raised by Haynes (1984): Does the exercise do more good than harm? In attempting to answer this, we must carefully weigh what Spodick (1982) has called behavioral pitfalls: general acceptance of a therapy; excessive zeal for the therapy; uncritical acceptance of poor data, or alternatively turning a blind eye to good data; and finally, the rationalization that the therapy can't hurt. The literature suggests that exercise rehabilitation may be associated with a lower mortality but that it apparently does not reduce non-fatal recurrence (Naughton, 1985), and that light- and moderate-intensity exercise appear to be equally effective in reducing recurrent infarction (Rechnitzer et al., 1983). Multifactorial intervention (exercise, health education, psychosocial counseling) after the initial myocardial infarction has resulted in significantly reduced recurrence rates (Kallio, Hamalainen, Hakkila, & Luurila, 1979). The physiological and psychosocial benefits have previously been identified.

The answer to Haynes' question is that in large populations of *selected* patients, exercise rehabilitation does do more good than harm. Although the question has not been adequately defined and investigated, the overall conclusion is that the reduction in risk factors along with the improvement in physiological and psychosocial outcomes with exercise rehabilitation amounts to an improved quality of life. It is not clear whether individual or group exercise programs are more beneficial. Certainly not every patient with an MI needs long-term supervision (DeBusk et al., 1985), but an equal number of patients derive considerable support knowing that they are not the only ones experiencing certain common problems. We have no data on long-term compliance with non-supervised exercise prescription; in the short-term (i.e., less than six months), the dropout rate from one clinical investigation is 29% (DeBusk et al., 1985). If exercise compliance is low and exercise is beneficial, then compliance-enhancing strategies are important.

The World Health Organization (WHO) (1964) definition of cardiac rehabilitation is: "the sum of activity required to ensure the best possible physical, mental, and social conditions so that [cardiac patients] may *by their own efforts regain* [italics added] as normal as possible a place in the community and lead an active, productive life." This definition makes eminent sense; the emphasis placed on patient responsibility and the open-ended outcome expectations are central to the real concept of rehabilitation. If the WHO definition of rehabilitation is acceptable and we accept the association between compliance and adherence, the focus of further investigation into compliance-enhancing should be on strategies: to foster self-responsibility; to improve short-term compliance and so achieve long-term adherence; and to derive the broader benefits associated with exercise-centered rehabilitation.

A Theoretical Approach to Investigating Compliance With Exercise Rehabilitation

Gordis (1979) makes the point that there are both clinical and research reasons for measuring compliance. In clinical settings, if there is poor compliance there may be a need for substitution of a treatment or initiation of some potential compliance-enhancing strategy. In research the focus may be on the extent, the effects, or the dynamics of either compliance or noncompliance. In exercise rehabilitation there is no doubt that poor compliance is common; this is particularly true in clinical trials (Oldridge, 1982, 1984) although not as frequently reported to be a problem in clinical studies (Kavanagh, Shephard, Chisholme, Qureshi, & Kennedy, 1980). Whether this is generally a case of non-report of poor outcome or whether it is a real observation is unclear. The concern expressed by Dishman (1982) that insufficient attention has been given to examining the interaction between exerciser and behavioral characteristics as well as among exercise, provider, and setting characteristics is valid. There is also little doubt that, with the background and descriptive information on exercise compliance that has been developed, more attention will be given first to identifying and second to overcoming physical and non-physical, real and perceived barriers to (a) the adoption of, (b) compliance with, and (c) adherence to exercise rehabilitation.

With the distinction between compliance and adherence in mind, it becomes clear that the majority of the literature in the area of compliance has been descriptive, with rates and characteristics as the focus of attention. Expected rates of dropout and compliance have been identified. It has been determined that there are few consistent factors associated with dropout or compliance. Increasing short-term compliance with health behaviors (such as not smoking and weight reduction) by using behavioral strategies has been more successful than other techniques; unfortunately, the short-term success of behavioral strategies has not yet been translated into long-term success (Haynes, 1979).

The logical future for compliance enhancement research in the area of exercise and rehabilitation lies in a better understanding of both exercise compliance and the factors associated with behavioral change. While

self-responsibility is a central conceptual component of the WHO definition of cardiac rehabilitation, a distinction between self-care activities
undertaken with and without professional assistance must be made (Levin
& Adler, 1983). In the early stages of rehabilitation, the health care professional provides information, counsel, direction, and feedback with regard
to the "sum of activity" which is most appropriate at any particular time;
the individual accepts the responsibility for fulfilling the advice, treatment, or management, and takes some action (i.e., complies). The
progression thus is from self-responsibility with support within the relatively short-term rehabilitation context to one of self-care in long-term
behavior maintenance or adherence (e.g., individual treatment of mutual
aid groups). The patient must become the primary active agent in the
process, and it is this primacy that is the core concept underlying self-
responsiblity, self-regulation, or self-management (Conrad, 1985).

Self-management (self-control) strategies, incorporated into the program as a routine practice, have not been extensively investigated as
compliance-enhancing strategies in cardiac exercise rehabilitation. There
are a number of strategies which may have potential in enhancing compliance (Martin & Dubbert, 1984). While some of these strategies have
been investigated (Oldridge & Jones, 1983; Erling & Oldridge, 1985;
Daltroy, 1985; Hilbert, 1985), they have not been investigated as a part
of a larger theoretical model but rather as single strategies in a routine
clinical setting. The remainder of this chapter is devoted to the self-
regulatory prospective as a comprehensive and specific basis for the investigation and possible initiation of self-management strategies to improve compliance (Leventhal, 1985).

The Self-Regulation Model

In a discussion of the self-regulatory perspective of compliance
Leventhal, Zimmerman, and Gutmann (1984) argue that behavior change
is not the product of antecedent but rather that it should be future oriented
or goal directed. This means that the behavior is pulled toward a goal
rather than pushed by stimuli. In the self-regulatory perspective, they
argue that in health and illness behavior, this control theory approach
emphasizes three stages. First, a representation of a health threat is identified. The second stage involves coping with the health threat: this includes the acquisition of self-regulatory skills; the development of a
problem-solving approach for a repertoire of plans; the action to minimize
the threat; and the appraisal and interpretation of outcomes. Stage 3 in-
troduces the integration of the new habits into a personal lifestyle (see
Figure 2). The theoretical basis for the self-regulatory model is that self-

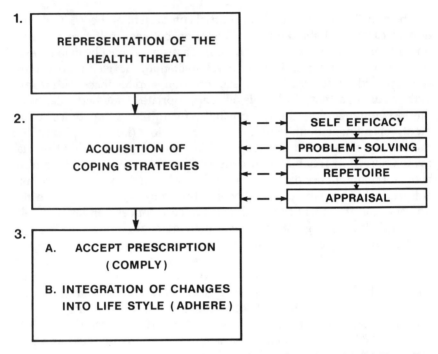

Figure 2   A schematic of the processes involved in the Self-Regulation Model. *Note.*   De-
rived from "Compliance: A Self-Regulatory Perspective" by H. Leventhal, R.
Zimmerman, and M. Gutman, 1984. In W. Gentry (Ed.), *Handbook of Behavioral
Medicine*, New York: Guilford Press.

regulated actions are internally oriented and have the best probability of
success (a) if the action or intervention is related to the representation
of the health threat, (b) if they are seen as one's own, and (c) if they make
sense in the overall context of the individual's life.

Representation of the Health Threat

The representation of the health threat (see Figure 3), both concrete and
abstract, is initially short-term for the patient with documented coronary
artery disease. The symptom of chest discomfort and the manifestation
of myocardial infarction are acute examples of the health threat with pain
and death as possible consequences. All contribute to the outcome of or
compliance with palliative treatment by acquiring coping skills such as
learning to be active, stopping smoking, and taking medications regularly, thus reducing the likelihood of symptoms and consequences. In the

	SHORT - TERM (Immediate)	LONG - TERM (Future)
1. REPRESENTATION OF HEALTH THREAT		
a.) Identify - concrete - abstract	Symptoms Diagnosis	Function Probability
b.) Consequences	Pain Disability Death	⬆ Functional impairment ⬇ Quality of life
c.) Treatment	Palliative Curative	Preventive
2. ACQUISITION OF COPING SKILLS	Seek treatment Adopt new behaviors	Lifestyle changes
a.) Objectives	Symptom reduction Reduce disability Increase control	Improve function Improve quality of life Increase control
3. OUTCOME	Compliance	Adherence

Figure 3   Compliance (short-term or present) and adherence (long-term or future)—as outcomes of the self-regulatory process consisting of (1) representation of the health threat, (2) acquisition of coping skills, and (3) acceptance of the prescription and integration of changes into a personal lifestyle.

long-term, however, there must first be an acceptance of the future threat and the real probability of reduced function before adherence to preventative strategies for dealing with the more abstract representation of the threat occurs.

The representation or perception of the health threat presumably determines the individual's willingness to consider different strategies to reduce the threat. Information about the health threat is collected: there may be new information which is actively sought by the patient or provided by some other person; there may be regeneration of previous knowledge and experience (or both); and there may be intuitive, emotional responses. If the information is sufficiently compelling and the symptoms threatening enough, new or different behaviors may be considered. Adoption of new behaviors such as regular physical activity and compliance with or adherence to them appear to be under different influences; enrollment in cardiac rehabilitation may signify the intention to be active whereas dropout may be determined by other factors.

The Health Belief Model (HBM) was originally an attempt to explain patient preventive health behaviors. The behaviors are seen as the result of perceived goals as well as the result of the perceived likelihood of specific strategies being able to achieve these goals under specific circumstances (Rosenstock, 1966). The HBM has been expanded and used to predict health behaviors and as such may have some validity in determining the probability of compliance with particular behaviors (Becker & Maiman, 1975). The HBM has not been extensively tested in cardiac rehabilitation but recent unpublished results from McMaster University suggest that there are significant differences between dropouts and compliers and, perhaps most interestingly, between avoidable and nonavoidable dropouts. These differences were seen in the scales of perceived severity, susceptibility, and treatment effectiveness, each of which is an important component of the individual's representation of the health threat.

As the representation of the health threat is an integral part of the patient's ability both to relate to the problem and to consider alternative strategies in an attempt to reduce the threat, it can be used by the program director or exercise specialist to gain an idea of the patient's own representation of the health threat. In this way the patient can best communicate concerns and hopes. The patient and the health professional can then join as colleagues to consider different strategies to optimize meeting stated objectives such as: to be able to climb the stairs without chest discomfort; to be able to perform my job without feeling exhausted; to be able to go for walks without getting short of breath.

Coping

Coping, which Leventhal et al. (1984) see as planning and action, is directed by the representation of the threat and consists of the individual's a) self-efficacy level, b) capacity to relate to problem situations, and c) repertoire of coping and appraisal skills (see Figure 3).

Self-efficacy. *Self-efficacy*, or self-perception of the capability to perform specific tasks in specific situations, apparently governs behaviors such as choice of a task to be attempted and perseverance with the tasks as well as governing the extent of emotional response to stressful events (Bandura, 1977, 1982). The judgment of capability and the degree of confidence to perform the particular action or task are two cognitive processes involved. Three recent reports, two specifically investigating self-efficacy (Ewart, Taylor, Reese, & DeBusk, 1983; Taylor, Bandura, Ewart, Miller, & DeBusk, 1985) and one indirectly implying self-efficacy (Newton,

Siverajan, & Clarke, 1985), have demonstrated the importance of self-perceived ability or self-confidence in subsequent behaviors such as physical activity. The initial perception of capacity for physical activity has been shown to be predictive of performance on the treadmill; performance on the treadmill modified the original self-perception. In addition, the modified self-perceptions were highly predictive of subsequent physical activity (Ewart et al., 1983; Taylor et al., 1983). For smoking change, weight loss, and return to sexual activity, attitude in the hospital was a good prediction of subsequent behavior change (Newton et al., 1985). These observations provide increasing support for the importance of self-efficacy as a factor in the self-regulation process for enhancing compliance with behaviors to reduce the health threat represented by coronary artery disease.

Problem Solving. The individual's ability to relate to *problem situations* is the second aspect of coping. A given situation may seem to be manageable under certain circumstances but quite unmanageable under others. Simple examples frequently seen in cardiac rehabilitation illustrate this point: good attendance at a 7:00 a.m. exercise program may be no problem but can become one if (a) the patient suddenly has to depend on a car pool for transportation, (b) there is a change of seasons (i.e., summer and winter), or (c) there is a change in the patient's working hours. Under these circumstances the individual can choose to stop exercising or to join another, more convenient program such as an evening program in a group setting, or to start an at-home-exercise program. The important point to keep in mind is that a program dropout does not automatically mean an exercise dropout (Oldridge & Spencer, 1985).

There are barriers to regular participation. Some of the self-report barriers may not in fact be real but may be self-fulfilling prophecies. Examples are: "My spouse does not support my participation" and "The exercise interferes with my job." Inconvenience, inaccessibility, time conflict, and lack of spouse support are frequently cited as reasons for dropping out of programs (Oldridge, 1982, 1984). While these may be reasons given for dropout from cardiac rehabilitation programs, there is evidence to suggest that this may be more of a perceived than an actual barrier to exercise compliance as opposed to program compliance.

These problem situations can often be dealt with by environmental engineering which will allow the patient to meet expectations. The patient may have to change, the program can be modified in some way, or an alternative exercise environment may have to be considered. Whether the patient changes or the program is modified, the success will to a large degree be dependent on the individual's perception or representation of the health threat; level of self-efficacy; and awareness of, exposure to, and skill with various coping strategies.

Repertoire of Coping Strategies.   *A repertoire of personal and program strate-gies* which may have application in enhancing compliance with exercise rehabilitation has been proposed by Martin and Dubbert (1984). Few of these have been tested in the rehabilitation setting although they have been shown to be effective to varying degrees in other health behavior management efforts. It is important, however, to be aware of the fact that exercise behaviors are not necessarily complementary with other health behaviors. It has been pointed out that exercise, while associated with better weight control despite higher caloric intake (Wood, Haskell, Terry, Ho, & Blair, 1982), is poorly correlated with smoking (Blair, Cooper, Gibbons, Gettman, Lewis, & Goodyear, 1983; Hickey, Mulcahy, Burke, Graham, & Wilson-Davis, 1975), and that too few data are available to evaluate the association between physical exercise and various other health behavior managements (Blair, Jacobs, & Powell, 1985).

The strategies outlined by Martin and Dubbert (1984) were derived from the field of behavioral psychology. They include strategies which are suitable for both the acquisition and the maintenance of exercise. According to Martin and Dubbert there are several acquisition strategies. Shaping is "the process by which behavior is dissected into a series of approximations that are gradually progressed to the desired end behavior." A second strategy is reinforcement control: "a stimulus or event that is presented during or following the behavior that increases the future rate [or probability] of the behavior upon which it is contingent." Reinforcement control includes social support, lottery, token reinforcement, and feedback. Stimulus control, a third strategy, involves the "use of cues and prompts that stimulate, or are reliably followed by the behavior, i.e., exercise." Other strategies listed include behavioral contracting (contingencies being specified for compliance or noncompliance), written agreement (no contingencies), and cognitive strategies (goal setting, associative/dissociative strategies, and coping thoughts). The evidence for these strategies in improving exercise compliance in cardiac rehabilitation programs is limited (Martin & Dubbert, 1984).

Maintenance or adherence strategies include (a) generalization training (preparation for the transit from adoption to long-term maintenance); (b) reinforcement fading (gradually diminishing the reinforcement being used); (c) self-control procedures (self-monitoring and contracting); and (d) relapse prevention training. Similarly, these have not been extensively investigated in cardiac rehabilitation (Martin & Dubbert, 1984).

Appraisal of Coping Strategies.   *Appraisal or evaluation skills* are necessary to permit the patient to decide which of the alternative strategies is most appropriate and which is most effective. The outcome measure against which the skill or strategy is evaluated is the achievement or non-achievement of the objective. The first consideration is to determine whether the objective was realistic. If it was realistic, what has not been done in order to meet the objective? If it was not realistic, why was it not realistic, how can it be made realistic, and what strategy is most likely to result in meeting the objective?

It is important that patients be given the freedom to define their own outcome or measure of success. For techniques in which the patient is an observer objectively assessing the effectiveness of a strategy, then the failure of a specific strategy is more likely attributed to an inappropriate choice of strategies rather than a failure of the individual. This approach may reinforce the individual's self-efficacy rather than the individual's self-inadequacy. The result may have a positive effect on enhancing the probability of compliance.

Acceptance and Integration of Changes

The ultimate objectives of the self-regulatory process are the *acceptance of the prescription and the integration of changes into a personal lifestyle* (see Figure 3). A patient's acceptance of prescription, or compliance with treatment is determined by (a) the representation of the immediate health threat, (b) the patient's perception of the consequences of the existing symptoms, and (c) the patient's available coping strategies to reduce the symptoms. The long-term adherence to a particular lifestyle is based on (a) the probability of future symptoms, (b) the impairment of function, (c) the associated reduction in quality of life, and (d) the individual's perception of the consequences of not adhering neither to health or medical advice nor to lifelong positive health behaviors.

Implications for the Self-Regulatory Perspective in Supervised Programs

The awareness of the self-regulatory perspective depends on the patient's exposure to behavior management techniques. If the patient is attempting to meet and respond to the challenges of a relatively hostile environment (e.g., job pressures, inconvenient hours, little social support, and little or no exposure to behavioral management strategies), there is probably a greater likelihood of long-term compliance in a support group setting. But care must be taken not to overemphasize the health professional's role in the supervised setting where exposure to behavioral strategies is more likely than in the unsupervised setting. If the patient perceives the health professional to be in charge, the long-term effectiveness of the behavior change may be minimized. If the structure of the program is such that the patient perceives himself or herself to be on a collegial footing with the health professional, then long-term effectiveness can probably be optimized. Though this has not been investigated in exercise rehabilitation, the perception of being in control of both the development and the progression of an exercise plan has been shown to increase compliance (Thompson & Wankel, 1980).

Together the health care professional and the patient set short-term expectations for specific behavior modifications with the explicit understanding that long-term behavior management and goal achievement must be the primary responsibility of the patient and not the health care professional. Long-term maintenance requires acquisition of problem-solving skills which focus on self-management strategies.

Self-management strategies can be learned. Inherent to self-management and problem-solving, however, is the central role of the patient as his own keeper. This has been previously discussed in this paper. If we argue that this concept of self-responsibility has the potential for enhancing compliance, then it is important to encourage patients to develop their own meaningful representation of the health threat based on sound evidence. They must be exposed to various alternative behavioral strategies as well as appraisal or evaluation skills so that they are able to determine the most effective strategies for integrating the new behaviors into a new, life-long, personal, lifestyle which is likely to be maintained.

Summary

The effectiveness of risk factor reduction has not been unequivocally established in the secondary prevention of CHD. However, there is sound logic for incorporating strategies to reduce risk factors such as hypertension, hyperlipidemia, smoking, and sedentary living habits in the management of documented CHD. Without extended compliance or adherence, however, there can be little hope of success. Extended compliance with health behavior changes after documentation of CHD is a major medical problem. Health professionals must attempt to maximize the collegial nature of the patient-professional role; this encourages self-responsibility for extended compliance and stabilization of the new health behavior. One of the benefits of this method of using self-responsibility and the self-regulatory perspective to encourage long-term compliance or adherence is that the practical strategies suggested also lend themselves to research (Leventhal et al., 1985).

From the perspective of self-regulation, some practical suggestions for the health professional include the following:

1. Identify the patient's objectives.
2. Assist the patient in making them as realistic as possible.

3. Provide access to and use various techniques and strategies to increase self-efficacy.
4. Provide exposure to alternative self-control or self-management strategies.
5. Instruct staff members in the use of motivational techniques.
6. Incorporate social support systems into the program.
7. Ensure rapid feedback of results.
8. Provide follow-up visits after graduation.

Potential research implications of the self-regulatory model include: What are the links between the individual compliers and dropouts and their social support systems? Can these be fostered or manipulated? What effects do patient perceptions of the health threat have on compliance? Does patient involvement in the management process improve compliance? Is there a difference between real and perceived involvement? Do health professionals' perceptions and attitudes affect compliance? Can self-efficacy be increased? Are certain strategies more frequently used by compliers than dropouts? Are certain problem-solving and self-management strategies more effective than others? In whom? Under what conditions? In the short-term? In the long-term? Do the strategies work in isolation? Are they more effective when combined? What are the most effective combinations?

Obviously the above suggestions demonstrate that there are many unknowns about self-management strategies designed to improve compliance with cardiac rehabilitation. The self-regulatory perspective does provide a theoretical framework for asking questions about coping strategies and their effect on compliance and adherence. Some of these questions may have been asked in isolation. They will make considerably more sense if investigated in a coherent fashion. The self-regulatory framework provides an interdisciplinary opportunity to investigate and enforce our understanding of compliance-enhancing strategies in exercise-centered rehabilitation for patients with coronary artery disease.

Acknowledgments

I would like to acknowledge Mary Gutmann, PhD, for her constructive comments and to thank Karn Korek, Pat Bodine, and Judy Steffan for their help.

References

American Heart Association Committee Report. (1980). Risk factors and coronary disease. *Circulation, 62*, 449A–455A.

Bandura, A. (1977). Self-efficacy: Toward a unifying theory of behavior change. *Psychological Review, 84*, 195–215.

Bandura, A. (1982). Self-efficacy mechanism in human agency. *American Psychologist, 37*, 122–147.

Becker, M.H., & Maiman, L.A. (1975). Sociobehavioral determinants of compliance with health and medical care recommendations. *Medical Care, 13*, 10–24.

Blair, S.N., Cooper, K.H., Gibbons, L.W., Gettman, L.R., Lewis, S., & Goodyear, N. (1983). Changes in coronary heart disease risk factors associated with increased treadmill time in 753 men. *American Journal of Epidemiology, 118*, 352–359.

Blair, S.N., Jacobs, D.R., & Powell, K.E. (1985). Relationships between exercise or physical activity and other health behaviors. *Public Health Reports, 100*, 172–180.

Carson, P., Philips, R., Lloyd, M., Tucker, H., Neophytou, M., Buch, N.J., Gelson, A., Lawton, A., & Simpson, T. (1982). Exercise after a myocardial infarction: A controlled trial. *Journal of the Royal College of Physicians of London, 16*, 147–151.

Castelli, W.P. (1984). Epidemiology of coronary heart disease: The Framingham study. *American Journal of Medicine, 76*, 4–12.

Conrad, P. (1985). The meaning of medications: Another look at compliance. *Social Science in Medicine, 20*, 29–37.

Daltroy, L.H. (1985). Improving cardiac patient adherence to exercise regimens: A clinical trial of health education. *Journal of Cardiac Rehabilitation, 5*, 40–49.

DeBusk, R.F., Houston, N., Haskell, W., Fry, G., & Parker, M. (1979). Exercise training soon after myocardial infarction. *American Journal of Cardiology, 44*, 1223–1229.

DeBusk, R.F., Haskell, W.L., Miller, N.H., Berra, K., Taylor, C.B., in cooperation with Berger, W.E., III, & Lew, H. (1985). Medically directed at-home rehabilitation soon after clinically uncomplicated acute myocardial infarction: A new model for patient care. *American Journal of Cardiology, 55*, 251–257.

Dishman, R.K. (1982). Compliance/adherence in health related exercise. *Health Psychology, 1*, 237–267.

Elveback, L.R., Connolly, D.C., & Kurland, L.T. (1981). Coronary heart disease in residents of Rochester, Minnesota. II. Mortality, incidence and survivorship, 1950–1975. *Mayo Clinic Proceedings, 56*, 665–672.

Erling, J., & Oldridge, N.B. (1985). Effects of a spousal-support program on compliance with cardiac rehabilitation. *Medicine and Science in Sports and Exercise* (abstract), **16**, 284.

Ewart, C.K., Taylor, C.B., Reese, L.B., & DeBusk, R.F. (1983). Effects of early post myocardial infarction exercise testing on self-perception and subsequent physical activity. *American Journal of Cardiology*, **51**, 1076–1080.

Gordis, L. (1979). Conceptual and methodological problems in measuring patient compliance. In R.B. Haynes, D.W. Taylor, & D.L. Sackett (Eds.), *Compliance in health care* (pp. 23–45). Baltimore: The Johns Hopkins University Press.

Haynes, R.B. (1979). Introduction. In R.B. Haynes, D.W. Taylor, & D.L. Sackett (Eds.), *Compliance in health care* (pp. 1–7). Baltimore: The Johns Hopkins University Press.

Haynes, R.B. (1984). Compliance with health advice: An overview with special reference to exercise programs. *Journal of Cardiac Rehabilitation*, **4**, 120–123.

Hickey, N., Mulcahy, R., Burke, G.J., Graham, I., & Wilson-Davis, K. (1975). A study of coronary risk factors related to physical activity in 15,171 men. *British Medical Journal*, **ii**, 507–509.

Hilbert, G.A. (1985). Spouse support and myocardial infarction patient compliance. *Nursing Research*, **34**, 217–220.

Kallio, V., Hamalainen, H., Hakkila, J., & Luurila, O.J. (1979). Reduction in sudden deaths by a multifactorial intervention programme after acute myocardial infarction. *Lancet*, **ii**, 1091–1094.

Kavanagh, T., Shephard, R.J., Chisholme, A.W., Qureshi, S., & Kennedy, J. (1980). Prognostic indexes for patients with ischemic heart disease enrolled in exercise-centered rehabilitation. *American Journal of Cardiology*, **44**, 1230–1240.

Kuller, L. (1984). Risk factor reduction in coronary heart disease. *Modern Concepts of Cardiovascular Disease*, **53**, 7–11.

Leventhal, H. (1985). The role of theory in the study of adherence to treatment and doctor-patient interactions. *Medical Care*, **23**, 556–563.

Leventhal, H., Zimmerman, R., & Gutmann, M. (1984). Compliance: A self-regulation perspective. In W. Gentry (Ed.), *Handbook of behavioral medicine* (pp. 369–436). New York: The Guilford Press.

Levin, L.S., & Adler, E.L. (1983). Self-care in health. *Annual Review of Public Health*, **4**, 181–201.

Martin, J.E., & Dubbert, P.M. (1984). Behavioral management strategies for improving health and fitness. *Journal of Cardiac Rehabilitation*, **4**, 200–208.

Mayou, R. (1983). A controlled trial of early rehabilitation after myocardial infarction. *Journal of Cardiac Rehabilitation*, **3**, 397–402.

Mayou, R., MacMahon, D., Sleight, P., & Florencio, M.J. (1981). Early rehabilitation after myocardial infarction. *Lancet*, **ii**, 1399–1401.

Naughton, J. (1985). Role of physical activity as a secondary intervention for healed myocardial infarction. *American Journal of Cardiology*, **55**, 21D–26D.

Newton, K.M., Sivarajan, E.S., & Clarke, J.L. (1985). Patient perceptions of risk factor changes and cardiac rehabilitation outcomes after myocardial infarction. *Journal of Cardiac Rehabilitation*, **5**, 159–168.

Nye, G.R., & Poulsen, W.T. (1974). An activity programme for coronary patients: A review of morbidity, mortality and adherence—After five years. *New Zealand Medical Journal*, **79**, 1010–1013.

Oldridge, N.B. (1982). Compliance with intervention and rehabilitation exercise programs—A review. *Preventive Medicine*, **11**, 56–70.

Oldridge, N.B. (1984). Compliance and dropout in cardiac exercise rehabilitation. *Journal of Cardiac Rehabilitation*, **4**, 166–177.

Oldridge, N.B., Donner, A., Buck, C., Andrew, G., Jones, N.L., Parker, J.O., Cunningham, D.A., Kavanagh, T., Rechnitzer, P., & Sutton, J.R. (1983). Predictors of dropout from the Ontario Exercise-Heart Collaborative Study. *American Journal of Cardiology*, **51**, 70–74.

Oldridge, N.B., & Guyatt, G.H. (1986). Mortality and morbidity after combining trials of cardiac rehabilitation. *Circulation* (abstract), **74**, 9.

Oldridge, N.B., & Jones, N.L. (1983). Improving patient compliance in cardiac exercise rehabilitation: Effects of written agreement and self-monitoring. *Journal of Cardiac Rehabilitation*, **3**, 257–262.

Oldridge, N.B., & Jones, N.L. (1986). Preventive use of exercise rehabilitation after myocardial infarction. *Acta Medica Scandinavica*, (Suppl. 711), 123–129.

Oldridge, N.B., & Spencer, J. (1985). Exercise habits and perceptions before and after graduation or dropout from supervised cardiac exercise rehabilitation. *Journal of Cardiac Rehabilitation*, **5**, 313–319.

Oldridge, N.B., & Stoedefalke, K. (1984). Compliance and motivation in cardiac exercise programs. *Clinics in Sports Medicine*, **3**, 443–454.

Oldridge, N.B., Wicks, J.R., Hanley, C., Sutton, J.R., & Jones, N.L. (1978). Non-compliance in a post myocardial infarction exercise rehabilitation program. *Canadian Medical Association Journal*, **118**, 361–364.

Pell, S.,& Fayerweather, W.E. (1985). Trends in the incidence of myocardial infarction and in associated mortality and morbidity in a large employed population, 1957–1983. *New England Journal of Medicine,* **312,** 1005–1011.

Prosser, G., Carson, P., Gelson, A., Tucker, H., Neophytou, M., Phillips, R., & Simpson, T. (1978). Assessing the psychological effects of an exercise training programme for patients following myocardial infarction: A pilot study. *British Journal of Medical Psychology,* **51,** 95–102.

Rechnitzer, P., Cunningham, D.A., Andrew, G., Buck, C., Jones, N.L., Kavanagh, T., Oldridge, N.B., Parker, J.O., Shephard, R.J., & Sutton, J.R. (1983). The relationship of exercise to the recurrence rate of myocardial infarction in men. Ontario Exercise Heart Collaborative Study. *American Journal of Cardiology,* **51,** 65–69.

Rosenstock, I.M. (1966). Why people use health services. *Millbank Memorial Fund Quarterly,* **44,** 94–124.

Roviaro, S., Holmes, D.S., & Holmes, D.R. (1984). Influence of a cardiac rehabilitation program on cardiovascular, psychological and social functioning of cardiac patients. *Journal of Behavioral Medicine,* **7,** 61–81.

Shaw, L.W., for the project staff. (1981). Effects of a prescribed supervised exercise program on mortality and cardiovascular morbidity in patients after a myocardial infarction. *American Journal of Cardiology,* **48,** 39–46.

Shephard, R.J., Corey, P., & Kavanagh, T. (1981). Exercise compliance and the prevention of a recurrence of myocardial infarction. *Medicine and Science in Sports and Exercise,* **13,** 1–5.

Spodick, D.H. (1982). Randomized clinical trials: The behavioral case. *Journal of the American Medical Association,* **247,** 2258–2260.

Stamler, J. (1985). Coronary heart disease: Doing the "right things" (Editorial). *New England Journal of Medicine,* **312,** 1053–1055.

Stern, M.J., & Cleary, P. (1981). National Exercise and Heart Disease Project. Psychosocial changes observed during a low-level exercise program. *Archives of Internal Medicine,* **141,** 1463–1467.

Stern, M.J., & Cleary, P. (1982). National Exercise and Heart Disease Project. Long-term psychosocial outcome. *Archives of Internal Medicine,* **142,** 1093–1097.

Taylor, C.B., Bandura, A., Ewart, C.K., Miller, N.H., & DeBusk, R.F. (1985). Exercise testing to enhance wives' confidence in their husband's cardiac capability soon after clinically uncomplicated acute myocardial infarction. *American Journal of Cardiology,* **55,** 635–638.

Thompson, C.E., & Wankel, L.M. (1980). The effects of perceived activity choice upon frequency of exercise behavior. *Journal of Applied Social Psychology*, **10**, 436–443.

Wilhelmsen, L., Sanne, H., Elmfeldt, D., Grimby, G., Tibblin, G., & Wedel, H. (1975). A controlled trial of physical training after myocardial infarction. Effects on risk factors, nonfatal reinfarction and death. *Preventive Medicine*, **4**, 491–508.

Wood, P.D., Haskell, W.L., Terry, R.B., Ho, P.H., & Blair, S.N. (1982). Effects of a two-year running program on plasma lipoprotein, body fat and dietary intake in initially sedentary men. *Medicine and Science in Sports and Exercise* (abstract), **14** 102.

World Health Organization. (1964). *Rehabilitation of patients with cardiovascular disease. Report of a WHO expert committee* (Technical Report Series No. 270). Geneva: World Health Organization.

CHAPTER *11*

Exercise Adherence in Corporate Settings: Personal Traits and Program Barriers

Roy J. Shephard

Despite occasional overly optimistic claims, no more than 20% of eligible workers are usually recruited to a corporate fitness program, and only about a half of those who are recruited become long-term program adherents (Beck, 1982; Fielding, 1982; Morgan, Shephard, Finucane, Schimmelfing, & Jazmaji, 1984; Shephard, 1985, 1986; Shephard, Morgan, Finucane, & Schimmelfing, 1980; Song, Shephard, & Cox, 1982). Although there may be some trickle down of improved lifestyle to other employees of the corporation, the potential impact of the corporate exercise class upon overall industrial and community health is seriously limited by problems in both recruitment and retention of participants (Brennan, 1982; Pomereau, 1983).

The issue of compliance with such programs is important because of a continued growth in the number of companies that provide exercise facilities and resources for employees, and because of commitments by both the U.S. and the Canadian federal governments to facilitate developments of this type in the future. The primary key to both recruitment and retention of program participants plainly lies in modifying the behavior of the individual worker. This chapter examines current rates of participation among eligible employees and considers behavioral correlates originating in both the program and the individual. Where possible, similarities and contrasts with adherence to clinical and community programs are noted, and research-based suggestions for increasing the effectiveness of corporate programs are advanced.

Participation Rates

Patterns of recruitment to corporate fitness programs have been remarkably similar in Canada and in the United States. Details of the process are illustrated by seven years of experience at the Canada Life Assurance Company in Toronto (Cox, Shephard, & Corey, 1981; Marsden & Youldon, 1979; Song et al., 1982). The Canada Life Program was initiated at the headquarters office of the company in January of 1978 with the enthusiastic support of senior management. Employees (who are predominantly white-collar workers) had opportunity to register for either two or three 30-minute exercise sessions per week, held in a converted basement area of the office block. Attendance was on the worker's own time (before work, during the lunch hour, or immediately following work). The cost was a $10.00 registration fee, payable at the beginning of each two-month session. The fitness coordinator applied the money received to the purchase of promotional materials such as door prizes and T-shirts for those who met certain standards of program adherence and exercise participation.

The program was initiated in January of 1978 and over the first six months of operation some 600 out of about 1280 employees made at least transient contact with the fitness coordinator (Marsden & Youldon, 1979). The inquirers quickly sorted themselves into four rather equally-sized categories (Cox et al., 1981): (a) non-participants who did not join the formal exercise classes but were nevertheless interested in having a fitness test; (b) drop-outs; (c) low adherents whose attendance continued, but averaged less than two class sessions per week; and (d) high adherents whose attendance averaged two or more sessions per week. Two months after initiation of the program, the fitness coordinator reported 402 immediate registrations for the second series of classes, while late enrollments boosted this total to 486 employees (37.9% of the company). At 6 months the overall adherence of the initial recruits was 80.5% (high adherents, 45.6%; low adherents, 34.9%). A further analysis of attendance at 18 months (Song et al., 1982) showed that 176 of the 307 individuals who had been active at 6 months were still involved in the program, 6 as exercise class leaders, 52 as high adherents and 118 as low adherents. The sustained adherence rate was thus 46.1% (176/307). In subsequent years, membership has been boosted by continuing recruitment, including new employees of the company. Thus, towards the end of its seventh year of operation (September, 1984), the program had some 400 active members (C. West, personal communication, September 25, 1984). A particularly interesting feature of the program was that approximately 100 of the 1280 employees were now supplementing the in-hours gymnasium sessions with regular, long-distance running. Moreover, many of those who had dropped out of the formal classes claimed to have begun exercise programs in their home communities. The long-term experience at Canada Life has thus exceeded the generalized expectation of 20% recruitment and 10% adherence; however, several features have favored a successful outcome, including (a) enthusiastic support of management, (b) health orientation of the company, (c) predominance of white-collar employees, and (d) a high-profile experimental program.

U.S. experience is illustrated by the General Foods study (Shephard et al., 1980; Morgan et al., 1984). This program originated at the head-quarters office of the General Foods Corporation, in White Plains, N.J. The recently constructed Health Fitness Center of this corporation included medical and exercise testing facilities, a large, covered, indoor/outdoor jogging track, a gym, a weight-training room, outdoor jogging and skiing trails, and shower/locker areas. Membership was by a payroll deduction, initially set at $4.00 per month, and the employees attended on their own time. Trained professionals directed organized programs featuring jogging, aerobic sports, aerobic dance, strength-building, flexibility, and relaxation. Participants had access to the facility 2 1/2 days per week, with use separated according to gender.

Initially, 535 head-office employees registered in the program: 22% of those with ready access to the facility, and 13.4% of all eligible employees. A follow-up evaluation at 20 months showed that 53% of the men and 62% of the women who had been inactive when first recruited were still participating regularly in class sessions.

The experience of other corporations has been similar. At the U.S. Exxon Corporation, 65% of executives initially recruited to a fitness facility still exercised two or more times per week after one year (Yarvote, McDonagh, Goldman, & Zuckerman, 1974) while at the National Aeronautics and Space Administration (NASA) only 38.4% continued to exercise two or more days per week (Durbeck et al., 1972).

To date, most studies of adherence to corporate fitness programs have focused on white-collar employees. By analogy with the response patterns observed in community programs, it has been hypothesized that blue-collar workers would be less readily recruited and would show poorer adherence rates to exercise classes. Limited personal experience has also shown (a) a preference of blue-collar employees for sports rather than exercise programs, (b) a wish of such individuals to exercise on company rather than personal time, and (c) if company time is made available, a tendency to see an exercise class as an opportunity for work avoidance. Although traditional blue-collar work is a rapidly declining segment of the North American labor force, it is important to recognize that there is a similar socioeconomic gradient of recruitment and adherence rates within white-collar exercise programs (Marsden & Youldon, 1979).

It is difficult to ascertain the impact of corporate programs compared with that of community-based initiatives. Where companies have sponsored formal, off-site programs, initial recruitment has been no more than 10 to 25% (Fielding, 1982). On the other hand, the Canada Fitness Survey (1983) reported that 54% of adults aged 20 to 39 years and 47% of those aged 40 to 59 years performed 3 or more hours of deliberate leisure activity per week during 9 or more months of each year. Self-reports are notoriously unreliable, but if the findings from the Canada Fitness Survey are taken at face value, it would appear that in Canada at least, there is a substantial community involvement in physical activity. In support of this view, about a half of those recruited to both the Canada Life Program and the General Foods Program reported that they had previously been active elsewhere. Likewise, many employees who took only a fitness test or soon dropped out of formal classes at the company headquarters indicated a continuing exercise involvement in the community. Whether the vigor and frequency of such activity was sufficient to obtain any health benefit is uncertain. More importantly, the remaining 50% of recruits to corporate fitness programs had previously been inactive.

The 46.5% sustained adherence rate observed after 18 months operation of the Canada Life Program is very similar to that which has been reported for some cardiac rehabilitation programs. The correspondence, however, is probably fortuitous. The decision to enter a corporate fitness program is personal and unrelated to any critical incident, whereas entry into a post-coronary exercise class is usually at the urgent behest of a physician, and immediately follows a life-threatening medical emergency. Furthermore, there are substantial medical incentives to continued participation in the cardiac program, including the opportunity for evaluation of any residual symptoms and discussion of a safe return to normal patterns of daily living. Because of such favorable influences, well-designed post-coronary classes have had adherence rates as high as 82% for 3 years (Shephard, Corey, & Kavanagh, 1981).

Program Correlates of Recruitment and Adherence

As in clinical and community-based programs, the most commonly cited reason for not participating in a corporate exercise class is "lack of time.'' Given that most white-collar employees have 3 to 4 hours of free-time per day, such an explanation must generally be regarded as an excuse rather than a reason. Nevertheless, a corporate program does present some time constraints which are not encountered in a community-based exercise program. Travel arrangements may be set by a car-pool system or an infrequent train service, children may require feeding or meeting after school, and a standard 60-minute lunch hour may not allow time for eating, any necessary shopping, and exercise. Executives may face problems from out-of-town commitments and unavoidable meetings arranged at the scheduled exercise hour. Program features which favor adherence thus include provision of flexible working hours and a free-time activity area adjacent to the main gymnasium, where executives can exercise as their business commitments permit.

''Lack of suitable facilities'' is a second common excuse for inactivity in a community setting. Members of corporate programs may complain of minor structural details; for example, ''lack of air'' in the Canada Life basement gym, or too much air in the General Foods Indoor/Outdoor facility. However, once a certain minimum investment has been made in space and equipment (probably about 0.25 m² of gymnasium floor area per employee), any further increase in the size or luxury of the facility has little influence upon program adherence.

Continued class participation depends heavily upon leadership and program content. Different individuals react favorably to differing styles of leadership, from the charismatic and authoritarian through the motherly to those who believe in self-direction. If the size of the corporation permits, it is thus useful to have parallel classes where lay group leaders can offer several different styles of leadership and supervision. Given a provision for periodic re-registration of all participants, it becomes possible for any given employee to seek a personally appropriate type of class leader without unnecessary discussion of motives for changing classes.

It seems logical that employees will be attracted to a program that matches their level of ability; if the demands of the exercise class are too rigorous or too limited, participants will become dissatisfied. The aim should be to form groups that are roughly homogenous with respect to age and initial fitness level, and within these given fitness categories subjects should be given a personalized exercise prescription. Particularly if their condition is poor, older employees may be uncomfortable exercising in the presence of the opposite sex; at least one segregated class should be offered in addition to coeducational sessions.

The content of corporate exercise classes is commonly built around progressive endurance exercise in the gymnasium, with an appropriate warm-up and a cool down. It is interesting to compare this focus with the opinions expressed to the Canada Fitness Survey (1983). The most popular current activities, with the percent participation at least once during 1981 by Canadians over 10 years of age, were walking (57%), cycling (38%), swimming in a pool (36%), jogging or running (31%), gardening (30%), and home exercises (28%). An "exercise class" of the type featured by most corporate fitness programs ranked sixteenth in terms of participation (8% of the population). Moreover, activities that showed rapid growth over the previous five years were cross-country skiing (+142%), alpine skiing (+69%), golf (+32%), and tennis (+23%). An increase in the number of conventional corporate fitness classes would have done little to satisfy such interests, and it could be argued that a more effective tactic would be for a company to invest in exercise testing, counseling, and shower facilities, encouraging employees to develop their current interests, and to walk, jog, or cycle to work. Some support for this view can be found in responses to a further question of the Canada Fitness Survey; this concerned activities the individual would like to begin over the next 12 months. Again, formal exercise classes were well down the list relative to such pursuits as jogging, swimming, tennis, cycling, and home exercises. Further evidence favoring a relatively simple approach to exercise comes from the listing of activities that were halted over the past year (Canada Fitness Survey, 1983). Walkers reported the smallest loss of interest (2% of initial participants), and in their case much of the attrition was unavoidable because the subjects concerned had developed an illness or an injury. The experience with formal exercise classes was much less favorable, with a 10% loss of participation admitted over the immediately preceeding year.

The Canadian Home Fitness Test (Shephard, 1979) was originally conceived as a means of motivating subjects to engage in regular exercise. It was reasoned that the demonstration of an improving test score would provide motivation for continued involvement in physical activity. While this type of feedback seems logical, one practical problem is that as physical condition improves, the gains from a given investment of effort diminish in logarithmic fashion. The difficulty can be circumvented if scores are presented in percentile fashion. Nevertheless, one recent controlled experiment suggested that a formal exercise testing and counseling sessions had little influence upon the intention of employees to undertake regular endurance exercise once such an intention had been formed (Godin & Shephard, 1983).

Policies regarding payment for exercise classes have been divided rather equally between total, partial, and zero subsidization by the corporation. Some corporations have argued (without any strong supporting evidence) that a modest financial stake ($4–$5/month) provides an incentive to use the facility. Others suggest that a charge of this order is hardly noticed among other payroll deductions. In the General Foods Study 80% of employees agreed with the statement that a charge of $48.00 per year was not a significant obstacle to participation. More important (and not yet evaluated) is the notion (encouraged by sports entrepreneurs) that regular physical activity demands a major investment in an athletic wardrobe, with the purchase of much expensive ancillary equipment. The value that workers place upon totally subsidized programs can be estimated in terms of the equivalent variation of consumer surplus economics: the alternative benefits needed to retain employees if an exercise program were discontinued. In the special case of the U.S. Navy, Morey (1983) estimated that the government would need to spend $3.20 to $4.60 on alternative benefits to compensate for every dollar that might be saved by a discontinuation of its fitness program.

Many corporate fitness programs invest a good deal of effort in the circulation of newsletters and similar forms of publicity. Recent studies of human behavior, however, have emphasized the substantial gap that separates awareness from actual behavior (Godin, Valois, Shephard, & Desharnais, 1985). The Canada Life Assurance Program followed this pattern, developing a well-designed monthly fitness/lifestyle newsletter. A large proportion of company employees claimed to read the newsletter, and most of them stated that at least some of the information contained in it was valuable to them (Marsden & Youldon, 1979); this response seemed characteristic, whether they participated in the program or not. However, such assertions made in response to leading questions must be weighed against the fact that most respondents to the Canada Fitness Survey (1983) did not believe that either the organization of more fitness classes or the provision of information on the benefits of physical activity would increase their exercise habits. Some 18% of currently active Canadians and 32% of sedentary Canadians insisted that no changes would make them increase their physical activity.

Some exercise programs have applied a Skinnerian system of rewards to encourage class members (Danielson & Danielson, 1979). Such an approach is particularly helpful in the early stages of participation when the internal rewards of exercise (i.e., ''feeling better,'' and the development of an attractive body) are not yet realized. During this time there may be substantial negative influences: costs of clothing and equipment; investment of time; expenditure of effort with possible pain and injury; discouragement; failure to realize goals; fatigue; and even alienation of the family. The type of reward provided to the exerciser may be symbolic (badge, pin, T-shirt, award, or membership), material (money, prize, release time, payment of club dues), or psychological (attention, recognition, encouragement, and friendship).

The extent to which corporate fitness programs should adopt behavioral modification techniques to encourage attendance is a difficult ethical decision (Godin & Shephard, 1984). While there is increasing evidence that the health experience of regular exercisers is better than that of sedentary employees, the individual benefits of class participation are not unequivocally established; and a case could be argued for allowing a free and informed personal choice. Unfortunately, the interests that push workers to adopt a sedentary and unhealthy lifestyle have fewer scruples about using the techniques of hidden persuasion; consequently, a moderately vigorous advocacy of exercise is appropriate. Additional techniques favored by clinical exercise programs, such as innoculation against occasional failures (Wankel, 1984), and the contracting of a specific performance (Oldridge, 1984) could be usefully considered in the occupational setting.

Personal Correlates of Recruitment and Adherence

Early research on recruitment and adherence emphasized the physical characteristics of exercise program participants. Relative to dropouts, they apparently had a higher standard of cardiorespiratory fitness, less excess weight, and less subcutaneous fat. They were also much less likely to be regular cigarette smokers (Massie & Shephard, 1971; Sidney & Shephard, 1977). More recent experience with corporate fitness programs has shown some variation from this pattern. In the Canada Life project, neither initial recruits nor continuing participants were an especially fit subsample of the population. Indeed, particularly among male employees, the non-compliers and the dropouts were apparently more fit, and they also had a greater likelihood of prior involvement in a community fitness program than did the adherents. Moreover, we did not see a progressive defection of the obese as the program continued. There seem three main reasons for this apparently anomalous pattern of response: (a) initial publicity was deliberately aimed at recruitment of the unfit; (b) classes were graded according to the physical ability of the participants, so that there was less likelihood of discouragement because of failure to realize the expectations of the instructor; and (c) the rate of progression of classes was deliberately held to a slow pace in order to avoid injuries and allow an eventual lay leadership of the program.

The General Foods Program had a somewhat heavier focus upon endurance exercise, and probably for this reason the typical recruit was a fairly fit, middle-aged non-smoker. The men had an above-average maximum oxygen intake and muscle strength, although they were somewhat overweight. The women (who had a woman instructor) were closer to the actuarial ideal weight and showed relatively lower initial levels of cardiorespiratory and muscular fitness than the men.

In neither the Canada Life Program nor the General Foods Program was injury a significant reason for ceasing to exercise. This finding mirrors the experience of clinical programs in which less than a quarter of defections have been attributable to musculo-skeletal or cardiac problems (Bruce, Frederick, Bruce, & Fisher, 1976). A formal behavioral study indicated that the intention to exercise was actually stronger in those who had previously sustained an injury while exercising than in those who had not (Godin & Shephard, 1985). Among several explanations of this finding, we conclude that (a) those who sustained injury may have had a greater intrinsic commitment to exercise, (b) the danger inherent in sport may have been one of its attractions, or (c) the injury may have been perceived as a random occurrence, unlikely to affect the outcome of future bouts of exercise.

The Canada Fitness Survey (1983) explored perceived motives for exercising in both men and women. Cited reasons for being active were to feel better physically or mentally (58% of men and 62% of women of the national sample rating this as "very important"), to control weight (33%, 51%, respectively), and for fun or excitement (44%, 43%). Doctor's orders (20%, 24%), the advice of a fitness leader (17%, 21%), the desire to learn (18%, 21%), and the desire to challenge personal abilities (23%, 19%) were seen as much less important motivators. Such findings stress the importance of the feelings generated by exercise and suggest that, unless it gives rise to a rewarding experience, an exercise counseling service for employees might have only limited success.

Kenyon (1968) devised the Attitudes Towards Physical Activity Inventory as a more formal method of soliciting similar information. The instrument has recently been criticized on the grounds that it makes an aggregate assessment of attitudes toward "physical activity", stressing neither the type of activity nor the need for personal participation. Bearing in mind this caveat, we consider information that has been collected by the Kenyon inventory in the context of employee fitness programming. Scores have been consistently highest for exercise as an aesthetic, cathartic, social, and health experience.

At first glance, the aesthetic element suggests a need for such activities as dancing and figure-skating, a conclusion at variance with the perceived ambitions of people questioned in the Canada Fitness Survey. The two sets of information, however, can be reconciled if aesthetics is interpreted in terms of personal appearance (i.e., the body beautiful). The objectives of "weight" control and a slim, graceful figure call for a combination of moderate endurance activity with dietary counseling, including, if possible, the presentation of nutritional advice through an appropriate labeling of food in the company canteen. Likewise, the wish to "feel better, physically or mentally" can probably be equated with the catharsis of tension. The program content may interact either positively or negatively with these objectives. Thus, in the General Foods program, men who adopted regular exercise had a lesser interest than non-compliers in exercise for socializing; factors reinforcing the exercise habit included a continued sense of trying to improve their health and perceived long-term benefits (including the relief of tension and an improvement of health). Among the women, feelings of robustness and acceptance of the discipline of aerobic exercise were keys to continued participation. Non-compliers initially recognized exercise both as a self-discipline and as a means of reducing their shortness of breath, but they did not experience any reinforcement of these attitudes as the program continued. The negative associations between adherence and a desire for "fun" or socializing suggests that these attributes may not have received sufficient emphasis in the programming at General Foods.

Health beliefs are a second important facet of attitudes towards physical activity. Such beliefs can be explored by the health belief model of Becker and Maiman (1975). This model holds that rational health behaviors such as voluntary leisure activity are initiated and sustained by the belief that they will correct a perceived threat to health. Thus, if a subject is convinced that physical inactivity has adverse consequences for health, adherence to an exercise program is likely. This model has proven relatively useful in interpreting clinical health behaviors, but in the setting of a corporate exercise program there is a much less strong relationship between general or specific beliefs in the health value of exercise, the practice of physical activity, and outcomes as indicated by fitness status (Shephard et al., 1980; Morgan et al., 1984). One problem is that the threat of an event such as a coronary attack seems a very remote contingency to a 20-year old office worker. In the Canada Life Program, the fitness instructor arranged lectures on topics such as heart disease, but it was soon noted that these were attended largely by older male employees. The Canada Fitness Survey (1983) examined differences in the importance attached to health related behaviors by active and sedentary individuals. There was a large difference in the value attributed to regular physical activity (55% vs. 26%), suggesting that people were indeed acting on their beliefs about the need for exercise. The active members of the community, however, also attached more importance to other health behaviors, especially not smoking (62% vs. 51%) and weight control (60% vs. 50%). It makes economic sense to offer employees a total lifestyle package rather than a specific exercise program, and the results of the Canada Fitness Survey suggest that such a package should appeal to active or potentially active workers. A number of corporate programs in the U.S., such as the Johnson & Johnson *Live-for-Life* Program, are now adopting this approach.

A further variable influencing exercise compliance is what Dishman (1982) calls self-efficacy. Others have spoken of self motivation, or of an internal versus an external locus of control (Rotter, 1975). In operational terms, the key issue is whether the individual's behavior is governed by personal attitudes and beliefs or by the views of significant others. If personal attitudes and beliefs are dominant, then the program can usefully embark upon long-term educational plans to shape attitudes and beliefs. If social norms are the dominant influence, however, then the main focus should be upon creating an ambience where an active lifestyle is the accepted norm of corporate behavior. In the working environment, social facilitation begins with senior management; the key to success is their committed participation, and there may be good grounds for special programming which accommodates their demanding schedules. Displays in lobby areas and canteens, interdepartmental contests, T-shirts, and lapel buttons all help to build peer pressure to participate. In the Canada Fitness Survey (1983), the interest of a partner (22%), family (18%), or friend (17%) were noted as potential incentives to greater physical activity. Likewise, spousal involvement or approval has proven very important in clinical exercise programs. Some corporations have thus opened their exercise classes to families, with varying success. Much probably depends upon the size of the city; if it is necessary to travel an hour each way to a downtown office block, the high "opportunity cost" of travel militates against family participation, except perhaps in extended-weekend classes. An alternative, adopted in the Canada Life Program, is to prescribe supplementary home exercises such as walking and cycling, with the intent that these be pursued in family groups.

There have been some attempts to relate program adherence to more fundamental personality traits. While some have found a poor attendance of Type A subjects, more often such individuals have the tenacity to stay with a program once they are convinced of its value. Extraverts tend to be attracted to group programs with high levels of social interaction, whereas introverts prefer a less structured, endurance-type program or the opportunity to exercise on their own.

Modeling of Exercise Behavior

The factors shaping exercise behavior are quite complex; practical application of modern behavioral theory to the problem of compliance with corporate exercise programs is still in its infancy (Godin et al., 1985). There is probably a whole series of predisposing factors such as knowledge, attitudes, beliefs, values, and perceptions which create an intention of involvement in physical activity. A series of enabling factors then encourages the translation of intentions into action; key variables are the individual's repertory of activity skills as well as personal and corporate resources. Finally, a series of reinforcing factors ensures persistence of the behavior.

Predisposing factors potentially offer the most effective plan of attack for those interested in modifying behavior, because the impact is felt by 100% of the workers, rather than the 20% or so who have been recruited to a program. On the other hand, the manipulation of attitudes and beliefs has an Orwellian aura, which is avoided if one concentrates upon sustaining a behavior the employee has already chosen. Predisposing factors are currently analysed using the models of Fishbein and Ajzen (1974) and Triandis (1977). These models envisage intention as being formed by an appropriately weighted combination of attitudes and social norms. Within the setting of a major university, attitudes had a much stronger impact upon the intention to exercise than did social norms (Godin et al., 1985). Further research is needed in other occupational units differing in both size and average level of intelligence. The university, with its strong emphasis upon independent thought, may not provide data which can be readily extrapolated to other industrial settings. The university experiments have further shown, contrary to the original Fishbein model, that prior experience of exercise has an effect upon intention, which is independent of both attitudes and the social norm. This reinforces the conclusion noted above that one of the most effective ways of changing attitudes and securing participation is to get the employee to sample the program. Other work within the university community has established, by an appropriate form of path analysis, that there are causal relationships running from attitudes through behavioral intentions to actual behavior (Godin et al., 1985).

Enabling factors, such as flexible hours of work to counter the argument of a "lack of time," operate mainly by converting an intention into overt behavior. Perhaps the greatest practical interest to date has centered on reinforcement of the exercise behavior, once initiated. It has increasingly been recognized that the factors sustaining adherence differ from those involved in recruitment. Suitable external rewards must be provided until the class member begins to perceive the intrinsic rewards of the program. There has been much recent discussion of exercise addiction, possibly linked to the secretion of beta-endorphins during vigorous physical activity. If the phenomenon of exercise addiction does indeed exist, it seems restricted to the enthusiast who spends several hours per day in his or her chosen activity. A chemical dependence upon exercise is thus unlikely to influence general adherence to a corporate fitness program; nevertheless, it could be a factor in the 6 to 8% of Canada Life enthusiasts who have become heavily involved in long-distance running.

Conclusions

Surveys of entire corporations, current exercise class participants, and dropouts are all helpful in establishing the type of activity employees want, the rewards they are seeking from physical activity, and the influence of personal characteristics upon such needs. Recruitment depends first upon an appropriate shaping of behavioral intentions. Attitudes and beliefs about the value of exercise must be developed by a long process of education; a social norm should be established whereby regular physical activity becomes an accepted part of corporate life. Better exercise programs and an effective manipulation of external rewards will help to support the employee who samples a corporate fitness program up through the point where adherence is sustained by the internal rewards of exercise participation. Enabling factors such as flexible work hours, child care, and family programs help to convert intentions to behavior, and subsequently boost class recruitment. In order to reach that 50% of the labor force who participate in little or no exercise, a more fundamental attack on corporate attitudes and beliefs is required. The average office or factory is important to the health professional as an established, coherent, social unit within which regular physical activity and other lifestyle changes important to community health may be initiated.

Acknowledgments

The work discussed in this chapter has been conducted in collaboration with a number of colleagues, including S. Keir, B. Ferris, and T. Stephens (Fitness Canada); C. West and V. Marsden (Canada Life Assurance Co. Ltd.); R. Finucane and L. Schimmelfing (General Foods Corporation); and P. Morgan, G. Godin, M. Cox, and V. Jazmaji (University of Toronto). The contribution of these individuals is acknowledged with appreciation, as is the financial support of the Fitness & Amateur Sport Branch, Health & Welfare Canada.

References

Beck, R.N. (1982). IBM's Plan for Life: Toward a comprehensive health care strategy. *Health Education Quarterly,* **9** (Suppl.), 55–60.

Becker, M.H., & Maiman, L. (1975). Socio-behavioural determinants of compliance with health and medical care recommendations. *Medical Care,* **13**, 10–24.

Brennan, A.J.J. (1982). Work site health promotion [Special Supplement]. *Health Education Quarterly,* **9**, 1–91.

Bruce, E.H., Frederick, R., Bruce, R.A., & Fisher, L.D. (1976). Comparison of active participants and dropouts in CAPRI cardiopulmonary rehabilitation programmes. *American Journal Cardiology,* **37**, 53–60.

Canada Fitness Survey (1983). *Fitness and lifestyle in Canada.* Ottawa: Fitness & Amateur Sport.

Cox, M., Shephard, R.J., & Corey, P. (1981). Influence of an employee fitness programme upon fitness, productivity and absenteeism. *Ergonomics,* **24,** 795–806.

Danielson, R.R., & Danielson, K.F. (1979). On-going motivation in employee fitness programming. In R.S. Wanzel (Ed.), *Employee fitness— The how to . . .* Toronto, Ontario: Ministry of Culture & Recreation.

Dishman, R.K. (1982). Compliance/adherence in health-related exercise. *Health Psychology,* 1(3), 237–267.

Dishman, R.K., & Ickes, W.J. (1981). Self motivation and adherence to therapeutic exercise. *Journal of Behavioral Medicine,* **4,** 421–438.

Durbeck, D.C., Heinzelmann, F., Schachter, J., Haskell, W.L., Payne, G.H., Moxley, R.T., Nemiroff, M., Limoncelli, D., Arnoldi, L., & Fox, S. (1972). The National Aeronautics and Space Administration—U.S. Public Health Service Health Evaluation and Enhancement Program. *American Journal of Cardiology,* **30,** 784–790.

Fielding, J.E. (1982). Effectiveness of employee health improvement programs. *Journal of Occupational Medicine,* **24,** 907–916.

Fishbein, M., & Ajzen, I. (1974). Attitudes towards objects as predictors of single and multiple behavioural criteria. *Psychological Review,* **81,** 59–74.

Godin, G., & Shephard, R.J. (1983). The impact of physical fitness evaluation on behavioural intentions towards regular exercise. *Canadian Journal of Applied Sport Sciences,* **8,** 240–245.

Godin, G., Valois, P., Shephard, R.J., & Desharnais, R. (1985). The direction of causality between attitude, past behavior, intention and future behaviour. *Canadian Journal of Applied Sport Sciences* (abstract), **9,** 152.

Kenyon, G.S. (1968). Six scales for assessing attitudes towards physical activity. *Research Quarterly,* **39,** 556–574.

Marsden, V., & Youlden, P. (1979, May). Report to Health and Welfare Committee on Employee Fitness Programme. Ottawa: Health and Welfare Canada.

Massie, J.F., & Shephard, R.J. (1971). Physiological and psychological effects of training. *Medicine and Science in Sports,* **3,** 110–117.

Morey, R.C. (1983). Cost-effectiveness of an employer-sponsored recreational program: A case study. *Omega,* **14,** 67–74.

Morgan, P.P., Shephard, R.J., Finucane, R., Schimmelfing, L., & Jazmaji, V. (1984). Health beliefs and exercise habits in an employee fitness programme. *Canadian Journal of Applied Sport Sciences,* **9,** 87–93.

Oldridge, N.B. (1984). Compliance and dropout in cardiac exercise rehabilitation. *Journal of Cardiac Rehabilitation, 4,* 166–177.

Pomereau, O.F. (1983). Proceedings of the University of Connecticut Symposium on Employee Health and Fitness. *Preventive Medicine, 12,* 598–681.

Rotter, J.B. (1975). Some problems and misconceptions related to the construct validity of internal versus external control of reinforcement. *Journal of Consulting and Clinical Psychology, 43,* 56–67.

Shephard, R.J. (1979). Current assessment of the Canadian Home Fitness Test. *South African Journal of Sports Science, 2,* 19–35.

Shephard, R.J. (1985). Factors influencing the exercise behaviour of patients. *Sports Medicine.*

Shephard, R.J. (1986). *Fitness and health in industry.* Basel: Karger.

Shephard, R.J., Corey, P., & Kavanagh, T. (1981). Exercise compliance and the prevention of a recurrence of myocardial infarction. *Medicine and Science in Sports and Exercise, 13,* 1–5.

Shephard, R.J., Morgan, P.P., Finucane, R., & Schimmelfing, L. (1980). Factors influencing recruitment to an occupational fitness program. *Journal of Occupational Medicine, 22,* 389–398.

Sidney, K.H., & Shephard, R.J. (1977). Attitudes towards health and physical activity in the elderly. Effects of a physical training programme. *Medicine and Science in Sports, 8,* 246–252.

Song, T.K., Shephard, R.J., & Cox, M. (1982). Absenteeism, employee turnover and sustained exercise participation. *Journal of Sports Medicine and Fitness, 22,* 392–399.

Triandis, H.C. (1977). *Interpersonal behaviour.* Monterey, CA: Brooks-Cole.

Wankel, L.M. (1984). Decision-making and social support strategies for increasing exercise involvement. *Journal of Cardiac Rehabilitation, 4,* 124–135.

Yarvote, P.M, McDonagh, T.J., Goldman, M.E., et al. (1974). Organization and evaluation of a physical fitness program in industry. *Journal of Occupational Medicine, 16,* 589–598.

CHAPTER *12*

Who Are Corporate Exercisers and What Motivates Them?

William B. Baun and
Edward J. Bernacki

Exercise adherence is the most critical issue facing directors of corporate health and fitness programs. In contrast to commercial health clubs where the constant selling of memberships is of prime interest, corporate programs must be concerned with initiation and maintenance of participation. Unlike YMCAs, cardiac rehabilitation centers, and health clubs, worksite health and fitness programs can only draw their membership from a relatively small, fixed population. Therefore, to be successful these programs must aim both at retaining current exercising employees as regular exercisers and for growth, the addition of new employees and hard core non-exercisers into the exercising group.

This chapter discusses the primary goals of a corporation in allocating company resources to promote exercise adherence. It addresses practical programming issues concerned with sustaining participation by describing the Tenneco Health and Fitness experience. This chronological description provides details concerning program start-up and the transition into program maintenance. Activity patterns are discussed in relation to promotional and motivational techniques that have been used and evaluated. Current corporate exercise adherence strategies are also examined.

Program Justification

The primary aim of a corporation is to generate profits and increase assets for shareholders. Secondary goals are to provide employment and increase the material wealth of the society in which a corporation operates. High priority is placed on achieving the first objective and although the second is deemed beneficial, it is of understandably lower priority.

It is obvious that fitness programs do not directly increase corporate profits or assets. How then are these programs justified by corporate managers? Driver and Ratliff (1982) postulate that managers perceive that exercise decreases health care claims and absenteeism by reducing illness. This increases profitability. They also feel that physical fitness programs, by increasing organizational cohesiveness or satisfaction with the corporation, leads to desirable work behaviors such as increased productivity, decreased turnover, decreased absenteeism, and decreased frequency of sick days. This in turn increases profitability and the perception that the corporation is a socially responsible one committed to the well-being of its employees.

Is there additional data to support these perceptions? It has been well demonstrated that increased exercise activity is strongly associated with a reduction in cardiovascular disease risk factors from heart disease (Cooper, Pollock, & Martin, 1978; Paffenbarger, Wing, & Hyde, 1983; Fox, Naughton, & Haskell, 1971) as well as morbidity and mortality (Peters, Cody, & Bischoff, 1983; Paffenbarger, Hyde, Wing, & Hsieh, 1986). Because employers in the United States, through disability and group health insurance policies, pay almost all of their employees' absenteeism and health care costs, any reduction in these expenses would reduce operating costs and increase profitability. There is ample evidence that in the short term, participants in an exercise program are absent less often and expend less on health care when compared to non-exercising co-employees (Baun, Bernacki, & Tsai, 1986; Bowne, Russell, Morgan, Optenburg, & Clarke, 1984). In almost all instances where initially positive studies have been extended for longer periods of time, the beneficial effects of exercise on absenteeism and health care costs are reduced primarily because of high dropout rates (secondary to employee turnover) and cessation of exercise among participants. Does this suggest that exercise programs may not be shown to be financially beneficial to an organization even though there is a reduction in illness and its attendant costs? In our experience, the population of a company is constantly changing primarily among employees most likely to exercise (those under age forty) and sustained exercise adherence is unusual. Because of this, the beneficial effects of exercise in reducing cardiovascular morbidity is likely to be realized only in a small group of long-term employees who continually exercise. Our studies (Baun et al., 1986) and others dealing with this subject (Cox, Shephard, & Corey, 1981; Hoffman & Hobson, 1984), indicate clear differences between exercisers and non-exercisers over such short periods of time that the medical benefits of exercise in reducing disease incidence and disability could not have been realized.

There are three chief factors operating to produce desirable effects among exercisers: (a) a satisfaction with the organization resulting in better attendance and performance, (b) a personality factor that proceeds and accounts for both exercise and good work, and (c) exercise induced reductions in cardiovascular disease incidence. The latter factor is difficult to document because of the long duration from exercise onset to an effect and turnover rates. A small cohort of dedicated exercisers, however, does exist in any fitness program and eventually their number will be great enough to study.

We feel it is not necessary to justify programs by demonstrating long-term exercise induced effects in an exercising cohort. Rather, they may be supported by the fact that exercisers possess attributes that are beneficial to a corporation. This point is made in our study of job performance and exercise (Bernacki & Baun, 1984) in which we found that performance did not materially change over time. Individuals who were high- or low-performers before they began an exercise program continued in the same category upon becoming exercisers. A significantly greater proportion of high-performers were seen among exercisers than among non-exercisers. In essence, exercise was not causally related to performance, but associated with it. This does not imply that exercise has no effect on subjective perceptions of increased performance, there is plenty of evidence for this (Pauly, Palmer, Wright, & Pfeiffer, 1982), but overall performance does not seem to change with exercise status.

While relating performance to exercise adherence, we found that performance levels among low-level exercisers were similar to those of non-exercisers. The implication of these findings suggests that a positive attribute of exercisers (high performance) is weakly or not associated at all with the occasional or low-level exercisers. It is therefore dangerous to extrapolate the beneficial effects and savings seen among high-exercise adherences to the whole employed population. Also it suggests that there will be few short-term financial gains if sedentary individuals become occasional exercisers.

What does all this mean? It appears that the managers' perceptions of the benefits of an exercise program are on the whole correct: fitness programs are associated with reductions in medical costs and absenteeism. We feel, however, that (in the short run) this effect is primarily due to the attributes of particular exercisers and not secondary to the beneficial effects of exercise. Because individuals choose to work for a corporation, we feel that the provision of an exercise facility by a company will increase the probability that highly motivated persons will select the company increasing their representation in the work force. The primary goal of a corporation interested in fitness programs would be to hire and retain high-exercise adherers; the secondary goal would be to induce non-exercisers to become exercisers in order to reduce the incidence of illness over time and to realize the optimal benefits of the program. Exercise programs cannot exist in situations where the corporation's survival is at issue. These programs will always be confined to well-managed, stable, and profitable corporations.

Program Initiation

The initiation or start-up phase of a worksite health and fitness program is the most critical period. It is during this time that philosophy and core program offerings are determined. This is the only chance the organizers have to sell a program to a large audience. If done correctly, growth from a large starting base can almost be guaranteed. Many models have been advanced offering systematic approaches to development and implementation of worksite programs (Haskell & Blair, 1980; Wilson, 1982; Dickerson & Mandelblit, 1983; Felix, Stunkard, Cohen, & Cooley, 1985). In the start-up planning and developmental stages several key components can be identified as common to all models. These are: establishing goals and objectives, determining needs, defining membership, creating employee ownership, coordinating with other departments, staffing, and programming.

Inevitably, the decision to offer a worksite health and fitness program requires senior-management support. Senior management provides not only the financial resources for the program but the perception that exercise is acceptable in the corporate culture. Tenneco's program was developed with the full support of the Chief Executive Officer. His own positive fitness experience made him realize that an important way to preserve "Tenneco's most important asset, its innovative, skilled employees" was to provide such a program. The corporation's goal for an exercise program became the education and motivation of employees to improve the overall quality of their lives.

Program Goals and Objectives

The first step in establishing a health and fitness program is to identify the program goals that reflect the corporation's humanistic desires for its work force. To be of value, however, these goals must have appropriate timetables and be supported by specific measurable objectives. These will serve as achievement benchmarks which when attained, will move the program forward throughout the start-up year.

Creation of Employee Ownership

The second step is to create the notion that this is the employees own program; they own it and have a say in its operation. Parkinson (1984) has shown that employee involvement and participation in the early development of the program promotes exercise adherence. At Tenneco this took the form of a health and fitness committee. The committee provided the newly organized health and fitness department with an audience to which it could propose ideas and from which it could expect realistic feedback. Committee members consisted of a cross section of the employee work force. Because of this, accurate and representative desires were incorporated into the program at its developmental stages.

Assessment of Needs and Interests

The third start-up step is to determine employee needs and interests by using interest and health practices surveys. Although this may seem obvious, it is important to remember that the success of a worksite exercise program depends on addressing the exercise interests of employees. This is a basic principle in program planning which, when violated results in a tremendous amount wasted effort to promote unpopular programs. The goal is first to attract, and then to begin working towards changing behaviors. Understanding population makeup has always been important in any marketing strategy (Wiener, 1983). This is true not only in planning for current initiatives but also for future ones. Organizers of employee fitness programs must analyze the same type of information. Table 1 provides some examples of potential factors that will establish a profile of the employee population.

There are many different examples of needs and interests surveys in the literature (Shephard, Morgan, Finucane, & Schimmelfing, 1980a; Wilson, 1982; Godin et al., 1985) that can be administered to employee populations. They generally provide detailed knowledge of employee interests, needs, preference for physical activities, and health promotional programming.

Tenneco's health and fitness committee distributed the initial interest survey, accompanied by a transmittal letter, to all employees. The approximately 5,100 employees within the Houston area received both letter and survey in personally addressed envelopes. The response of 61.5%

Table 1 Significant Demographic Variables

Age/sex/job	Business	Work schedule	Location	Commuting methods
Mean age by sex	Divisions represented	Work schedule	Location of office buildings serviced	Van pool
Number within each age and sex group	Number within each division	Break times	Distance between work location and fitness facility	Carpool
Mean age within each job category	Reporting structure	Lunch time	Job categories at locations	Bus
Mean age within each job category by sex				Personal car
Number within each job category				

(3,132 employees) was much greater than expected. Downtown Houston employees (3,415 total) indicated even greater interest with over 68% (2,316) responding to the questionnaire. Eighty percent (2,507) of the 3,132 employees who returned the survey expressed interest in becoming members of the health and fitness program. Among respondents from the downtown area (2,316) over 84% (1,951) expressed interest in membership, with more females, 54% (1,043), responding positively than males, 46% (908).

This profile of the Tenneco employee population also provided information concerning employee preference for various fitness and health promotional activities. Tables 2 and 3 reflect these preferences by quantifying interest in the various program options offered in the survey. The results of the survey provide a good indication of the number, age, and sex of employees who expressed interest in the health and fitness program. Correlated with this information were the different types of activities in which individual age and gender groups were interested. This information facilitated the planning and development of our initial program offerings. We also found that the survey served not only as an information gathering tool but also as a promotional device, providing the employees with their first glance at program offerings.

Health practices surveys generally provide information concerning lifestyle factors and chronic illnesses within the given population.

Table 2 Percent Distribution of Employee Interest in Health and Wellness Programs

Program activity	Number of employees	Percent
Weight control	1470	59
Stress relief	1390	55
First aid	1267	51
Nutrition	1261	30
CPR	1164	48
Hypertension control	992	40
Back care	858	34
Cancer detection	767	31
Smoking cessation	481	19
Diabetes	457	18
Drug abuse	251	10
Alcohol abuse	240	9

Note. Based on population of 2,507.

Table 3 Percent Distribution of Employee Preference for Physical Activity

Program activity	Number of employees	Percent
Weight lifting	1727	69
Jogging	1278	51
Exercise class	1207	48
Racquetball	1087	43
Aerobic dance	971	39
Bicycle	885	35
Walking	715	29

Note. Based on population of 2,507.

Dickerson and Mandelblit (1983) have suggested that because of the common health risk factors shared by a substantial portion of the population, health practices surveys can be eliminated. This information is invaluable during the planning and developmental phase, and it also serves to stimulate interest and provide true program ownership for employees who have identifiable risk factors.

Our own health practices survey indicated some specific health problems in several selected groups. Table 4 shows that we found profes-

Table 4 Tension Levels

Variable	More tension than desired (%)
Sex	
Male	71.0
Female	29.0
Job category	
Clerical/secretary	18.9
Management/supervisory	24.6
Professionals/administrative	53.6
Other	2.9
Back pain	
Frequently	13.2
Occasionally	63.2
Never	23.6

sionals who occasionally have back pain, perceive more job tension than desired. Males also reported more tension than females. This prompted the development of a stress-management program which was initially targeted for male professionals. The information also supported the need for a healthy back program as one of the initial health promotional offerings.

Coordinated Planning

The next step in the start-up process is to collaborate with other departments to achieve workable fitness programming; this links the previous three steps together into a plan of action. The process involves many departments within the corporation. At Tenneco these departments consisted of health and fitness, health services, safety and health, epidemiology and health research, personnel, realty, purchasing, financial controls, and computer services.

Facility and Staffing Considerations

Finally, decisions concerning facility and staffing needs must be addressed. The extent to which the company commits its resources to the project ultimately decides whether the program will use existing community resources (local fitness centers, YMCAs, university facilities, and recreation centers) or construct an on-site facility. Following this decision, the number of staff necessary to run an effective program is determined, based on the number of employees expected to participate in the program.

The health and fitness center, the foundation of the Tenneco program, occupies 25,000 square feet of the general employee center. The employee center sits atop a seven-story parking garage and is comprised of a cafeteria, a conference center, an executive dining room, and the health and fitness center. The fitness facility is equipped with weight-lifting equipment, stationary bicycles, rowing machines, and stretching areas. There are four racquetball/wallyball courts and a multipurpose room used for activity classes. The most frequently used area is the one-fifth mile indoor running track that circles the entire center. Program participants record their fitness activities using computer terminals located in the fitness center. Exercise activity is recorded as mode, duration, and intensity, and converted by a computer program into caloric expenditure. Males in the program expended an average of 421 calories per exercise session and females, an average of 292 calories per session. The system provides not only immediate caloric feedback, but also a Monthly Activity Report to each participant. Figure 1 is an example of the Monthly Activity Report each participant receives. The system serves as an exercise diary/training record as well as helping participants set and achieve goals.

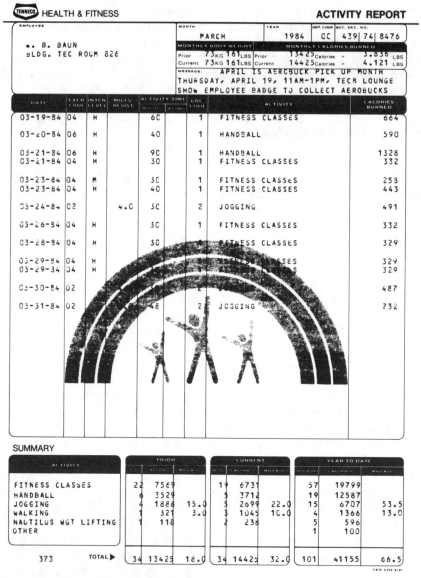

DATE	EXER CODE	INTEN LEVEL	MILES RESIST.	ACTIVITY TIME MIN/SET	SEC/REPS	LOC CODE	ACTIVITY	CALORIES BURNED
03-19-84	04	H		60		1	FITNESS CLASSES	664
03-20-84	06	H		40		1	HANDBALL	590
03-21-84	06	H		90		1	HANDBALL	1328
03-21-84	04	H		30		1	FITNESS CLASSES	332
03-23-84	04	M		30		1	FITNESS CLASSES	253
03-23-84	04	H		40		1	FITNESS CLASSES	443
03-24-84	02		4.0	30		2	JOGGING	491
03-26-84	04	H		30		1	FITNESS CLASSES	332
03-28-84	04	H		30			FITNESS CLASSES	329
03-29-84	04	H					SES	329
03-29-84	04	H						329
03-30-84	02							487
03-31-84	02			48		2	JOGGING	732

TENNECO HEALTH & FITNESS — ACTIVITY REPORT

EMPLOYEE: M. B. BAUN / BLDG. TEC ROOM 826

MONTH: MARCH   YEAR: 1984   DEP. CODE: CC   SOC. SEC. NO.: 439 74 8476

MONTHLY BODY WEIGHT: Prior 73KG 161LBS   Current 73KG 161LBS

MONTHLY CALORIES BURNED: Prior 13425 Calories = 3.836 LBS   Current 14425 Calories = 4.121 LBS

MESSAGE: APRIL IS AEROBUCK PICK UP MONTH THURSDAY, APRIL 19, 11AM-1PM, TEC8 LOUNGE SHOW EMPLOYEE BADGE TO COLLECT AEROBUCKS

SUMMARY

ACTIVITY	PRIOR			CURRENT			YEAR TO DATE		
	SESSIONS	CALORIES	MILEAGE	SESSIONS	CALORIES	MILEAGE	SESSIONS	CALORIES	MILEAGE
FITNESS CLASSES	22	7569		19	6731		57	19799	
HANDBALL	6	3529		5	3712		19	12587	
JOGGING	4	1888	15.0	5	2699	22.0	15	6707	53.5
WALKING	1	321	3.0	3	1045	10.0	4	1366	13.0
NAUTILUS WGT LIFTING	1	118		2	238		5	596	
OTHER							1	100	
TOTAL	34	13425	18.0	34	14425	32.0	101	41155	66.5

373

TEN 5354 8/81

Figure 1 Participants Monthly Activity Report is sent to all employees who log exercises.

The Tenneco health and fitness staff consists of seven teaching professionals and three administrative positions. The manager of the department reports to a physician who serves as Vice President of Health, Environmental Medicine and Safety. The program is divided into separate fitness and wellness components that share many programming activities. The fitness program is coordinated by a health and fitness coordinator who is assisted by two health and fitness specialists. An exercise physiologist coordinates all the physiological testing and provides the rehabilitation expertise necessary to coordinate the sports medicine program with the health services department. Wellness programming is coordinated by the assistant manager/wellness administrator of the health and fitness department; however, the entire Health, Environmental Medicine and Safety staff share in the delivery and organization of these activities.

Our corporate fitness staff is continually challenged to initiate new programs or repackage old programs in order to stimulate usage and help participants develop new skills. This continuing challenge causes high levels of burnout among fitness professionals. The most significant management concern is providing them with developmental opportunities that will stimulate them to maintain high quality programming. This challenge may be met by a commitment to evaluate programming and use these evaluations to plan and implement other program options. This in turn provides feedback to the professionals regarding their own performance.

The current ratio of staff to participant is 1 to 600. We have found this to be sufficient for initiating and sustaining fitness knowledge. During program start-up, the ratio of staff to participant was 1 to 300 (additional part-time testing personnel were hired to perform fitness orientations).

Membership Criteria

After the designation of staff and exercise facility, membership specifications must be determined. Should a corporate fitness program include only executives or the whole population? The history of the health and fitness movement in the United States provides many good examples of both. It is our opinion that executive fitness programs have little impact on the corporation's health care costs and incidence of illness because too few people can be influenced by the program. Naisbitt (1983) observes that the American business professional of today is increasingly becoming an advocate of preventive medicine for the work force through physical fitness. Consequently, it is important to make a strong effort to include all employees in any fitness offering.

At Tenneco it was not a question of who would be given the opportunity to participate in the program, rather of how the initial membership process could be handled fairly (because there was no question that all employees would be eligible). The fairness issue was complicated by the fact that an initially large number of employees (2,507) desired membership in a facility designed to serve approximately 700 (400 participants per day). One solution to this problem would have been to limit membership to a set number of employees, using exercise adherence as the criterion for continued membership. Although this solution offered an efficient way of solving the problem, its limited membership had the potential of biasing the program to serve employees who were disciplined enough to meet adherence standards. The people who would need the program most, in terms of support systems, instruction, and time to make difficult behavioral changes, would be the first to be eliminated according to this solution. We chose the option of limiting time of entry into the program rather than total number of participants. All employees received a registration card by mail and had to return the card within a period of several weeks. These cards were randomly drawn to determine the order of entry. The drawing of the registration cards established a 6-month screening backlog for medical and fitness testing. There were 1,200 individuals processed at the time of opening, the maximum number we could handle at the time. Over the next 18 months, approximately 400 individuals were processed each month and added to the membership. With this system we achieved a steady state of 425 exercisers a day. This assured a timely entry and manageable programming throughout program start-up.

Screening Process

Corporate fitness programs derive a great deal of their legitimacy from the fact that employees are exercising for their health; medical and fitness assessments are crucial to furthering that perception and achieving that goal. During testing employees begin to understand the philosophy and goals of the program as well as their personal health objectives. Shephard (1985) suggests that recruitment and adherence into corporate programs could be improved if we could better understand and manipulate the factors shaping beliefs and behavior regarding exercise. During these initial screening sessions, past and current exercise behaviors are recorded, and an employee's exercise beliefs become apparent. At Tenneco both the initial and continued medical screening process is conducted by nurse practitioners supervised by a physician who not only collect and analyze findings, but also initiate a health prescription: the first educational component. This is followed by a fitness assessment and program planning session with a health and fitness staff professional. It has been our experience that by using Tenneco personnel as opposed to contractors to do the processing, an immediate bond is established between the staff person and employee; this enables the new participant who is out of shape, sensitive, and lacking in fitness knowledge, to feel safe and comfortable.

The fitness assessment and program planning sessions have objectives other than collecting initial physiological data and providing an exercise prescription. Our data have shown that 51% of the employees who joined our program were currently involved in an exercise program, whereas 49% were individuals who either had not been active for many years or had never been involved in a supervised health and fitness program. The sedentary group needed not only a clear explanation of what their exercise options were, but also the chance to experience their lack of conditioning during physiological testing. This feeling of physical inadequacy provides an opportunity to gain the attention and trust of these individuals by offering a variety of ways in which fitness can be achieved. We feel that through this process the employees obtain a new perspective of their own bodily health and establish a bond with the staff member that facilitates continued participation in the program.

Another factor in deciding the criteria for membership should be safety. The assurance that little harm will come to a potential exerciser through exercise can be accomplished by admitting only healthy individuals to membership and requiring members to maintain a certain level of fitness by participating on a regular basis (e.g., twice weekly or 8 times per month). These requirements achieve two purposes: safety plus high attendance rates. Unfortunately, because of the size of Tenneco's program (over 3,000 initial members) and the travel schedules of its work force, this strategy was not acceptable (i.e., regular weekly or monthly attendance was not possible). We adopted instead the concept of supervised and unsupervised exercise. If after the medical screening process the individual exhibited no identifiable medical problems he or she was allowed full center privileges and could exercise without supervision. Individuals who exhibited health problems were placed in a supervised exercise group and monitored until it was determined they could exercise safely on their own. Upon entry, all males 40 and over, postmenopausal females, and high-risk individuals identified at physical examination, took a maximum exercise stress test. If the test results showed no abnormalities, then the employee, because of presumed low risk of developing a significant cardiovascular problem during exercise, received full center privileges and exercised without supervision. Throughout the four years that the program has been in operation not one acute cardiovascular event has occurred to persons found acceptable for exercise in this manner. Individuals found to have problems were medically evaluated and treated and possibly admitted to a supervised-exercise group.

Of the 5,000 employees screened since the program's initiation, less than one percent needed to enter the supervised program. Almost all of these individuals graduated to unsupervised exercise programs after 6 months of participation. The supervised program is directed by a fitness staff person and consists of both group and individual exercise activities. Individuals with significant cardiac problems are placed into one of several cardiac rehabilitation programs in the area. After discharge from these programs they enter the supervised program for a short period of time and then are admitted into the unsupervised program. Individuals 55 years and above and high-risk individuals are evaluated in depth every two years; the remainder of the population are evaluated on a case-by-case basis.

Exercise Prescriptions and Fitness Orientation

Both exercise and behavioral prescriptions are given at orientation. The behavioral prescription provides a member with factors that have been linked to successful exercise. The first is support group adequacy. Do the employees interact with individuals who will support their exercise habit? If the employee is married, is that person's spouse supportive? If the employee is single, are there individuals within the company or at home who can help support the types of changes he or she is planning to make?

The second factor is fitness skill level. Employees who have been successful at fitness will more likely be successful again. Therefore the type of prior involvement in health and fitness is important. The third factor is injury. Does the employee have a current or past injury that will hinder exercise efforts? Many times employees will choose fitness routines that aggravate past injuries and lead to unsuccessful outcomes. If encountered early enough, these problems can be circumvented by giving the employee alternate routines that will provide positive fitness outcomes with low risk. The fourth factor is convenience. Are programs and exercise facilities convenient in terms of time and location? If not then a realistic opportunity for the employee to take advantage of a program is limited. The fifth concerns an employee's understanding of the satisfaction derived from regular exercise. Individuals who relate exercise to losing weight, gaining strength, and relieving tension are more likely to be successful. It is important for individuals to renew these feelings. The final factor is the employee's motivation for enrolling in the program. Dishman (1980) has shown that self-motivation is the most important factor in predicting who will be successful in an exercise program. At Tenneco we strongly feel that employees should understand their motivations for exercising and translate these into realistic short-term goals and eventually a long-term commitment. Including this six-pronged behavioral prescription with a general exercise prescription increases the probability that the decision to exercise will be followed by adherence to the exercise program.

The start-up of a corporate health and fitness program is critical to its long-term success. The program's philosophy which is instilled during the first year sets the tone for the future. How well employees are oriented and advised will determine their future participation. These two processes must be done correctly.

Program Maintenance

At the end of the first year, program planning shifts toward maintenance. Rather than nurturing the status quo, we see maintenance as planning for growth which includes the enrollment of hard core non-exercisers and recently hired employees while maintaining the participation of current exercisers. Maintenance strategies support the initial goals of the program and expand them by developing specific objectives for various segments of the exercising population. The focus becomes selective programming and specific motivational support for special groups. This ultimately determines the continued success of the program.

Shephard and Cox (1980) have suggested that no more than 15% to 20% of an employee population are recruited for most corporate fitness programs. A review of our initial statistics shows that in February of 1982 the program began with 1,221 members representing 35% of the total employee population (3,415). One year later we had a membership of 3,005 employees, representing 85% of the employee population.

Employees lose their membership in the Tenneco program if they have not participated for a full year. Each month members who did not use the program are divided into three-month categories. Individuals who have not participated in the program for three months receive a post card. The card has a comic illustration and a simple note written by a staff member suggesting that the employees have been missed and that there are some new programs they might enjoy. Persons who do not attend for a six-month interval receive a letter describing new program changes and a warning that they will lose their locker if they do not wish to participate. At nine months a letter informs them that they have lost their locker and that if they fail to participate in the next three months they will lose their membership. At twelve months membership is taken away and they are informed of the steps necessary to become a member again. With this system membership at Tenneco has stabilized at approximately 75% of employed persons for the last three years.

Tenneco's monthly membership participation rates vary from 55% to 60% at the beginning of the year to a low of 45% during December. Conversely, 40% to 55% of the membership can be viewed as non-participants. This system allows for a relaxation of participation standards as well as defining a true dropout as an employee who has not participated for twelve months. The strength of the system is that it views nonparticipation as a temporary state. We feel the system is organized so that it maintains contact with the non-participant and offers suggestions and motivation for renewed participation.

Participation Assessment

Each month at Tenneco a monthly report reviews participation statistics. These statistics are derived from computer-generated reports of program activity. These reports provide participation rates for various age and sex groupings, and summarizes attendance for each activity. These data permit the evaluation of specific programming efforts and their effects on attendance.

One of the most useful measures of success or failure is the penetration rate: the number of employees who exercise in a given month (i.e., active members) divided by the total employee population. It is important that the denominator be the total population because the ultimate success of the program is determined by its ability to attract a large percentage of the entire work force rather than just members (which form a self-selected group). Figure 2 indicates that since the program's initiation Tenneco's program penetration rates have been consistent at 40%(+). Note that the lowest penetration rates occurred in December, a month when many individuals are on vacation.

Figure 3 is a plot of the penetration patterns of Tenneco employees for the past two years. Quite evident is the cyclical increase at the first of the year with a significant drop in penetration over the holiday season. Young male exercisers (males less than 40 years of age) have the highest penetration rates. These rates change very little over time. Young females also have consistently high penetration rates, but during the holiday season (November, December) their rates drop approximately 10%. The plot for older females (females above 39 years of age) also shows a significant decrease during the holiday season. The most difficult group to motivate has always been male employees above the age of 39 whose penetration rates range between 27% and 37%.

Adherence rate, or the number of employees exercising at certain weekly frequencies during a month, is another important index. We divide adherence into four different rates: (a) members who did not exercise, (b) participants who exercised on an average of less than 1 day a week, (c) participants who exercised between 1 and 2 days a week, and (d) participants who exercised an average of over 2 days a week. We collect these data using the sessions recorded on the exercise logging system mentioned previously. To simplify analysis a session of exercise is defined as 1 day of exercise. For example, a member plays handball in

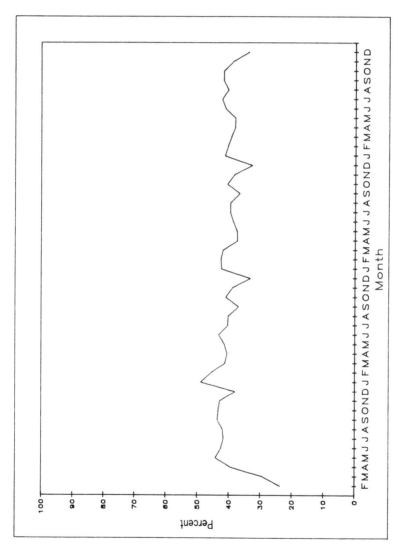

Figure 2 Penetration rate from February 1982 (initiation) to December 1985.

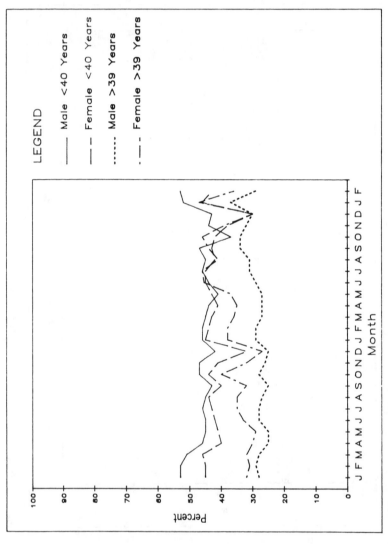

Figure 3 Penetration rate by age and sex for 1984 and 1985.

the morning and jogs at home the same evening; though the computer stores all the recorded exercise activity, the summary report enumerates it as only 1 exercise session. Of those employees who work out at Tenneco's exercise facility, 93% log their exercise activities. Although the system is set up to allow individuals to also log outside exercise, only 20% do so. Because of this, any analysis we conduct using these data underestimates the true exercise habits of the Tenneco population. This discrepancy is taken into account in our planning process.

Other research (Shephard & Cox, 1980; Shephard, 1985) indicates that there is a progressive increase in the number of employees who drop out of a corporate program during the first 3 months of its operation. Because these studies do not provide an in-depth look at adherence rate changes over time, we decided to analyze the changes during Tenneco's initial 8 months of operation in relation to age and sex. At 3 months, we found that more females dropped out of the program than males, relative to their proportion in the population. The number of individuals who became members but never participated in the program during the first 3 months was approximately 10%. Individuals who had initially been categorized as high adherers (greater than 2 days of exercise a week) decreased by 9%. The low-adherer group (less than 1 day of exercise a week) decreased by 19.8%, and the number of employees in the middle-adherence group (1–2 exercise days a week) increased by 6.2%.

Analysis after 8 months of participation (October, 1982) showed that an average of 44.5% of the membership did not exercise in the month of October. However, employees who had not used the program for 3 or more months still represented only 10% of the entire membership. This indicates there is a great amount of variability in exercise adherence. During October, 1982, 39% of the exercising employees reported participating less than 1 time a week, 33% reported 1–2 times a week, and 28% reported exercising on the average more than 2 times a week. A close look at the adherence changes that occurred since March, 1982, indicate that fewer employees reported low adherence levels (March, 75.2%; October, 39%), more employees reported middle adherence (March, 12.5%; October, 33%) and high adherence (March, 12.1%; October, 28%) levels. At this early stage in our program's history there appear to be no effects of age or sex on exercise adherence. Table 5 depicts the fluctuation in adherence rates over two years of programming. The effect of age is apparent: as age increases adherence rates increase. Among males the positive correlation between age and exercise adherence holds true almost every month.

The last element we use to measure program dynamics is daily attendance. This statistic gives us day-to-day feedback on the effectiveness

Table 5 Adherence Levels by Age and Sex

Age groups	Exercise adherence groups					
	1 X/week (%)		1-2 Xs/week (%)		2 Xs/week (%)	
	Male	Female	Male	Female	Male	Female
< 30	54	45	29	35	17	20
30–39	37	81	31	31	32	28
40–49	35	38	30	30	35	32
50+	31	28	30	31	39	41

of our program in attracting individuals. It is extremely sensitive to temporal influence on adherence, such as weather conditions, sales in local stores, epidemics, and holidays.

The Tenneco corporation operates on a flexible working schedule; specific times for exercise are agreed to between the employee and his or her supervisor. This allows for great flexibility in participation. Early morning participation in 1983 was 15%; by 1986 it was 17% of the total daily participation. Usage during the noon hour (11:00 a.m. – 1:00 p.m.) was 41% in 1983 and 45% in 1986. After-work attendance was 22% in 1983 and 24% in 1986. Since 1983 the number of employees exercising during traditional work hours has decreased from 22% to only 14% of daily participation.

In our experience Mondays are always the busiest in terms of usage and recorded exercise. As the week progresses the number of employees using the facility and recording exercise decreases. Fridays have the least amount of daily usage along with those days which precede major holidays. The average daily attendance for Fridays averages in the low 400s, representing only 10% to 12% of the total population. Facility use on Mondays is usually over 600 employees representing between 18% to 20% of the total population. Because of these fluctuations, we evaluate monthly attendance by averaging attendance on Monday – Thursday, Monday – Friday, and Fridays.

Motivational Strategies

Howell and Alderman (1967) have indicated that the single most important psychological deterrent to regular exercise is lack of motivation.

It appears that self-motivation is strongly related to exercise adherence (Dishman, Ickes, & Morgan, 1980). Shephard (1985) suggests that only 20% of the eligible employees will join a fitness program. At Tenneco the majority of employees are members and each year between 60% and 75% of them participate in some aspect of the program. We have not experienced the initial disinterest that many programs have faced. Our major problem has been to continually challenge members to maintain or increase their exercise adherence levels. New employees at Tenneco immediately experience the corporate culture that says its OK to be fit and healthy. The peer pressure to belong to the program is an extension of this culture and is an important factor in maintaining our large membership and frequency rates.

Successful health and fitness programs offer more than just the promise of good health. They market the healthy image along with the ideas that exercise is fun, enjoyable, and provides the opportunity to be with other people. We feel that the key to good programming is the ability to offer a variety of opportunities from which to choose; this variety enhances not only their health but also other positive emotions.

Thompson and Wankel (1980) have shown that participants who perceive they have a choice in fitness activities will adhere better to exercise programs. Exercise options within the Tenneco program are planned around the basic components of an exercise prescription: cardiovascular fitness, muscular strength and endurance, flexibility, and body composition. These basic program areas are supported by activities for either an individual exerciser or groups. Eighty percent of the logged exercise activity at Tenneco occurs in the form of individual programming. Walking and jogging account for almost 60% of all recorded activity, followed by weight lifting, and exercise classes. Only 20% of all recorded activity is among individuals attending group activities (exercise classes, wallyball, etc.). The majority (85%) of these individuals are females. Contract teachers conduct 40% of the exercise classes. This gives our professional staff the time to work with the individual exercisers and provide the personalized attention and enthusiasm needed by many participants to be successful.

Extrinsic Motivation

Almost all corporate fitness programs use extrinsic motivational campaigns to provide excitement and challenges for their participants. These motivational campaigns are designed to reward individuals for maintaining or improving their exercise adherence with some external sign of success. Shephard (1985) suggests that extrinsic reward systems are particularly important in the early stages of developing good exercise adherence. In August of 1982 (six months after the Tenneco program began we initiated our first motivational campaign called "fitness challenge." The challenge was designed to require participants to exercise a minimum number of sessions per week, and burn a minimum number of calories per exercise session. The caloric expenditure requirements were based on the participant's body weight. The challenge also provided for different levels of exercise participation, progressively rewarding employees for more exercise sessions and larger number of calories expended. Fitness challenge lasted from August of 1982 until December of 1983; T-shirts of various designs were used as rewards. The level of participation was evident by the color and design of the T-shirts. Every three months fitness center personnel evaluated exercise adherence; individuals who had met the challenge criteria could present their monthly activity report for evaluation and be rewarded with a T-shirt. Figure 4 illustrates the average daily frequency of the fitness facility for the past four years; note that in challenge months (August and November, 1982; February, May, August, and November, 1983) usage was generally higher than it was during non-challenge months.

Figure 5 is a plot of the different levels of adherence groups throughout the challenge period. It is evident that during the challenge months the highest adherence group experienced its highest levels. The peaks (i.e., more participants) in the high-adherence groups are generally matched by valleys (i.e., less participants) in the low- and middle-adherence groups. This suggests that motivational campaigns increase adherence among individuals most committed to exercise but do not attract new exercisers into the program. They do, however, increase daily attendance and substantially affect exercise adherence patterns during the early phase of a program's development. For this reason, motivational campaigns are to be encouraged.

In 1984 we altered the fitness challenge to a bimonthly program. Participants were rewarded for different levels of participation and caloric expenditure with "Aerobucks." Aerobucks are wooden coins worth one dollar each and are redeemable for athletic clothing at the company store or for meals in the company cafeteria. Following completion of the year, we conducted a random sample of participants and analyzed their exercise adherence. Employees who were high-adherers (averaging greater than 2 exercise days a week) and middle adherers (averaging between 1 and 2 exercise days a week) significantly increased ($p < .05$) their exercise participation with the challenge programs. Those individuals who were categorized as low-adherers (averaged less than 1 day a week) did not significantly improve their attendance. These results suggest that the aerobuck program only provided support to already successful participants.

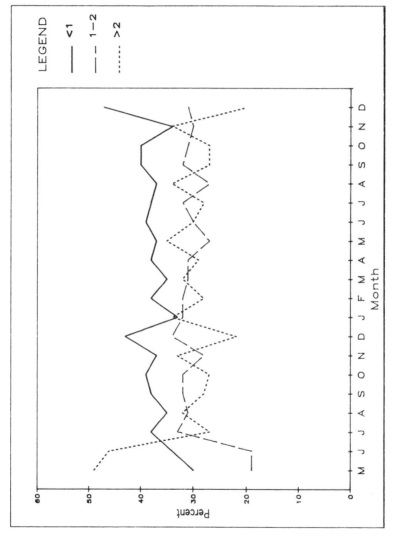

Figure 4 Average daily attendance from February 1982 (initiation) to December 1985.

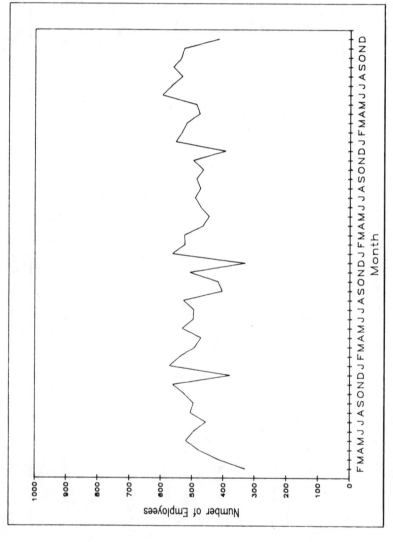

Figure 5 Levels of exercise adherence by adherence groups from March 1982 through December 1983.

There are some trends regarding incentive programs. They must be structured by a set of rules which are announced in an opportune manner and in language that is easily understood. The general goal of the program should be to reward individuals for levels of participation which can be realistically reached through regular exercise. If the standards for participation are set too high, then the majority of the employees will not participate. Individuals will only participate if the challenge is realistic and will lead to a reward. The reward must be something that the participant can visualize; the item should let others know that the participant is a winner. The redemption process should also be orchestrated so that the rewards are given out in a timely manner.

In 1985 the fitness challenge was restructured so that individuals had to exercise on a regular basis for three months before they received a T-shirt. Approximately 300 employees or only 15% to 20% participated in the challenge campaign during 1985. There are two possible explanations for this low turnout. First, the 3-month commitment may have been too long and thus was not appealing as a fun event. Second, because this occurred during the program's fourth year, many of the original members may no longer have been dependent on extrinsic rewards for adherence to their exercise routines.

We feel that extrinsic rewards are a very important part of a corporate fitness program. As indicated they can be used effectively to increase daily attendance and adherence levels in new programs. They should be introduced not immediately but only after initial momentum has slowed. Longstanding programs need incentive campaigns to challenge a portion of their membership. At Tenneco the numbers of individuals needing this type of support appears to be growing smaller. Instead of depending on extrinsic rewards, the emphasis of a program should be on retesting and counseling. This serves to underline the successes that each individual is experiencing, and then to set new, realistic goals. Consequently, participants move from extrinsic rewards to behaviors that are internally motivated.

Target Marketing

Since 1984 we have been experimenting with the effectiveness of targeting our promotional material and incentive programs to specific populations. Professional marketers have used this technique successfully for many years; it is now starting to appear in the social marketing literature (Bloom & Novelli, 1981). The tremendous sorting power of our computer system allows us to send promotional flyers on programs that will appeal to specific age, sex, and adherence-level groups. This has not only increased the effectiveness of these types of campaigns but also saved time and money. At Tenneco organized employee support groups exist for a variety of activities; we have found that after some initial nurturing they can be quite effective. Some examples of these groups are the running club, the wallyball committee, weight watchers, and a smoking-cessation support group.

Relapse Prevention

Another exercise adherence strategy is relapse prevention (Goodrick, Hartung, Warren, & Hoepfel, 1984). This strategy aims at training exercisers to recognize behaviors (e.g., thoughts, feelings, life situations) that lead to relapse or nonadherence; relapse prevention provides interventions that impede the process. This information is best presented at the orientation session and updated as employees are retested. When a dropout is reinitiated into the program, one of the major tasks is to identify the reasons for unsuccessful maintenance to that individual's previous program. The staff member presents the dropout with strategies for minimizing these problems and together they establish new physiological and behavioral goals. As our population becomes more sophisticated in their understanding of health, relapse prevention is becoming an important component of Tenneco's exercise adherence strategy.

Conclusion

The challenge for the corporation that initiates a fitness program is ultimately to change the corporate culture so that exercise and good health become an inherent employee desire and responsibility. This takes many years to develop and can only be accomplished with the support of all levels of management as well as staff dedicated to evaluation and service. The rewards are many: stronger, healthier employees who are absent less, consume fewer health care dollars, and are more productive and happier at work.

References

Baun, W.B., Bernacki, E.J., & Tsai, S.P. (1986). A preliminary investigation: Effect of a corporate fitness program on absenteeism and health care cost. *Journal of Occupational Medicine, 28*, 18–22.

Bernacki, E.J., & Baun, W.B. (1984). The relationship of job performance to exercise adherence in a corporate fitness program. *Journal of Occupational Medicine, 26,* 529–531.

Bloom, P.N., & Novelli, W.D. (1981). Problems and challenges in social marketing. *Journal of Marketing, 45,* 79–88.

Bowne, D.W., Russell, M.L., Morgan, J.L., Optenberg, R.N., & Clarke, A.E. (1984). Reduced disability and health care costs in an industrial fitness program. *Journal of Occupational Medicine, 26,* 809–816.

Cooper, K.H., Pollock, M.L., & Martin, R.P. (1978). Physical fitness levels vs. select coronary risk factors: A cross sectional study. *Journal of the American Medicine Association, 236,* 116–169.

Cox, M., Shephard, R.J., & Corey, P. (1981). Influence of an employee fitness programme upon fitness, productivity and absenteeism. *Ergonomics, 24,* 795–806.

Dickerson, O.B., & Mandelblit, C. (1983). A new model for employer-provider health education programs. *Journal of Occupational Medicine, 25,* 471–474.

Dishman, R.K., Ickes, W., & Morgan, W.P. (1980). Self-motivation and adherence to habitual physical activity. *Journal of Applied Social Psychology, 10,* 115–132.

Driver, R.W., & Ratliff, R.A. (1982, August). Employers' perceptions of benefits accrued from physical fitness programs. *Personnel Administrator,* 21–26.

Felix, M.R., Stunkard, A.J., Cohen, R.Y., & Cooley, N.B. (1985). Health promotion at the worksite. *Preventive Medicine, 14,* 99–108.

Fox, S.M., Naughton, I.P., & Haskell, W.L. (1971). Physical activity and the prevention of coronary heart disease. *Annals of Clinical Research, 3,* 404–432.

Godin, G., & Shephard, R.J. (1985). Psycho-social predictors of exercise intentions among spouses. *Canadian Journal of Applied Sport Science, 10,* 36–43.

Goodrick, G.K., Hartung, G.H., Warren, D.R., & Hoepfel, J.A. (1984). Helping adults to stay physically fit preventing relapse following aerobic exercise training. *Journal of Physical Education, Recreating and Dance, 55*(2), 48–49.

Haskell, W.L., & Blair, S.N. (1980). The physical activity component of health promotion in occupation settings. *Public Health Reports, 95,* 109–118.

Hoffman, J.J., & Hobson, C.J. (1984). Physical fitness and employee effectiveness. *Personnel Administrator, 4,* 101–126.

Howell, M.L., & Alderman, R.B. (1967). Psychological determinants of fitness. *Proceedings of the International Symposium on Physical Activity and Cardiovascular Health,* **96,** 721–726.

Naisbitt, J. (1983). *Megatrends: Ten new directions transforming our lives.* New York: Warner Books.

Paffenbarger, R.S., Hyde, R.T., Wing, A.L., & Hsieh, C. (1986). Physical activity, all-cause mortality, and longevity of college alumni. *New England Journal of Medicine,* **314,** 605–614.

Paffenbarger, R.S., Wing, R.T., & Hyde, R.T. (1983). Physical activity and the incidence of hypertension in college alumni. *American Journal of Epidemiology,* **117,** 245–257.

Parkinson, R. (1984). Participation: Keystone in health promotion evaluation. *Corporate Commentary,* **1,** 30–35.

Pauly, J.T., Palmer, J.A., Wright, C.C., & Pfeiffer, G.J. (1982). The effect of a 14-week employee fitness program on selected physiological and psychological parameters. *Journal of Occupational Medicine,* **24,** 457–463.

Peters, R.K., Cody, L.D., & Bischoff, D.P. (1983). Physical fitness and subsequent myocardial infarction in healthy workers. *Journal of American Medical Association,* **249,** 3052–3056.

Shephard, R.J. (1985). Motivation: The key to fitness compliance. *The Physician and Sportsmedicine,* **13,** 88–101.

Shephard, R.J., & Cox, M. (1980). Some characteristics of participants in industrial fitness programme. *Canadian Journal of Applied Sport Science,* **5,** 69–76.

Shephard, R.J., Morgan, P., Finucane, R., & Schimmelfing, L. (1980). Factors influencing recruitment to an occupational fitness program. *Journal of Occupational Medicine,* **22,** 389–398.

Thompson, C.E., & Wankel, L.M. (1980). The effects of perceived activity choice upon frequency of exercise behavior. *Journal of Applied Social Psychology,* **10,** 436–443.

Wiener, N. (1983, May). Customer demographics for strategic selling. *Business Marketing,* pp. 78–82.

Wilson, M.R. (1982). The selling of a program. *Corporate Fitness and Recreation,* **3**(6).

CHAPTER *13*

Occupation-Related Fitness and Exercise Adherence

Larry R. Gettman

While the major focus of this volume deals with health-related outcomes of adhering to regular physical activity programs in a population base or in supervised medical settings, this chapter addresses the unique fitness and exercise requirements of high-risk occupations such as law enforcement and petroleum exploration and production. Although data are not provided for fire fighting, construction, and other jobs requiring strenuous physical performance, the fitness and exercise requirements discussed in this chapter apply to these high-risk occupations as well.

Employees in these types of occupations present unique behavioral problems for implementing fitness programs. For example, Price, Pollock, Gettman, & Kent (1978) stated that police officers are enigmatic in their attitudes and practices toward physical fitness. There is universal agreement that on-the-job physical requirements in law enforcement are extremely high at times and that officers should be capable of performing these physical feats when the occasion arises. Yet, police officers show little initiative to keep themselves prepared to perform the varied physical requirements of the job.

In addition to these behavioral issues is the question of cost-effectiveness. Implementing and perpetuating fitness programs in employee settings usually depends on the acceptance by management that the programs are financially worthwhile.

This chapter contains a discussion of the rationale for job-related fitness, a description of results from studies on exercise adherence in law enforcement personnel, a pragmatic view of promoting exercise adherence, and a cost-benefit analysis of an employee fitness program in a petroleum exploration and production company.

Rationale for Job-Related Fitness

The concept that an individual's fitness status can affect job performance has been discussed in detail by Collingwood (1985). Though the principle is generally accepted as reasonable, its application has been either too general or too specific. For example, some job standards are stated in a very general way such as requiring employees to ''be fit to carry out duties of the job.'' On the other hand, standards may be stated specifically as in ''having the ability to lift 45 lb bales continuously.''

In the past, law enforcement agencies have not been able to link specific fitness status to specific job performance tasks. It is difficult to quantify the relationship between law enforcement jobs and fitness scores in the attempt to validate the fitness tests. Most job analyses on law enforcement groups (Smith, Pehlke, & Weller, 1976) indicate low and infrequent physical demands. Consequently, it is difficult to *validate* that a high level of fitness is necessary to perform specific job tasks on a regular basis.

This situation, however, can be viewed differently when the concepts of physical readiness and health risk are considered. One of the important functions of law enforcement is to protect public safety; the officer should be physically ready to perform in an emergency. In addition, health risks such as experiencing a heart attack during an emergency may be avoided if law enforcement officers are physically prepared to handle the situation. The focus should be on the importance of having good fitness levels and regular activity programs to insure readiness for performing physically demanding tasks as well as reducing health problems that may occur as a result of the physically demanding tasks.

Job-related physical fitness is perhaps viewed most appropriately as a health status concept. In this way, it incorporates the physiological functioning of the individual in terms of efficiency of the heart, peripheral vascular system, respiratory system, musculoskeletal system, and endocrine, metabolic, and nutritional systems. Health risk is especially important due to codification (i.e., ''heart laws'') recognizing that heart disease of law enforcement officers is job-related.

In designing a physical fitness program with consequent fitness standards, the Kentucky Department of Justice defined physical fitness in terms of health status rather than physical ability testing (Collingwood, 1985). This provided a clear focus for the purpose and design of the total fitness program because physical ability standards have caused much legal controversy in the past. Job relatedness of physical ability standards needs only to be shown if adverse impact is demonstrated. Adverse impact is defined as any type of testing process in which the failure rate is greater than 30% of a protected class; a protected class includes female, black, Hispanic, or American Indian (Maher, 1984).

In the attempt to validate fitness requirements for police work, it was not always possible to specify the frequency and criticality of law enforcement tasks due to the spurious nature of emergency situations. Police functions have not been well quantified. Energy cost studies have not been done and most data are in terms of frequency of tasks per year. For example, it has been reported that approximately 20% of law enforcement officers can expect one physical assault per year (Horstman, 1973). It has also been noted that chasing offenders is a major physical activity for officers and is a major precipitator of injuries and death (Callanan, 1982). Subjective reports indicate that an officer may be involved in a chase situation one to three times per year with an average distance of 100 to 500 feet. Physically subduing a suspect may occur one to three times per year (Mostardi & Vrychi, 1983). Other physical tasks that have been reported are included in Table 1. The tasks listed in Table 1 require some level of physical ability; physical fitness is necessary to perform them.

Table 1   Frequency of Physical Tasks in Law Enforcement

Physical task	Frequency (no. per year)
Pushing a vehicle (average distance = 30 ft)	3 to 4
Chasing offenders (average distance = 100 to 500 ft)	1 to 3
Physically subduing a suspect	1 to 3
Fence climbing	1 to 3
Dragging people or objects	1 to 3
Physical assault (20% of all officers)	1
Stair climbing	< 1
Lifting people or objects (average weight = 100 to 200 lbs)	< 1

A problem emerging for law enforcement agencies is a legal issue called vicarious liability, that is, negligence in having an unfit law enforcement officer. An individual who is hurt in a situation related to an officer's lack of fitness may hold the agency liable for not doing anything about the officer's fitness level. The plaintiff in such a case may be any citizen, including the officer involved and/or a family member. A law enforcement organization is liable for having an unfit officer in terms of negligent retention, negligent assignment, failure to supervise, failure to train, and failure to direct an officer to maintain a status of health which can have a bearing on that officer's functioning in an emergency situation. The organization is caught in a double bind: adverse impact and discrimination on one side and vicarious negligence on the other.

As mentioned previously, a high-risk occupational group should consider emphasizing physical fitness status as health- rather than task-related. The physical fitness program then becomes an employee health promotion benefit program. The functional goal of the program is to help personnel develop and maintain physical fitness and good health habits.

Physical fitness has four health-related components that can be job-related: (a) aerobic power or cardiovascular-respiratory endurance, (b) strength, (c) flexibility, and (d) body composition. The four health-related aspects of physical fitness have both general and specific implications for high-risk jobs; these include physical readiness to perform strenuous physical tasks along with health and disability risks. Cardiovascular-respiratory endurance concerns the efficient functioning of heart and blood vessels and the performance of endurance activities. It determines work capacity and fatigue tolerance and has a bearing on disease risk (especially heart disease). Strength is the physical ability to generate force. It is related to musculoskeletal injuries and performance of motor tasks. Flexibility refers to joint range of motion and the extensibility (elasticity) of muscles, tendons, and ligaments. Flexibility has a direct bearing on the efficient performance of many motor tasks. In terms of health risk, it is essential for the prevention of musculoskeletal injuries (especially of the lower back). Body composition refers to the relationship between lean tissue and fat tissue. The greater the amount of body fat the less efficient the body movements. Obesity is also a risk factor for cardiovascular disease.

Due to the nature of law enforcement work as well as other high-risk occupations, a majority of the time on the job is spent doing sedentary tasks. As a consequence, personnel develop a sedentary lifestyle which minimizes physical readiness and maximizes health risk. This places employees in a state of jeopardy at two levels: they are (a) unable to perform maximally in a demanding situation, and (b) at high risk for developing cardiovascular disease. When a sedentary police officer responds to an emergency situation requiring a high degree of physical exertion, the officer's life as well as the lives of others may be in greater jeopardy than in situations where the officer is physically fit. In addition, the officer's sedentary lifestyle is related to the possible development of back problems. Price et al. (1978) reported that the major causes of both early retirement and limited-duty assignment among police officers were back trouble and heart-related conditions. The main concern, therefore, in developing a physical fitness program for public safety personnel should be fitness for both physical readiness and reduced health risk. The same principle may be true for other high-risk occupations such as fire fighting, construction, and petroleum exploration and production.

On a cross-sectional basis, fitness in public safety officers has been shown to be positively correlated with ratings of job performance and physical task performance, lower frequency of complaints, and less incidence of sick leave (Collingwood, 1984). Fitness has also been shown to predict recruit academy performance, not only in physical abilities but in academic performance as well (Collingwood & Stockwell, 1973).

Adherence to Unsupervised Exercise

Most of the high-risk occupations such as law enforcement, fire fighting, construction, and petroleum exploration and production entail rotating shifts. Due to the necessity of unusual work and rest hours, the employees often participate in unsupervised exercise programs. Though it is logical to assume that individuals exercising under direct supervision will adhere to a program better than those under no supervision, Gettman, Pollock, & Ward (1983) found no difference between supervised and unsupervised exercise programs for improving physical fitness. They compared 17 police officers who participated in an unsupervised exercise program to 10 sedentary officers (control group) and 20 officers in a supervised exercise program. Both exercise groups increased significantly compared to the control group in treadmill performance time and maximum oxygen uptake and decreased significantly in resting heart rate, heart rate response to a step test, percent body fat, total skinfold fat, and waist girth. Adherence rates were 65% for the unsupervised group, 55% for the supervised group, and 70% for the controls. Most of the officers who dropped out of the unsupervised exercise program reported that it took too much time and interfered with their jobs and family life, even though they exercised at a location they felt was convenient. Dropouts from the supervised program reported five reasons for attrition:

1. Program involved too much time
2. Program interfered with job responsibilities
3. Family illness prevented participation

4. Lack of interest
5. Travel to exercise center was too time-consuming and expensive

Researchers did not expect the relatively high attrition rates because most of the police officers were at the middle-management level (supervisors and administrators). They anticipated that the officers would have sufficient control over their schedules to plan enough time for exercise. This illustrates a unique behavior pattern in dropouts from an exercise program. Most of the attrition reasons listed by the dropouts in this particular study involved time limitations. Oldridge (1979) and Andrew and Parker (1979) also found that lack of time was a major determinant of exercise program attrition in post-myocardial infarction patients. The subjects also listed lack of enthusiasm for the program as a cause of attrition. Lack of time and lack of enthusiasm most likely coincide; employees may indicate that lack of time is the major obstacle to participation when, in actuality, lack of enthusiasm is the problem. For example, in the study by Gettman et al. (1983), the dropouts from the unsupervised exercise program indicated "too much time required to travel to the exercise location" as the problem. In reality, the dropouts traveled less distance (2.0 miles) than the unsupervised compliers (2.9 miles). The dropouts travel-time problem may have been used as an excuse for the actual reason of lack of enthusiasm or other attrition reasons. The importance of isolating true barriers to exercise adherence from perceived barriers and motivation deficits is discussed in detail by Dishman and Dunn in chapter 6 of this book.

In another police study, Price et al. (1978) reported that officers who had dropped out of a three-day-per-week fitness program also indicated that their main reasons for attrition was too much time traveling to and from a centrally located exercise center. Other factors which led to attrition from the exercise program included (a) a second job, (b) school attendance, (c) court appearances, (d) injuries, and (e) family commitments. These answers were perplexing because a similar number of officers who completed the exercise programs also held second jobs, attended school, traveled comparable distances, and experienced some injuries. To clarify the results of the study the researchers conducted personal interviews with many of the dropouts. The interviews revealed disappointment among some officers with the random selection process of the study design and dislike of the exercise program to which they were assigned. Dropouts identified a lack of communication with the exercise staff even though the program directors designed a closely supervised program. For some reason the dropouts did not list these factors on the attrition questionnaire. This illustrates that the role of the exercise staff is extremely important for the support of participants in supervised programs; communication should be of primary concern as well as close attention to participant fitness development.

The findings from exercise adherence studies conducted on police officers and myocardial infarction patients in the 1970s are similar to recent results obtained by a Gallup Survey of the general population in the 1980s (Harris & Gurin, 1985). In the 1984 Gallup Survey, 54% of 1,019 telephone households indicated that they exercise regularly (i.e., at least 1.5 hours per week). Reportedly exercise does not take people away from work or family and 60% of the exercisers said that exercise has become "a natural part of daily life." Of those who did not exercise, 40% listed "no time, too busy" as the major reason for not exercising (see Table 2). In

Table 2 What's Keeping You From Fitness?

Reason for not exercising	Response (%)
No time, too busy	40
Get enough exercise at work or home	20
Too lazy	15
Health problems	15
No interest, exercise is boring	12
Too old	10
Exercise is not necessary	9
Too tired	7

Note. Nonexercisers asked, "What are the two or three most important reasons you don't exercise?" Adapted from "The New Eighties Lifestyle: Look Who's Getting It All Together" by T.G. Harris and J. Gurin, 1985, *American Health,* 4(2), p. 46. Copyright by American Health Partners. Reprinted by permission.

our time-conscious, hurry-up society many people (18% in the Gallup Survey) say they have no time for exercise. In contrast, 26% in the Gallup Survey indicated that time for workouts is still hard to find during the week, but the time is easier to find now than it was in the past. The new fitness generation is probably making more time for exercise because of its health-related importance rather than simply using available idle time for exercise.

Promoting Exercise Adherence in High-Risk Occupational Groups

The lower attrition rate for the unsupervised exercise group in the police study conducted by Gettman et al. (1983), suggests that designing an exercise program at a convenient location near the home has an advantage over a fixed, central location. It saves time and may lead to better adherence. A suggested model to improve adherence in an unsupervised exercise program includes several characteristics.

1. Encourage the use of a home program because it may be more convenient for the individual.
2. Teach the individual how to start an exercise program.
3. Provide some supervision in the early stages of the program.
4. Have the individual report the types and amount of activity participation every two weeks.
5. Maintain good communication with the participants by regularly scheduled follow-up sessions.

Price et al. (1978) describe three basic administrative approaches to physical fitness programs in law enforcement agencies (see Table 3). The most common administrative method observed during site visits to vari-

Table 3   Administrative Approaches to Fitness Programs in Law Enforcement Agencies

Voluntary approach	Revolutionary approach	Evolutionary approach
The department provides exercise equipment and promotes participation through encouragement and educational materials. Although the voluntary approach is the most widely used, it appears to be the least effective in promoting adherence.	The administration indicates that the employees will meet certain criteria within specified times to show that they are capable to perform their duties. Failure to comply with the requirements results in negative disciplinary action. Usually no assistance is offered and there is no regular program for the employees to maintain their conditioning.	In this method, employees receive (1) indoctrination concerning the program, (2) testing to determine current status, and (3) assistance in meeting the requirements. After a time when all personnel have had the opportunity to comply, the program may become mandatory. This method is the most effective and creates less friction with employees and with collective bargaining groups.

Note.   From *Physical Fitness Programs for Law Enforcement Officers: A Manual for Police Administrators* by C.S. Price, M.L. Pollock, L.R. Gettman, and D.A. Kent, Washington, DC: National Institute of Law Enforcement and Criminal Justice. Copyright 1984. Reprinted by permission.

ous agencies was *voluntary*. The major finding from the site visits was that in the most successful agencies the chief administrator and staff become actively involved in the implementation of the fitness program. Those top-level managers promoted the program by example. These principles may apply to other high-risk occupations such as fire fighting.

The involvement of the department's leaders in the program cannot be overemphasized. A chief administrator who complies with weight and conditioning requirements has a much greater ability to encourage the participation of the employees. The display of leadership is responsible for the success or failure of the program (Patton, Corry, Gettman, & Graf, 1986). In addition to top management support, well-qualified fitness staff counseling is essential for the encouragement of participants.

According to the information collected by Price et al. (1978), it was recommended that departments desiring to implement fitness programs begin with an evaluation of the current fitness levels of their officers. In this manner, programs can be designed to help individuals reach desired levels of performance. Program directors do not require extensive facilities, equipment, and budgets either to successfully test physical fitness or to implement a fitness program. Low-budget health promotion and physical fitness programs are described by Price et al. (1978) and the American Heart Association (1985). The American Heart Association's health promotion program for the worksite is called *Heart At Work*. Several suggestions are offered in *Heart At Work* for implementing exercise programs at low-cost levels. For example, the use of nearby parks and recreation facilities as well as other available community resources may be convenient and inexpensive ways to promote exercise adherence.

Cost-Effectiveness of Employee Fitness Programs

Companies which have implemented employee fitness programs have invested anywhere from less than $5 per employee for awareness and promotional programs to over $600 per employee for highly organized programs with extensive exercise facilities (Patton et al., 1986). Companies which have reported their investments in physical fitness programs for employees have indicated an interest in helping to improve the health of their employees; they also expect a return on their investment in terms of an increase in productivity and savings in medical costs (Gettman, 1983). Few companies, however, have documented their exercise participation levels in order to analyze the cost-effectiveness of their programs.

Mesa Petroleum Company, an oil and gas exploration and production firm in Amarillo, Texas, formalized an employee fitness program by providing guidance in the implementation of personal fitness programs

(Gettman, 1986). The company made the program available to all employees, including those in the high-risk field of exploration and production. All field employees were encouraged to participate in the company-sponsored fitness testing program and to receive a personalized exercise prescription. If convenient to the home, the company purchased health club memberships for the field employees. Otherwise, they were encouraged to carry out home programs.

Activity levels were documented by having the employees voluntarily submit monthly exercise log cards which included records of type, intensity, and duration of activity as well as body weight for each day of activity recorded. Data from the exercise log cards were entered into computer software programs in which caloric output was calculated for each exercise recorded.

In several respects the field employees displayed exercise adherence behavior characteristics similar to those discussed for law enforcement personnel. Although convenient exercise programs were provided by management, only 27% (n = 34 of 127) of the field workers who were engaged in physically vigorous, high-risk petroleum exploration and production participated in the company's exercise program during 1982. In contrast, 59% (n = 165 of 278) of the other employees (e.g., managers, accountants, secretaries, and clerks) in the company's field locations participated in the exercise programs during that same year (Gettman, 1986).

The 34 field workers who exercised averaged 13.2 kcal per kilogram body weight per week (kcal/kg/week) which is equivalent to exercising regularly 2.8 days per week or 924 kcal per week per person. The 165 managers, accountants, secretaries, and clerks averaged 12.0 kcal/kg/week which is equivalent to 2.5 days per week or 840 kcal per week per person.

Overall participation in the company's fitness program including the headquarter personnel is represented in Figure 1. The percentage of sedentary employees (0 kcal/kg/week) decreased from 42% in 1982 to 37% in 1983 while the percentage of active (exercising) employees increased from 58% in 1982 to 63% in 1983. Most of the active employees were in the low level of 1 to 10 kcal/kg/week. This corresponds roughly to exercising 1 to 2 days per week on a yearly average. An activity level of 14 kcal/kg/week, or 1,000 kcal/week would correspond to 30 minutes of aerobic exercise performed 3 days per week on a yearly average. Paffenbarger, Wing, and Hyde (1978) reported that 1,000 kcal/week corresponds to an average activity program and that 2,000 kcal/week may be vigorous enough to be protective in preventing heart disease. In this study of Harvard alumni, individuals who expended fewer than 2,000 kcal/week at work and play had a 64% higher risk of heart attack than more active alumni. Individuals averaging 2,000 kcal/week or roughly 28 kcal/kg/week would be considered highly active. For the Mesa Petroleum Company,

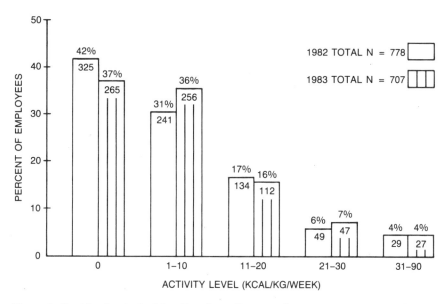

Figure 1 Participation in the Mesa Petroleum Company fitness program, 1982 and 1983.

only 5% (n = 36) of the employees exercised at highly active levels, averaging 28 kcal/kg/week or more in 1982.

In addition to activity patterns, Mesa Petroleum documented yearly absenteeism rates. Administrators recorded only personal sick time for analysis, and determined the annual medical cost for each employee by totaling the amount of money paid by the company for medical claims. Only illness claims were analyzed; pregnancy reimbursements were omitted from the study.

A cross-section analysis of the relationship between absenteeism and activity level is presented in Figures 2 and 3. In 1982 and 1983, 325 and 265 sedentary employees (0 kcal/kg/week) averaged 41 and 41 hours, respectively, of absenteeism per employee. The trend for the active employees during both years showed that the higher the activity level, the lower the absentee rate. The active employees were grouped into four categories and the average absenteeism for each group is represented in Figures 2 and 3. When considered as a group, all 453 active employees in 1982 averaged only 29 hours of sick time. The 442 active employees in 1983 averaged only 20 hours of absenteeism.

The hourly difference in absenteeism between active and sedentary employees may be interpreted from the standpoint of productivity. In 1982, the 12-hour difference in sick time between active and sedentary employees represented 0.6% of the total work time available for the year

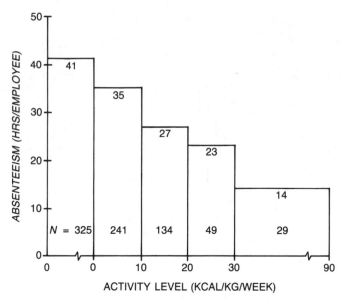

Figure 2 Relationship between absenteeism and activity level, 1982.

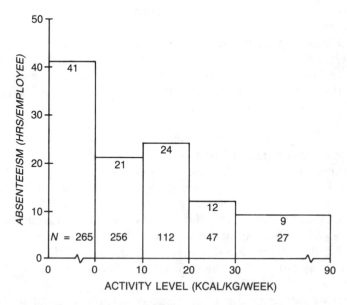

Figure 3 Relationship between absenteeism and activity level, 1983.

(see Table 4). Assuming that the active employees were on the job 0.6% more of the time during the year and that this time was directly related to productivity resulting in net income to the company, the 0.6% represents $700,000 more in net income to the company having active employees. The value is even more substantial in 1983 where the 21-hour difference in absenteeism represents 1.1% of the total work time and $1.3

Table 4 Estimated Productivity Increase by Having Employees Who Exercise

	1982	1983
Sedentary sick time (hours per employee)	41	41
Active sick time (hours per employee)	29	20
Difference (hours per employee)	12	21
% of total work time	0.6	1.1
Company's net income	$116 million	$115 million
Productivity increase (net income × work time %)	$0.7 million	$1.3 million

million of net income to the company. The potential to reduce absenteeism by encouraging more employees to become active in a regular exercise program is suggested by the Mesa data. The active employees of Mesa exhibited lower absenteeism and presumably higher productivity than the sedentary employees. This type of analysis represents one way of estimating the productivity in a company in which there are several job classifications that are especially hard to quantify such as management, professional/technical, secretarial/clerical, and maintenance.

The analysis compares the average absenteeism experienced within sedentary and active employee groups. Some of the sedentary and active employees had no sick time at all throughout the year. In 1982 the proportion ($n = 118; 15.2\%$) of the sedentary employees reporting no absenteeism for the entire year was similar to the proportion ($n = 115; 14.8\%$) of active employees. However, in 1983 a greater proportion ($n = 184; 26\%$) of active employees reported no sick time for the year compared to sedentary employees ($n = 57$; 8%). The 1983 data indicated that more sedentary employees and less active employees were absent compared to 1982. This is a positive trend for the company and shows a relationship between being active and having no absenteeism from work.

The 12- and 21-hour differences between active and sedentary employees in 1982 and 1983 represent $156 and $303, respectively, per employee in salary paid for sick time (see Table 5). This may be considered as the amount of money saved by having active employees as compared to having sedentary employees.

Table 5 Cost Effectiveness of the Mesa Petroleum Company Employee Fitness Program

	1982	1983
Absenteeism savings (per active employee)	$156	$303
Medical cost savings (per active employee)	$217	not available
Total savings (per active employee)	$373	$520
Budget costs (per employee)	$494	$485
Amount recovered (%) (savings/budget)	76%	107%

Table 5 also indicates that the medical cost differences between active and sedentary employees in 1982 averaged $217. No medical cost data were available from the company for 1983; to compensate the average savings of $217 from the previous year was used. If the medical cost data followed the same trend as the absenteeism data, the savings would have been much greater. The relationship between activity level and medical cost for 1982 is illustrated in Figure 4. The active employees averaged $173 per person in medical cost while the sedentary employees averaged $390 per person.

The analysis appearing in Table 5 represents one way to determine the cost effectiveness of an employee fitness program. The estimated savings in absenteeism and medical cost per active employee were combined resulting in total savings per active employee of $373 in 1982 and $520

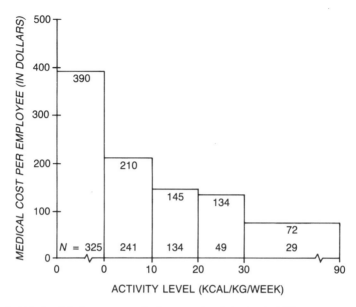

Figure 4   Relationship between medical cost and activity level, 1982.

in 1983. The total budget spent by the company on the fitness program averaged $494 in 1982 and $485 in 1983. Therefore, 76% of the budget spent in 1982 was theoretically recovered through savings in absenteeism and medical costs by having active employees. In 1983, the fitness program paid for itself by recovering 107% of the budget spent on each employee.

One important consideration to examine in an analysis of this type is the selection effect. Did the healthy employees who started exercising in 1982 lower their absenteeism and medical costs? Or would the lower absenteeism rate and medical costs have existed in those employees regardless of exercise patterns? There is no absolute proof that exercise *causes* a decrease in absenteeism but there are some interesting data available from Mesa Petroleum in this regard.

To analyze the relationship between exercise and absenteeism, 579 Mesa employees who were with the company both in 1982 and 1983 were examined. Of the 579 employees, 338 were active both in 1982 and 1983 and averaged 13.0 and 12.7 kcal/kg/minute, respectively, each year. This indicates that they did not increase their exercise levels the second year, yet the average absenteeism decreased from 28 hours to 21 hours per employee in 1982 and 1983, respectively (see Figure 5). Furthermore, 154 employees who were sedentary both years also decreased in absentee-

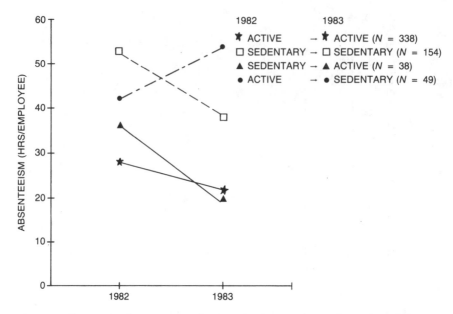

Figure 5   Changes in absenteeism and activity level in employees from 1982 to 1983.

ism from 53 hours to 38 hours per employee in 1982 and 1983, respectively. Therefore, both the active and the sedentary employees decreased in absenteeism from 1982 to 1983. Although exercise may not necessarily *create* a decrease in absenteeism, it is an interesting fact that employees who exercised had lower absenteeism rates than did the sedentary employees.

A further analysis revealed that 38 employees who were sedentary in 1982 and then became active in 1983, decreased their absenteeism rates from 36 hours to 20 hours per employee (see Figure 5). And, most interestingly, 49 employees who were active in 1982 and became *sedentary* in 1983 *increased* in absenteeism from 42 hours to 54 hours per employee, respectively. These results favor the claim that exercise leads to lower absenteeism and becoming sedentary leads to increased absenteeism. More research is needed to verify a possible cause-effect between exercise and absenteeism.

The study conducted at Mesa Petroleum involved just two tangible (measurable) benefits of having active employees—reduced absenteeism and lower medical costs. The study did not take into account any financial outcomes from having intangible (immeasurable) benefits of a fitness program such as higher employee morale and higher levels of self-confidence and energy leading to greater productivity. The tangible benefits of lower absenteeism rates and lower medical costs alone appear to pay for the fitness program in terms of theoretical money saved. Adding the intangible benefits of having active employees leads to the conclusion that both the tangible and intangible benefits of an employee fitness program more than justify the investment.

Summary

This chapter addressed the issue of job-related fitness and exercise adherence for high-risk occupations such as law enforcement and petroleum exploration and production. The fitness and exercise requirements discussed for high-risk law enforcement would also apply to other high-risk occupations such as fire fighting, construction, and other jobs involving strenuous physical performance. In these types of jobs, development and maintenance of physical fitness should be viewed from a physical readiness and health risk standpoint—not necessarily from a validated job task analysis.

Attrition from exercise programs in high-risk occupations is similar to other occupational groups in the population. The main reason for dropping out of an exercise program is "lack of time." However, this reason may often be listed to mask other reasons such as lack of enthusiasm, poor communication with members of the fitness staff, and lack of leadership in the department.

Because high-risk occupations often have scheduling problems due to shift rotation, it is extremely important to design exercise programs to be as convenient as possible. Encourage the use of home programs or the use of nearby facilities. Teach the individual how to start an exercise program and then provide some supervision in the early stages of the program. Have the individual report the types and amount of activity participation every two weeks or so. Maintain good communication with the participant by regularly scheduled follow-up sessions.

Top management support for the exercise program and their participating leadership are perhaps the most important factors for promoting exercise adherence among the employees. In addition to management leadership is the importance of having well-qualified exercise staff counseling and encouraging the employees.

Cost-analysis studies of corporate fitness programs show cross-sectional relationships between exercise and absenteeism and medical costs. Active employees experience lower absenteeism rates and lower medical costs compared to sedentary employees. Intangible benefits of having active employees include the possibility that the employees enjoy higher morale levels, they may feel better about themselves, have more confidence, and therefore, produce more for the company.

The tangible benefits of lower absenteeism and lower medical costs alone appear to pay for the company fitness program in terms of potential financial savings. Adding the intangible benefits of having active and alert employees leads to the conclusion that both the tangible and the intangible benefits of an employee fitness program more than justify the investment.

References

American Heart Association. (1985). *Heart at work*. Dallas: Author.

Andrew, G.M., & Parker, J.O. (1979). Factors related to dropout of post myocardial infarction patients from exercise programs. *Medicine and Science in Sports*, **11**, 376–378.

Callanan, J. (1982). Officer survival. *ACADS Dispatcher*, **2**.

Collingwood, T. (1984). *Final report: Physical fitness standards and fitness program project*. Alexandria, VA: Alexandria Police Department.

Collingwood, T. (1985). Rationale for job-related fitness in law enforcement. In *Kentucky justice cabinet report*. Richmond, KY: Kentucky Department of Criminal Justice.

Collingwood, T., & Stockwell, D. (1973). The importance of physical fitness for law enforcement selection. *Consortium Monograph Series on Fitness*, **1**(1).

Gettman, L.R. (1983, November). Reduced costs, increased worker production are rationale for tax-favored corporate fitness plans. *Employee Benefit Plan Review*, pp. 11–13.

Gettman, L.R. (1986). Cost benefit analysis of a corporate fitness program. *Fitness in Business*, **1**, 11–17.

Gettman, L.R., Pollock, M.L., & Ward, A. (1983). Adherence to unsupervised exercise. *The Physician and Sportsmedicine*, **11**, 56–66.

Harris, T.G., & Gurin, J. (1985). The new eighties lifestyle: Look who's getting it all together. *American Health*, **4**(2), 42–47.

Horstman, P. (1973, December). Assaults on police officers. *Police Chief*, p. 44.

Maher, P. (1984). Police physical ability tests: Can they ever be valid? *Public Personnel Management Journal*, 173–183.

Mostardi, R., & Vrychi, S. (1983). *Construction and validation of a police officer physical fitness battery as a substitute for maximum age requirement.* Akron, OH: Akron Police Department.

Oldridge, N.B. (1979). Compliance of post myocardial infarction patients to exercise programs. *Medicine and Science in Sports,* **11**, 373–375.

Paffenbarger, R.S., Wing, A.L., & Hyde, R.T. (1978). Physical activity as an index of heart attack risk in college alumni. *American Journal of Epidemiology,* **108**(3), 161–175.

Patton, R., Corry, J., Gettman, L.R., & Graf, J. (1986). *Implementing health/ fitness programs.* Champaign, IL: Human Kinetics.

Price, C.S., Pollock, M.L., Gettman, L.R., & Kent, D.A. (1978). *Physical fitness programs for law enforcement officers: A manual for police administrators.* Washington, DC: National Institute of Law Enforcement and Criminal Justice, Law Enforcement Assistance Administration.

Smith, C., Pehlke, D., & Weller, C. (1976). *Role performance and the criminal justice system: Vol. II. Detailed performance objectives.* Cincinnati, OH: Anderson.

CHAPTER 14

Exercise Adherence and Leisure Activity: Patterns of Involvement and Interventions to Facilitate Regular Activity

Leonard M. Wankel

As described in a number of the preceding chapters, the 1970s saw an increased recognition of the importance of physical activity for well-being. Convincing evidence indicated that easier and more sedentary lifestyles were having harmful effects on general health. The trend toward more mechanization and automation seems inevitable, as few individuals are prepared to give up modern conveniences and return to the more frugal, ascetic lifestyle of their forefathers. There is growing recognition, however, that at least a minimal amount of vigorous exercise is essential to healthy living. More particularly, it has been recognized that if exercise is no longer a significant part of one's occupation or normal daily routine, then active recreational pursuits might be an appropriate substitute. This chapter, focuses on the role of community-based sport and physical activity programs in providing such opportunities, with specific emphasis on the following topics: participation patterns, governmental campaigns to promote physical activity, factors affecting involvement in activity programs, and program interventions for increasing involvement.

"Sport for All" Programs

The 1960s and 70s saw the widespread initiation of governmental programs that fostered public involvement in sport and physical activity. Although this was not the first time that governments had initiated programs to promote physical activity for the general populace, this was by far the most widespread movement (McIntosh, 1980). In 1966, "Sport for All" was adopted as the major long-term objective for the sports programs of the Council of Europe, an organization formed to foster unity among the member countries, to facilitate their economic and social progress, and to promote European culture (Council of Europe, 1976). In 1968, the Council formed a planning group to define the concept "sport for all." "Sport" was used in a broad sense to refer to "free, spontaneous physical activity engaged in during leisure time to include sports proper and various other physical activities provided they demand some effort" (Council of Europe, p. 2).

The first Sport for All national program was initiated by Norway in 1967. The mass media publicized and promoted the general values of sport and physical activity, and attempts were made to encourage more widespread involvement in vigorous physical activity (Palm, 1978). Similar programs soon sprung up in Holland, Austria, The Federal Republic of Germany, and Belgium. The Sport for All movement received more international impetus in 1975 when the United Nations Educational, Scientific, and Cultural Organization (UNESCO) began to encourage Sport for All. In April 1976, Sport for All was a central topic at a Ministers of Sport Conference held at UNESCO house in Paris with 101 of 150 member states represented (McIntosh, 1980). At the General Conference of UNESCO meeting in Nairobi, Kenya later that year a series of recommendations with implications for Sport for All were passed. In November 1978, the General Conference of UNESCO adopted the International Charter of Physical Education and Sport.

Article 1.1 of the Charter states that "every human being has a fundamental right of access to physical education and sport, which are essential for the full development of his personality" (cited in McIntosh, 1980, p. 8). Throughout the 1970s Sport for All programs spread throughout the industrialized world and into a number of third-world countries (McIntosh, 1980). These programs differed somewhat from country to country and adopted different titles. They all adopted the same basic format, however. Although generally government-initiated, they were very much dependent upon nongovernmental agencies and private donations for funding. They all cooperated with, and relied considerably upon, the mass media (especially television) for publicity.

In Canada, a promotional agency called "Participaction" was established in 1971 to "inform, inspire, encourage and motivate Canadians to get active, to get fit" (Participaction Brochure, undated). This agency was meant to be an "arms length agency" which received some government funding but also relied to a large extent on private and corporate sponsorship. Relying heavily on the mass media as well, Participaction has attempted to encourage public involvement by creating an awareness of the importance of physical activity. More recently the agency has also become a source of general information on the subjects of physical activity and sport, distributing educational materials to various organizations and to the general public.

The Australian "Life Be In It" program, which began as a state program in Victoria in 1975, is also a media-based program designed to increase awareness of the need for regular physical activity and to encourage public involvement. After commissioning an initial study of people's attitudes toward physical activity and fitness, the program designed some promotional strategies based on these findings. These strategies achieved considerable success in Victoria, and as a result the program was adopted nationwide in 1977. Thereafter, a number of public organizations (e.g., municipal recreation departments and public schools) and voluntary organizations (e.g., service clubs) began to sponsor and promote Life Be In It activities (Dixon, 1978).

In the United States no nationwide governmental program as such has been undertaken; however, governmental support does exist indirectly through such programs as the President's Council on Sport and Fitness and the National Recreation and Park Association, which has adopted the Australian-produced Life Be In It program. Although these organizations operate autonomously, they do receive some governmental financial assistance.

Evidence indicates that media campaigns can indeed influence public awareness. A 1976 evaluation of the Australian Life Be In It campaign indicated that 79% of the people who were sampled recalled the Life Be In It ads (Becker, 1977). By 1977, another evaluation revealed that that figure had increased to 97% and that 87.8% of the national sample recognized the 1977 Life Be In It television commercials (Department of Youth, Sport and Recreation, 1979). Similar studies conducted in Canada and West Germany indicated that 94% and 93% of the respective populations sampled were aware of the promotional campaigns (Jackson, 1979; Dixon, 1977).

As might be expected, the impact of these programs on behavior falls far short of the figures reflecting public awareness. In Australia, 47% of the 1977 sample responded positively to the question, "Has the Life Be In It message caused you to think about how you could be more active?" Thirty-eight percent indicated that they did exercise more often, 8% indicated that they got out of the house more often and 10% indicated that they often substituted walking for driving (Department of Youth, Sport and Recreation, 1979).

In Canada, corresponding evidence indicated that 27% of respondents in one city and 10% in another reported that Participaction had a positive effect on their involvement in physical activity (Jackson, 1979). Similarly, 19% of the respondents to a West German survey indicated that the Trimm campaign had caused them to be more active (Palm, 1978).

One problem with all of the available information on promotional campaigns is that it is subjective: There is a lack of well-controlled data. The campaigns can clearly be effective in increasing awareness of the campaigns; it is also clear that a general increase in physical activity has occurred over the years. What is not clear, however, is the extent that this increase can be attributed to the promotional campaigns. Involvement in physical activity has increased markedly in a number of countries in recent years; however, the fact that such gains have not been restricted to countries with national promotional campaigns calls into question the causal nature of the relationship between such campaigns and increased physical activity.

Agency Involvement at the Local Level

People can engage in physical activity and sport in a number of different places. Whereas statistics indicate that most recreational activity takes place at or near the home, the particular place that an activity occurs depends upon both the equipment and the personnel necessary to perform that activity. Jogging, running, and individual calisthenics programs can be easily practiced in the home environment. Weight lifting, formal exercise classes, and organized sporting events, on the other hand, tend to operate out of a variety of agencies. There are a number of public, semiprivate, and commercial agencies that provide opportunities for sport and exercise at the local level. These include public recreation departments which provide a wide range of sport programs as well as more exercise-oriented aerobics, calisthenics, and weight-lifting classes and programs. Semiprivate agencies such as the YMCA and YWCA and voluntary agencies and service clubs also offer a variety of such programs. Finally, a number of private and commercial clubs offer sport and exercise activities for their members or clients. The individual therefore has the advantage of selecting from programs and activities that are offered by a wide variety of agencies. Such programs might vary considerably in cost and ancillary services, but the activities offered are basically the same.

Although most studies have not identified the site or agency where a given activity takes place, the Ontario survey conducted in the fall of 1982 did collect the following information: Thirty-five percent of those surveyed said that they participated in recreational activity out-of-doors using no special facility; 23% used public, nonprofit facilities and clubs; 18% exercised at home; and 4% exercised at work or at school. As might be expected, the type of activity and place of activity were related. Most jogging (65%) took place out-of-doors with no special facility, while calisthenics were performed in different settings, 26% at commercial or private facilities and clubs and 20% in public recreation facilities (Fitness Ontario, 1983).

Whereas in North America most opportunities for activity are provided by municipal recreation departments, public schools, commercial clubs, and private and voluntary clubs, in Europe the mass sport movement is based largely on the sport club concept. Sport clubs, which are generally supported by government and/or business funding plus modest membership fees, provide a variety of sporting opportunities for all age levels and at a very reasonable cost.

Many Eastern European countries have developed a unique system of sport festivals for promoting widespread involvement in sport (McIntosh, 1980). The German Democratic Republic has operated *Spartakiades* since 1965 under the patronage of sport organizations, youth organizations, and the National Ministry of Education. The pyramidally structured *Spartakiades* foster youth participation in a number of sports. After initial selection at the school or club level, participants engage in regional competitions. Successful competitors at the regional level then progress to district competitions and ultimately to the national *Spartakiade*. The district and national festivals are held biannually on alternating years.

Participation Patterns

Research indicates that in recent years there has been a marked increase in the number of people who exercise regularly. Whereas in 1961, only 24% of Americans reported that they "did something on a daily basis apart from their work, to keep them physically fit," the corresponding figures for 1977, 1980, and 1983 were 47%, 46%, and 47% (Gallup Polls, 1961, 1977, 1980, 1983). The 1983 Miller Lite study of sport in the United States found that 44% of Americans 14 years and older engaged in athletic activity daily or almost daily. In Canada, participation in sport increased from 54% in 1976 to 77% in 1981 while participation in exercise (walking, jogging, cycling, calisthenics, exercise classes, etc.) increased from 63% to 66% (Canada Fitness Survey, 1983). These later figures, however, are based on a minimal level of involvement, "involvement" being defined simply as having participated in an activity at least once in the past year. When a more stringent criterion of involvement was used (a minimum of 3 hours per week for at least 9 months per year) 56% of the population reported being "active."

The Canadian province of Ontario provides a more detailed look at changing activity patterns during recent years (Fitness Ontario, 1984). In November 1981, 56% of Ontario adults reported being active at least once a week—a 7% increase from November 1978. Since 1978, the same information has been collected in the spring and fall of every year. Figure 1 depicts the results of these surveys from 1978 to 1983. The figure illustrates the seasonal variations with generally higher participation in spring, a general increase in activity levels over the years 1978 to 1981, and a stabilizing effect after that.

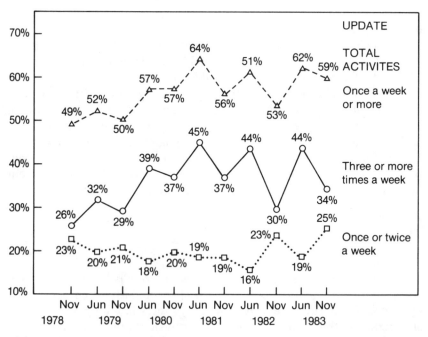

Figure 1 Percentages of Ontario adults engaging in physical activity, 1978–1983. *Note.* From *Physical Activity Patterns in Ontario—IIa (1982–83 Update)* by Fitness Ontario, 1984, Toronto: Ministry of Tourism and Recreation, Government of Ontario. Copyright 1984 by Ministry of Tourism and Recreation. Reprinted by permission.

Aside from the general trends, a number of differences among particular groups are also evident. Although males have traditionally been more active than females, recent surveys indicate little difference between the sexes in this regard. Whereas 57% of Canadian males 14 years and over were active in 1981, the corresponding figure for females was 55% (Canada Fitness Survey, 1983). The most recent Ontario studies (Fitness Ontario, 1984) indicate 63% and 61% participation for males and females respectively in June 1983, and 54% and 51% respectively in November 1983. Similar shifts are also evident in the results of U.S. Gallup polls. Fifty percent of men and 45% of women reported doing some type of daily exercise in 1977, while in 1980 the figures for men and women were 70% and 71% respectively. Although the gap in the numbers of the two sexes who are active has narrowed considerably, the Ontario studies still indicate that more men than women exercise at a high-intensity level. These differences in exercise intensity levels are especially marked in the fall.

Gender differences are also evident in the popularity of different activities. According to the 1983 Gallup study, 18% of American men participated in jogging while 11% of American females did so. In 1977 the corresponding figures were 16% and 7%. According to the Canada Fitness Survey (1983), 56% of Canadian males and 44% of Canadian females participated in jogging, while 16% and 13% respectively were regular joggers. Ontario figures (Fitness Ontario, 1981a) indicate that more females than males participated in swimming (29% vs. 19%), bicycling (18% vs. 11%), and walking (31% vs. 21%). Also more women than men participated in organized exercise classes, 11% versus 9% in June and 17% versus 8% in November 1981. More men than women participated in organized team sports according to the Ontario survey (10% vs. 3% for baseball; 12% vs. 4% for skating and hockey), and tennis was equally popular for men and women with 6% of each participating.

Statistics also indicate that the amount of time an individual spends in physical activity declines with age after adolescence. The November 1982 Gallup Poll reported the following percentages of different age groups to be active daily: 59% of 18- and 24-year-olds; 50% of 25- to 29-year-olds; 44% of 30- to 49-year-olds; 39% of 50- to 64-year-olds; and 48% of those aged 65 and older. A study of jogging yielded similar results: 53% of 13- to 15-years-olds participated in jogging; 50% of 16- to 18-year-olds; 30% of 18- to 24-year-olds; 24% of 25- to 29-year-olds; 12% of 30- to 49-year-olds; 6% of 50- to 64-year-olds; and 2% of those 65 and older.

Comparable information for Canadians is provided by the 1983 Canada Fitness Survey which includes the percentages of different age groups participating in exercise three or more times a week for at least a nine-month period: 75% of 10- to 14-year-olds; 68% of 15- to 19-year-olds; 54% of 20- to 39-year-olds; 47% of 40- to 59-year-olds; 53% of those

60 and older. These statistics, however, are based on cross-sectional data, and can yield only limited conclusions. As McPherson (1984) notes,

> Cross-sectional designs can only indicate differences between age groups at a specific point in time. They can not be used to conclude that changes have occurred because of aging phenomena, or to explain why the pattern varies by age. Nor is this design suitable for determining whether a curvilinear relationship exists between two variables over time. (p. 9)

Researchers interested in studying the topics of aging and physical activity should carefully examine McPherson's discussion in this article concerning the apparent decrease in physical activity with age. For the purposes of this discussion, however, it is important to note only that most older people have both the need for, and the ability to engage in, physical activity. There are a number of psychological and sociological explanations, which might account for the decline in activity with age, but these are incomplete. McPherson clearly identifies the need for further research in this area. He states,

> While chronological age per se does not appear to be a barrier to participation in physical activity, we have yet to derive a complete explanation as to why participation rates decrease by age, and why some elderly persons are active, while most are not. Herein lies a challenge to sport scientists so that policies and programs might be developed and initiated to change existing patterns. (pp. 19–20)

The interrelated factors education, occupation, and income levels are all related to an individual's level of physical activity. The 1977 Gallup Poll indicated that 59% of Americans with a college education participated in daily physical activity, compared to 47% of high school graduates, and 30% of those with only a grade school education. Fifty-six percent of professional and business people reported daily activity, compared to 57% of clerical sales workers and 45% of manual workers. Sixteen percent of those with an annual income in excess of $19,999 reported daily physical activity compared to 10% of those between $15,000 and $19,999, 14% of those between $10,000 and $14,000, 9% of those between $5,000 and $9,999, and 7% of those with an income of less than $5,000 a year.

Information from the Canada Fitness Survey indicated that for Canadians 15 years of age and over the following percentages apply for regularly active people: those with a university degree, 63%; those with a certificate or diploma, 58%; those with a secondary education, 56%; and those with an elementary education, 41%. Sixty percent of people in managerial professional occupations reported themselves to be regularly active, compared to 53% of white-collar workers; and 48% of blue-collar workers. Again, "regular activity" in this survey was defined as involvement at least three times a week for at least nine months.

Marital status also appears to be related to an individual's level of physical activity. In the 1977 Gallup Poll, the percentage of married and single persons who regularly engaged in physical activity were 45% and 60% respectively, while the Canada Fitness Survey showed comparable percentages of 49% and 63%. Although these differences might be partially attributable to the different age levels of the two samples, it is also known that recreational involvement is affected by different life stages and family life cycle stages.

The following excerpt from the 1980 Gallup Poll provides a capsule summary of the demographic characteristics of the active individual.

> Those most likely to say they exercise daily are basically the up-scale socioeconomic groups, the college educated, those in the upper and upper-middle income brackets, and professional, business people, and others in white collar positions. In addition, young people (under 30 years old) are more likely to say they exercise than are their elders, men are more likely than women, and people living in the Northeast and Far West are more likely than middle westerners and southerners. (p. 111)

As mentioned earlier, with respect to interpreting data on the relationship of aging and physical activity, considerable caution must be used when interpreting statistics pertaining to characteristics of those who are active versus those who are not. These particular statistics are based on correlational data; they are descriptive, not prescriptive, and cannot be used in isolation to justify particular program offerings. However, program planners should be aware of these patterns so that they can determine whether or not their program leads to, or reinforces them.

Program planners must also take care not to interpret patterns as reflecting demand when in fact they may simply reflect present supply. To avoid this possibility, it is essential to gather information from people not currently in programs, for if program planning is based largely on input from program participants, a built-in bias may perpetuate existing participation patterns.

Barriers to Participation

The 1983 Canada Fitness Survey and the 1983 Fitness Ontario survey both provide information regarding barriers to participation in physical activities. The Canada Fitness Survey gathered information on people who claimed that they wanted to participate more, while the Ontario study asked respondents for the reasons that they were not active. In both cases, lack of time was by far the most frequently reported obstacle for all groups responding to the survey. In the Canada Fitness Survey, 62% of males and 48% of females reported lack of time due to work, while 22% of males and 15% of females reported lack of time due to other leisure activities. In the Ontario study, 31% of the women and 30% of the men who were active less than once a week reported lack of time as a reason. Although lack of time is the most consistently reported obstacle in a number of studies, it may simply be a rationalization rather than a reflection of reality: The observation that there is never enough time for everything is fairly common. The problem may well be, then, a question of priorities—a question of what a person wants to make time for. Those who exercise likely have no more time than those who do not exercise; nevertheless, this factor should be treated seriously and attempts made to help individuals overcome the problem, whether real or perceived. This might take the form of simply making individuals aware of their priorities, when programs are available, or of how they might schedule things differently. As Goodrick, Warren, Hartung, and Hoepfel (1984) suggest, time management training might also be beneficial: "Participants would learn how to assess their use of time using diaries, how to schedule and set priorities, how to discover the cause of exercise procrastination and to think about what value they place on being physically fit relative to other uses of time" (p. 49).

Lack of interest, motivation, or encouragement ranked second in these studies as obstacles to regular physical activity. In the Canada Fitness Survey, 27% of males and 37% of females reported being "too lazy" or "lack[ing] energy" as an obstacle. Eighteen percent of the male respondents and 16% of the females in the Ontario study reported "the need for more encouragement" as a reason, while 7% of the males and 14% of the females reported "have tried but find it difficult." These reasons indicate the importance of environmental factors and of the programs themselves in fostering participation, a subject which will be discussed further in the final section of this chapter.

Inadequate facilities were another obstacle reported by 20% of both male and female respondents in the Canada Fitness Survey, while 9% of males and 8% of females reported "no skills or no leaders" as a reason for not participating. Six percent of both males and females in the Ontario study reported "no opportunity" as the main reason for inactivity. Physical disability was reported to be an obstacle by 18% and 21% of males and females respectively in the Canada Fitness Survey and 11% and 13% of males and females in the Ontario study. The Ontario study also found that lack of time and encouragement were more important factors for groups under 40 years of age, whereas physical disability became a more predominant obstacle with increasing age.

An interesting element of the Canada Fitness Survey was its breakdown of respondents into active and sedentary groups. Although the same barriers existed for both groups, more of the sedentary group than the active group (30% vs. 22%) indicated a lack of desire to increase physical activity. These results are consistent with the Ontario study, which found that increased involvement in physical activity over the years 1978 to 1981 was entirely due to already active people becoming more active. The number of people who were minimally active (only once per week) actually declined over this period.

The Canada Fitness Survey, regarding possible changes that might encourage activity, found that more females than males placed emphasis on "having a partner" (25% vs. 18%) and "family interest" (20% vs. 15%), while more males than females placed emphasis on "organized sports" (10% vs. 4%) and "activities sponsored by employer or union" (10% vs. 4%). A greater percentage of the people who were already active than those who were sedentary indicated that each of the suggested changes would encourage them to be more active. Further, thirty-two percent of the sedentary group and only 18% of the active group indicated that nothing would increase their activity level. Program organizers who assume that everyone wants to be, and should be, active should remember this. Although injury or illness accounts for some of this inactivity, 39% of the sedentary individuals indicated that the reason that they were not active was injury or illness, 30% of the sedentary individuals indicated that they "did not want to participate more." Although lack of interest might reflect a negative early exposure to sport and physical activity, and might perhaps be overcome by providing a new enjoyable exposure to activity (Department of Youth, Sport and Recreation, 1975), the fact that 32% of the sedentary individuals indicated that "nothing would increase activity" provides little room for optimism. Perhaps resources might better be spent in trying to help those who want to be active rather than trying to convince those who do not.

Reasons for Being Active

Surveys have consistently shown that people participate in physical activity for two main reasons—health benefits and enjoyment (Canada Fitness Survey, 1983; The Miller Lite Report on American Attitudes Toward Sports, 1983; Palm, 1978). Which of the two is more important will depend on the individual, and different programs will probably attract individuals with different priorities. For example, a recreational sport program would probably cater more to enjoyment than to fitness goals, whereas the opposite would be true for a formal exercise program. A participant's goals may have important implications for continued interest in a fitness program. A retrospective study of participants in an employee fitness program (Wankel, 1985) revealed that both continuing participants and dropouts rated health objectives as the most important reasons for joining the program. Continuing participants, however, reported stronger social and recreational interests than did the dropouts. Contrary to this, Olson and Zanna (1982), in a study of commercial fitness clubs, found that subjects who had health- or fitness-oriented goals persisted longer in the program than did subjects who stated enjoyment-oriented goals. These conflicting results might simply indicate that to persist in a program, an individual must receive satisfaction from the program—must realize his or her objectives, whatever they may be.

Initial reasons for joining an exercise program are often not the same as the reasons for continuing (Heinzelmann, 1973; Oldridge, 1982; Perrin, 1979; Wankel, 1985). Whereas initial involvement is often related to a desire to obtain some health-related benefits (e.g., improvement in cardiovascular fitness, loss of weight), continued involvement is more dependent on enjoyment of the program, its convenience, and the social support received. In one of the early studies of factors affecting exercise involvement, Heinzelmann and Bagley (1970) found that the most important reasons for joining an adult fitness program were a desire to feel better and healthier and a concern about reducing the chances of having a heart attack. On the other hand, when participants were later asked what helped them stay with the program, the most frequently reported reasons were the program's organization and leadership (31%), recreational games (29%), and social aspects or camaraderie (26%). Similarly, Perrin (1979) reported that whereas new exercise participants claimed health benefits were their main reason for being active, long-term participants emphasized enjoyment as the primary reason for their continued involvement in physical activity.

Wankel (1985) found that people who dropped out of a program and people who stayed with it both rated health benefits (prevention of cardiovascular disease, loss of weight, reduction of anxiety) as the most important reasons for joining the program, and both agreed on the relative importance of these goals. The participants who continued in the program, however, scored higher than the dropouts on other goals such as competition, curiosity, enjoyment, recreational skills, and going out with friends. The long-term participants reacted more positively to the program than did the dropouts and reported developing a greater degree of friendship with other participants in the program. Social support was related to continued involvement in a program in that continuing participants reported greater levels of encouragement from their families, friends, and work supervisors than did dropouts. Andrew et al. (1981)

and Andrew and Parker (1979) have also demonstrated that family support is important to continued involvement in postcardiac exercise programs. In addition, both the 1983 Canada Fitness Survey and the various Ontario Activity studies provide further evidence that social support is indeed important. Fifteen percent of the males who responded to the Canada Fitness Survey and 20% of the females claimed that family interest would encourage them to be more active, while 17% of the males and 18% of the females said that a friend's interest would do the same. Sixty-three percent of the respondents to the Ontario survey of physical activity patterns (1981a) indicated that the encouragement of family and friends was either "very important" or "somewhat important" to their involvement in physical activity.

Other social factors are also important to involvement. Eighteen percent of the males and 25% of the females who responded to the 1983 Canada Fitness Survey reported that having an exercise partner would encourage them to be more active. Furthermore, 14% of the females, but only 8% of the males, indicated that fitness classes would encourage them to participate more. This result is consistent with the common observation that the vast majority of participants in community fitness classes are women. Males tend either to exercise on their own or go to a club or activity center alone and exercise with the people there, while females tend to prefer going with someone to exercise classes. Later in this paper, when intervention techniques are discussed, more will be said of the importance of social support and how it might be developed.

Withdrawal From Activity Programs

Although dropping out of a program or giving up regular physical activity might appear simply to be the opposite of participation, this is not necessarily the case. Just as there may be substantial differences between reasons for initial involvement and reasons for long-term involvement, so there may be very different reasons for terminating physical activity.

Inconvenience is one of these reasons, and a major one. Forty-two and one-half percent of the people who dropped out of an industrial exercise program (Wanzel, 1977, 1978) gave as their primary reason for doing so the fact that the program was located too far from their home. Over 40% claimed that they dropped out due to the interruption of their daily schedule. Wankel (1985) obtained similar results when he found that inconvenient time and inconvenient location were two of the most important reasons given for withdrawing from an employee fitness program. Earlier research by Teraslinna, Partanen, Koskela, and Oja (1969) and Hanson (1976) indicated that proximity of an exercise program to one's place of work influenced involvement in the program. This evidence of the importance of convenient time and location is consistent with the previously reported observation that "lack of time" is one of the greatest obstacles to increased physical activity. Opportunities for physical activity, then, should not only be easily accessible but must be *perceived* as easily accessible by participants and potential participants. This is one of the strongest arguments supporting the development of exercise facilities and programs at the work-place and in residential communities.

Accessibility and convenience, then, are both necessary if physical activity is to become a popular leisure-time activity. Research has clearly indicated that perceived freedom is the most essential defining characteristic of what people view as "leisure" (Iso-Ahola, 1979; Neulinger, 1974). The nature of the activity itself is not as crucial to the idea of leisure as is the attitude toward that activity. If the individual perceives that he or she is free to choose an activity, and to engage in that activity when it is convenient, then the activity will likely be considered a leisure activity. Another important part of the definition of leisure is that it involve activities that are intrinsically interesting. The enjoyment that the individual derives from an activity must be regarded as an end in itself, and the activity is not viewed as a means to some other, external end.

Studies from the United States (Gallup Poll, 1980), Canada (Canada Fitness Survey, 1983), and Australia (Department of Youth, Sport and Recreation, 1978) all indicate that people participate most frequently in activities that are unstructured and easily accessible. The importance of accessibility is borne out by research on television viewing as a form of leisure activity. Surveys consistently report that, in terms of hours watched, television viewing is one of the most popular of all leisure activities. The degree of enjoyment that people experience watching television, however, is low compared to a number of activities that are participated in less often (Csikszentmihalyi & Larson, 1984).

Convenience, however, does not ensure involvement. Although lack of convenience is definitely a limiting factor and is frequently reported as the reason for withdrawing from an activity, convenience in itself is not a sufficient motivating influence for most people to become involved in a program. Obviously, there are activities that can easily be practiced at home or near the work-place, but that people still do not choose to practice. Clearly, then, further research is needed on other factors that may influence involvement.

A number of studies (e.g., Boothby, Tungatt, & Townsend, 1981; Wankel, 1985) have reported lack of enjoyment or loss of interest as factors influencing withdrawal from a program. The 1983 Canada Fitness Survey reported that "being too lazy" or "lack[ing] . . . energy" and having "no skills or leaders" were obstacles to increased activity. The lack of social support has also been identified as a factor contributing to an individual's withdrawl from sport or activity programs (Boothby et al., 1981; Heinzelmann, 1973; Oldridge, 1982; Wankel, 1985). The following sections will discuss these factors and others which influence interest and involvement in a program.

Attitude Toward the Activity or Program— The Importance of Individual Differences

Intrinsic interest in or enjoyment of an activity is very important to long-term involvement in that activity. Although frequently an individual might initiate an activity program for instrumental reasons such as becoming more fit, if that person is to continue the activity over an extended period of time, he or she must come to enjoy the activity or at least some aspects of it. Evidence indicates that the desire to be healthy is not sufficient motivation to sustain involvement in an activity that is otherwise regarded as aversive. Motivation and attitudes can change, however, and many individuals who begin an activity program with an instrumental purpose come to genuinely enjoy the activity in time.

If involvement is to be long-term, then, the program must be "fun," satisfying, or enjoyable. Although this idea is widely accepted, (e.g., Ferris, 1985; Henderson, 1980), it provides no guidelines on what it is that leads to these conditions. People may generally agree on some of the characteristics of fun, that is, feeling good, or having a smiling face; however, what is needed is information on the conditions that lead to these feelings. Although there are some general guidelines that might be useful and that will be discussed presently, what constitutes "fun" is very much an individual thing. There are always individual differences in what is considered enjoyable or satisfying.

Just as one individual may prefer vanilla ice cream, another chocolate, and another strawberry, while a fourth doesn't like ice cream at all, so it is with physical activity. Different people prefer different activities, different ways of structuring activities, different social groupings for activity, or they may simply dislike activity altogether! Because people are looking for different things, they will gain enjoyment or satisfaction from different programs or different aspects of the same program.

Programs must be flexible enough to adapt to individual interests. As no one program can be all things to all people, there should be made available a variety of programs ranging from formally organized groups to self-designed individual activities. Effective education and/or counseling services can guide individuals into the type of program best suited for them. Some type of personal interview or specially designed questionnaire might be useful in obtaining information about an individual's interests and expectations. Good communication between the leader and the participant must exist if a program centered on the individual is to be effective. Finally, the leader's demonstration of personal interest in the participant is also important to the success of a program (Henderson, 1980).

While the overriding principle for developing a program should be to accommodate individual differences as much as possible, there are a number of general guidelines that can also be useful in designing exercise programs.

Activity Considerations— The Importance of Challenge

Recent research has demonstrated that testing one's skills or competencies against realistic task challenges is important to intrinsic interest in or enjoyment of any activity (Csikszentmihalyi, 1975; Deci, 1975; Iso-Ahola, 1980). Deci posits that humans have a basic need to be self-determining and competent, which results in seeking out challenging situations in which to test and develop one's competencies. Physical activities are one area in which individuals may test their abilities and capacities. The following quotation clearly illustrates how important physical challenge can be to personal development and self-image.

It was a very vivid incident. I had been running for about six months. I was probably running sixty or seventy kilometers a week and I was running with serious runners—although I didn't consider myself a serious runner at the time. I went to a conference and an old friend and I started talking about how I'd started running and we thought "wouldn't it be a real life accomplishment to do something major?" I don't know how it came up, but somebody suggested doing the Boston marathon, and I thought, "Wouldn't it be incredible to run the Boston marathon in the year I turn forty?" . . . Then I started to train really hard. I went out and got my training up to a hundred kilometers a week . . . I did qualify for Boston—by the skin of my teeth— and that was a real high. I mean, I can still remember the agony of that hotel room in Seattle. Just sitting there thinking, "I did it, I really did it." I don't know if I've ever had as deep and strong a feeling of satisfaction as sitting exhausted in that hotel room. With all the Ph.D. and appointments and all that crap, it was almost as if it was the most satisfying thing that I had ever done. I think it was because it was me, it was only me. It wasn't the luck of the draw or the result of all the fortuitous things that can happen in life. I went out and I trained and I did it. (Dixon, 1985, p. 1)

Csikszentmihalyi (1975, 1978) developed the concept "flow" to refer to a state wherein an individual is intrinsically interested in and fully absorbed by an activity. He describes the flow experience as "a contraction of the perceptual field, a heightened self-awareness that sometimes results in a feeling of transcendence, or a merging with the activity and the environment" (1978, p. 213). Csikszentmihalyi has also studied the environmental conditions that are conducive to experiencing "flow," or intrinsic interest. He states "The central requirement seems to be that his or her actions are meeting a set of challenges in the environment" (1978, p. 209). Other key factors identified by Csikszentmihalyi include a merging of action and awareness, a total concentration on a limited stimulus field, a loss of ego, a sense of being in control of one's actions and the environment, and clear, unambiguous feedback.

A number of these features can feasibly be incorporated into activity programs—indeed, a number of them are characteristic of sport situations. Sport participants are well aware of the importance of realistic challenge. Facing opponents who are either too easy to challenge or too difficult leads to boredom or worry rather than to an enjoyable contest. Sport also meets the criterion of providing clear feedback to the person on the results of his or her actions. The rules are clearly specified and success according to these rules is clearly and immediately evident to both participants and observers. The fact that optimum challenge and immediate feedback are intrinsic in most sport situations makes sport an excellent source of enjoyment and intrinsic motivation. Accordingly, many participants enjoy playing a game of tennis, racquetball, or hockey more than they enjoy jogging or attending an exercise class.

There are some general guidelines, however, that might make any activity more enjoyable. What appears to be very dull, monotonous activity to some might be a very interesting and pleasant experience for others. Csikszentmihalyi (1978) outlines how an apparently boring activity can be made more enjoyable by introducing realistic challenges and by providing clear feedback. People who enjoy running or other such activities seem to intuitively incorporate many of Csikszentmihalyi's principles into their approach to activity (cf. Sheehan, 1978). The running experience changes from an aversive to a very positive experience for many individuals, but typically only after they have been running for some time (Keefe & Blumenthal, 1980). The central problem is often how to make vigorous activity sufficiently attractive in the initial stages so as to encourage continued participation until some of the more distant benefits might be realized.

Recent research on youth sports has demonstrated the importance of perceived competence and testing to enjoyment and involvement (Feltz & Petlichkoff, 1983; Roberts & Duda, 1984; Wankel & Kreisel, 1985). Similarly, interview data for adults also indicates the importance of perceived competence to involvement in exercise. One of the greatest barriers to involvement in physical activity as an adult appears to be a youthful, negative experience associated with sport (Department of Youth, Sport and Recreation, 1975; Fitness Ontario, 1981b).

Providing participants with a choice, or at least a perceived choice, of activities also seems important for both enjoyment and involvement. Thompson and Wankel (1980) investigated the effect of perceived choice of activity on attendance in an adult activity program, and found that the perception that one was allowed to select one's own activities resulted in increased participation in a drop-in program. This is consistent with Iso-Ahola's findings (1980) that perceived choice or freedom is fundamental to leisure and to the enjoyment of leisure experience. Similarly, Pennebaker and Lightner (1980) demonstrated that environmental factors which alter the amount of external and internal information available to exercise participants can significantly affect both the performance and enjoyment of the activity. In one study, reported fatigue due to walking on a treadmill was found to be significantly affected by the use of an auditory tape. In a second study, jogging on a cross-country course was found to lead to different reactions from running on a lap course: participants ran a standardized distance faster and preferred running on the cross-country course, and were more bored and frustrated when running laps.

The Social Context

Equally important as the physical environment for enjoyment is the social environment. Research has indicated that the social group can be just as important as the nature of the activity itself, or the place that the activity is performed (Cheek & Burch, 1976). The people with which one engages in physical activity will greatly influence not only the type of activity, but the degree to which one enjoys that activity. A mother who goes swimming with her young children may do so for entirely different reasons than when she goes swimming alone or with an adult friend. Similarly, an individual who jogs alone may have a quite different experience from one who jogs with a good friend or with a group. Most recreational engagements take place in four major social contexts: alone, with friends, with family, and with fellow workers (Alberta Recreation and Parks, 1984).

Although there is no evidence proving as much, it seems likely that these same four contexts would also apply to any physical activity. Evidence does indicate that although most people prefer to exercise with someone else or with a group, some individuals prefer to exercise alone. Heinzelmann and Bagley (1970) found that 90% of the adult male participants in a program preferred to exercise either with a group or with another person. Wanzel (1977) found that for a drop-in program there was a greater tendency for females (62%) than for males (26%) to exercise with a friend or spouse.

People may become involved in group activity for a number of reasons including group identification and commitment, social reinforcement, competitive stimulation, and the opportunity for team activities (Brawley, 1979). Camaraderie among exercisers and the support of the leader have been shown to positively influence continued involvement (Wankel, 1985; Wankel, Yardley, & Graham, 1985). Similarly, the social support of those outside of the program can play a critical role in regular involvement. Heinzelmann & Bagley (1970) found that 80% of husbands whose wives had positive attitudes toward the program had excellent patterns of attendance. The corresponding figure for husbands whose wives had neutral or negative attitudes was only 40%. More recently, Andrew & Parker (1979) and Andrew et al. (1981) have reported that spousal support is an important influence on adherence to an activity program.

Social support from family and others, can provide moral support and reinforcement for desired behaviors. It can also provide more tangible and immediate support in that family and friends can help to accommodate the exercise program by rearranging schedules and other commitments. To encourage such support it is important that the planning of an activity program include other people who are in an important position to influence the participant's attitudes and behavior. In this regard Heinzelmann (1973) states:

> Those persons who serve as significant others should be adequately informed about the nature of the program and be involved in the program on a continuing basis to ensure that their reactions provide social support, and reinforce the individual's participation, rather than influence it negatively. (p. 279)

Spouses, families, and friends might be included in related social events, and mixed-adult or family-based activity programs might also be offered. Because different approaches will have more appeal to different groups, input from the individuals involved should guide the practices for a particular program.

The author and his colleagues have developed a program of structured social support to encourage regular program attendance (Wankel,

1984; Wankel, Yardley, & Graham, 1985). This program includes family, friend, buddy, group, and leader support elements. The program which is typically introduced during the first exercise class is outlined in a self-instructional booklet. Charts are provided to assist participants to monitor their own behavior as well as the social support they receive.

The program has been found to facilitiate program attendance and has been generally well received by both exercise leaders and exercise class participants. Participants have indicated that leader and class support, in-class buddy support, and the class monitoring chart are the most valuable components of the program. Exercise leaders have generally reacted positively to the program and have indicated that it helped to build a positive social environment for the class. Although more research is needed to refine this program, the indisputable importance of social support to any ongoing involvement in a physical activity program argues strongly for the development of such a program.

Decision-Making Approaches to Motivating Participants

One technique that has consistently facilitated attendance of an exercise program is the use of a decision balance sheet (Hoyt, & Janis, 1975; Wankel & Thompson, 1978; Wankel, Yardley, & Graham, 1985). This technique developed by Janis and his associates is designed to assist individuals to think through the benefits and costs of any potentially stressful decision so that their commitment to the decision is strengthened. Typically, the balance sheet is introduced to an individual by an interviewer after the desired change of behavior has been defined (e.g., involvement in exercise) and the potential difficulties of the change acknowledged. The interview may take place either by telephone or in person. The individual is asked to complete a balance sheet of the following categories: utilitarian gains or losses (i.e., instrumental goals for oneself); utilitarian gains or losses for significant others; self-approval or disapproval; approval or disapproval from significant others. After the individual has completed the balance sheet, the interviewer asks that the responses be read aloud, and the interviewer then responds in a positive, supportive manner.

The decision balance sheet technique has been shown to facilitate exercise behavior in regularly scheduled classes (Hoyt & Janis, 1975; Wankel, Yardley, & Graham, 1985) as well as in a drop-in context (Wankel & Thompson, 1978). Wankel (1980) summarizes some of the advantages of the technique.

The fact that the technique is easy to administer and requires only ten to fifteen minutes per individual makes it a viable technique for most exercise programs. Although research on the technique, with respect to exercise, has exclusively used a telephone interview, it would seem that a personal interview conducted at the exercise site might be more advantagous. If administered by a program leader it could allow for more effective reinforcement over time which should provide a more efficient treatment. (p. 28)

Janis (1983) demonstrates how the technique can be used effectively in a variety of decision-making contexts. Furthermore, whereas the technique has been used strictly as an independent technique in the exercise literature, Janis has incorporated it as one of several intervention techniques in an integrated approach to short-term counseling and helping behavior. Researchers in exercise science may also find it desirable in the future to adopt a more integrated approach to exercise motivation. In the absence of any unique theory of exercise motivation, it seems worthwhile to investigate the applicability of Janis' theoretical framework for helping relationships to exercise counseling and leadership.

Conclusion

Participation patterns indicate that more kinds of people are becoming involved in physical activity. Old stereotypes and inhibitions are weakening as more females and older individuals engage in vigorous activity. However, the democratization of sport and activity still has a long way to go. Kirshenbaum and Sullivan (1983) make the following commentary on the "American Fitness Boom":

This boom is in large part illusory. To begin with, it's much more of a factor in some social, economic and age groups than others. The much ballyhooed growth in the number of private health clubs and employee fitness programs has been paralleled by a less widely recognized decline in the availability of traditional fitness programs in parks, recreation departments and, above all, schools. This shift in emphasis from the public to the private sector is reflected in the fitness boom demographics: Participants in it are more likely to be rich than poor, executives than blue-collar workers, white than non-white, college graduates rather than high school graduates, adults than children. The myth that the boom is a democratic phenomenon has been nurtured in part by the gratifying increase in the number of women participating in it. But women have moved into fitness activities largely to the extent that they've advanced into the upper middle class, to which the boom is geared. Poor women, like poor men, aren't exercising; cuts in phys ed programs put schoolgirls on the sidelines just as they do schoolboys. (p. 63)

Although participation in physical activity must be voluntary and freely chosen to qualify as leisure actitivy, and although it is quite likely that some groups and individuals will choose to participate more or less than others, it cannot be assumed that current differential participation rates reflect different choices. It is likely that current participation reflect opportunities and encouragement as well as preferences. If the premise is accepted that all groups can benefit from involvement in physical activity, then those in charge of program delivery should ensure that their program practices are not discriminatory, promoting the involvement of certain groups at the expense of others. An examination of current participation patterns suggests that special attention should be paid to providing physical activity opportunities for lower socio-economic groups, older persons, those with less formal education, and women—especially women of middle age or older.

Regardless of the kind of group involved, the attrition rate from exercise programs is high. Continuing efforts should be made to help individuals stay in programs that they have voluntarily selected. This can be more easily accomplished if the program includes the following services: choice of activities, graduated progression of exercise intensity, initial completion of a decision balance sheet, realistic goals, feedback and individual encouragement, social support both in the home environment and in the exercise program. The key to making these services work is the enthusiasm and sincerity of the program's leader. As Oldridge (1977) notes, "Whether or not the participant's attitudes toward the program will be positive primarily depends on the exercise leader" (p. 87). Participants should also be involved in any decision made to encourage adherence. Trust, personal involvement, and commitment are essential if an individual is to persist in a program.

Recreational programs may have certain advantages in promoting physical activity. Although most adults believe that physical activity is good for them, these beliefs are generally not sufficient in themselves to enable one to remain in an exercise program that is not otherwise regarded as enjoyable, and whose benefits are not immediately attainable. On the other hand physical activity that is regarded as a means of socializing, that is intrinsically enjoyable, or that provides some other immediate pleasure might be used to involve individuals gradually in successively greater levels of activity (Palm, 1977b). Some individuals involved in sporadic recreational activity never engage with sufficient regularity and/or intensity to obtain health benefits (Fitness Ontario, 1981b), but many individuals have moved on to quite intense involvement in physical activity after very modest recreational beginnings.

The use of recreational sport and activity for promoting general health, fitness, and happiness lies at the heart of the Sport For All movement. If success is to be achieved in this mission, an appropriate perception of "sport" must exist. Such a perspective is succinctly described by McIntosh (1980) in his report, " 'Sport for All' Programmes Throughout the World."

> So long as sport is thought of in terms of stereotypes of the Olympic Games, the World Cup Football Competition and other championship events, Sport for All will appear to be a dream that will never come true. Such thinking is misguided and perverse. There are many sports and recreations and many variations on the championship stereotypes which require little equipment and very simple facilities. Many indigenous dances, games and recreations of primitive societies are of this kind. Jogging is an obvious example in the industrialized world and there are many others. A change of attitude is needed in many quarters. Governments would do well to conduct research on what programmes and projects can be organized with whatever facilities are now available as well as assessing what facilities are needed for the future. (p. 55)

References

Alberta Recreation and Parks. (1984). *1980–81 public opinion survey on recreation*. Edmonton, Alberta: Government of Alberta, Recreation and Parks.

Andrew, G.M., Oldridge, N.B., Parker, J.O., Cunningham, D.A., Rechnitzer, P.A., Jones, N.L., Buck, C., Kavanagh, T., Shephard, R.J., Sutton, J.R., & McDonald, W. (1981). Reasons for dropout from programs in post coronary patients. *Medicine and Science in Sports and Exercise*, **13**, 164–168.

Andrew, G.M., & Parker, J.O. (1979). Factors related to dropout of post myocardial infarction patients from exercise programs. *Medicine and Science in Sports*, **7**, 376–378.

Becker, R. (1977). Introduction and development of 'Life Be In It' campaign, *Minister's Paper, Government of Victoria, Melbourne*. Paper presented at the International TRIMM Conference, Paris.

Boothby, J., Tungatt, M.F., & Townsend, A.R. (1981). Ceasing participation in sports activity: Reported reasons and their implications. *Journal of Leisure Research*, **13**, 1–14.

Brawley, L.R. (1979). Motivating participation in the fitness group. *Recreational Research Review*, **6**, 35–39.

Canada Fitness Survey. (1983). *Fitness and lifestyle in Canada*. Ottawa, Ontario: Fitness and Amateur Sport, Government of Canada.

Cheek, N.H., & Burch, W.R. (1976). *The social organization of leisure in human society*. New York: Harper & Row.

Council of Europe. (1976). *European sport for all charter*. Resolution (76)41, Strasbourg, France.

Csikszentmihalyi, M. (1975). *Beyond boredom and anxiety: The experience of play in work and games*. San Francisco: Jossey-Bass.

Csikszentmihalyi, M. (1978). Intrinsic rewards and emergent motivation. In M.R. Lepper & D. Green (Eds.), *The hidden costs of reward: New perspectives on the psychology of human motivation* (pp. 205–216). Hillsdale, NJ: Erlbaum Associates.

Csikszentmihalyi, M., & Larson, R. (1984). *Conflict and growth in the teenage years*. New York: Basic Books.

Deci, E. (1975). *Intrinsic motivation*. New York: Plenum.

Department of Youth, Sport and Recreation. (1975). *Attitudinal study: Fitness and recreation in Victoria*. Melbourne: Department of Youth, Sport and Recreation, Government of Victoria.

Department of Youth, Sport and Recreation. (1978). *Recreation in Australia. An enquiry into the present patterns of participation in recreation. 3.1. Kew.* Melbourne: Department of Youth, Sport and Recreation, Government of Victoria.

Department of Youth, Sport and Recreation. (1979). *Life Be In It: National evaluation study, 1979*. Melbourne: Department of Youth, Sport and Recreation, Government of Victoria.

Dixon, B. (1977). Official opening. In *Department of Youth, Sport and Recreation/Conference Report (Life Be In It). People and Participation* (pp. 1–4). Melbourne: Department of Youth, Sport and Recreation, Government of Victoria.

Dixon, B. (1978, October). *'Life Be In It.' An Australian campaign to involve people in sport and active recreation*. Address presented at the International Trimm and Fitness Conference, Tokyo, Japan.

Dixon, M. (1985). *Psychosocial influences on male involvement in physical activity at mid-life: Theoretical considerations*. Unpublished doctoral dissertation, University of Alberta, Edmonton.

Feltz, D., & Petlichkoff, L. (1983). Perceived competence among inter-scholastic sport participants and dropouts. *Canadian Journal of Applied Sport Sciences*, **8**, 232–235.

Ferris, B. (1985). Let's put some fun back into fitness. *Recreation Canada*, Special Issue, 16–20.

Fitness Ontario. (1981a). *Physical activity patterns in Ontario*. Toronto: Ministry of Culture and Recreation, Government of Ontario.

Fitness Ontario. (1981b). *Physical activity: Reaching adults who know, but don't do*. Toronto: Ministry of Culture and Recreation, Government of Ontario.

Fitness Ontario. (1983). *Physical activity patterns in Ontario—II*. Toronto: Ministry of Tourism and Recreation, Government of Ontario.

Fitness Ontario. (1984). *Physical activity patterns in Ontario—IIa (1982-83 Update)*. Toronto: Ministry of Tourism and Recreation, Government of Ontario.

The Gallup Poll (1961).

The Gallup Poll (1977). Exercise, pp. 1200–1202.

The Gallup Poll (1980). Sports, pp. 109–111.

The Gallup Poll (1983). Jogging/Exercise, pp. 16–17.

Goodrick, G.K., Warren, D.R., Hartung, G.H., & Hoepfel, J.A. (1984). Helping adults to stay physically fit: Preventing relapse following aerobic exercise training. *Journal of Physical Education, Recreation and Dance*, **55**(2), 48–49.

Hanson, M.G. (1976). *Coronary heart disease, exercise, and motivation in middle-aged males*. Unpublished doctoral dissertation, University of Wisconsin, Madison.

Heinzelmann, F. (1973). Social and psychological factors that influence the effectiveness of exercise programs. In J. Naughton & H.K. Hellerstein (Eds.), *Exercise testing and exercise training in coronary heart disease* (pp. 275–287). New York: Academic Press.

Heinzelmann, F., & Bagley, R.W. (1970). Response to physical activity programs and their effects on health behavior. *Public Health Reports*, **85**, 10, 905–911.

Henderson, J. (1980). Rolling out the red carpet with F.I.T.N.E.S.S. In R.R. Danielson & K.F. Danielson (Eds.), *Fitness motivation: Proceedings of the Geneva Park Workshop*. Toronto: Ontario Research Council On Leisure.

Hoyt, M.F., & Janis, I.L. (1975). Increasing adherence to a stressful decision via a motivational balance-sheet procedure: A field experiment. *Journal of Personality and Social Psychology*, **35**, 833–839.

Iso-Ahola, S. (1979). Basic dimensions of definitions of leisure. *Journal of Leisure Research*, **11**, 28–39.

Iso-Ahola, S. (1980). *The social psychology of leisure and recreation.* Dubuque, Iowa: W.C. Brown.

Jackson, J.J. (1979). Promoting physical recreation in social systems. *Recreation Research Review*, **6**(4), 66–69.

Janis, I.L. (1983). *Short-term counseling: Guidelines based on recent research.* New Haven: Yale University Press.

Keefe, F.J., & Blumenthal, J.A. (1980). The life fitness program: A behavioral approach to making exercise a habit. *Journal of Behavior Therapy and Experimental Psychiatry*, **11**, 31–34.

Kirshenbaum, J., & Sullivan, R. (1983). Hold on there America. *Sports Illustrated*, **58**(5), 60–74.

McIntosh, P. (1980). *'Sport for all' programmes throughout the world* (Report prepared for UNESCO, Contract No. 207604). New York: UNESCO.

McPherson, B.D. (1984, July). *Sport, health, well-being and aging: Some conceptual and methodological issues and questions for sport scientists.* Paper presented at the Olympic Scientific Congress, Eugene, OR.

Miller Brewing Company. (1983). *The Miller Lite report on American attitudes toward sports.* Milwaukee, WI: Author.

Neulinger, J. (1974). *The psychology of leisure: Research approaches to the study of leisure.* Springfield, IL: Charles C Thomas.

Oldridge, N. (1977). What to look for in an exercise class leader. *The Physician and Sportsmedicine*, **5**, 85–88.

Oldridge, N. (1982). Compliance and exercise in primary and secondary prevention of coronary heart disease: A review. *Preventive Medicine*, **11**, 56–70.

Olson, J.M., & Zanna, M.P. (1982). *Predicting adherence to a program of physical exercise: An empirical study.* Toronto: Government of Ontario, Ministry of Tourism and Recreation.

Palm, J. (1977a). Participation in physical activity. In *Department of Youth, Sport and Recreation/Conference Report (Life Be In It). People and Participation* (pp. 7–13). Melbourne: Department of Youth, Sport and Recreation, Government of Victoria.

Palm, J. (1977b). Role of sporting and recreation associations in considering ways to increase participation in physical activity. In *Department of Youth, Sport and Recreation/Conference Report (Life Be In It). People and Participation* (pp. 111–118). Melbourne: Department of Youth, Sport and Recreation, Government of Victoria.

Palm, J. (1978). Mass media and the promotion of sports for all. In F. Landry & W. Orban (Eds.), *Physical activity and human well being* (pp. 273–279). Miami, FL: Symposium Specialists.

Participaction (undated brochure). *We're talking about action.* Toronto: Participaction.

Pennebaker, J.W., & Lightner, J.M. (1980). Competition of internal and external information in an exercise setting. *Journal of Personality and Social Psychology,* **39,** 165–174.

Perrin, B. (1979). Survey of physical activity in the regional municipality of Waterloo. *Recreation Research Review,* **6**(4), 48–52.

Roberts, G.C., & Duda, J.A. (1984). Motivation in sport: The mediating role of perceived ability. *Journal of Sport Psychology,* **6,** 312–324.

Sheehan, G.A. (1978). *Running and being: The total experience.* New York: Simon and Schuster.

Teraslinna, P.T., Partanen, T., Koskela, A., & Oja, P. (1969). Characteristics affecting willingness of executives to participate in an activity program aimed at coronary heart disease prevention. *Journal of Sports Medicine and Physical Fitness,* **9,** 224–229.

Thompson, C.E., & Wankel, L.M. (1980). The effects of perceived choice upon frequency of exercise behaviour. *Journal of Applied Social Psychology,* **19,** 436–443.

Wankel, L.M. (1980). Involvement in vigorous physical activity: Considerations for enhancing self-motivation. In R.R. Danielson & K.F. Danielson (Eds.), *Fitness motivation: Proceedings of the Geneva Park workshop.* Toronto: Ontario Research Council On Leisure.

Wankel, L.M. (1984). Decision-making and social support strategies for increasing exercise adherence. *Journal of Cardiac Rehabilitation,* **4,** 124–135.

Wankel, L.M. (1985). Personal and situational factors affecting exercise involvement: The importance of enjoyment. *Research Quarterly for Exercise and Sport,* **56**(3), 275–282.

Wankel, L.M., & Kreisel, P. (1985). Factors underlying enjoyment of youth sports: Sport and age comparisons. *Journal of Sport Psychology,* **7,** 51–64.

Wankel, L.M., & Thompson, C.E. (1977). Motivating people to be physically active: Self-persuasion vs. balanced decision-making. *Journal of Applied Social Psychology,* **7,** 332–340.

Wankel, L.M., Yardley, J.K., & Graham, J. (1985). The effects of motivational interventions upon the exercise adherence of high and low self-motivated adults. *Canadian Journal of Applied Sport Sciences,* **10**(3), 147–156.

Wanzel, R.S. (1977). *Factors related to withdrawal from an employee fitness program.* Paper presented at the American Association for Leisure and Recreation National Conference, Seattle, WA.

Wanzel, R.S. (1978). Toward preventing dropouts in industrial and other fitness programmes. *Recreation Canada, 36*(4), 39–42.

PART 5

Methodological Issues and Future Directions for Research

Several conceptual and methodological problems in the study of exercise adherence remain unresolved and confuse our efforts to answer important questions. Each of the authors of the preceding chapters has carefully scrutinized his or her topic in terms of scientific merit, and several conceptual and methodological problems were noted. In each instance future directions for research and applied interventions have been shaped. This section focuses attention on these concerns in specific and integrated ways to promote future inquiry.

Chapter 15

"Methodology in Exercise Adherence Research" by Kenneth A. Perkins and Leonard H. Epstein examines the behavioral definition of adherence and the measurement of physical activity. The populations sampled and the variables and time frames examined have not generally been standardized from study to study. Follow-ups of spontaneous activity outside supervised settings after interventions and/or after drop-out have been infrequent. This chapter addresses these issues and their importance for past and future research.

Chapter 16

"Epilogue and Future Directions" follows chapter 15 and attempts to summarize the key themes about the state-of-knowledge underlying exercise adherence and public health presented in this book. Important questions and directions for exercise adherence research and promotion are also posed. These include recommendations from the Workshop on Epidemiologic and Public Health Aspects of Physical Activity and Exercise sponsored by the U.S. Department of Health and Human Services and held on September 24-25, 1984 at the Centers for Disease Control in Atlanta, Georgia. Included as the Appendix to chapter 16 are excerpts from the Midcourse Review of the U.S. Public Health Service 1990 Objectives for Physical Fitness and Sports and the Behavioral Epidemiology and Evaluation Branch of the Centers for Disease Control. These excerpts include revised national public health objectives for physical fitness and exercise for the year 2000. Of particular note is the recommendation that the determinants of physical activity be known by 2000. This objective was not included in the original 1990 objectives for the nation, and its inclusion signals the increased need to understand and promote exercise adherence within public health.

CHAPTER 15

Methodology in Exercise Adherence Research

Kenneth A. Perkins and Leonard H. Epstein

A large percentage of people who are prescribed medical treatments for chronic diseases do not comply with these treatment programs (Haynes, Taylor, & Sackett, 1979; Epstein & Cluss, 1982). This problem is not limited to pharmacological treatments, but extends also to behavior change, including adopting an exercise program, controlling one's diet, and giving up smoking. In fact, adherence rates may be even lower for these types of programs than for medication regimens (Haynes, Taylor, Snow, & Sackett, 1979), since the behavioral requirements of these programs are generally much greater than the requirements of drug-taking. The focus of this book is on one type of behavior change that may improve health: increased exercise.

Interest in exercise compliance is guided by one of two general concerns. First, research that is designed to investigate the health benefits of regular aerobic exercise may be hampered by problems with participant compliance. Paramount among these has been the imperfect compliance of subjects to exercise prescription, which reduces differences in exercise levels between the exercise treatment group and nonexercise controls. Such imperfect compliance reduces the power of any clinical outcome study (Goldsmith, 1979).

Despite the problems in getting people to exercise, a growing number of studies have shown that exercise may be beneficial for physical and mental health. Thus research has also been conducted with compliance as the main objective, trying to identify individual difference or treatment variables that may influence compliance. These studies are not as concerned with documenting the medical benefits of exercise as they are with focusing on compliance as the main dependent variable.

This chapter addresses methodological issues that may be important for both types of research, where exercise adherence is a mediator of health benefits, or exercise adherence is itself the primary variable of interest. The methodological issues that are discussed include the following: setting goals for exercise adherence; lack of appropriately and clearly defined criteria for measuring adherence; variations across studies in subject selection; sample size considerations influenced by adherence; incomplete description and heterogeneity of samples; failure to randomly assign subjects to treatment and control groups; inadequacy of control procedures; specificity of adherence intervention effects on exercise versus other health behavior change; and assessment of program and individual cost-benefit analyses. While some researchers have suggested that the term "compliance" be reserved for studies of clinical groups who are prescribed exercise and that the term "adherence" be used in studies of healthy groups who voluntarily seek exercise participation (Oldridge, 1984), these two terms are used interchangeably in this chapter.

Setting Goals for Exercise Adherence

The exercise prescription, which usually includes *frequency, duration,* and *intensity* components, should be that level of exercise which is optimum for producing the desired physiological or psychological benefits *without* exposing the subject to excessive risk of injury (see the following section on cost-benefit). Thus appropriate frequency, duration, and intensity of exercise will vary across subjects depending on age, health, current functional capacity, previous experience with exercise, and the particular benefit that is desired. When cardiovascular fitness is the goal, asymptomatic adults should exercise 3 to 5 times per week, 15 to 60 minutes per session, at 50% to 85% of their maximum functional capacity (American College of Sports Medicine, 1980). However, participants with a low functional capacity (e.g., cardiac patients) may initiate exercise at *higher* frequencies (e.g., 1 or 2 daily sessions) but at shorter duration (5 minutes) and lower intensity (40% to 60% of functional capacity) (ACSM, 1980). On the other hand, if psychological changes are desired, a greater emphasis on nonfitness aspects of exercise may be more appropriate (Simons, McGowan, Epstein, Kupfer, & Robertson, 1985). Therefore, criteria for adherence will vary across subjects, unless the sample is particularly homogeneous, and should vary across time as the functional capacity of subjects improves with physical training.

Unfortunately, many of the health benefits for specific clinical groups attributed to regular aerobic exercise have not been proven (Haynes, 1984). Therefore, before exercise is prescribed and methods to promote adherence/compliance applied, it should be empirically determined that regular exercise for the particular group to be studied holds greater benefits than risks (Haynes, 1984). This point is discussed further in the section on cost-benefits.

Measurement of Exercise Adherence

While several authors have lamented the variability of adherence measures across studies (e.g., Dishman, 1982; Martin & Dubbert, 1982; Oldridge, 1984), surprisingly little attention has been paid to the issue of how best to *define* exercise adherence/compliance, the dependent measure that is of interest in this research area. It is important that this issue be resolved, as differences in measurement of adherence increase variability across studies, thus limiting generalizability. In addition, assuming that the lasting benefits of regular exercise generally require continuous, long-term participation, it would seem critical to develop adherence measures that can be used longitudinally during follow-up after intervention has ceased.

There has been wide variability in operational definitions of adherence in research studies. For example, some studies (e.g., Wysocki, Hall, Iwata, & Riordan, 1979) have used weekly Cooper aerobics points (Cooper, 1977) to define adherence. Other studies have used the number of consecutive absences from exercise sessions as an indication of dropout status (Ward & Morgan, 1984), while some have required attendance at a specified proportion of sessions (Epstein, Wing, Thompson, & Griffin, 1980; Perkins, Rapp, Carlson, & Wallace, 1986). Some have recognized that adherence may be considered a continuous variable and have used the proportion of weeks that an exercise goal was met to indicate degree of adherence (Epstein, Koeske, & Wing, 1984). To complicate matters further, some of these studies have made allowances for "reasonable absences" (e.g., travel, illness) in determining a subject's adherence (Ward & Morgan, 1984). Although independent observation of *all* components of exercise behavior is the only *direct* measure of exercise adherence, it is rarely, if ever, practicable. The following methods, with the possible exception of attendance, must all be considered *indirect* measures of exercise adherence.

Self-Report

The most obvious method of assessing adherence is to ask the subject if he or she is performing the exercise as prescribed. This assessment or self-report, may take many forms. First, there are several possible types of retrospective assessments. These may range from a simple question asking the subject if he or she is adhering, to the use of structured questionnaires (Taylor et al., 1978). These retrospective assessments are often flawed due to the subject's faulty memory and to the difficulty in specifying day-to-day or week-to-week fluctuations in adherence (Washburn & Montoye, 1986).

A better method is the use of self-monitoring in which subjects keep track of their exercise behavior on a continuous basis. Although self-report of the frequency, duration, and intensity of exercise can provide the information necessary to measure adherence, researchers have long recognized that subjects react to the very process of recording their behavior and tend to channel that behavior, at least initially, in socially desirable directions (Kazdin, 1974). Thus it is difficult to use self-monitoring as the only measure of adherence.

Corroboration of a subject's self-report by collaterals (spouse, friend) has seldom been used as a measure of adherence, despite its use in other research involving behavior change (e.g., Best, 1975). Reports from collaterals may help identify the relatively uncommon instances of a subject's deception, but the collateral report is also subjective and thus may suffer from the same problems of inaccuracy and unreliability.

Attendance

Attendance at sessions in formal exercise programs is the most common index of adherence and the most direct method for assessing adherence. Continued attendance presumes continued participation in the exercise program and adherence to the experimenter's specified exercise objectives outside of the session. Infrequent or a complete lack of attendance is assumed to indicate less involvement in, or a cessation of, exercise outside of the program.

At first glance, attendance would appear to be an adequate measure of adherence because of its apparent objectivity and face validity. However, it is adequate only if the exercise performed at these sessions is by itself sufficient to achieve the training objective of the program and if each participant is supervised at every session to determine intensity and duration of exercise. On the other hand, as Oldridge (1982; 1984) has clearly pointed out, decreased attendance at a formal program may not mean decreased level of exercise, but simply that the individual has joined another exercise program or is exercising independently. Finally, attendance by itself provides no information about intensity of exercise and often little information about duration of exercise, both necessary factors in judging the adequacy of exercise behavior in producing the desired training (or health) effect. Surprisingly, even among programs in which subjects exercise on site, adherence to exercise intensity is rarely monitored.

Therapeutic Outcome

The physiological changes that are expected from ongoing participation in exercise are often used to estimate adherence. However, the occurrence or nonoccurrence of physiological changes may be due to a number of factors other than the exercise program itself (Haynes, 1984). For example, Kavanaugh, Shepherd, Pandit, and Doney (1970) found changes in physical fitness for groups who participated in exercise treatment equal to changes for groups who practiced meditation control. In addition, outcome research involving other medical treatments has sometimes shown that patients who do not comply with either treatment or placebo show improvement while a substantial number of those who do comply with treatment fail to show improvement (Sackett, Haynes, Gibson, & Johnson, 1976). Finally, the physiologial effects of training may not be linearly related to exercise participation in that low levels of exercise may not produce a significant change in fitness, while extremely high levels of exercise may produce changes no greater than more moderate levels. Thus, degree of adherence may not be related to degree of change in fitness.

The fallacy of using outcome measures to infer adherence is also demonstrated by the finding of a main effect for compliance (Epstein, 1984; Epstein & Cluss, 1982). Those who comply with any intervention— whether active treatment or inactive placebo—may show more improvement at the end of the intervention trial than those who do not comply. If treatment outcome is proposed as a measure of compliance with treatment regimen, what is one to make of the improvement shown by those complying with an inactive placebo? Assuming that the placebo is truly inactive, other factors unrelated to compliance with treatment must be involved in determining outcome. In addition, the use of outcome to estimate adherence provides no information on frequency, duration, and intensity.

Mechanical/Electronic Methods

Assessment of activity or movement can be made by a variety of mechanical devices, such as the pedometer (Gayle, Montoye, & Philpot, 1977) and actometer (Tryon, 1984), or electronic monitoring devices such as the Large-Scale Integrated Sensor (LSI) (LaPorte et al., 1979) or Caltrac (Montoye et al., 1983). These devices are designed to assess the amount of movement or caloric expenditure integrated over a specific period of time, such as an hour or a day. Despite their promise of objectivity and reliability, these devices generally require individualized calibration for such factors as stride length and proper body location, and they are usually limited to measurement of specific types of activities. For example, some of these devices can be used for walking but not running, and none can be used for bicycle riding.

It should be emphasized that each of these devices, as well as the odometer for bicycle riding, measures only distance over some length of time, which in and of itself provides no information on frequency, duration, or intensity of exercise without concurrent recording of the time of each exercise session. The resulting distance per unit time does provide an indication of intensity averaged over the session but does not account for variations in intensity within the session. Furthermore, each of these devices may be hampered by the same problems of subject reactivity to self-monitoring.

Heart rate may be measured by a variety of devices (e.g., Exersentry) that can be used to assess intensity and caloric expenditure (McGowan, Bulik, Epstein, Kupfer, & Robertson, 1984). These heart rate monitors provide no direct information on duration and frequency of exercise, but may be profitably used in combination with other devices or other measures of adherence.

In sum, it appears that no single measure of adherence is adequate. It may be best to use combinations of measures to obtain the most accurate and reliable information on frequency, duration, and intensity of a subject's exercise. Multiple measures may also provide consensual validation of adherence. For example, adherence to exercise could initially be determined by the combination of frequency of attendance, session performance at desired intensity for desired duration, and self-monitoring of extrasession exercise using an electronic device such as Caltrac or the LSI plus a "guide" for intensity such as the Exersentry Heart Rate

Monitor. Obviously, expense of the device and sophistication of the participant may limit the use of some of these methods.

Sample Size Considerations in Documenting the Effects of Exercise

One of the most important considerations in documenting the health benefits of exercise is the "power" of exercise as a treatment for the particular problem. Power refers to the probability of detecting that a truly effective treatment intervention is more significant than a control procedure. The power of a treatment is a function of both the efficacy of the treatment and the rate of compliance (Goldsmith, 1979). Using blood pressure as an example, assume that exercise lowers blood pressure, on the average, 10 mmHg more than a control procedure, and that the standard deviation of the change is also 10 mmHg. If all the patients adhered to both procedures as prescribed, then observation of significant differences between the treatment and control group would require 23 patients per group. However, if the rate of compliance with each procedure was about 50%, which is more likely, 88 subjects per group—almost four times as many—would be needed in order to observe significant differences between treatment and control. Thus extrapolating from laboratory studies of exercise effects, in which the adherence to exercise is controlled, to clinical outcome studies, where compliance is problematic, is often difficult due to the greater number of subjects required in clinical research.

Subject Characteristics

While it is tempting to generalize about factors that may influence exercise adherence, the results of most of this research are likely to be applicable only to populations that are similar to those from which the particular study subjects are drawn. For example, one important subject characteristic is stage of disease. Oldridge (1982) has demonstrated that people who have disease are more adherent to exercise programs than those who exercise to prevent disease. One-half of the people who exercise to prevent disease will drop out after a year, while the same proportion of people who exercise to treat disease will not drop out until after two years. The effectiveness of specific methods designed to encourage adherence may also be related to certain characteristics of the patient. For instance, educated participants may respond best to complex goal-setting and self-monitoring, while less educated participants may work best with single prompts. Similarly, Perkins et al. (1986) found that an intervention of self-monitoring and positive reinforcement produced increased exercise which was maintained in medical patients but not maintained in psychiatric patients after withdrawal of the intervention. Therefore, careful identification of subject characteristics is important in determining applicability of results.

Aside from demographic descriptors such as age, sex, education, socioeconomic status, and marital status, it is important to note the manner in which the subjects were recruited. Even if groups are matched on all other characteristics, potentially critical differences may still exist among: (a) a group of exercise study subjects who seek to join an exercise group without being solicited; (b) a group whose members respond to an experimenter's recruiting efforts (especially if certain inducements are offered, e.g., monetary reimbursement or descriptions of benefits of exercise); and (c) a group whose members are *prescribed* exercise for a specific health problem. Expectations and motivations may differ substantially between these groups, as well as initial attitudes toward regular exercise. For example, the first group, which incurs some response cost by seeking out a program, will include subjects who already believe exercise is likely to benefit them and are invested in the notion that participation in a formal program will help them initiate and maintain exercise behavior. At first glance, this might seem to be a group which would potentially be the most likely to adhere and the least likely to drop out. However, although these subjects are in fact interested in improving their fitness, it is possible that they have previously been unable to initiate and/or maintain exercise. They would more than likely be exercising on their own, if this were not so, and would not need a formal program. The second group, those responding to the experimenter's recruiting efforts, may be less invested in the notion that they will benefit from exercise in general and the exercise research program in particular, and they may be unwilling to participate at a response cost as high as that of the first group. The third group, those who are prescribed exercise, is the most common subject of research on the effects of exercise in rehabilitation. These subjects may derive substantial benefits from exercise, and the prospect of obtaining such benefits (e.g., symptom relief) may enhance the likelihood of adherence. Indeed, previous research has revealed better adherence for patients who are prescribed exercise than for those who are attempting to prevent illness (Oldridge, 1982). On the other hand, some members of a group prescribed exercise may feel unable to perform (e.g., "cardiac cripple"), or may be resistant to coercive attempts to make them exercise.

Specifying subject characteristics is particularly critical in compliance research that involves clinical populations, especially when the ultimate objective is to determine the treatment effects of exercise on specific clinical disorders. Intervention and control groups should be equivalent with respect to distribution of disorders; stage and/or severity of disorders, including degree of disability; chronicity; current functional capacity; and current and previous exposure to other treatment modes. If diagnosis and determination of severity are unreliable, then substantial heterogeneity could be introduced within and between study groups. Sackett et al., (1976) recommend employing inception cohorts for study whenever possible, or a group of patients who have recently been diagnosed and have no experience with the treatment.

The setting of the exercise program (e.g., worksite, community) and relationships among subjects (e.g., co-workers, neighbors) may also determine the potential influence of intended or unintended social factors on exercise adherence (Cox, 1984; Wankel, 1984). For example, exercise adherence in a worksite exercise program would probably be influenced to some extent by social support within and outside the exercise sessions. Of course, degree of social support for exercise may vary between groups in the absence of previously existing relationships among participants. It would be necessary to equalize the degree of this influence across intervention and control groups, if this potentially powerful factor is not included as part of the experimental manipulation.

All subjects identified and selected should then be *randomly* assigned to treatment and control groups. Assigning to groups on the basis of their characteristics or preferences would obviously complicate the interpretation of observed group differences in adherence outcome. Randomly assigning all subjects to groups should produce groups with a balanced number of subjects who have characteristics that are predictive of adherence or nonadherence. An alternative would be to stratify the initial cohort on the basis of preintervention subject characteristics considered strongly related to adherence, and then forming treatment and control groups matched on those characteristics. This procedure is warranted with a heterogeneous sample that is relatively small in size, as long as the variables that are used for stratification have been demonstrated to predict adherence. But unless these relationships are very strong, stratification may not reduce between-group variability enough to increase the power that is necessarily lost when subject sample size is small.

Once the sample characteristics, selection criteria, and research setting have been carefully identified and subjects randomly assigned, it is important to include in statistical comparisons *all* subjects meeting those selection criteria. One strategy often used when the effects of exercise on disease are being assessed is to reduce the probability of nonadherence by screening procedures and lengthy pretreatment periods to identify and exclude those who are likely to be nonadherers (Taylor, Buskirk, & Remington, 1973). While these procedures are advantageous for evaluating the effects of exercise on disease, they increase the likelihood that subjects remaining in the study may differ from the original sample in substantial ways, thus limiting the generalizability of results. These procedures should certainly not be used in research that focuses on adherence as the end point. Excluding from study the early, preintervention dropouts and those dropping out before completion of the adherence intervention likely would inflate the adherence rate of the remaining study sample.

Defining Treatment and Control Procedures

Identification of the particular components of the treatment and control procedures is essential to determine the active ingredient(s) being manipulated, whether the research is aimed at demonstrating health effects of exercise or changes in exercise adherence. The most common type of exercise outcome study involves the random assignment of subjects to an exercise treatment group and to a no-exercise control group. This strategy may maximize the likelihood of identifying outcome differences, but it does not allow for specification of the variable that determined the differences.

While it is commonly accepted that outcome differences are a result of differential fitness changes in the exercising treatment group versus the sedentary control group, this is often not the case. For example, Kavanaugh, et al. (1970) randomized post-MI subjects to one of two groups, aerobic exercise or meditation. Although very different changes in fitness would be expected, results showed equivalent effects of each procedure on fitness and cardiovascular endpoints. It is plausible that components common to both the exercise and meditation procedures—namely the credibility of the procedure, experimenter attention, and social support—may have had more significant effects on the endpoints than the manipulation of exercise. Rechnitzer et al., (1983) showed no difference in reinfarction rates between high-intensity and low-intensity exercise, despite significant improvements in fitness for only the high-intensity group. Finally, we have shown that aerobic and calisthenics groups matched for attention did not differ in weight loss over a 2-year period even though there were significant differences in energy expenditure for the two groups (Epstein, Wing, Koeske, & Valoski, 1985).

The demonstration of a main effect of compliance (Epstein, & Cluss, 1982; Epstein, 1984) further highlights the importance of accounting for nonspecific influences on outcome. As described earlier, the main effect of compliance is based on research showing that those who are compliant with any prescribed treatment or placebo procedure tend to show greater health changes in the desired direction compared with those who are noncompliant with any intervention. This effect has been demonstrated in five studies in a variety of problems, including heart disease, cancer, schizophrenia, alcoholism, and obesity. The observation that patients may improve based on nonspecific aspects of treatment emphasizes the importance of adequate controls for these factors. In the absence of these controls, effects are often unjustifiably attributed to particular components of the treatment intervention groups.

In general, treatment and control procedures should be equivalent regarding all nonspecific factors (e.g., amount of experimenter contact, social support) to ensure that the experimental comparison is between the presence and absence of the specific treatment component. It is preferable that only one treatment component be manipulated at a time unless the sample is sufficiently large to allow for a complete examination of several components and all possible interactions among components. Otherwise, partialling out the effects due to the specific treatments can be very complicated.

Often, little attention is paid to the development and execution of adequate control procedures because change in the control group is of little interest to the experimenter. The term "control group" carries with it the connotation of "nonintervention" or "hands off." Consequently, most control procedures consist of minimal contact or information only, which are often substantially less involving than treatment procedures. Such control procedures are generally not adequate as the sole control condition but may be included along with other, more appropriate control conditions, as well as with other comparison treatment groups.

Treatment and control procedures should be conducted by the same personnel to eliminate experimenter differences, at generally the same time of year to eliminate seasonal influences (e.g., hot or cold weather), and at roughly the same time of the day and week to allow for equal ease of attendance by participants. Treatment and control procedures should also have equivalent credibility with subjects as legitimate methods of increasing adherence, if the purpose of the intervention is presented to subjects as such. Subjects doubting the efficacy of the intervention procedure they receive would be less likely to adhere from the outset prior to any significant exposure to the procedure (Kazdin, 1980).

A related issue involves avoiding "contamination" between treatment and other groups (comparison and control). Communication about program procedures between members of different groups could expose treatment versus control differences in complexity or experimenter attention which would jeopardize the credibility of control procedures. Such communication could also lead to control participants adopting treatment procedures (e.g., goal-setting) without the experimenter's knowledge and thus complicate outcome comparisons between groups. Avoiding this contamination requires conducting separate intervention sessions in different locations or at different times, or otherwise preventing communication among members of different groups.

Determining Effects of Interventions on Other Health Behaviors

When the target of research is the effects of increased exercise compliance on health outcome in patient populations, it is important to separate the degree of health change due to increased exercise per se from that due to concurrent changes in other health behaviors which might influence the target health outcomes (Blair, Jacobs, & Powell, 1985; Sallis, Haskell, Wood, Fortman, & Vranizan, 1986). For example, compliance interventions with cardiac patients may be successful in increasing exercise behavior, but they also may lead to decreased smoking, changes in diet, or increased compliance with previously prescribed medications. Therefore, observed changes in health cannot be attributed solely to the increased exercise behavior brought about by the compliance intervention, and one would have to monitor changes in these other health behaviors in order to detect this potential confound. Such a generalization of compliance behavior could help explain the main effect for compliance on health outcome previously described. Subjects who comply with placebo or active treatment may be more likely to change other health behaviors and thus show greater improvements in target health outcome. Those who do not comply with placebo or active treatment may be less likely to change other health behaviors and thus may show less or no improvement in target health outcome.

Program and Individual Cost-Benefit

Most researchers concern themselves with the health benefits of increased exercise, but a complete evaluation of adherence should also include the cost-benefit of program participation. However, few researchers report information on the financial cost-benefit of the exercise programs or adherence interventions, which is as important as health cost-benefit in determining the public health value of widespread use of these adherence-improving methods. In other words, researchers ultimately must examine whether or not the allocation of financial resources to exercise adherence programs achieves equal or greater health benefit per dollar than allocation of those resources to some other mode of intervention. Given the relatively small increases in adherence reported by most researchers, determination of program cost-benefit may be an important outcome in the assessment of adherence research.

Improved efficiency and lowered cost-benefit ratio might be obtained by initially employing minimal interventions to increase adherence, and then using more costly and complex strategies afterwards. Such an approach does not need to be taken at the expense of scientific rigor, as the subject sample could be randomly split into three subgroups, with the low-cost interventions presented to two subgroups followed by the high-cost intervention to one of those two subgroups. The third subgroup would serve as controls. This design would test low-cost plus high-cost intervention, versus low-cost alone, versus no intervention. Programmatic research using this approach could lead to the identification and prediction of types of individuals who respond to minimal interventions and also, therefore, those types of individuals requiring more intensive interventions.

The initial compliance distribution (Goldsmith, 1979) may provide some clue as to the cost-benefit of choosing low- versus high-cost interventions, or both, to improve adherence. For example, if the compliance distribution is negatively skewed (i.e., most participants show relatively high adherence, a group mean of perhaps 70%), then the potential benefits (up to 30% improvement for the group) obtained from an intensive intervention are less likely to be worth the high cost, and a minimal intervention is probably more prudent. However, if the adherence distribution is positively skewed (i.e., most participants show low adherence, a group mean of perhaps 30%), then an intensive intervention will most likely be needed either alone or following a minimal intervention.

In a related vein, adherence interventions may be differentially efficacious for improving initial adherence (e.g., increasing adherence from 0% to 30%) versus enhancing adherence in currently exercising participants (e.g., increasing adherence from 60% to 90%). Furthermore, the health changes accrued from these two different increases in exercise adherence may also be different. Thus, cost-benefit analyses should take into account the specific range of improved adherence (e.g., from 0% to 30%, from 60% to 90%) generated by the particular intervention and the corresponding expected health benefits of exercising at that new level of adherence compared to the previous level. It is quite possible that the health benefits of exercising at 30% of full adherence may not be greater than those of exercising at 0%, indicating that an intervention producing such a change in adherence, regardless of its reproducibility and statistical strength, may have no clinical value.

The medical benefits of exercise for the individual must also be weighed against the costs of exercise. The need for this participant cost-benefit evaluation is rather obvious for clinical populations. For example, it has long been advised that cardiac patients be thoroughly evaluated as to their initial functional capacity and examined for the presence of any physical contraindications (e.g., aneurysm) before exercise is prescribed (American College of Sports Medicine, 1986). This precaution applies to any clinical group as well as to certain types of individuals in the general population (e.g., previously sedentary males over 35; those with a history of cardiac irregularities; severely obese individuals).

The need for such an individual participant cost-benefit evaluation does not seem so obvious for participants in the general population who are known to be healthy. However, as previously indicated, expected benefits from regular exercise in this group are generally not very great (Haynes, 1984), thus magnifying the importance of documenting the costs of participating. Exercise prescription, or even recruitment of participants for study, must be made with reasonable expectation of clearly defined benefits. Even those who seek participation in an exercise program without being solicited must be apprised of what benefits they may and may not expect.

The costs of participating in exercise would not be expected to be great for healthy subjects. Yet aerobic exercise—especially certain forms, such as running—does carry some risk of injury (Pollock et al., 1977). Besides the risk of injury, exercise participation exacts costs in terms of time, physical effort (fatigue), money for equipment (shoes, etc.), accessibility (travel to and from exercise site), and convenience (disruptions in daily schedule). Some of these may not be trivial costs for certain people, and are in fact often cited by some program dropouts as reasons for not adhering (Oldridge, 1984). Therefore, prospective participants for exercise adherence research should be: (a) those for whom exercise clearly holds greater potential benefits than risks, and (b) those who agree to participate after being fully and accurately informed of the expected benefits and potential risks of participating.

Once these healthy individuals or clinical patients have been determined to be more likely to benefit than to suffer from exercise and have agreed to participate, it is important to determine the *minimum* compliance standards necessary to achieve the desired benefit. In other words, given the strong relationship between exercise level and injury, why insist on exercise participation at an intensity, duration, or frequency higher than that necessary to produce the target benefit? This is particularly important since maximum treatment gains are often obtained at lower exercise intensities (Haynes, 1984), and adherence is likely to be better at lower intensities, especially at the beginning of an exercise program (Epstein et al., 1984).

Conclusions

Exercise adherence is a limiting factor in determining the effects of exercise in preventing, treating, or rehabilitating people from health problems. This chapter was designed to provide an overview of general methodological issues that may be important in exercise adherence research. One major point that applies to all exercise adherence research is that the goal of exercise adherence must be clearly defined. It is often convenient to state that the frequency, duration, and intensity should be sufficient to produce a fitness effect. However, the amounts of exercise must be related to the benefits expected for the particular disease being studied. In addition, exercise adherence should be advocated only for problems or diseases in which the effects of exercise have been documented.

One of the major problems in exercise research is the measurement of adherence. The only reliable way to assess adherence is to directly measure exercise on site. However, this type of assessment is practical only as short-term assessment during limited programs. More research is needed on the validity of self-monitoring and the utility of mechanical methods. In addition, increased attention should be paid to exercise intensity and duration, as well as to the more typical measurement of frequency.

Considerations concerning research design must include subject characteristics and carefully developed treatment and control procedures. Control procedures must be equivalent to treatment procedures with respect to nonspecific aspects of exercise programs, such as experimenter attention and expectations of success (i.e., procedure credibility).

Finally, one possibility often not considered in evaluating the effects of exercise adherence procedures is a comprehensive assessment of the program and individual participant cost-benefits of exercise. This assessment is very complex, since the efficacy of adherence-improving strategies may vary depending on the population studied, the initial compliance distribution, and the desired health benefit, while there are numerous potential individual costs of increasing exercise. Such an assessment, however, may be more important in determining the usefulness of an adherence intervention than the actual amount of increased adherence produced by the intervention.

Acknowledgments

Preparation of this manuscript was supported by grant HL07560, and by grants HD16411 and HD12520 awarded to the second author.

References

American College of Sports Medicine. (1986). *Guidelines for graded exercise testing and exercise prescription* (3rd ed.). Philadelphia: Lea & Febiger.

Best, J. (1975). Tailoring smoking withdrawal procedures to personality and motivational differences. *Journal of Consulting and Clinical Psychology*, **43**, 1–8.

Blair, S.N., Jacobs, D.R., & Powell, K.E. (1985). Relationships between exercise or physical activity and other health behaviors. *Public Health Reports*, **100**, 172–180.

Cooper, K. (1977). *The aerobics way*. New York: Bantam.

Cox, M. (1984). Fitness and life-style programs for business and industry: Problems in recruitment and retention. *Journal of Cardiac Rehabilitation*, **4**, 136–142.

Dishman, R. (1982). Compliance/adherence in health-related exercise. *Health Psychology*, **1**, 237–267.

Epstein, L. (1984). The direct effects of compliance on health outcome. *Health Psychology*, **3**, 385–393.

Epstein, L., & Cluss, P.A. (1982). A behavioral medicine perspective on adherence to long-term medical regimens. *Journal of Consulting and Clinical Psychology*, **50**, 950–971.

Epstein, L., Koeske, R., & Wing, R. (1984). Adherence to exercise in obese children. *Journal of Cardiac Rehabilitation*, **4**, 185–195.

Epstein, L., Wing, R., Koeske, R., & Valoski, A. (1985). A comparison of lifestyle exercise, aerobic exercise, and calisthenics on weight loss in obese children. *Behavior Therapy*, **16**, 345–356.

Epstein, L., Wing, R., Thompson, J.K., & Griffin, W. (1980). Attendance and fitness in aerobic exercise. *Behavior Modification*, **4**, 465–479.

Gayle, R., Montoye, H., & Philpot, J. (1977). Accuracy of pedometers for measuring distance walked. *Research Quarterly*, **48**, 632–636.

Goldsmith, C. (1979). The effect of compliance distributions on therapeutic trials. In R.B. Haynes, D.W. Taylor, & D.L. Sackett (Eds.), *Compliance in health care* (pp. 297–308). Baltimore: Johns Hopkins Press.

Haynes, R. (1984). Compliance with health advice: An overview with special reference to exercise programs. *Journal of Cardiac Rehabilitation*, **4**, 120–123.

Haynes, R., Taylor, D., & Sackett, D. (1979). *Compliance in health care*. Baltimore: Johns Hopkins Press.

Haynes, R., Taylor, D., Snow, J., & Sackett, D. (1979). Annotated and indexed bibliography on compliance with therapeutic and preventive regimens. In Haynes, R., Taylor, D., & Sackett, D. (Eds.), *Compliance in health care* (pp. 337–474). Baltimore: Johns Hopkins Press.

Kavanaugh, T., Shephard, R., Pandit, V., & Doney, H. (1970). Exercise and hypnotherapy in the rehabilitation of the coronary patient. *Archives of Physical Medicine and Rehabilitation*, **51**, 578–587.

Kazdin, A. (1974). Self-monitoring and behavior change. In M.J. Mahoney & C.F. Thoresen (Eds.), *Self-control: Power to the person* (pp. 218–246). Monterey: Brooks/Cole.

Kazdin, A. (1980). *Research design in clinical psychology*. New York: Harper & Row.

Laporte, R., Kuller, L., Kupfer, D., McPartland, R., Matthews, G., & Caspersen, C. (1979). An objective measure of physical activity in epidemiological research. *American Journal of Epidemiology*, **109**, 158–168.

Martin, J., & Dubbert, P. (1982). Exercise applications and promotion in behavioral medicine: Current status and future directions. *Journal of Consulting and Clinical Psychology*, **50**, 1004–1017.

McGowan, C., Bulik, C., Epstein, L., Kupfer, D., & Robertson, R. (1984). The use of the Large-Scale Integrated Sensor (LSI) to estimate energy expenditure. *Journal of Behavioral Assessment*, **6**, 51–57.

Montoye, H., Washburn, R., Servais, S., Ertl, A., Webster, J., & Nagle, F. (1983). Estimation of energy expenditure by a portable accelerometer. *Medicine and Science in Sports and Exercise*, **15**, 403–407.

Oldridge, N. (1982). Compliance and exercise in primary and secondary prevention of coronary heart disease: A review. *Preventive Medicine*, **11**, 56–70.

Oldridge, N. (1984). Adherence to adult exercise fitness programs. In J.D. Matarazzo, St.M. Weiss, J.A. Herd, N.E. Miller, & Sh.M. Weiss (Eds.), *Behavioral Health* (pp. 467–487). Somerset, NJ: Wiley & Sons.

Perkins, K.A., Rapp, S.R., Carlson, C.R., & Wallace, C.E. (1986). A behavioral intervention to increase exercise among nursing home residents. *The Gerontologist*, **26**, 479–481.

Pollock, M., Gettman, L., Milesis, C., Bah, M., Durstine, L., & Johnson, R. (1977). Effects of frequency and duration of training on attrition and incidence of injury. *Medicine and Science in Sports and Exercise*, **9**, 31–36.

Rechnitzer, P., Cunningham, D., Andrew, G., Buck, C., Jones, N., Kavanaugh, T., Oldridge, N., Parker, J., Shepherd, R., Sutton, J., & Donner, A. (1983). Relation of exercise to the recurrence rate of myocardial infarction in men: The Ontario exercise-heart collaborative study. *American Journal of Cardiology*, **51**, 45–69.

Sackett, D., Haynes, R., Gibson, E., & Johnson, A. (1976). The problem of compliance with antihypertensive therapy. *Practical Cardiology*, **2**, 35–39.

Sallis, J.F., Haskell, W.L., Wood, P.D., Fortmann, S.P., & Vranizan, K.M. (1986). Vigorous physical activity and cardiovascular factors in young adults. *Journal of Chronic Diseases*, **39**, 115–120.

Simons, A., McGowan, C., Epstein, L., Kupfer, D., & Robertson, R. (1985). Exercise as a treatment for depression: An update. *Clinical Psychology Review*, **5**, 553–568.

Taylor, H., Buskirk, E., & Remington, R. (1973). Exercise in controlled trials of the prevention of coronary heart disease. *Federation Proceedings*, **32**, 1623–1627.

Taylor, H., Jacobs, D., Schucker, B., Knudsen, J., Leon, A., & DeBacker, G. (1978). A questionnaire for the assessment of leisure time physical activity. *Journal of Chronic Diseases*, **31**, 741–755.

Tryon, W. (1984). Measuring activity using actometers: A methodological study. *Journal of Behavioral Assessment*, **6**, 147–153.

Wankel, L. (1984). Decision-making and social support strategies for increasing exercise involvement. *Journal of Cardiac Rehabilitation*, **4**, 124–135.

Ward, A., & Morgan, W. (1984). Adherence patterns of healthy men and women enrolled in an adult exercise program. *Journal of Cardiac Rehabilitation*, **4**, 143–152.

Washburn, R.A., & Montoye, H.J. (1986). The assessment of physical activity by questionnaire. *American Journal of Epidemiology*, **123**, 563–576.

Wysocki, T., Hall, G., Iwata, B., & Riordan, M. (1979). Behavioral management of exercise: Contracting for aerobic points. *Journal of Applied Behavior Analysis*, **12**, 55–64.

CHAPTER *16*

Epilogue and Future Directions

Rod K. Dishman

Predominant strategies used to study exercise adherence have been limited because they have not described exercise behavior as a process. It may be as reasonable to continue the search for invariant (i.e., generalizable) influences on exercise adherence by describing more transient behavioral processes common to exercise settings than to focus exclusively on invariant traits from various populations and programs on the assumption that they operate in a common way across diverse settings, participants, and time periods. Suggestions were advanced throughout this book for encouraging a process approach that entertains the importance of interactions among person and setting characteristics, physical activity itself, time stages during which different behavioral influences may predominate, and the possible influence of behavioral and psychological states on chronic behavior patterns.

Epilogue

It has become increasingly clear that physical activity and exercise consist of various behaviors and subcomponents that are more complex than many other health-related behaviors. Studies repeatedly show that adoption (initiating) and maintenance (adherence) of an exercise routine are independent acts and are associated with different determinants. The search for effective interventions to increase exercise adherence among sedentary and low-active segments of the population will likely benefit from creating new models or selecting existing models that best explain specific exercise behaviors (e.g., type and intensity of activity) and their subcomponents (e.g., deciding to begin, actually adopting a routine, maintaining or adhering, planning for setbacks or relapse, the ability to modify original plans). These models will also explain general exercise (e.g., supervised attendance, compliance with exercise prescription, fitness gains, or free-living energy expenditure) and enabling factors (e.g., time management, barriers such as inconvenient scheduling and facilities, seasonal changes) that mediate the expression of interest and intention into observable acts.

Application of general models of behavior to exercise adherence adopts a deductive approach. This should be useful because exercise shares common dimensions with many other behaviors. Because exercise also has uniqueness (e.g., exertion), conceptual and practical views for its explanation should also benefit from inductive approaches that integrate empirical data from exercise studies into new conceptual frames. These may or may not overlap with theories of other behaviors. This need for exercise adherence theory stems from the limited success of previous approaches toward predicting exercise dropouts and using behavior modification principles to increase exercise adherence.

Predicting Dropouts

The use of entry profiles to predict adherence has been a prevalent approach, but participant characteristics alone have not given rise to predictions that are accurate enough for practical use. Reports by Oldridge and his colleagues (Oldridge et al., 1983) from the Ontario Exercise Heart Collaborative Study (OEHCS) of 751 post-myocardial infarction (MI) patients have been the most impressive to date. In analyses at several different times up to three years after program entry, blue-collar work status and smoking remained strongly associated with dropout. After two years (Oldridge, 1979), a blue-collar worker who smoked and was inactive in his leisure time had an 80% likelihood of dropping out. If he also was employed in light occupational work, this increased to a 95% chance of dropping out. Yet the predictive use of these findings is actually limited. Only 57 of the original 751 patients fit the first profile, while just 22 fit the latter. Because there were 335 dropouts, these models were useful only for a select few, and at best accounted for less than 7% of all dropouts. Moreover, whether or not these findings can be generalized to other samples is not known, although smoking has been associated with dropout in several similar programs.

We also have had modest success in using entry characteristics. A light, lean body composition and a low exercise tolerance test were stable predictors of adherence in two random groups of 181 male patients drawn from a 5-year sample at the University of Wisconsin-Madison (Dishman, 1981); their predictive use in distinguishing between those who dropped out in one month and those who stayed for more than one year was 30% better than chance. But only half of the adherence rates in these extreme groups was explained and the prediction rates for other time periods were about 25%. We later boosted the prediction accuracy in a 20-week study to nearly 80% by adding a psychological test of self-motivation (Dishman & Ickes, 1981). Though other studies have also shown body weight, body fat, and self-motivation to be independent correlates of adherence, an equal number show no relationships. Ward & Morgan (1984) found that our original equation predicted adherence by both males and females in their program with nearly 90% accuracy, but it was worse than a chance guess for predicting dropout.

Samples vary in the presence and in the range of scores on medical, fitness, and sociodemographic parameters. Oldridge's findings among post-MI patients that exercise angina (Oldridge et al., 1983) and multiple recurrences of an infarction (Oldridge, 1979) were associated with dropout, has been replicated in another post-MI sample (Kavanagh et al., 1980) but it obviously could not be expected to be seen in apparently healthy groups. In fact, our own study (Dishman, 1981) of a heterogeneous cardiac prevention and rehabilitation group including healthy, at-risk, and documented coronary artery disease (CAD) patients showed no association between MI occurrence and adherence. Further, our observation that the dropouts were more likely to be disease free, with longer treadmill time, would not likely be seen in samples where all subjects are diseased and thus show a restricted range on entry treadmill performance. Similarly, while several studies agree with our findings that excess body weight correlates with dropout, this cannot be seen in samples of only lean or only obese subjects. Likewise, several studies have not replicated Oldridge's finding of blue-collar work status as a correlate of dropout, but many exercise rehabilitation programs have a low proportion of blue-collar patients.

A summary of predictive approaches using entry profiles suggests that select groups of patients, in certain types of programs, who are prone to adhere or to drop out can be identified with fairly high accuracy. But biomedical profiles explain only a portion of total dropout or adherence, and their applicability to other programs and groups of patients remains undemonstrated. A recent comprehensive test of entry traits as adherence predictors by Gale, Eckhoff, and Mogel (1984) confirms this, and illustrates the practical problem of predicting a behavior that has an a priori occurrence likelihood of 50% (the typical dropout rate) using tests that have low behavioral sensitivity.

Planning Interventions

Although exercise adherence has neither been predicted nor explained, there remains hope that it can be reliably controlled. In case-controlled comparisons, behavior modification and cognitive behavior modification techniques seem equally effective when used singly or in combination, but their specific effects, beyond any form of social reinforcement, are not known. Collectively, a 10% to 25% increase in frequency of activity can be expected, but this has been shown mainly for short time periods (3 to 10 weeks) and the few follow-up studies suggest this effect is largely lost within 6 months to a year after the intervention is removed. The usefulness of behavior change for increasing intensity and duration of activity remains undemonstrated, but available estimates (Dishman, 1987; Cantwell, Watt, & Piper, 1979) show that the increased volume of activity due to behavioral interventions is less than one-half of the 1,500 to 2,000 kcal per week needed to reliably increase aerobic fitness, reduce CAD risk factors, and lower risk for mortality.

Much more must be learned about how alternative activity plans might offset self-regulatory failures in those individuals who are behaviorally unable to adapt to the fitness model of healthy exercise, and about those who may benefit by health improvements from other forms of physical activity. A recent 12-month community surveillance study of 1,400 Northern California adults (Sallis et al., 1986) showed that over twice as many added more moderate activity to their daily routines such as walking or stair climbing instead of riding (26% of men and 33% of women), than adopted vigorous activity such as planned fitness activity (5% of women and 11% of men). While 50% quit vigorous exercise during the year, just 25% to 35% stopped their moderate activity routines. An equal number reported increased (9%) and decreased (7%) global activity (leisure plus work), and these changes were associated with altered physiological risk factors for CAD.

Future Prospects

First, while the apparent goal is to control the dropout rate, the prevailing outcome-oriented research philosophy in exercise adherence research has in effect described, not predicted or explained, exercise behavior. The history of science shows the goal of control is an elusive one if it precedes prediction and explanation. Second, most of today's essential questions were actually posed by the very earliest studies of exercise compliance. They have resurfaced not so much because research cannot answer them, but because they have largely gone unasked. Third, as happens in many areas, the progress made has not been in solutions to the problem but in a clearer definition of what the problem is: How is exercise adherence measured? What influences are reliable and which interventions may prove most fruitful? What portion of nonadherence can be changed? What portion should be changed? Finally, it becomes clearer that the questions of exercise adherence will most likely be resolved, and must be asked, not only in the settings of supervised exercise but in the broader context of public health where exercise is largely a personal choice. This will necessitate consideration of the impact of major areas of health intervention on physical activity patterns throughout the population. These areas include the following: political/social (policy makers and citizen groups); lifestyle (behavioral scientists, teachers, mass media); health programs (community, worksite, and national service agencies); and the medical office (physicians, nurses, and allied health professionals).

Recent findings in exercise epidemiology are, in fact, encouraging. They suggest that patterns of free-living physical activity in the population can be increased. Although activity levels decline with age, recent analyses (Powell and Paffenbarger, 1985) from the Harvard Alumni study discussed by Paffenbarger and Hyde in chapter 2 reveal this activity decline can in part represent an age group effect (i.e., cross-sections of earlier born people are less active) rather than a birth-cohort effect (individuals born in the same year individually decline as they age). As Table 1 shows, Harvard alumni who were followed individually from year to year do not show the decline in activity seen for cross-sectional age group comparisons.

Recommendations for Research

As part of the implementation plans to attain the Public Health Service physical fitness and exercise goals for 1990, The Workshop on Epidemiologic and Public Health Aspects of Physical Activity and Exercise was sponsored by the U.S. Department of Health and Human Services and held on September 24–25, 1984 at the Centers for Disease Control in Atlanta, Georgia.[1]

---

[1]Excerpts from the Midcourse Review of The U.S. Public Health Service 1990 Objectives for Physical Fitness and Exercise, including objectives for the year 2000, are in the Appendix.

Table 1   Changes Over Time in Specific Physical Activities Among Harvard Alumni by Cross-Sectional Age Group and by Cohort, 1962–77

Activity and survey year	Percentage of subjects by age						
	35–39	40–44	45–49	50–54	55–59	60–64	65–69
Climbed 50 or more steps per day:							
1962	67	68	a 57				
1966	68	70	64	67	65	65	58
1977		66	69	62	60	60	57
Walked 5 or more blocks per day:							
1962	78	76	a 78				
1966	77	74	75	77	79	79	76
1977		72	75	75	72	77	73
Participated in any sport activity:[b]							
1962	50	52	a 38				
1966	54	52	55	54	47	38	34
1977		91	93	88	85	82	81
Participated in vigorous sport activity:[b]							
1962	38	38	a 27				
1966	46	42	40	38	26	18	14
1977		83	82	70	71	62	55

Note. From "Workshops on Epidemiologic and Public Health Aspects of Physical Activity and Exercise: A Summary" by K.E. Powell and R.S. Paffenbarger, Jr., 1985, Public Health Reports, 100, p. 125. Copyright 1985 by U.S. Public Health Service. Reprinted by permission. [a]Based on less than 10 subjects. [b]Sports activity included sports generally considered to require comparatively little energy output (for example, bowling, golf, yardwork). Vigorous sport activity included sports generally considered to require more energy (for example, running, skiing, swimming).

The goal of the workshop was to provide summaries of the status of knowledge about, and recommendations for future research on, the relationships between physical activity, public health, and epidemiology (Powell & Paffenbarger, 1985). After review and discussion by a panel of 33 experts from the fields of public health and exercise science, the following recommendations and questions for the future study of exercise adherence were agreed upon as important ones for public health (Dishman, Sallis, & Orenstein, 1985, pp. 168–170):

First, there remains a need to conceptualize and in a general way rank determinants according to priority. Our knowledge will continue to benefit from replication, extension, and direct comparison of factors implicated by previous studies. Therefore, we need to:

1. Determine factors that lead to the decision or intention to begin a physical activity program.
2. Specify the cognitive and behavioral skills or physical abilities needed to initiate and maintain a physical activity program.
3. Identify and put in priority the critical interactions, within and among personal and environmental factors, that determine a person's willingness and ability to be active.
4. Determine the degree to which influences on participation may vary for different activity behaviors.
5. Determine the behavioral significance of perceived barriers to activity and, likewise, excuses for inactivity.
6. Examine the degree to which known health-risk factors precede or follow inactivity, and why.
7. Determine how perceived exertion during and after activity influences future activity.

Second, as our general knowledge grows, it will also be necessary to specify major activity determinants for certain populations and settings. Therefore, we need to:

8. Study how activity determinants differ according to a person's age, gender, ethnicity, socioeconomic level, and health or fitness status.
9. Investigate possible differences in determinants of lifestyle (routine leisure) and vigorous (exercise for fitness) activities.
10. Establish whether determinants of participation in supervised and unsupervised programs differ.

11. Determine if history of previous activity or sports, family or peer influences, socioeconomic status, education level, and age represent true influences on activity or if these represent a selection bias.
12. Determine who is most likely to follow and benefit from programs of vigorous exercise, from routine physical activity, and from activity modified for disabling conditions.
13. Investigate the extent to which physical activity and other health behaviors may reinforce or negate each other.

Third, advancing age and elapsed time after initial adoption of an activity are among the most reliable predictors of inactivity. Thus, it seems likely that past activity environments and experiences are strong influences on present and future participation. Yet, little is now known in these areas. Therefore, we need to:

14. Examine when and how preference for types and intensities of activity are formed and how they influence future activity.
15. Establish what determinants at one age (for example, childhood) can be altered to increase the likelihood that the person will be active at another age (for example, adulthood).
16. Determine if certain types of individuals are predisposed to activity or inactivity and if this changes at definable stages across the lifespan.
17. Examine why activity seems to diminish with advancing age and what might be done to retard this decline.
18. Investigate how self-motivation and intrinsic reinforcements for regular participation develop, what the time course is for their impact, and whether it is realistic to change them to increase activity.
19. Determine if definable stages or patterns of participation exist in which different determinants operate or vary in their influence, making specific interventions uniquely effective at different times.

To address the preceding questions and to provide guidance to those planning intervention programs, the following recommendations for research and program design are offered.

1. Most population studies of determinants are retrospective and cross-sectional. Current knowledge suggests

that a longitudinal population study should be conducted. A representative sample (including all sex, age, ethnic, socioeconomic, health, and regional groups) should be assessed at intervals of 3 to 4 years. A natural history of activity and factors associated with changing patterns will be useful, but measures should be chosen based on probable relevance to interventions targeted for people and environments.

2. Small descriptive and experimental studies, testing the application of behavioral science theories to determinants of activity habits, should be carried on concurrently. These studies should focus on selected groups (such as children, blue-collar workers, working mothers, Hispanics, blacks, Asians, those with high-risk health profiles, and the habitually active), or should test intervention hypotheses, assess the interaction of selected determinants, or validate survey reports of activity and its determinants.

3. Study questions, variables, and measurement methods should be standardized, or their disparities quantified and reconciled, to allow researchers to examine whether the results of studies of behavioral patterns and determinants can be generalized across settings, activities, and population segments. Standardized questions concerning determinants should be added to population surveys.

4. Most studies have been guided by applied concerns rather than by theory. Although some attempts to conceptualize existing evidence have helped form predictive hypotheses, there is a need to continue bridging applied questions with theory. This is important if physical activity, exercise, and fitness are to be examined in relation to other health behaviors and outcomes. Standardized theories and technologies will allow us to determine if common determinants exist or if models unique to physical activity are needed.

References

Cantwell, J.D., Watt, E.W., & Piper, J.H. (1979). Fitness, aerobic points and coronary risk. *The Physician and Sportsmedicine, 7*(8), 79–84.

Dishman, R.K. (1981). Biologic influences on exercise adherence. *Research Quarterly for Exercise and Sport, 52*, 143–159.

Dishman, R.K. (1987). Exercise adherence and habitual physical activity. In W.P. Morgan & S.N. Goldston (Eds.), *Exercise and mental health* (pp. 55-83). Washington, DC: Hemisphere Publishing.

Dishman, R.K., & Ickes, W. (1981). Self-motivation and adherence to therapeutic exercise. *Journal of Behavioral Medicine, 4*, 421-438.

Dishman, R.K., Sallis, J.F., & Orenstein, D. (1985). The determinants of physical activity and exercise. *Public Health Reports, 100*(2), 158-171.

Gale, J.B., Eckhoff, W.T., & Mogel, S.F. (1984). Factors related to adherence to an exercise program for healthy adults. *Medicine and Science in Sports and Exercise, 16*, 544-549.

Kavanagh, T., Shephard, R.J., Chisholme, A.W., Qureshi, S., & Kennedy, J. (1980). Prognostic indexes for patients with ischemic heart disease enrolled in an exercise-centered rehabilitation program. *American Journal of Cardiology, 44*, 1230-1240.

Oldridge, N.B. (1979). Compliance of post myocardial infarction patients to exercise programs. *Medicine and Science in Sports and Exercise, 11*, 373-375.

Oldridge, N.B., Donner, A., Buck, C.W., Jones, N.L., Andrew, G.A., Parker, J.O., Cunningham, D.A., Kavanagh, T., Rechnitzer, P.A., & Sutton, J.R. (1983). Predictive indices for dropout: The Ontario exercise heart collaborative study experience. *American Journal of Cardiology, 51*, 70-74.

Powell, K.E., & Paffenbarger, R.S., Jr. (1985). Workshop on epidemiologic and public health aspects of physical activity and exercise. *Public Health Reports, 100*, 118-126.

President's Council on Physical Fitness and Sports and Behavioral Epidemiology and Evaluation Branch, Division of Health Education, Center for Health Promotion and Education, Centers for Disease Control. (1985). *Midcourse Review, 1990 Physical Fitness and Exercise Objectives* (1986-636-688 Region 4). Washington, DC: U.S. Government Printing Office.

Sallis, J.F., Haskell, W.L., Fortmann, S.P., Vranizan, K.M., Taylor, C.B., & Solomon, D.S. (1986). Predictors of adoption and maintenance of physical activity in a community sample. *Preventive Medicine, 15*, 331-341.

Ward, A., & Morgan, W.P. (1984). Adherence patterns of healthy men and women enrolled in an adult exercise program. *Journal of Cardiac Rehabilitation, 4*, 143-152.

APPENDIX

Physical Fitness and Exercise Objectives for the Year 2000*

This document summarizes the current status of the 1990 Physical Fitness and Exercise Objectives and proposes objectives for the year 2000. The document was prepared in draft form by The President's Council on Physical Fitness and Sports and the Behavioral Epidemiology and Evaluation Branch of the Centers for Disease Control. Over 300 copies were sent for comment to public and private agencies, concerned citizens, and experts in the field. Open discussions were held at national meetings of the American Alliance for Health, Physical Education, Recreation and Dance, and the American College of Sports Medicine. A third open discussion was held primarily for representatives of interested federal agencies. The original draft has been revised based on the oral and written input from many people who received a copy and/or attended an open meeting.

Eleven of the 223 1990 Objectives are in the area of physical fitness and exercise (PFE). Available data indicate that 2 of the 11 are likely to be achieved by 1990; 4 are not likely to be achieved; 2 have insufficient data to predict; 1 is not quantifiable; and 2 have 2 distinct components, (1 component of each of those objectives will be achieved, and the other component of each has insufficient data to predict) (Table 1).

*From *Midcourse Review, 1990 Physical Fitness and Exercise Objectives* (pp. 4–6, 72–83) by President's Council on Physical Fitness and Sports and Behavioral Epidemiology and Evaluation Branch, Division of Health Education, Center for Health Promotion and Education, Centers for Disease Control (1986-636-688 Region 4), 1985, Washington, DC: U.S. Government Printing Office. Reprinted by permission.

Table 1 Current Status and Projected Likelihood of Achieving the 1990 Physical Fitness and Exercise Objectives

Category	Objectives	Best estimate of current status 1990	Likelihood of achievement by 1990
a. Appropriate physical activities, ages 10–17	90%	66% (No trend data)	Poor
b. Participation in daily school physical education	60%	36% (Stable over 10 years)	Poor
c. Appropriate physical activities, ages 18–64	60%	10–20% (No trend data)	Poor
d. Appropriate physical activities, ages 65+	50%	10–20% (No trend data)	Poor
e. Knowledge about exercise for cardiovascular fitness	70%	70%-duration and frequency 50%-intensity	Good
f. Exercise history by primary care physicians	50%	47% (Local surveys)	Good

(Cont.)

Table 1 (Cont.)

Category	Objectives	Best estimate of current status 1990	Likelihood of achievement by 1990
g. Fitness programs at worksites of 500 or more employees	25%	Data not available	Unknown
h. (1) Practical fitness test for youth, ages 10–17	(1) Establish one	(1) Three available	(1) Achieved
(2) Participation in test	(2) 70%	(2) Data not available	(2) Unknown
i. Long- and short-term health effects	Will be known and evaluable	Data vary with specific health effect	Not quantifiable; progress will be made; questions will remain
j. Fitness program effects on job performance and health care costs	Data will be available	Data not available	Unknown
k. (1) Monitor trend of activities	(1) Data will be available	(1) Baseline data are available	(1) Good
(2) Use of public programs and community facilities	(2) Data will be available	(2) Data not available	(2) Unknown

One of the most firmly established health benefits resulting from in-creasing levels of physical activity is a reduced risk of coronary heart dis-ease (CHD). The 11 PFE objectives for 1990 assume that the types of physical activity that reduce the risk of CHD are the same as those that produce cardiorespiratory fitness. Therefore, the objectives have been designed to encourage activities known to produce cardiorespiratory fit-ness and having the following four characteristics:

1. rhythmic contractions of large muscle groups;
2. require 60 percent or more of maximal aerobic capacity;
3. are performed 3 or more times per week;
4. are performed 20 minutes or more per session.

Few of the surveys or reports that might have provided information about our progress toward the 1990 PFE Objectives obtained information compatible with this definition. In addition, few of the definitions of physi-cal activity used in past surveys are similar enough to compare the results. Therefore, one major impediment of our efforts to track our progress toward the 1990 PFE Objectives is the use of inadequate and varying defi-nitions of activity in previous surveys.

An important future concern is whether the next round of PFE Ob-jectives should be expanded to encompass health benefits likely to ac-crue from activities other than those known to produce cardiorespiratory fitness, even though the benefits may be less firmly established in the scientific literature. For example, osteoporosis appears to be retarded by weight bearing activity; weight control may be related to overall energy expenditure regardless of the intensity of the activity; and activities of daily living may be best maintained in the elderly through exercises designed to promote flexibility and strength. We recommend that for the year 2000, the behavioral objectives be expanded to include low intensi-ty physical activity and strength and flexibility exercises in addition to the activities that promote cardiovascular fitness.

Efficiently and effectively promoting increased levels of physical ac-tivity in our society requires knowledge and understanding of the com-mon and important predisposing, enabling, and reinforcing factors, as well as the common and important impediments to that goal. Although reasonable suppositions about these factors have been made, more com-plete information about the determinants of an active lifestyle would be very valuable. We recommend the addition of objectives designed to focus attention on this important topic.

Finally, we recommend that the objectives be expanded to include children six to nine years old. The suggested objectives for the year 2000 encompass this age group where appropriate.

Summary List of 1990 Objectives and Recommended Objectives for 2000

1990 Objectives	Recommended objectives for 2000
a. By 1990, the proportion of children and adolescents ages 10 to 17 participating regularly in appropriate physical activities, particularly cardio-respiratory fitness programs which can be carried into adulthood, should be greater than 90 percent.	a.1. By 2000, 75 percent or more of children and adolescents ages 10 to 17 years will participate 3 or more times per week for at least 30 minutes per session in activities requiring 50 percent or more $\dot{V}O_2$ max and which are most commonly or easily performed by adults. (This assumes the criterion for year-round participation is removed.)
	a.2. By 2000, 90 percent or more of children and adolescents ages 10 to 17 years will participate 3 or more times per week for at least 30 minutes per session in an activity at least as vigorous as a sustained slow walk.
	a.3. By 2000, 75 percent or more of children and adolescents ages 10 to 17 years will participate 3 or more times per week for at least 15 minutes per session in activities that promote the development and maintenance of flexibility and muscular strength and endurance.
	a.4. By 2000, population-based descriptive information about the levels of physical fitness and physical activity patterns of children ages 6 to 9 years will be available. (If available before 1990, a more specific behavioral objective should be made for this age group.)
b. By 1990, the proportion of children and adolescents ages 10 to 17 participating in daily school physical education programs should be greater than 60 percent.	b.1. By 2000, 50 percent or more of children and adolescents 6 to 17 years of age will participate in daily school PE programs.
	b.2. By 2000, 90 percent or more of high schools will have PE classes devoting at least 50 percent of class time to activities that are commonly done by adults.

(Cont.)

Summary List of 1990 Objectives and Recommended Objectives for 2000 (Cont.)

1990 Objectives	Recommended objectives for 2000
c. By 1990, the proportion of adults 18 to 64 participating regularly in vigorous physical exercise should be greater than 60 percent.	c.1. By 2000, 30 percent or more of adults 18 to 64 years old will participate in a physical activity 3 or more days per week for 30 or more minutes per session at 50% or more $\dot{V}O_2$ max.
	c.2. By 2000, 75 percent or more of adults 18 to 64 years old will participate in a physical activity at least as vigorous as a sustained slow walk, 3 or more days per week, for 30 or more minutes per session.
	c.3. By 2000, 40 percent or more of adults 18 to 64 years old will participate 3 or more times per week for at least 15 minutes per session in activities that promote the development and maintenance of flexibility and muscular strength and endurance.
d. By 1990, 50 percent of adults 65 years and older should be engaging in appropriate physical activity, e.g., regular walking, swimming, or other aerobic activity.	d.1. By 2000, 30 percent of adults 65 years of age or older will be participating in physical activity 3 or more days per week, 30 or more minutes per session, at 50 percent or more $\dot{V}O_2$max. (This is an intensity equivalent to walking about 3 miles per hour.)
	d.2. By 2000, 50 percent of adults 65 years of age or older will be participating in physical activity at least as vigorous as a sustained slow walk 3 or more days per week, 30 or more minutes per session.
	d.3. By 2000, 50 percent of adults 65 years of age and older will be participating 3 or more times per week for 30 minutes or more per session in activities designed to promote or maintain flexibility, ambulatory skills, arm and hand strength, or other skills of daily living.
e. By 1990, the proportion of adults who can accurately identify the variety and duration of exercise thought to promote most effectively cardio-vascular fitness should be greater than 70 percent.	e.1. By 2000, 80 percent or more of persons 10 years of age and older will be able to correctly identify the variety, frequency, and duration of exercise thought to promote most effectively cardiorespiratory fitness for their age group.

(Cont.)

Summary List of 1990 Objectives and Recommended Objectives for 2000 (Cont.)

1990 Objectives	Recommended objectives for 2000
	e.2. By 2000, 80 percent or more of persons 10 years of age and older will know that regular physical activity reduces the risk of heart disease, helps maintain appropriate body weight, and reduces the symptoms of depression and anxiety.
f. By 1990, the proportion of primary care physicians who include a careful exercise history as part of their initial examination of new patients should be greater than 50 percent.	f.1. By 2000, 65 percent or more of primary medical care providers will inquire about the frequency, duration, type, and intensity of most new patients' exercise habits.
g. By 1990, the proportion of employees of companies and institutions with more than 500 employees offering employer-sponsored fitness programs should be greater than 25 percent.	g.1. By 2000, the proportion of companies and institutions with more than 500 employees on site offering employer-sponsored fitness programs should be greater than 35 percent.
	g.2. By 2000, the proportion of companies and institutions with more than 50 employees on site offering employer-sponsored fitness programs will be known. (If known before 1990, this objective can be modified to set a specific proportion to have programs by 2000.)
	g.3. By 2000, 75 percent of all companies and institutions with more than 50 employees that have a fitness program will make the fitness program available to all of their employees.
h. By 1990 a methodology for systematically assessing the physical fitness of children should be established with at least 70 percent of children and adolescents 10 to 17 participating in such an assessment.	h.1. By 2000, practical methods to measure the health-related components of fitness and desirable and reasonable norms for those measures will be established for age- and sex-specific groups for both children and adults.
	h.2. By 2000, the levels of achievement of the health-related components of fitness for various age- and sex-specific segments of children and adults will be known.

Summary List of 1990 Objectives and Recommended Objectives for 2000 (Cont.)

1990 Objectives	Recommended objectives for 2000
	h.3. By 2000, 70 percent of children and adolescents, 10–17 years of age, will receive recognition for their participation in a test of physical fitness without regard to their level of achievement.
i. By 1990, data should be available with which to evaluate short and long term health effects of participation in programs of appropriate physical activity.	i.1. By 2000, the effect of becoming regularly and vigorously active at various stages in life on the incidence of cardiovascular disease will be established.
	i.2. By 2000, the effect of regular activity of various intensities on the incidence of cardiovascular disease will be known.
	i.3. By 2000, the effect of regular weight-bearing activities on the incidence of osteoporosis-related hip fractures will be established.
	i.4. By 2000, the effect of regular flexibility and strength exercises on the incidence of disability resulting from low back pain will be known.
	i.5. By 2000, the effect of regular flexibility and strength exercises on the ability of persons 65 years of age and older to perform activities of daily living will be known.
	i.6. By 2000, the effect of regular activity of low or high intensity on the incidence of depressive episodes among depressed persons will be known.
	i.7. By 2000, the effect of regular vigorous physical activity on prevention and cessation of smoking and on treating alcohol and drug abuse will be known.
	i.8. By 2000, the effect of regular vigorous physical activity on the incidence of and disability from osteoarthritis will be known.
	i.9. By 2000, the incidence of exercise-related injuries for the most popular adult exercises (e.g., running, swimming, cycling, aerobic dancing, tennis, racketball) will be known.

(Cont.)

Summary List of 1990 Objectives and Recommended Objectives for 2000 (Cont.)

1990 Objectives	Recommended objectives for 2000
j. By 1990, data should be available to evaluate the effects of participation in programs of physical fitness on job performance and health care costs.	j.1. By 2000, data should be available to evaluate the effects of participation in worksite exercise programs on job performance, health care costs, employee absenteeism, and turnover rates.
k. By 1990, data should be available for regular monitoring of national trends and patterns of participation in physical activity, including participation in public recreation programs in community facilities.	k.1. By 2000, 50 percent or more of counties will maintain a current inventory of physical activity programs, facilities, and special events within the community.
	k.2. By 2000, information will be available about the type, location, and frequency of use of facilities most commonly used for leisure time physical activity.
l. No previous objective.	l.1. By 2000, the relationship between participation in various types of physical activities during childhood and adolescence and the physical activity practices of adults will be known.
	l.2. By 2000, the relationship between the accessibility of facilities and physical activity practices of adults will be known.
	l.3. By 2000, the behavioral skills associated with a high probability of adopting and maintaining a regular exercise program will be known.

Index